INTERNATIONAL BUSINESS

THE ACADEMY OF INTERNATIONAL BUSINESS

Published in association with the UK Chapter of the Academy of International Business

Titles already published in the series:

International Business

Adjusting to New Challenges and Opportunities

Edited by

Frank McDonald

Heinz Tüselmann

and

Colin Wheeler

palgrave

First published 2002 by
PALGRAVE
Houndmills, Basingstoke, Hampshire RG21 6XS and
175 Fifth Avenue, New York, N.Y. 10010
Companies and representatives throughout the world

PALGRAVE is the new global academic imprint of
St. Martin's Press LLC Scholarly and Reference Division and
Palgrave Publishers Ltd (formerly Macmillan Press Ltd).

ISBN 0–333–98411–0

This book is printed on paper suitable for recycling and made from fully managed and sustained forest sources.

A catalogue record for this book is available from the British Library.

A catalogue record for this book is available from the Library of Congress.

10 9 8 7 6 5 4 3 2 1
11 10 09 08 07 06 05 04 03 02

Printed and bound in Great Britain by
Antony Rowe Ltd, Chippenham, Wiltshire

Contents

List of Figures

List of Tables

Preface

Interest in international business in the UK has been growing as more institutions teach specialist classes in international business and incorporate aspects of the subject in existing curricula. The popularity of international business has created the opportunity for the AIB to hold annual conferences at a number of new venues, and the UK Chapter of the Academy of International Business was very pleased that in 2001 it was able to hold the 28th annual conference at Manchester Metropolitan University.

The theme of the conference, 'Adjusting to new challenges and opportunities', reflects not only the changing global environment but also concerns about the environment and the actions of MNCs. For the first time these issues were the subject of Keynote addresses by speakers from Oxfam and Friends of the Earth. At the time of writing talks on the implementation of the Kyoto Accord on climate change have been taking place in Genoa and concerns about the environment and the role of the MNCs are prominent. It seems only fitting that these issues were a focal point of the AIB conference.

Acknowledgements

Many thanks to the team at the International Business Unit, Manchester Metropolitan University for holding the 28th annual conference of the Academy of International Business. Thanks also to Barbara Cousins and Chris Bagley, who acted as conference secretaries, to Kevin Boles, who coordinated operations, to the PhD students of Manchester Metropolitan University Business School for their practical help during the conference, and to Simon Downes, who put together the material for the proceedings.

Notes on the Contributors

Maureen Berry is a Senior Lecturer at the University of Strathclyde. Her present research interests are the globalization of smaller firms, entrepreneurship and strategic management in smaller firms, and the strategic management of technology.

Dev K. Boojihawon is a Doctoral Researcher at the Strathclyde International Business Unit (SIBU). His teaching and research interests focus on the internationalization strategies of professional service firms.

Keith D. Brouthers is a Reader in Strategic and International Management at the University of East London. His research interests are international strategic decision making and factors that influence strategic decisions.

Lance Eliot Brouthers is Professor of International Business at the University of Akron, USA. His research has involved the exploration of international strategy theories.

Trevor Buck is Professor of Business Policy at the Graduate School of Business, Leicester De Montfort University. His research interests are corporate governance, strategies and performance in the former Soviet Union; business history in Russia, Japan and Germany; executive pay in the US and UK; and executive share options in large German firms.

Chris Carr is Professor of Corporate Strategy at the School of Management, University of Edinburgh.

Rajesh Chakrabarti is an Assistant Professor of Finance at the DuPree College of Management, Georgia Institute of Technology, Atlanta. Besides e-commerce, his areas of interest include international financial markets, exchange rate movements and informational issues in financial markets.

Sumi Dhanarajan is a Policy Adviser to the Private Sector for Oxfam GB.

Jody Evans is a Senior Research Fellow at the Department of Retailing and Marketing, Manchester Metropolitan University Business School. Her teaching and research interests include international marketing and retailing, marketing strategy, consumer behaviour and research methods.

Pavlos Dimitratos is a Research Fellow at the University of Strathclyde. His present research interests are the globalization of smaller firms, internationalization strategies and international entrepreneurship. He has contributed to a number of edited volumes.

John R. Firn is Director of Firn Chrichton Roberts Ltd.

Mika Gabrielsson is Professor of International Business at the Helsinki School of Economics and Professor of International Marketing at Lappeenranta University of Technology. His teaching and research interests are international sales channel strategies, rapid globalization and e-commerce. Before joining the academic world he held several senior positions in high-tech marketing and purchasing.

Paul N. Gooderham is Professor of International Management at the Norwegian School of Economics and Administration. His research interest is the transfer of knowledge in multinational corporations.

Arne Heise is Professor of Economics at the University of Cologne. His research interests include the impact of DFI flows on the German economy.

Neil Hood is Professor of Business Policy at the University of Strathclyde and Deputy Chairman of Scottish Enterprise. His research interests include the strategic development of subsidiaries, international business strategy and public policy.

Kevin Ibeh is Lecturer in the Department of Marketing, University of Strathclyde, Glasgow, UK. He has also taught and researched marketing at the University of Uyo and Abia State University, both in Nigeria.

Marian V. Jones is a Senior Lecturer at the Department of Business and Management, University of Glasgow. Her research interests are internationalization of small, high technology firms, export information and international entrepreneurship.

Felix Mavondo is an Associate Professor at the Department of Marketing, Monash University, Melbourne. His teaching and research interests are marketing strategy, market orientation, relationship marketing, retailing strategy and research methods.

Duncan McLaren is Head of Policy and Research at Friends of the Earth (England, Wales and Northern Ireland).

Michael McDermott is a Senior Lecturer at the University of Strathclyde. His present research interests are the globalization of smaller firms, international divestment strategies and East Asia's emerging economies.

Frank McDonald is a Principal Lecturer and Head of the International Business Unit at Manchester Metropolitan University Business School.

Zuhair Al-Obaidi has DSc, Licentiate and MSc degrees from the Helsinki School of Economics and a BA from the University of Reading. His business experience includes thirteen years of work and consultation for Middle Eastern and Finnish firms and governments, as well as international organizations. His current teaching and research interests include technology transfer, the global-ization of high-tech SMEs, IT applications to internationalization, and business in developing countries.

Robert Pearce is a Reader in International Business at the School of Business, University of Reading.

Philip Raines is a Senior Research Fellow at the European Policies Research Centre, University of Strathclyde. His research interests are cluster development and cluster policy, foreign investment policy and UK regional development.

Barry Scholnick is an Associate Professor of International Business at the School of Business, University of Alberta, Edmonton, Alberta. Besides e-com-merce, his research interests include international financial markets, banking and foreign direct investment.

Benedikt Schwittay is a Lecturer in Strategy at the Manchester Business School.

Stephen Tagg is a Lecturer in the Marketing Department at the University of Strathclyde. His teaches multivariate methods in marketing and his research interests include small firm internationalization, charitable giving and corporate communications.

James H. Taggart is Professor of International Business Strategy at the Department of Management Studies, University of Glasgow.

Jennifer M. Taggart is a Researcher in Strategy at the Department of Management Studies, University of Glasgow.

Ana Teresa Tavares is Assistant Professor of International Economics at the University of Porto, Portugal. Her main research interests are the strategy and evolution of multinational subsidiaries, and the impact of trading blocs on the strategy and structure of multinational corporations.

Heinz Tüselmann is a Senior Lecturer at the International Business Unit, Manchester Metropolitan University Business School.

Svein Ulset is an Associate Professor at the Norwegian School of Economics and Administration. He specializes in economic organization theory and his current research is the telecommunications industry.

Colin Wheeler is a Senior Lecturer at the International Business Unit, University of Strathclyde. His research interests are international marketing strategies in the food and drink industry, and export marketing strategies and performance.

Stephen Young is Professor and Director at the Strathclyde International Business Unit, University of Strathclyde. His research interests include international business strategy, foreign market servicing methods, the impact of multinational firms on host countries, and public policy and multinational firms.

List of Abbreviations

ADR	American Depository Receipt
A–PJ	Autonomy–procedural justice (model)
AS	Autarkic subsidiary
CEO	Chief executive officer
CG	Corporate governance
DTI	Department of Trade and Industry
EU	European Union
FDI	Foreign direct investment
FIGs	Financial–industrial groups
GATS	General Agreement on Trade in Services
GDP	Gross domestic product
HQ	Headquarters
IDV	International Distillers and Vintners
IMF	International Monetary Fund
IT	Information technology
MNC	Multinational company
MNE	Multinational enterprise
OECD	Organization for Economic Cooperation and Development
PM	Product mandate
PSF	Professional service firm
R & D	Research and development
RS	Rationalized subsidiary
RTS	Russian trading system
SG	Strategic group
SIC	Standard Industrial Classification
SMEs	Small and medium-sized enterprises
SOE	State-owned enterprise
SSTP	Strategic stable time period
UDG	United Distillers Guinness
WTO	World Trade Organization

1 Introduction: Adjusting to New Challenges and Opportunities

Colin Wheeler

NEW CHALLENGES AND OPPORTUNITIES

This volume of the Academy of International Business series organized around the theme of adjusting to new challenges and opportunities. Part One of the book is devoted to the best paper at the AIB's 28th annual conference, which investigated the nature of the contact that small high technology firms have with foreign markets. Part Two is concerned with ethics, environmental issues, corporate governance and the MNC. Part Three deals with the strategic development of subsidiaries and the rapid changes that are occurring in the changing environment. Part Four is broadly based on the theme of performance assessment of international business operations. Part Five deals with the internationalization of SMEs.

Chapter 2, on the relationship between a firm's performance and the management of its points of contact in overseas countries, won the Best Paper Award at the conference. In a previously under-researched area, Marian Jones argues that it is debatable whether small entrepreneurial firms adopt specific internationalization strategies. Rather it is more likely that firms that have succeeded in internationalizing, will have developed strategies to form international linkages, and will have devoted time and resources to seeking, developing and maintaining these linkages. The study indicates that contact and frequency of contact are linked to the performance of the firm, whilst predisposing factors (the founder's linguistic ability, education, overseas work experience and educational attainment), though not directly associated with performance, are significantly associated with the establishment of certain overseas links and the frequency of contact made. This chapter has strong links with Part Five, 'The Internationalization of SMEs'.

Chapter 3 is the keynote address by Sumi Dhanarajan, Policy Advisor for Oxfam, UK. After outlining how Oxfam decided to lobby for business responsibility in respect of development and human rights, she discusses a number of issues of world-wide concern in international business. She focuses on the economic and political responsibilities of firms and argues, for example, that firms in the pharmaceutical industry have a duty to reduce the cost of medicines to treat HIV in poorer countries. She is also concerned about the influence that industry groupings have in developed countries.

Chapter 4 is the second keynote address. Duncan McLaren, Head of Policy and Research at Friends of the Earth, is critical of the stance taken by the US government on climate change and argues that much of the blame for climate change should be placed on the activities of corporations, and that the neoliberal model of trade and investment liberalization externalizes environmental and social costs. He concludes that public opinion is changing and that calls for corporate responsibility, accountability and liability are likely to increase.

In Chapter 5 Trevor Buck charts the 'Americanization' of corporate governance in Russia. He addresses two questions: has the reform of Russian corporate governance been significantly constrained by Russia's historical institutional arrangements and national culture; or can a gradual evolution towards US-style corporate governance be observed and expected to continue? In 1991 the break-up of the former Soviet Union and the abandonment of central planning demanded the reform of Russia's corporate governance system. Under pressure from Western (mostly US) creditors, Russia therefore embarked on a mass programme of privatization, ostensibly with a view to creating US-style corporate governance. This type of governance involves full information disclosure and enterprise ownership by outside investors who have no relationship with the firm other than through the purchase and sale of its shares. In practice, however, a very different pattern has emerged, with potential conflicts of interest among 'relational' investors (managers and other employees, banks and other firms linked horizontally or vertically), little stock liquidity, continued hostility towards Western and other outside investors, and the persistence of strong state influence.

In Chapter 6 Steven Young, Neil Hood and John Firn address the issues of globalization, corporate restructuring and influences on MNC subsidiaries. They assess the nature and extent of corporate restructuring among a sample of MNCs with subsidiaries in Scotland. They offer a framework that distinguishes between changing firm locations, boundaries, structures, processes and practices to provide a useful basis for analyzing restructuring at the corporate and subsidiary levels in the global knowledge economy. Their findings suggest that there has been extensive MNC headquarters-led restructuring, which in the Scottish case reflects the characteristics of overseas-owned companies. They note that externally there are few examples of innovative regional clusters that might encourage spatial immobility. They conclude that in the future Scotland and other UK regions are unlikely to be competitive in respect of high-volume production and assembly operations. Hence radical policy changes will be required to attract investment that is higher up the value chain.

In Chapter 7 Ana Tavares and Robert Pearce address two related propositions, based on a survey of MNC subsidiaries in four EU countries: (1) mandate-type subsidiaries are more common in the UK than in other EU countries; and (2) UK-based subsidiaries tend to have higher value-added scope and conduct more sophisticated technological activities than their counterparts in other EU host economies. Both propositions receive considerable support, and the authors give further consideration to the coexistence and evolution of distinct subsidiary roles/strategies in the UK, particularly in terms of value-added scope.

In Chapter 8 Paul Gooderham and Svein Ulset provide a conceptual framework to address knowledge transfer between parent company and low-knowledge subsidiaries in developing countries. The move from knowledge recipient to centre of innovation is divided into four levels. A level 1 subsidiary is only capable of absorbing explicit knowledge of an elementary type, while a level 4 subsidiary is capable not only of absorbing tacit knowledge, but also of independently generating knowledge that can be transferred to the parent or other parts of the firm. Various knowledge transfer mechanisms are identified in the move from level 1 to level 4. These vary in terms of the social interaction they are intended to generate, which in turn is contingent on the degree of tacitness in the knowledge that is to be transferred.

In Chapter 9 James and Jennifer Taggart set out an empirical test of the autonomy–procedural justice framework. The A–PJ framework proposes four types of subsidiary strategy: vassal (low autonomy, low procedural justice), collaborator (low autonomy, high procedural justice), militant (high autonomy, low procedural justice) and partner (high autonomy, high procedural justice). Their research draws on a sample of 265 MNC manufacturing subsidiaries in Scotland, Wales, Ulster and the Republic of Ireland. Using factor analysis and cluster analysis, a four-group solution emerges that appears to be both robust and insightful. The framework is validated across a range of strategic issues, and a number of implications are developed.

Chapter 10, by Frank McDonald, Heinz Tüselmann and Arne Heise, focuses on regional specialization as MNCs concentrate on supplying all or large parts of Europe from fewer sites and on developing or creating new markets. This should lead to the creation of pan-European industrial structures. However there is evidence to suggest that the European subsidiaries of MNCs based in large European economies such as Germany, France and the UK tend to grant lower-level mandates to their subsidiaries than is the case with non-European MNCs and those based in the smaller economies of Europe. Granting low-level mandates to subsidiaries in regions that do not offer a wide range of desirable assets is understandable, but it is not clear why there should be a country-specific effect based on the home base of the MNC. The authors provide a theoretical explanation of low-level subsidiary development in regions with few desirable resources and a reason for the observed country-specific effect from the largest economies of Europe.

In Chapter 11 Philip Raines examines the use of public–private partnership in the development of local industrial clusters. Based on research on cluster policies in three European regions – Östergôtland (Sweden), Scotland (UK) and Tampere (Finland) – the author considers the roles of government and business in three aspects of policy making: its overall scope, its design, and its implementation. He concludes that the partnership model is used not only commonly but also more intensively in cluster policies because of the need for close cooperation between the public and private sectors at most stages of policy development. However, while allowing a more targeted form of industrial policy, the approach does carry the danger that institutional policy making will be captured by private sector interests.

In Chapter 12 Colin Wheeler and Kevin Ibeh review UK export behaviour research conducted between 1990 and 2000, drawing on some 64 research publications based on 41 research projects. A notable development during the period was the recognition that the resources and competences embodied in firms provide a good indication of export behaviour. It seems that well-developed product/service competences, relationship-building skills and export market knowledge and its management are particularly strong indicators of positive export behaviour. The research also indicates that, in comparison with other 'indigenously owned' UK firms, Asian SMEs are less aware of government export promotion programmes and have a generally negative attitude towards organizations outside their ethnic grouping.

In Chapter 13 Dev Boojihawon and Stephen Young examine international strategy and development in the professional services industry. Based largely on a case study of a multinational advertising agency, they present a conceptual framework (drawing on the resource-based view, the network-based view and the industrial organization view) and offer propositions for future research. The international development of professional services centres on effective client servicing in foreign markets, the generation of new business activities through established networks, and the development and nurturing of the expertise and skills of professionals to provide local solutions within a global framework.

In Chapter 14 Colin Wheeler, Stephen Tagg and James Taggart investigate the extent to which elements of a US model linking export marketing strategy to performance can be applied to a different country, namely Scotland. The US model was chosen because it uses a comprehensive set of variables and appropriate statistical techniques to model direct and indirect effects on export performance. Because much of the research on export performance has been carried out in the US, it seems reasonable to see whether a US model can be applied to a non-US context. Drawing on data from a mail survey of Scottish exporters, an attempt has been made to replicate the US model of export performance. Some commonalities are evident, with management competence, support for individual export market ventures and relative business intensity being similar. However it also seems likely that a different model of export marketing performance would fit the data. The results of the study lend support to the view that commonalities rather than identical results are likely to be found across studies conducted in different environments.

Using data from a pan-European survey of the largest companies in the EU, in Chapter 15 Keith Brouthers and Lance Brouthers investigate whether there is a relationship between performance and transaction costs, institutional context, cultural context, and entry mode choice. After examining both financial and non-financial performance measures, they conclude that transaction costs, institutional context and cultural context are all related to performance, but that mode choice is not. However, their sample was drawn from large international firms and data on the last target country entered means that the study focuses on smaller, less developed markets because these were the last target countries. In this context, mode of entry does not seem to be important from a performance standpoint. Their results indicate that superior firm performance is more likely to occur in higher-risk markets, and thus to improve their performance firms must be willing to face additional risks.

In Chapter 16 Rajesh Chakrabarti and Barry Scholnick investigate the supposed borderlessness of the new e-commerce economy by examining the nature of price competition in book retailing between a world leader in Internet retailing, Amazon.com, and the largest on-line retailer in Canada, Chapters.ca. The Internet allows Canadian consumers to circumvent protectionist barriers by purchasing directly on-line from US booksellers. However Canadian on-line booksellers still enjoy considerable protection in the form of significant shipping cost advantages when selling to Canadian customers. The authors construct a large panel data set on the prices, delivery schedules and popularity ratings of more than 5000 books over 21 weeks, all collected from the Internet. Using this data they demonstrate that in spite of the shipping cost differential, the Canadian company sets prices that on average are remarkably close to the US prices, when adjusted for the exchange rate.

In Chapter 17 Benedikt Schwittay and Chris Carr consider the use of strategic groups within the context of globalization. They suggest that in the new global competitive environment the old strategic group concepts are losing their explanatory power and new dynamic strategic group concepts are needed that take account of the turbulent transformation of global industries. Their study of the spirits industry during the period 1982–95 uses statistical industry data, 47 company interviews and questionnaires completed by senior executives from 21 UK, US and German spirit companies and trade associations. Their findings suggest that the old strategic group concepts are indeed becoming less useful for predicting the behaviour and performance of companies, and that account needs to be taken of dynamic industry changes.

Using mail survey data collected from senior executives in the US, the UK, Europe and the Asia-Pacific region, in Chapter 18, Jody Evans and Felix Marondo examine the relationship between psychic distance and organizational performance in an international retailing context. Research in this area has focused on a number of topics, ranging from export development to international retailing, and reported conflicting findings. The authors suggests that the perception of psychic distance has no significant effect on financial performance, but it does reduce the strategic effectiveness of foreign operations in close markets, and has however, had a positive effect on organizational performance in distant markets. The relationships between a disaggregated dimension of psychic distance and organizational performance are also investigated. The results indicate that the dimensions differ in their importance in close and distant markets: cultural distance is the most important influence on organizational performance in close markets, while the perception of economic differences is the most important predictor of organizational performance in distant markets.

In Chapter 19 Maureen Berry, Pavlos Dimitratos and Michael McDermott examine the extent to which globalization and the smaller firm can be seen as compatible concepts. They argue that the disagreement in the literature regarding these concepts stems from the fact that ideas from the themes of global strategy, multinational enterprise and the 'born global firm' are being mixed up. They seek to alleviate this confusion by suggesting that the globalization of smaller firms is a valid notion, and they offer a comprehensive framework with five dimensions of the smaller global firm. These dimensions relate to three chronological stages of the internationalization route of the smaller global firm.

In Chapter 20 Mika Gabrielsson and Zuhair Al-Obaidi examine multiple sales channel strategies in the export marketing activities of small and medium-sized design companies. The development from single to multiple sales channel structures is described and analyzed on the basis of four theoretical approaches, namely the internationalization process, sales channel economic structure, long-term channel relationships, and the product life cycle the multiple channel. They present a framework consisting of three independent factors: the internationalization process, product markets and other environmental aspects, and long-term channel relations. Using four case studies the authors identify a variety of channel structures and explain why they are chosen.

In conclusion, the chapters on the strategic development of subsidiaries, the performance of international business operations and the internationalization of SMEs have explored the ways in which international firms and governments are adjusting to new challenges and opportunities. At the managerial level a number of chapters have identified and explored aspects of relationships in the internationalization process (for example Marian Jones' chapter on firms' management of contacts in foreign markets). There is also evidence that a resource-based view of the firm is gaining increasing attention (for example Dev Boojihawon and Stephen Young's conceptualization of international strategy and development in professional service industries).

At the policy level, perhaps the greatest challenges are those outlined by the keynote speakers (Chapters 3 and 4). They firmly argue that corporations and politicians are facing new and demanding social, political and environmental responsibilities, which will continue to attract public support. This has been highlighted by the recent agreement at Genoa, on the implementation of the Kyoto Accord on Climate Change which, whatever its outcome, will present significant challenges and opportunities to international business.

Part One

Best Paper

2 The Importance of International Predisposition and Contact with the Foreign Market: Empirical Evidence from UK High Technology Small Firms

Marian V. Jones

INTRODUCTION

Whether small entrepreneurial firms form strategies specifically in order to internationalize is debatable. It is likely, however, that the firms that are most successful in internationalizing will develop strategies aimed at forming international linkages with external bodies, and will spend time and resources on seeking, developing and maintaining these linkages. Firms are likely to be better at or more active in developing linkages overseas if they are predisposed to internationalize. Small entrepreneurial firms may be more predisposed to internationalize if their founders have an international orientation (Dichtl, 1990), or have experience that enables them to cross the cultural divide between country markets (Reuber and Fischer, 1999). Firms that have founders who are fluent in foreign languages, are themselves foreign nationals or have received education or work experience overseas will be more predisposed to make contact with organizations or bodies overseas (Wiedersheim-Paul *et al.*, 1976; Cromie *et al.*, 1997; Westhead *et al.*, 2001) and are likely to put more effort into developing those links.

Whether firms make economically rational market entry decisions, psychically safe entry decisions or evolve gradually into foreign markets on the back of existing networks of relationships, it is likely that at some point most will make contact with individuals or organizations in the foreign market. The relationship between a firm's performance and the management of its points of contact in overseas countries, is the focus of this chapter.

CONTACTS AND LINKS WITH THE FOREIGN MARKET

Cross-border links and contacts have been examined in a number of ways across a relatively wide range of topics that are loosely or specifically associated with internationalization or exporting. Turning first to theory, discussion of the role of knowledge and information in high technology firms and in internationaliza-

9

tion has some relevance to a study of the contacts and links made by internationalizing firms.

Penrose (1959) states that both an automatic increase in knowledge and an incentive to search for new knowledge are fundamental to the nature of firms that possess entrepreneurial resources. Knowledge is also fundamental to a number of theories of internationalization. In both internalization and transaction costs, information – or knowledge – is seen less as a market imperfection than as an exploitable asset if concentrated in the industry or the firm. The internalization of knowledge and other exploitable assets such as technology are what gives the MNE its unique advantage (Hood and Young, 1979; Buckley, 1995; Caves, 1996).

Casson (1992) suggests that the uniqueness of international expansion, as compared with domestic growth, might be demonstrated by emphasizing the difference between technical and market know-how. Kogut and Zander (1992) go further and suggest that it is a firm's ability to 're-combine knowledge' that determines its expansion into new markets. Kogut and Zander (1993) reason that knowledge, learning, technology transfer and the ability to recombine knowledge are important to the theoretical explanation of firms' competitiveness, growth and internationalization. Internalized knowledge is a self-limiting growth prospect however, and studies of small firm internationalization, have emphasized external links as important both to knowledge development and to performance and international growth.

Behavioural and export process models of internationalization have identified lack of knowledge as a major inhibiting factor in internationalization (Johanson and Vahlne, 1977, 1990; Cavusgil, 1984) and the attainment of experiential knowledge as fundamental to international growth and expansion. In general, network approaches support the idea of international growth through the development of external links and relationships that maximize the opportunities for knowledge exchange. O'Farrell *et al.* (1998a: 35) suggest that a basic assumption of the network model is that the individual firm is dependent on resources controlled by other firms, and it gains access to those external resources through its network position. They criticize behavioural approaches for their lack of emphasis on the strategic motivations of firm relations, and specifically the strategic importance of project-based links with clients. They suggest that a principal asset of small firms be their established pattern of external contacts.

Contacts and links with the foreign market have been examined as a source of information before export commences. Hart and Tzokas (1999) have identified a gap in empirical research that examines the relationship between the collection of marketing information by exporting firms and their export performance. Despite widespread acknowledgement that information collection should lead to less risky decisions, links between the use of information and performance are under-researched. Some studies have examined sources of export information used by exporters, the organization of research activities, the data collection methods employed and factors affecting the use of export information (Hart *et al.*, 1994; Crick *et al.*, 1994).

The emphasis in the latter studies is on contacts and links as sources of marketing research information rather than as sources of informal information or potential business contacts. These studies acknowledge, however, that personal networks and contacts are more likely to be used by small firms as sources of information than are formal sources of information provision. In fact Crick and Czinkota (1995) have found that UK exporting SMEs are largely unaware of what governmental programmes are available to assist their export activities. Hart and Tzokas (1999) have found that the use of export marketing information is associated with export success and that higher export profits are strongly related to export usage patterns. They recommend, however, that scholars should look beyond the export information required, to softer issues such as the managerial approach adopted for its collection and use.

Crick *et al.* (1994) and Jones (1990) suggest that there might be other reasons for making links and contacts than merely the formal collection of export market information. Informal, interpersonal contacts are thought to be important to the internationalization of small firms. At present so much quality information is supplied by governments, trade and industry publications and libraries that personal contact in a foreign market as a means of collecting information seems inefficient and unreliable, to say the least. However as Hart and Tzokas (1999) suggest, the apparent reluctance to use formal sources of information may be due to managements' lack of appreciation of its usefulness or their inability to collect and utilize relevant information.

Contacts and links have been examined in relation to firms' entry into foreign markets. A number of traditional export studies suggest that a considerable amount of exporting activity is initiated by the customer (Coviello and Munro, 1995). This mode of initiation tends to rely on personal contact between the partners to the agreement. It is widely acknowledged that small firms may lack the resources needed for international expansion (Buckley, 1989; Lindmark, cited in Holmlund and Kock, 1998). Holmlund and Kock (1998) have established that small Finnish firms gain access to and mobilize external resources through established long-term relationships, but according to Christensen and Lindmark (1993), international value chain linking by small firms through tight relationships is often not taken into account in the internationalization literature.

Value chain connections have also been identified as important to small firm internationalization by Oviatt and McDougall (1997), Jones (1999) and Jones and Tagg, (2000). Firms whose business contains a service element may rely on existing contacts and networks during their internationalization (Erramilli and Rao, 1990; Coviello and Martin, 1999). O'Farrell *et al.* (1998a, p 15) suggests that small service firms' competitive advantage is defined not only by their internal resources but also by their external interactions: 'the institutional and social networks surrounding small business service firms are essential to gather information, mobilise new partners, gain access to other skills and specialised services, sustain their knowledge and client contacts, and adjust these networks to meet the tasks'.

Studies of the growth and expansion of small, innovative, high technology firms have long acknowledged that external links and particularly access to the science base are crucial to the development of technology as well as for the firms themselves (Rothwell, 1991). Where technologies have international or global markets, overseas contacts may be important in linking firms to the local science base.

Social networks can form the basis of successful business (Aldrich and Zimmer, 1986). Alliances may therefore be an important means by which small firms can gain access to and penetrate foreign markets (Buckley and Casson, 1988; Welch, 1992). With regard to the internationalization processes of Finnish SMEs, Holmlund and Kock (1998) have found that managements' social network abroad and their previous professional experience are important triggers. In their sample the most common way of doing business was through agents and the firms' own sales representatives. Amongst their SMEs' perceived strengths were their managers' personal contacts and a good knowledge of buyers, suppliers and competitors in the market. Language skill was listed as an area that needed improvement. Elsewhere, Ostgaard and Birley (1996) have found a correlation between the performance of new entrepreneurial firms and their professional networks. More recently, Reuber and Fischer (1999) have pointed out that the literature on founders' experiences does not indicate any consistent, direct relationship between founder experience and venture performance.

It has been consistently argued in the literature that language ability is likely to facilitate successful exporting; on the other hand it has been found that successful exporters do not always appreciate the need for foreign language ability. Cromie *et al.* (1997), Ford (1989) and Dichtl (1990) argue that foreign language ability is a form of empathy with an export partner and may provide 'psychological closeness'. Cromie *et al.* (1997) have found that exporting firms that lack foreign language ability compensate by using interpreters, translation agencies, intermediaries or foreign personnel. Most of the firms in their study acknowledged the importance of languages for exporting, but in practice, actual use and proficiency varied considerably.

The importance of contacts in and links to foreign markets is to a large extent under-researched as a specific topic in its own right. The literature reviewed here indicates that contacts and links are important as sources of both technological and market information, as a bridge foreign markets, as part of a firm or industry's value chain development and as a stage in network development. The literature also indicates that a firm's international orientation, professional experience and language ability are important in relation to the type of contact made overseas and possibly even the entry mode used.

The purpose of the study described below was to identify the types of overseas links and contacts made by small high technology firms, rather than to trace individual firm networks. Its focus was on the establishment of cross-border business activity and not the development of long-term relationships or networks. The factors examined were those that might predispose firms to internationalize, and the relationship of those factors to the overseas contacts made by firms and their subsequent performance. Interest was specifically on small firms in high technology sectors.

METHODOLOGY

The main part of the study consisted of a structured mail questionnaire. The questions were constructed after consulting the literature on small firms, on small firms and high technology, and an exporting and internationalization. The integrating theme derived from these strands of literature was the growth and development processes of small firms.

The questionnaire was tested for construct and content validity by academic experts in the fields identified in the literature, experts in research methods, and industry members and government officials involved in small high technology firms and sectors. The questionnaire was mailed to 1001 small firms. The firms were selected according to the standard industrial classification (SIC) codes for four high technology sectors that are known for rapid growth: plastics and composites, biotechnology, advanced surgical instruments, and advanced instruments for industry.

The questionnaires were addressed by name to the owners or chief executives of the firms. Reminders were sent out after two weeks. A total of 117 usable questionnaires were received from the first mailing, and 96 from the second. There were no significant differences between the answers to key questions across the two mailings. An export entry mode bias was avoided by using a database constructed from directories of firms other than export directories. These included the Dunn & Bradstreet Market Identifiers directory, and Scottish Enterprise directories of electronics firms and biotechnology firms. As high technology markets tend to be international in nature, it was assumed that most firms would have some involvement with international contacts. Only 10 of the sample claimed to have no international activity whatsoever.

The criteria for the selection of sample firms were that they should belong to one of the listed sectors (based on their SIC code), have fewer than 50 employees at the time of listing in the directory, and fewer than 200 current employees. Only 13 per cent of firms had their workforce to more than 50 employees since the time they were registered on the database. Completed questionnaires were included in the analysis if the firm had fewer than 200 employees (provided expansion to that size had taken ten years or less), could be classified as high technology based, was a manufacturer, and was not less than five years old. As 70 per cent of the respondents were founders of the firm and more than 85 per cent were chief executives, credibility in terms of corporate memory and overall knowledge of the firm was considered acceptable. A profile of the sample firms is presented in Table 2.1.

Table 2.1   Sample profile

	f	%
Size of firm (number of employees, n = 213):		
Fewer than 10	56	26
11–20	52	25
21–50	78	37
51–200	27	13
Age of firm (n = 212):		
New (5 years or less)	42	20
Young (6–10 years)	53	25
Adolescent (11–25 years)	80	38
Mature (26 years and over)	37	18
R & D Investments (% of turnover, 1993, n = 181)		
0	20	11
1–5%	84	47
6–20%	49	27
21–100%	28	16
Industry sector (n = 212):		
1. Plastics and composites	22	11
2. Biotechnology/pharmaceuticals	34	16
3. Advanced medical instruments/appliances	48	23
4. Electronic equipment instruments for industry	54	25
5. Other	54	25

Research Constructs and Analytical Procedures

Predisposition to internationalize was ascertained using four discrete dichoto-mous variables, each of which were considered important in their own right and were therefore not combined into a single composite measure. These variables were whether or not the founder or founders (1) were nationals of a foreign country, (2) were fluent in foreign language, (3) had been educated overseas and (4) had had overseas work experience prior to the establishment of their firm. The dependent variables consisted of 12 points of contact identified from the lit-erature as important external links for small high technology firms (Jones, 1990; Hart *et al.*, 1994; Leonidou and Adams-Florou, 1998). These points of contract were as chambers of commerce, trade or employers' associations, professional associations, university research departments, public research departments, company- or industry-based research units, trade fairs, academic conferences or seminars, research colloquia, customers, suppliers and distributors or agents. The performance indicators included the number of export markets, percentage growth in exports and turnover in the three-year period prior to the study and the current international ratio, that is, the ratio of all income generated from overseas business activities to total turnover.

Contact with overseas-based links was measured in the first instance as a dichotomous variable, that is, whether or not the firm had established contact with each type of link. Secondly, contact was measured on a seven-point scale: 7 (never), 6 (less than annually), 5 (annually), 4 (biannually), 3 (quarterly), 2 (monthly) and 1 (more frequently than monthly). The seven categories were subsequently collapsed into four for analysis.

Cross-tabulation and chi-squared analysis revealed a significant correlation between contact and frequency of contact, with international predisposition, but not with performance, apart from one exception. Three factors were extracted from the list of overseas contacts using a common factor analysis with varimax rotation. The three emerging factors were 'research contact', 'trade contact' and 'professional associations'. The factors confirmed the extent to which types of contact shared patterns of contact frequency (Alt, 1990; Hair *et al.*, 1998). Composite scales were constructed from the extracted factors, but 'chambers of commerce', which had a very weak factor loading, was excluded. Cronbach alpha tests produced scales that were well above the minimum acceptable level of reliability of 0.7 (Nunally, 1978). Kruskal–Wallis non-parametric tests established significant correlations between the contact frequency scaled by factor, and certain performance indicators.

Table 2.2   International predisposition

	f	%
Founders' overseas links:		
Foreign nationals as founders	24	12
(n = 206)		
Founders fluent in foreign language	54	26
(n = 206)		
Founders educated overseas	43	21
(n = 203)		
Founders with overseas work experience	108	52
(n = 209)		
Useful foreign languages in firm		
(n = 213):		
None/declined to answer	102	48
One language	111	52
Two languages	62	30
Three languages	27	13
Four languages	10	5
Five languages	6	3
Six or more languages	3	1

FINDINGS

International Predisposition

As can be seen in Table 2.2, very few of the firms had founders who were foreign nationals. A quarter had founders who claimed to be fluent in a foreign language, the founders of a fifth had had at least some of their education overseas, and just over half indicated that their founders had had overseas work experience before the founding of the firm. Hence at least half of the sample could be expected to be predisposed to international business activity through orientation or previous experience.

In addition to predisposing factors the firms were asked whether they currently had a foreign language capability that was useful to the firm's international business. Just under half of the firms stated that they had no such capability (Table 2.2). The remainder had a capability in that the firm had at least one useful foreign language. The language ranked as most important was French, followed by German.

Predisposition to Internationalize by Overseas Contact Made

The proportion of sample firms that had contact with overseas individuals and organizations ranged from 25 per cent (contact with public research institutions) to 84 per cent (contact with overseas-based customers) (Table 2.3). Overall, and as expected, more firms had contact with customers, suppliers, distributors/agents and trade fairs than with professional associations and research contacts. Surprisingly few firms (28 per cent) had contact with overseas chambers of commerce.

Predisposing variables that indicated significant correlations (at <0.05) in respect of whether or not contact was made with each type of overseas contact are also reported in Table 2.3. The foreign nationality of firm founders was found to play no significant part in whether or not contact was made with any type of overseas contact. However, founders' foreign language ability was to be an important factor in firms' contact with trade and professional associations and university research departments, in attendance at academic conferences, and in making contact with customers and suppliers, but not with distributors/agents.

Founders' overseas education was found to be important in relation to whether or not firms made contact with chambers of commerce, university research departments, customers, suppliers and distributors/agents, as well as attendance at academic conferences (Table 2.3). Founders' overseas work experience before founding their firms was significantly associated with contact with professional associations, university research departments and public research institutions, attendance at conferences and colloquia, and contact with customers and distributors/agents, but not suppliers (Table 2.3). Founders' prior overseas work experience was the only variable to indicate a significant correlation with any of the performance variables – it was found to be important to the firms' international ratio.

Table 2.3 Predisposition to internationalize by contact made

	Firms		Foreign nationals*		Foreign language*		Overseas education*		Overseas work experience	
	f	%	χ²	significance	χ²	significance	χ²	significance	χ²	significance
Overseas contacts:										
Chambers of commerce (n = 202)	57	28	–	–	–	–	3.90	0.04	–	–
Trade/employers associations	66	33	–	–	5.4	0.02	–	9.00	–	–
(n = 202)			–	–	1.0	0.00	–	–	5.27	0.02
Professional associations	80	40	–	–	6.2	0.01	10.50	1.00	9.35	2.00
(n = 201)			–	–	7.0	2.00	9.50	1.00	3.85	0.00
University research depts	83	41	–	–	7.6	0.00	–	–	–	2.00
(n = 202)			–	–	3.0	6.00	–	–	–	0.05
Public research institutions	50	25	–	–	–	–	4.57	–	7.46	–
(n = 201)			–	–	–	–	–	–	5.07	–
Company/industry based	81	40	–	–	–	–	5.25	0.00	5.17	–
research units (n = 202)			–	–	12.0	0.00	4.32	6.00	–	–
Trade fairs (n = 208)	162	78	–	–	9.0	0	4.24	0.02	7.91	6.00
Academic conferences seminars	109	54	–	–	–	–		3.00	–	0.02
(n = 202)			–	–	5.3	0.02		0.03	–	4.00
Research colloquia (n = 198)	54	27	–	–	7.0	1.0		8.00	–	0.02
Customers (n = 209)	176	84	–	–	6.6	0.01	–	0.04	–	3.00
Suppliers (n = 204)	152	75	–	–	1.0	0.0	–	0	8.63	–
Distributors/agents (n = 206)	151	74	–	–	–	–	–	–	–	0.00
										5.00
*Performance:**										
Number of export markets	–	–	–	–	–	–		–		–
Export growth	–	–	–	–	–	–		–		–
International ratio	–	–	–	–	–	–		–		–

Table 2.3 Predisposition to internationalize by contact made *cont*

	Firms		Foreign nationals*		Foreign language*		Overseas education*		Overseas work experience	
	f	$\%$	χ^2	*significance*	χ^2	*significance*	χ^2	*significance*	χ^2	*significance*
Turnover growth	–	–	–	–	–	–	–	–	0.03	
									5.00	
									–	

* Measured as dichotomous variables.
** Continuous categories

Table 2.4 Predisposition to internationalize by frequency of contact

	Foreign nationals*		Foreign language*		Overseas education*		Overseas work experience*	
	χ^2	significance	χ^2	significance	χ^2	significance	χ^2	significance
*Overseas Contacts:***								
Chambers of commerce (n = 202)	8.4	0.038	10.46	.015	13.04	.005	–	–
Trade/employers associations (n = 202)	0.08	0.008	–	–	–	–	–	–
Professional associations (n = 201)	–	–	16.46	.001	19.36	.000	11.15	.011
University research depts (n = 202)	–	–	–	–	–	–	–	–
Public research institutions (n = 201)	–	–	8.62	.035	–	–	8.24	.041
Company/industry based research units (n = 202)	–	–	13.80	.003	7.86	.049	–	–
Trade fairs (n = 208)	–	–	–	–	9.62	.022	10.26	.016
Academic conferences seminars (n = 202)	–	–	9.64	.022	–	–	–	–
Research colloquia (n = 198)	–	–	9.12	.028	–	–	–	–
Customers (n = 209)	–	–	–	–	–	–	–	–
Suppliers (n = 204)	–	–	–	–	–	–	–	–
Distributors/agents (n = 206)	–	–	–	–	–	–	–	–
Performance	–							

* Measured as dichotomous variables.

** Scaled items from 0 = 'never' to 3 = 'monthly or more frequently'.

Predisposition to Internationalize by Frequency of Contact

In addition to whether or not firms made contact with overseas bodies, the effect of frequency of contact was examined (Table 2.4). As discussed above, founders' foreign nationality played no significant part in whether or not firms established contact with chambers of commerce. When they did do so, however, they made contact more frequently than those without foreign national founders (Table 2.4), and foreign language ability made contact more important in the case of frequency of contact with chambers of commerce, university research departments, customers and distributors/agents, and attendance at trade fairs and academic conferences.

There was a significant correlation between founders' overseas education and frequency of contact with chambers of commerce, university research departments, customers and distributors/agents. Founders' overseas work experience was significantly associated with frequency of contact with university research departments and distributors/agents, and attendance at academic conferences and seminars. There was no direct association between any of the predisposing variables and firm performance (Table 2.4).

Patterns of Overseas Contact Frequency

It might be expected that different types of overseas contact will evoke different patterns with regard to the frequency with which firms approach or interact with them. For example trade fairs may be useful points of contact on a few discrete occasions, but customers may require more regular contact, and so on. A common factor analysis indicates three patterns of contact (Table 2.5).

The first factor, 'research contacts', includes contacts that suggest that R & D or the acquisition of scientific or technical knowledge are the underlying reasons for contact. The points of contact in question produce similar patterns of contact frequency. The second factor, 'trade contacts', includes customers, distributors/agents, suppliers and trade fairs. Here there is a common theme of commerce, as well as a similar pattern of contact frequency. The third factor, 'professional associations', suggests membership of or embeddedness in the local business community, and again there is a distinct frequency of contact pattern. Chambers of commerce loaded weakly on the third factor (0.331) and therefore was not included in the subsequent construction of scales.

Frequency of Contact Patterns and Performance

Kruskal–Wallis analysis indicated a significant correlation between frequency of contact with overseas research contacts and the firms' international ratio and number of export markets (Table 2.6). No correlation was found between frequency of contact with overseas research contacts and either export growth or turnover growth.

Significant correlations were found between the frequency of contact pattern of overseas trade contacts and international ratio, number of export markets and

Table 2.5 Factor matrix: patterns of overseas contact frequency

	Factor 1 (research contacts)	Factor 2 (trade contacts)	Factor 3 (professional associations)
University research departments	0.792	–	–
Company/industry R & D units	0.728	–	–
Research colloquia	0.665	–	–
Public research institutions	0.609	–	–
Academic conferences/seminars	0.543	–	–
Customers	–	0.890	–
Distributors/agents	–	0.769	–
Suppliers	–	0.642	–
Trade fairs	–	0.523	–
Trade/employers associations	–	–	0.764
Professional associations	–	–	0.759

Factor	Eigenvalue	% of var.	Cum. (%)
1	4.91	44.7	44.7
2	1.48	13.4	58.1
3	1.19	10.8	69.0

Keyser–Meyer–Olkin measure of sampling adequacy = 0.829
Bartlett test of sphericity = 1038.9; df = 55; significance = 0.000

Table 2.6 Pattern of contact frequency for research contact by firm performance (Kruskal–Wallis one-way analysis of variance)

	n	χ^2	df	Sig.
Number of export markets	168	30.02	3	0.000*
Export growth	141	4.46	2	0.107
International ratio	195	29.14	3	0.000*
Turnover growth	172	4.17	2	0.125

Scale reliability alpha = 0.8314

*Significant at ≤ 0.05. Scale constructed from factor groupings. Compound scale across variables includes contact with university research departments, company/industry based research units, research colloquia, public research institutes and academic conferences.

Table 2.7   Pattern of contact frequency for trade contact by firm performance (Kruskal–Wallis one-way analysis of variance)

	n	χ^2	df	*Sig.*
Number of export markets	175	65.24	3	0.000*
Export growth	145	17.43	2	0.000*
International ratio	202	53.65	3	0.000*
Turnover growth	180	3.79	2	0.151

Scale reliability alpha = 0.8401

*Significant at ≤ 0.05. Scale constructed from factor groupings. Compound scale across variables includes contact with customers, suppliers, distributors/agents and attendance at trade fairs.

Table 2.8   Pattern of contact frequency for professional association by firm performance (Kruskal–Wallis one-way analysis of variance)

	n	χ^2	df	*Sig.*
Number of export markets	168	16.51	3	0.001
Export growth	140	0.29	2	0.865
International ratio	195	11.37	3	0.010*
Turnover growth	173	0.20	2	0.906

Scale reliability alpha = 0.7570

*Significant at ≤ 0.05 Scale constructed from factor groupings. Compound scale across variables includes contact with trade and employers associations and professional associations.

export growth. There was no significant correlation between trade contact and turnover growth (Table 2.7).

The frequency of contact pattern of professional associations with performance indicators was significant only in respect of number of export markets and international ratio. No correlation was found with either export growth or turnover growth (Table 2.8).

DISCUSSION

The types of overseas contact that emerged in the analysis as significant *vis-à-vis* international predisposition tended to be those that would demand an appreciable amount of personal contact between the parties involved. The founder's language ability, education and overseas work experience all proved to be important in relation to the various types of research organization listed and to customers, suppliers and agents/distributors. Educational links proved to be important in respect of university contact, including attendance at seminars and conferences.

Work experience was a significant factor in the use a firm made of local professional associations. This might suggest that founders who had previously worked overseas may have been more aware of the opportunities offered by, or more willing to become embedded in, the professional and business infrastructure of their foreign markets. It might also be that founders with previous overseas work experience were more active in seeking international business based on their experiential learning.

The frequency with which firms made contact with overseas bodies was found to be important where there was likely to be repeated or on-going contact between or amongst individuals. Firms with foreign founders with a foreign language ability and overseas education made more frequent contact with chambers of commerce than those without these characteristics. Foreign language ability, education and work experience were also correlated with more frequent contact with agents/distributors, and the first two characteristics were correlated with more frequent contact with customers.

The association between contact frequency patterns and performance variables indicated that both the intensity of international activity and its geographic spread were important, especially in the case of research contacts. The greater the number of export markets a firm had, the larger the network of contacts it would have needed to keep in touch with. However, intuitively, research contact would not be the most obvious type of contact one would expect to increase because of an increase in the number of export markets. Together with the importance of the international ratio, the indications are that frequent contact with the science base in overseas markets expands the scope of internationalization in terms of geographic diversity and business intensity. Also worth noting is that R & D contact does not necessarily generate income directly. the international ratio is a measure of *all* income from overseas, not just that generated from export sales.

A significant relationship can be expected between patterns of trade contact frequency and international performance. The results of the analysis confirm that the more effort a firm puts into contacting those directly involved in marketing and distribution activities, the more impact there will be in terms of export expansion. Conversely it could be argued that firms that are more successful in terms of the extent of their international business will make more frequent contact with their overseas contacts. While frequency of contact with trade-related links can be expected to be associated with international performance indicators, it is worth pointing out that indirect modes of foreign market entry, often implicitly associated with small firms, require little if no contact between the firm and overseas-based individuals and organizations.

Following the latter argument through, small firms' choice of entry mode may be influenced by the extent to which they are predisposed towards international business. Several studies have found that small firms tend to prefer foreign agents/distributors or their own personnel to any form of domestic intermediary (Holmlund and Kock, 1998). For example foreign agents/distributors or own personnel were used by 70 per cent of the small software firms in Bell's (1995) study, 67 per cent of the service firms in O'Farrell *et al.*'s (1998) study and, in a sample of small high technology firms, agents/distributors were used by 60 per cent and own personnel by 30 per cent, although these were not not mutually exclusive (Jones, 2000). These modes of export by their nature require more commitment, more cultural affinity and more language ability or awareness than the less direct modes of export commonly associated with small firms.

Common sense dictates that the need for frequent contact with overseas bodies will increase as a firm's overseas business interests expand. Factor analysis has revealed, however, that patterns of contact frequency vary by type of activity. The emergent factors are suggestive of a value chain configuration, with distinct specialist or functional activities taking place through specific types of cross-border contact.

CONCLUSIONS AND RECOMMENDATIONS

This study has found no direct relationship between predisposition and performance. Like other studies that have examined the role of founder experience and performance and produced similar results, this chapter does not reject the possibility that predisposing factors may ultimately have a strong effect on performance (see Reuber and Fischer, 1999, for a discussion).

The data in this chapter have been limited to four predisposing factors, a predetermined list of overseas-based research contacts and the frequency with which firms make contact. The questions have been exploratory and were based on a study that focused in the first instance on internationalization patterns and processes. It would clearly be worthwhile to take a more in-depth look at predisposing factors and to determine the ways in which they are used by founders and developed over time. Future research should aim to determine modes of contact, the individuals who are involved in maintaining contact, the purpose of making contact and the value of this contact to firms with regard to the international development over time. This may require a qualitative methodology. This study has indicated that contact and frequency of contact are linked to the performance of firms. While predisposing factors have not been found to be directly associated with performance, predisposition does increase the likelihood that firms will make and keep contact with bodies or individuals overseas.

As Yeoh (2000) suggests, personal contact is developed with key people and sources of information in the primary environment. In his view performance is likely to be improved by using 'experiential information sources' such as trade fairs, potential customers and foreign representatives. External interaction is important for small firms as it is likely to supplement their internal knowledge resources and provide access to information they could not otherwise obtain (O'Farrell *et al.*, 1998 9; Yeoh, 1999). Finally, while small firms may not adopt specific internationalization strategies, they may have strategies to make and develop overseas contacts and links. The challenge for future research in this area is to establish whether this is the case.

Part Two

Ethics, Environment and Corporate Governance

3 Multinational Companies and Ethical Issues

Sumi Dhanarajan

Oxfam was founded in 1942 in response to the human crises caused by the blockades in Europe during The Second World War. Since then it has grown to become the largest British-based international development organization, with offices in over 70 countries. Its mandate is to work with others to find lasting solutions to poverty and suffering. Towards this end, it seeks to identify the root cause of poverty, lobby policy makers to make pro-poor decisions and empower communities to demand respect for their civil, political, economic, social and cultural rights.

In this context, Oxfam plays an active role in addressing the impact of business on the lives of poor people. It has recognized from its engagements at the grassroot and policy levels that it is no longer possible to concern itself solely with government activities as one of the biggest engines of development in today's world is the private sector. Oxfam's aim is to ensure that this engine generates advantages rather than harm for those who are vulnerable to exploitation or have been unable to reap the benefits of the current economic order. Show why Oxfam is taking this so seriously. The following data[1]

- Of the 100 largest economic entities in the world, over half are corporations.
- The combined sales of the world's 200 largest corporations are greater than the combined GDP of all but the 10 largest state economies.
- The sales of the top five corporations (General Motors; Wal-Mart, Exxon-Mobil, Ford Motor and Daimler Chrysler) are greater than the GDPs of 182 countries.
- These sales are also 18 times greater than the combined annual income of a quarter of the world's population, who live on less than one US dollar a day.

Whilst all companies have similar legal and ethical responsibilities, whether they are a small enterprise or a transnational, the size, economic power, political influence and structure of multinational companies mean they have more responsibilities and should be subject to greater accountability. There have been angry public demonstrations in support of this, such as those in Seattle, where big businesses were labelled miscreants. There have also been considered responses by citizens concerned about corporate behaviour in their own backyard and elsewhere in the world. In a poll conducted in 23 countries at the turn of the century, one in five of those surveyed reported either rewarding or punishing companies according to their perceived social performance. Those who had not taken such action reported that they had at least considered doing so.[2]

In the UK, before making investment decisions pension-fund managers are now required by law to report whether they have considered the social and environmental impacts made by the companies in question. A compelling wake-up call to corporations must be the confidence with which Al Gore pursued his US election campaign line: 'Stand up and say no to big tobacco, big oil, big polluters, the pharmaceutical companies and the HMOs.' The tide, it appears, has turned.

The concept of business ethics is not a new one. However its scope is evolving as the nature of the corporation and its interaction with people and governments changes. Even events of the past are coming under the spotlight because of this new take on the accountability and responsibilities of business. For example, in 2001 IBM was the target of a lawsuit filed in the US on behalf of Holocaust survivors. It was alleged that the company had aided genocide by developing and providing the punch-card system that had helped the Nazis to index those in the concentration camps and ultimately determine who should be exterminated. It was alleged that the company had known exactly what the technology was being used for, and that it had reaped profits to the tune of US$10 million in today's value. The action was subsequently dropped in order to speed up compensation payments by the German government. Compensation could be paid until there were no more outstanding legal actions.

This case highlights two developments: the application of human rights standards to the operations of business – such as the allegation that IBM was guilty of or at least complicit in genocide; and the establishment of a causal link between company activity and human rights violations. And this in the face of the traditional approach, which places the responsibility for human rights upon the state. A similar allegation to that levelled against IBM has been made against Royal Dutch Shell – a New York court has agreed to hear the substance of a case against the company, in which it is alleged that Shell was guilty of complicity in the killing of Ken Saro-Wiwa's and the Ogoni 9. Another allegation levelled against multinational retailers is that their products have been made under exploitative conditions.

We shall focus here on two particular responsibilities carried by companies – economic responsibility and political responsibility – and what they entail.

In a time of mergers between megacorporations, the combined economic power of multinational companies is huge. When Glaxo Wellcome and SmithKlineBeecham merged to become GSK in 2000, this pharmaceutical company's market capitalization was in the region of £107 billion. GSK now has manufacturing sites in 41 countries, its products are sold in 140 countries and it has a 7 percent share of the global pharmaceutical market.[3] It produces some of the world's best-selling drugs and has made significant inroads into antiretroviral treatment for HIV/AIDS.

Like other big pharmaceutical companies, GSK is conscious of the necessity to protect its market, but efforts to achieve these ends must be conducted responsibly when a product or service is meeting a basic human need. Oxfam, is very concerned about companies using a variety of mechanisms to achieve effective monopolies over markets that result in medicines being priced beyond the means of poor people and sometimes even their governments. The AIDS crisis has brought this to the forefront of public consciousness. In South Africa the situation is critical. Some 4.5 million people are already infected with HIV, and each day a further 1700 people are newly infected. Brand-name patented medicines necessary for treatment are very expensive, in some cases up to 12 times the price of the generic equivalent available from countries such as Brazil. The South African government tried to deal with this crisis by legislating for the use of safeguards that would allow intellectual property rights to be quashed in the face of a serious threat to human health. These safeguards would facilitate the importation of patented medicines from places where they were cheaper or enable the granting of compulsory licenses to allow generic producers to manufacture cheaper equivalents. In response, 39 of the largest pharmaceutical companies mounted a legal challenge for the law to be declared unconstitutional because it *inter alia*, breached their right to property. This lawsuit prevented the legislation from taking effect for three years. No wonder the public outrage. The attack on the pharmaceutical industry for its bullishness even prompted Business Week 12 Feb 2001 to suggest that, 'Sometimes protecting shareholder value has as much to do with doing the right thing as it does with pro-tecting drug patents'. The 39 drug companies subsequently withdrew their legal challenge because of the weight of public pressure both in South Africa and inter-nationally.

There are similar concerns about patents in the Western world. In the US there are complaints even at the governmental level about pharmaceutical firms arbitrar-ily seeking to prolong the patent period for key best-selling drugs through tactics such as 'evergreening'. For example, in order to extend the patent on its epilepsy drug Neurontin, Pfizer patented the way in which its epilepsy drug prevents this drug from degrading the patent – and it even offered pay-offs to companies to dis-suade them from marketing the cheaper equivalents that will doubtless be produced when the patent expires. Similar tactics have been identified in Thailand.

Oxfam is not calling for the demise of the intellectual property regime. It rec-ognizes that patent protection is a crucial precondition for innovation and R & D. It also recognizes that denied access to health care is a complex issue and that infrastructure and governments play a major role. However, if companies were to exercise their economic rights responsibly rather than on absolute, self-inter-ested terms, this would considerably aid the addressing of health crises.

The second and final issue to be addressed have is political responsibility. 'He who has the gold, makes the rules' – so says Samuel Jayson LeFrak, one of the richest real estate tycoons in the US. His words are pretty accurate. Economic power inevitably translates into political influence, be this gained through the corporate bankrolling of politicians or the overwhelming part played by corpo-rate coalitions in defining the global political and economic agenda. In countries desperate to attract foreign direct investment, multinational companies wield a tremendous influence and conditions are often be tailored to their benefit, such as tax concessions or the watering down of workers' rights in export processing zones. As companies grow in size and power, the use of such influence is being brought out of the shadows and institutionalized, or taken as a given. This does not sit well with the public, especially when it threatens democratic institutions and marginalizes those whom governments are supposed to represent.

To pick up the thread on the pharmaceutical industry, during the negotiations at the last Uruguay Round of GATT talks the industries most concerned about intellectual property rights formed a coalition called the Intellectual Property Committee. This committee was instrumental in the drafting of the Trade-Related Intellectual Property Agreement (TRIPS), which among other things extended the patent period to 20 years. Some observes even suggest that the committee drafted the agreement. In the US the Pharmaceutical Manufacturers Association (PhRMA) regularly lobbies the US Trade Representative to take action against countries that PhRMA feels are failing to protect intellectual property rights to its satisfaction. Usually, what the PhRMA wants, the PhRMA get. For example in Thailand a series of amendments were made to the Thai Patent Act at the behest of the US Trade Representative, with the result that flexibility in the law to balance patent protection against health needs has almost been removed.

The report of the UK Pharmaceutical Industry Competitiveness Task Force in 2001 makes one wonder if the industry has the same influence here. Signed by Tony Blair, the report highlights that a key priority of the UK government should be to maintain the level of investment by pharmaceutical companies in the UK. It then goes on to insist that the protection of intellectual property rights must remain a key plank, that such protection is not *per se* a barrier to access to medicines, and that attempts to weaken it would be counterproductive[4].

Oxfam believes that if a company is to demonstrate credible corporate responsibility it needs to take an integrated approach, and ensure that all aspects of its business are imbued with ethical commitment. Nowadays, public expectations of companies go right to the core of their business. There are concerns about the products or services, production operations, marketing, trading relationships, disposal of products and engagement by businesses with the government and community. These concerns are no longer arrested simply by adding a philanthropic arm to the business. Customers and, significantly, investors want more. Referring to the poll mentioned earlier in this chapter, the CEO of Burson-Marsteller asked: 'Does it really make business sense to say that the customer is wrong?'[5]

Notes

1. Institute of Policy Studies, report on the global power of the top 200 corporations, December 2000.
2. The Millenium Poll on Corporate Social Responsibility, conducted by Environics International Ltd in cooperation with the International Business Leaders Forum and the Conference Board, 1999.
3. 'Dare to Lead: Public health and Company wealth', Oxfam GB, February 2001.
4. Department of Health press release, 28 March 2001. See report at <<http:/www.doh.gov.uk>>
5. Allan Biggar, letter to the *Financial Times*, 19 March 2001.

4 Multinational Companies and Environmental Issues

Duncan McLaren

INTRODUCTION

Friends of the Earth is the largest environmental campaigning network in the world – a federation of national groups in 68 countries. In the UK, Friends of the Earth is one of the country's most influential environmental pressure groups and it aspires to find solutions to environmental problems that will make life better for all people. To this end it works with activists, communities, politicians and businesses.

It is a truism that the business world changes fast. One day dot-coms are a phenomenon, the next a bursting bubble. Today 'e' is no longer the most important letter in the business lexicon, whether it stands for electronic or the euro. Today the most important letter is the 'w' or 'Dubya' in the name of US President George W. Bush.

THE TOXIC TEXAN AND CLIMATE CHANGE

Is Bush junior really the friend of US multinational companies? Or is he their worst nightmare come true? In our view, because of his insensitivity to the changing social and global environment, the latter is more likely. To explain this we shall consider what he has done, and the context in which he has done it.

In March 2001 Bush declared that the US did not intend to sign up to the Kyoto Protocol, negotiated under the UN Framework Convention on Climate Change (FCCC). The protocol sets binding targets for the reductions of emissions of climate-changing gases by richer nations. The US ratified the FCCC in 1992 under George Bush senior. By repudiating the Kyoto Protocol, Bush junior has nailed his colours to the mast. This action is clearly a political pay back for the financial backers of the Bush presidential campaign – giant oil companies such as Exxon, Texaco and Chevron. Now, these companies believe they are the winners.

However the costs of putting short-term business interests and profits first means those costs will be borne not only outside the US, but also by the wider US public. As climate change takes hold, tropical diseases will spread northwards over the US, hurricanes will occur more frequently (and not just in Florida), and water shortages and other heat-generated effects will grow. At the

31

same time it will be come starkly clear that the US, and especially US business, is the main obstacle to a fair and effective agreement to tackle this most pressing global environmental concern.

This will be bad for business, for several reasons. First, economic analysis links sustained corporate success and productivity to energy efficiency and high energy prices. Similarly, low energy prices are a disincentive to investment in renewable and hydrogen technologies. Yet these will be the energy production technologies of the future (when oil resources are depleted, if not before). Those economies and companies that have invested in their development now will profit most in the future, as the Danes have already found with their booming export business based on their expertise in wind power.

Second, despite the fact that implementing the Kyoto Protocol will probably be good for business, Bush does not see it this way. Thus the EU has been given an excuse to impose (or at least threaten) border tax adjustments on US imports or even trade sanctions – either of which will worsen the existing US trade deficit and affect US company profitability.

Third, the Bush announcement has led to increased environmental activism and concern. Friends of the Earth's 'Flood Bush' email initiative resulted in more than 100 000 protest messages being sent to the White House over two weeks by individual activists all over the world. There have been many calls in Europe for consumer boycotts – not just of US oil companies (a coalition of environmental pressure groups, including Friends of the Earth and Greenpeace, have launched a 'Stop Esso' boycott campaign) but also of iconic American products such as Coca-Cola and McDonald's hamburgers. Such calls harm business reputations at a time when reputation is becoming increasingly important for financial success.

The changing nature of the investment market – with a growing share being taken by funds that engage actively with company directors – means that reputation management is more vital than ever to share values and the ability of companies to raise equity. At the same time, public trust in companies has been dramatically reduced by the process of 'hollowing out', in which employment in major companies has fallen and become much less secure. Permanent employment in the US fell by almost 700 000 in 1998 alone (despite growth in the total number of jobs). In 1997 the CEO of Kodak earned $60 million in share options for cutting 20 000 jobs. This trend means that companies now depend much more on consumer loyalty to their brands than on their employees' loyalty to them. Therefore good reputation is essential.

As a consequences companies risk losing their public 'licence to operate' and public pressure is bound to grow for tighter business regulation. Increased regulation is the worst nightmare of the US Council for International Business, which sees the mandatory verification of business participation in voluntary agreements as tantamount to a police state.

Climate Change

Climate change is not the only issue of concern to Friends of the Earth, but in several ways it is symbolic of the problems humankind faces in achieving sustainable development. Climate change demonstrates that economic growth has pushed the environment beyond its limit, with emissions of carbon dioxide and other greenhouse gases far exceeding the capacity of ecological and natural systems to absorb them. It also illustrates the accelerating use humans are making of the world's resources, and therefore the failure of eco-efficiency strategies (as promoted by the World Business Council for Sustainable Development and others) to address the absolute rates of resource use and relative efficiency. Despite cars and power plants that are more efficient, the growing number of them means that the absolute levels of emissions and environmental degradation are still rising.

Climate change also illustrates growing emission inequality at the global level. Although emissions are rising in many countries, to consider the equity implications of climate change we need to compare emissions with fair per capita shares of the ability of the world to absorb them, and to do so across time. For example, the US, with just 5 per cent of the world's population, currently accounts for 25 per cent of world emissions, and its historic share is even higher. Hence it is clear that the richer countries are still accumulating a vast 'carbon debt' that is owed to poorer countries. This is just one part of the wider ecological debt.

Finally, taking these together, climate change dramatically symbolizes the unsustainablity of the global economy. How can we sustain an economy, that relies so heavily on the – unequally distributed – burning of fossil fuels? Friends of the Earth has calculated the extent to which the consumption of fossil fuels must fall to meet the twin demands of global ecological stability and social equity (which combine to define sustainability constraints for the economy). In the UK a 90 per cent cut in per capita emissions is required to keep within scientifically recognized climatic constraints and to deliver the 'environmental space' needed by poorer countries to claim a fair share of the world's resources for their development.

PUBLIC PERCEPTION

The public perception is that corporate interests are to blame for accelerating climate change. Whilst this perhaps ignores the part played by individual actions and demands, it reflects the real power relations between companies and governments.

Members of the public have a low opinion of multinational enterprises, despite buying their products. Many see such companies as uncaring, exploitative, antagonistic, arrogant, corrupt and politically over-powerful. The reasons for this attitude are wide-ranging, and include the spread of low-wage temporary jobs, the use of corporate greenwash and strategic lawsuits against public participation to silence critics, and the strategies used by corporations to avoid paying, corporation tax.

These views are echoed by UK politicians: 91 per cent of UK members of parliament believe that corporate social responsibility activities are no more than public relations exercises. In addition 44 per cent believe that multinational companies are already more powerful than governments.

The reaction of the public has been instructive. Amongst the masses we see further disengagement from both companies and politics, and a growing minority have turned to protest, boycotts and other types of activism. Fifty thousand protesters took to the streets in Seattle, and thousands in Prague. Now we hear that the next World Trade Organization (WTO) ministerial marking will be held in the desert dictatorship of Qatar, where, according to human rights organizations, meetings of more than five people (excluding family members) are illegal.

The dangerous influence of corporations over political processes is highlighted by the nine million francs spent by the Swiss government to protect the annual meeting of the World Economic Forum in Davos in January 2001. The police were apparently instructed to prevent activists carrying 'subversive literature' from reaching Davos. 'Subversive literature' included the bestselling book *No Logo* by Naomi Klein.

THE REALITY

In some respects the public perception may be exaggerated, but in other respects the situation is even worse than perceived – as Bush's explicit support for big companies will make clear. Fundamentally, current corporate strategies cannot be sustained in the long term as the ecosystem's services and resources – such as climate stability and biological and genetic diversity – are becoming ever more stretched or scarce.

This is not to say that foreign direct investment (FDI) and multinational corporations cannot help improve the efficiency of resource use, transfer technology, generate (some) employment, and even contribute to economic and social development. Nor is it to claim that the people who direct, manage and work in corporations do not care about these issues. However it does mean that in the modern global economy these same activities (FDI and corporate practices and competition) are driving us away from sustainability by externalizing environmental and social costs. Moreover the neoliberal model of trade and investment liberalization, low taxation, privatization and deregulation, which is shaping the modern global economy, is not simply a product of governments.

In the South, debt and structural adjustment determine economic policy, whilst in the North the threat of corporate relocation is driving down taxes and putting pressure on regulatory standards, reinforced by the powerfully chilling effect of the WTO, whose practices are shaped by influential lobbying by Dialogue and similar business groupings working closely with governments. In practice the WTO has the power to overturn government regulations – but as challenges to agreed environmental measures have shown, in almost all such cases the dispute settlement panels have ruled in favour of trade interests over the environment. Furthermore it is often the case that such challenges are not even needed, as it is not unknown for governments to hold back from implementing agreed environmental and social measures – the so-called 'chill factor'.

A close look at the WTO reveals that corporate interests are represented in committees and dispute panels, and that WTO negotiations, tend to result in protective measures when this suits big business (for example trade-related intellectual property rights), and liberalization where it suits MNCs (for example in services). Privatization – in both North and South – is consistently driven by the liberalization of services (under the General Agreement on Trade in Services) or structural adjustment, regardless of its net impact on society. In the UK the private finance initiative has vastly increased long-term taxpayer costs in sectors such as transport and healthcare.

The consequences of the neoliberal model are destructive not simply because of the scale of the adjustment costs, but also because its assumptions are flawed. Its main faults have to do with environmental resources (which are largely upriced), competition (which is rarely fair between companies), market symmetry (where asymmetries in information and power are more common), comparative advantage (which relies on the highly unrealistic assumption of capital immobility) and the price – production relationship (which in the face of external debt, does not function to cut commodity production when prices fall).

The overall result is that we consume too much and protect the environment too little. Our economy actively manages and limits financial risks, but this also means that environmental risks are systematically increased. Our economy externalizes resource and environmental costs, and distributes them unfairly. The unacknowledged ecological debt owed by the North to the South now significantly exceeds the financial debt owed by the South to the North.

ANALYSIS AND CONCLUSIONS

Public distrust has already forced companies and governments to adopt a host of voluntary agreements and initiatives. The OECD recently catalogued 230 codes of conduct – covering everything from baby milk to bath water. In January 2000 the UN launched the 'Global Compact', which was quickly taken up by multinational companies with the worst reputations, such as Shell and Rio Tinto. In June 2000 the OECD concluded its review of the Guidelines for Multinational Enterprises – a review that the OECD hoped would invigorate a largely moribund and impotent instrument.

However these voluntary measures are failing. The OECD review provided no 'viagra' for the guidelines as there was strong opposition from companies to any form of verification of compliance with the guidelines. Public scepticism of companies' green claims is unabated, and even the widely lauded Dutch 'covenants system' – for which entry is voluntary but compliance is then legally binding – has been of limited impact as the courts have failed to levy the sanctions for non-compliance that the system requires. Four fifths of UK members of parliament believe that corporate social responsibility practice falls short of society's demands, and 93 per cent see a role in this for the government (although as yet only an minority think that legislation is essential).

It should come as no surprise that voluntary measures are failing. At best they are only likely to be used to overcome organizational failures in which companies fail to do what is in their own financial interests – such as failing to exploit significant financial savings from energy efficiency and waste minimization – because of lack of management attention and knowledge. The true scale of such potential is unclear, but it seems unlikely that the current voluntary initiatives can tackle even these problems. A good illustration is the current situation with e-business. Entrepreneurs in this sector stress the potential environmental gains that e-business could deliver, yet almost 80 per cent of e-businesses in the UK do not even measure environmental impacts. As the old maxim has it, what is not measured, is not managed.

The problems of business activity also include market failures arising, for example, from monopoly powers, asymmetry of information and unpriced inputs or outputs. Dealing with such failures requires government action, for example the imposition of taxes that internalize the costs of unpriced outputs of pollution, and the introduction of regulations that work with the grain of the market system – such as well-designed liability and accountability regulations.

However governments will only act when public pressure overwhelms business interests, which brings us back to George W. Bush. His decision on the Kyoto Protocol gave a strong incentive to citizen's movements (and progressive governments) to lobby for accountability – both political and corporate. A clear example is the way in which the legal challenge to Bush's big oil backers for compensation for the effects of climate change is rising up the agenda. This shift in public opinion is having not just a national but also an international impact. In the preparations for the world summit on sustainable development the call for corporate responsibility, accountability and liability is dominating the agenda of NGOs around the world. It will not go away.

5 Russian History and the 'Americanization' of Corporate Governance

Trevor Buck

INTRODUCTION

No single form of corporate governance (CG, the way in which managerial decisions are controlled by shareholders and/or other stakeholders) has yet emerged as being universally superior, and different forms have proved successful under different contingencies. For example the size of a firm, its industrial affiliation and technological level all have an influence in the effectiveness of different CG regimes, as do national institutions and culture (Noteboom, 1999). Furthermore, analysis of business histories in different environments suggests that even if national governments should wish to change the nature of CG, serious doubts must be cast on their ability to succeed. For example North (1990: 89) argues that institutional change is 'overwhelmingly incremental'. However he does go on to concede that circumstances of 'conquest or revolution' offer the best opportunity for discontinuous institutional change. Studies of German and Japanese CG reform (Buck and Tull, 2000) under (mostly) American military occupation after The Second World War have attributed to governmental actions some limited US-style CG changes, but these were under the most propitious circumstances, when the occupying authorities were free from local electoral pressure and the citizens were demoralized and helpless in defeat.

Given these conditions it seems appropriate to reflect on Russian business history in relation to CG in the 1990s. Although no military occupation was involved, the collapse of communism, the break-up of the former Soviet Union (FSU) and the enormity of Russia's indebtedness to the West after 1991 meant that in effect Moscow was 'occupied' by American (and other Western) creditors. These creditors, and the advisors they imposed on the Russian government, were able to demand the most drastic political and economic changes, many of which reflected US political democracy, company law, capital markets and price liberalization. Of course no German-style physical destruction of industry was involved, though in a few ways this turned out to be a mixed blessing.

In the event, some of the Russian regulatory changes that were partly made under Western duress had only temporary and insignificant effects because of the prevailing institutions and culture, but some subtle, long-term governance

37

changes were achieved. At the same time, terms such as 'semifeudal' and 'robber barons' have been used when speaking of the 'new' CG in Russia, which some extent reflects the earlier history of serfdom and exploitation.

The analysis in this chapter is presented in four sections. The first summarizes the alternative CG forms available to the central authorities in Russia during the 1990s. The second questions the effectiveness of 'top-down' state reforms in general, and in particular the assembly of a package of reforms based on the selective combining of elements from different national CG regimes. The third section deals with the historical antecedents of Russian CG that influenced the post-1990 reforms, and the fourth explains actual outcomes in the 1990s. The final section compares historical precedents with current outcomes, and speculates whether further 'Americanization' of Russian industry can be expected, or whether some CG regime of a peculiarly Russian type is likely to persist.

THE OPTIONS FOR RUSSIAN CG

Despite the recent emphasis on stakeholders, CG in the US and UK usually reduces to *the means by which important enterprise decisions made by professional managers are controlled by the firm's shareholders*. These shareholders are usually specialist suppliers of capital and they play no other role in the firm. Their sale and purchase of shares acts as the main disciplinary force on manager in that large-scale sales may facilitate hostile takeover and the replacement of managerial incumbents. Although independent or non-executive directors are supposed to represent the voice of shareholders, in practice outsiders have every incentive to free-ride in relation to the monitoring of managers, and they influence managers mainly through share exit (Noteboom, 1999). Noteboom (ibid.: 846) goes on to observe that market-driven discipline by capital markets invariably extends to labour relations and the internal divisionalization of the firm into profit centres. Other interested parties, besides shareholders, with stakes in the firm do not usually hold seats on company boards. For example senior managers, other employees, suppliers, customers, banks and the government are usually dealt with on a bilateral, market basis, although this does not of course preclude employees from being treated as human beings and human capital rather than as commodities.

The law in the US and UK has historically reinforced exit-based CG. For example judge made common law has arguably encouraged the protection of individual shareholders from expropriation by insiders, and from restrictions on the free tradability of stock (La Porta *et al.*, 1997). Until its recent abolition the Glass–Steagall Act in the US either prohibited banks from stock ownership, or permitted it subject to approval by the Federal Reserve Board, provided it was passive. Legislation has also restricted the holdings of other financial institutions to certain maximum levels in any one industrial firm, thus discouraging 'relational' investment (Roe, 1993). Furthermore, active shareholding has been discouraged by insider trading laws. Thus, shareholder interest based CG is deeply embedded in many legal institutions, and reforms to CG structures have broad consequences for the wider socioeconomic system (Noteboom, 1999: 845).

The negative aspects of such market-based CG are widely recognized. For example free-riding by dispersed outside shareholders is widespread, and Roe (1993) refers to the powerlessness felt by individual Anglo-American shareholders. Among its other alleged shortcomings, Anglo-American CG has been associated with short-termism (Dickerson *et al.*, 1995) and with firms' difficulty in raising funds for expansion, particularly in industries that are too complex to be transparent to outside shareholders (Noteboom, 1999: 858).

These alleged shortcomings are balanced by the potential strengths of market-based CG that are so appealing to countries such as Russia. In contrast to ministerial monitors, for example, capital markets offer dispassionate verdicts on the performance of professional managers and their firms, involving no significant personal relationship between decision makers and monitors. These verdicts demand substantial amounts of information, routinely gathered by analysts and the financial press, but they produce an extremely flexible, particularly downwardly flexible, industrial system, should capital markets take weak performance to indicate a need for retrenchment. With single-role, specialized input suppliers quite separate from specialized shareholders as suppliers of finance, there may be significant economies of scale to be enjoyed, but few economies of scope, since stakeholders do not conventionally become involved in governance.

Another CG approach in large industrial firms in Japan and Germany can be defined as *the means by which important managerial decisions are controlled by firm's stakeholders*. Such governance has been termed 'voice-based' CG, with shares and/or places on boards being held by dual-role stakeholders with an existing relationship with the firm, such as banks, suppliers to the firm, the state or employees. In Germany, banks can influence industrial firms through their own shares and those they hold for others, and banks (and employees) typically have places on separate supervisory boards. In Japan, relational investors take the form of banks and other financial institutions, and suppliers and clients are linked by cross shareholdings and cross-directorships. Although managers in countries with voice-based CG have not usually experienced the threat of hostile takeover, they are constrained by active monitoring by stakeholders with shares and/or board representation, especially during a financial crisis.

As with CG in the US and UK, regulations in Japan and Germany have buttressed their distinctive forms of CG. For example La Porta *et al.* (1997) note that French, Scandinavian and German law – and by definition Japanese law, which is modelled on the German system – belongs to the scholar- and legislator-made civil law tradition, where insiders have more opportunities to influence legislators than is the case with US/UK judge-based common law.

The positive and negative attributes of voice-based (relationship- or network based) CG are essentially the mirror image of market- or exit-based systems: specialized suppliers of credit and other banking services to particular firms and their competitors, are able to enjoy economies of scope in information collection as they combine this function with the monitoring of senior managers. Such dual-role monitors may be slow to demand rationalization unless there is a major crisis, but they can provide a ready source of funds for long term expansion, especially in technologically complex firms that are easily monitored by single-role, outside shareholders with no deep relationship with the firm (Noteboom, 1999: 855). While a second role may inform relationship investors in their monitoring capacity, shares for input suppliers (for example employees) may provide incentives for consummate performance.

Table 5.1 summarizes the modern debate on CG. Besides offering economies of scope, voice-based CG has generally been found to offer a comparative advantage during economic upturns, when relational investors are able to supply funds for expansion. Such investors, with a long relationship with and deep knowledge of the firm, can be expected to be most effective in a technologically complex industry whose operations are opaque to unrelated outside investors.

On the other hand, such a system is weakest when a severe downturn in the national economy requires dispassionate outside investors to demand downsizing and divestment. Of course such downsizing tends to destroy mutual trust, and a culture of trust is a necessary condition for effective relational CG, since stakeholders with dual roles in the firm, for example bankers who are also shareholders, must be trusted not to exploit information collected in one role to inform rent seeking in the other.

Russian firms and their reformers might look at Table 5.1 and ponder whether they could combine the strengths of both systems. It is suggested here, however,

Table 5.1 Corporate governance and contingencies

Level of contingency	Contingencies favoured	
	Voice-based governance	*Market-based governance*
National level	Culture of trust (Noteboom, 1999; Baums, 1993)	Culture of individual opportunism (Noteboom, 1999)
National/ business level	Expansion phase: need for new investment (Baums, 1993)	Contraction phase: need for downsizing (Franks and Mayer, 1997)
Business level	Businesses with long production cycles needing long-term investors (Baums, 1993)	Businesses with short production cycles needing short-term investors (Franks and Mayer, 1997)
Business level	Businesses that are technologically complex: rendering operations opaque for unrelated outside investors (Bolton and Von Thadden, 1998)	Businesses that are technologically routine, rendering operations transparent for unrelated outside investors (Noteboom, 1999)

that typical national governance regimes are deeply embedded in national culture and institutions, and that path dependency puts clear limits on a 'pick-and-mix' approach to governance reform.

CONSTRAINTS ON RUSSIA'S CHOICE OF CG REFORMS

Although the law can reinforce a prevailing form of CG, path dependency may also prevent the successful grafting of elements from alien CG systems (North, 1990: 99). Black (2000) goes further and argues that the role of the law in the context of CG may be trivial. In particular, other socioeconomic institutions and national culture may interact to block attempted grafts of regulatory reforms.

In general, as noted above, in countries such as France and Germany, law based on a civil code, as opposed to judge-based case law, can provide powerful institutional support for relational shareholders. The law can therefore underpin voice based CG and a civil code may constitute a barrier to proposed market reforms that amount to Americanization. In addition, pressure groups representing insiders in large firms may find it relatively easy to influence legislator-made laws in countries with civil codes, while judges and the common law may protect the rights of individual shareholders when governments try to introduce legislation that promotes the interests of relational shareholders. In any case, formal attempts to introduce elements of exit-based CG in a predominantly voice-based society (and *vice versa*) may simply provide entrepreneurs with new profit opportunities, since entrepreneurs' instinct is to seek profit by circumventing new formal rules with old patterns of behaviour (North, 1990: 87).

In Russia's case, a succession of top-down presidential decrees and parliamentary laws may effectively sabotage any attempts to introduce market-based economic reforms. Other potential institutional barriers will be reviewed in the historical section below. At this stage it should be noted that any distinctively Russian institutions must interact with national culture, though even the use of these terms is controversial: Lane (1989: 87) provides an excellent critique of the culturalist and institutionalist perspectives on societal forms and processes.

Following Hofstede's seminal work (1980a), national culture can be taken to mean the ideas, values, norms and meanings shared by members of a social entity that are transmitted through families and communities. Hofstede and Bond (1988: 419) have identified the crucial cultural dimension of power distance, or 'the extent to which the less powerful members of institutions and organizations accept that power is distributed unequally'. In Russia a culture of low tolerance of power distance combined with high levels of collective orientation (Naumov, 1996) has encouraged enterprise incumbents to demand a reform path that does not threaten their own power within enterprises. It also follows that a well-developed legal system may be weakly enforced locally in the face of organized interest groups, usually enterprise managers, other employees and their political contacts.

However such a view of cultural influence has been criticized as 'ideational' (Lane, 1989: 27; Whitley, 1992) and as a 'black box', catch-all term for all unexplained variations (Lane, 1992: 29). A naive culturalist view has therefore largely been replaced by an institutional perspective (Peng, 2000) that sees culture as being embedded in observable social, political and economic institutions such as education, training and workplace representation. From this perspective, institutions are perpetuated and modified by powerful actors in society according to their economic interests and cultural orientations (Lane, 1989: 32). For example Russia's gradual, post-Stalinist relaxation of central controls over enterprises between 1965 and 1990 gave decentralized power to local political and economic interest groups. Subsequent economic reforms in the 1990s had to appease these interest groups as well as Western creditors.

A crucial factor in CG regimes based on relationships between managers and stakeholders is that dual-role stakeholders, such as banks as owners and lenders, must be trusted not to abuse their privileged positions by seeking immediate, opportunistic advantage, but to take a long-term view in the interests of the firm as a community. Examples of stakeholders representing their own interest rather than those of shareholders as a whole include banks earning extra rents from companies in which they hold shares, incumbent managers entrenching their own positions as managers, and creditors encouraging managers to forego risky investment projects (Casson, 1993: 171; Shleifer and Vishny, 1997). Market-based CG may therefore be most suited to cultures with a low degree of trust, where such opportunism is anticipated and therefore preventable. Where different stakeholders in the firm have a history of adversarial relationships and opportunism, relational, voice-based CG (under capitalism or communism) may collapse into 'arbitrariness and delusion at the top, and corruption and deceit at the bottom' (Blackwell, 1970: 168).

In any case, deliberate CG reforms may founder when faced with vested interests. North (1990: 101) argues that although (military or financial) conquest and revolution provide the most efficacious conditions for institutional change, for cultural and historical reasons there is 'tenacious survival of institutional constraints in the face of radical alterations in the formal rules of the game'.

With these philosophical, institutional and cultural limits on the ability of market forces, governments and the law to modify the predominant national form of CG in large firms, it seems appropriate to study modern Russia's historical background. The 1990s were a unique and tumultuous decade when the CG regime in the FSU, previously founded on relational ownership and control by the state, came under the strong influence of the US, a country with the most exit based CG, bent on industrial 'democratization', openness and the introduction of a US style CG that was considered to be ideal. Whatever the practical consequences of such an idealized system, should the outcome of Russia's reforms be attributed to this attempted Americanization or to Russia's historical antecedents?

PRE-1990 ANTECEDENTS OF RUSSIAN CG

Although central planning under the Communist Party is usually identified as the main antecedent of the post-1990 reforms, it should not be forgotten that Russia had a rich history of industrial development before 1917. Although the revolution of 1917 (and of 1991 for that matter) had a large impact, the previous economic structures and their performance continued to exert an influence, and the 1917 revolution may be seen to some extent as the logical extension of trends established under successive tsars, or even earlier.

In the early 1930s, Stalin completed his reorganization of industry, featuring public ownership and resource allocations by central directive. This gave the state the necessary voice and power to control the operations of industrial enterprises, or at least their formal operations. It should not be assumed, however, that state ownership and control of industry was an innovation of the Communist Party. Rather state bureaucracy is 'one of the most deeprooted of Russian traditions . . . the machine grew over the centuries and developed a kind of independent and self-regenerative power. It was not smashed to pieces by the revolution, but in fact merged with the Communist Party bureaucracy . . . [and] resulted in the growth of even greater, more arbitrary bureaucratic power in The Plan . . . a natural expression of this long tradition' (Blackwell, 1970: 168).

According to Pipes (1995: xxxi) the communist era was just a logical continuation of what has been called Russia's 'patrimonial' tradition. Russian geography, and in particular its extensive borders, meant (militarily) that control over its people (that is, sovereignty) was highly centralized, with overspending on defence and an almost permanent state of military and/or financial emergency (Crisp, 1976: 9). In addition poor soil and the short growing season in agriculture meant that markets and property rights (and consequently towns and cities, with only 18 per cent of Russia's population being urbanized by 1914 – Falkus, 1972: 11) would be weakly developed, exerting little discipline on the central rulers. The result was patrimonial, not despotic, rule (Pipes, 1995: 23). While despotism implies an absolute sovereign violating the property rights of subjects, a patrimonial ruler simply does not distinguish between sovereignty and ownership, and does not even recognize the existence of property rights, let alone infringement of them. As in primitive societies, under patrimony authority over people and objects is combined, and political authority is conceived as an extension of the rights of ownership. The ruler is both sovereign (controller) and proprietor (owner). Pipes (ibid.: 23) concludes that from the twelfth century to the present day patrimony has characterized the Russian State, and particularly its relationship with industry.

It should be remembered that Russia's feudal agricultural system always involved more state influence than was the case in other European societies. Serfs were assigned to noblemen, who were in turn usually under strong state influence, and over half of all serfs were attached to estates belonging to the Russian government itself (Crisp, 1976).

The first major attempt at industrialization was made by Peter the Great before 1725, but already the state's power was reflected in government departments (*prikazy*) that overlapped and conflicted in the organization of the economy. While Peter the Great is widely acknowledged to have been a reforming Tsar concerned with Westernization, it should be remembered that industrialization involved the establishment of state factories to produce military goods, and that state monopolies were granted for consumer goods in the form of licences to private operators, who were required to fulfil state procurement orders at fixed prices, usually at cost (Pipes, 1995: 209). Serf labour and enterprise managers alike were requisitioned by the state, which provided most of the capital and routinely fleeced operators and serfs with fixed prices and taxes (ibid.: 208). Industries were administered through 'colleges' that also carried out centralized research programmes at the state's behest.

The Crimean War (1854–56) highlighted the acute backwardness of Russian industrial materials and transport infrastructure. Largely as a consequence, liberal reforms, including the formal abolition of serfdom in 1861 (which also occurred in Japan in the early 1870s), weakened the power of the state for a short while. However the new private railways were initially subsidized by the state and then taken over by it, and two state banks continued to dominate total deposits until around 1890.

At about that time the state opened up Russian industry to foreign capital, particularly French and British investors, in manufacturing and oil respectively. By 1903–5, economic growth was rapid and foreign capital was financing 81 per cent of new industrial investment (Gatrell, 1986: 228). The state continued to play a major role in the formation of new financial institutions (ibid.: 175) and 'any company in Russia could have their authority to operate withdrawn by the administration at will' (Crisp, 1976: 183).

From 1902 the state permitted and even encouraged the growth of syndicates/cartels on the German *Kombinat* model (Gatrell, 1986: 177) and vertical integration advanced, for example between mines and metallurgy, and so on. This meant that when yet another national emergency emerged – in the form of The First World War – it was a small step from concentrated private industries to state regulation and effective control. For example state councils were established to procure the products militarily strategic industries such as armaments, fuel, transport and food, and the state set the price of and issued orders for iron and steel (ibid., 185).

From regulation it was an easy step in 1916 to set up the pre-revolutionary branch ministries (*glavki*), which in the 1930s were to become a significant feature of Stalin's central planning. According to Blackwell (1970: 61), 'by the end of 1916, a degree of state control of industry unprecedented in Russian history had been attained', and seventy *glavki* were run by boards consisting in many cases of the old factory managers and technicians, but including a preponderance of trade union members, workers' representatives and party officials. In turn, the *glavki* appointed similarly composed boards, as well as directors and inspectors, for local plants (ibid.: 70). Despite this attempt at super-bureaucratization, in practice it was 'impossible in the conditions of the Civil War for one central agency to control hundreds of dispersed factories' (ibid.: 71)

It can therefore be appreciated that the wielding of power by the Russian state bureaucracy was a continuous and evolving feature of corporate governance for many centuries, and not just during the communist period. State control over industry is best viewed as a constant feature of Russian culture and institutions, and the generally patrimonial relationship between the state and industrial enterprises cannot be expected to have produced the high degree of trust needed for the state be an effective enterprise stakeholder and/or shareholder. Hence it would be surprising indeed if state influence did not continue to have a strong impact on modern enterprise decisions.

The experiences of managers and workers (enterprise incumbents) comprise a long catalogue of bullying and exploitation under successive regimes in the form of exhortations to produce more in existing workplaces and of forced migration to new places of employment. This disregard for employees' preferences provoked varying degrees of defensive resistance. According to Naumov (1996) Russia was characterized by the low degree of individualism (that is, a high degree of collectivism) found in most Asian societies, but unlike in Asia there was little tolerance of power distance. This implies that enterprise incumbents exhibited solidarity towards each other but hostility towards distant state bureaucrats, unless they were embraced by the personal networks of enterprise managers (Peng, 2000: 158).

Pipes (1995: 17) argues that these cultural features can be connected to Russia's poor soil, harsh climate, and short growing season, which meant that individual subsistence farming was difficult and survival meant reliance on collective, cooperative action to sow and tend crops and harvest them quickly. Thus private land ownership was never a significant feature, and Pipes argues that the collectivist nature of Russia's agricultural institutions is echoed in modern industry.

By the nineteenth century ancillary production carried out in villages by cottagers (*kustari*), mostly during the winter, was providing a useful 'appendage' to the factory, according to Lenin (see Gatrell, 1986: 115). By the 1880s, this non-factory manufacturing sector was employing up to 15 million individuals (ibid.: 154). Despite having to pay rent and taxes to noblemen and the state, *kustari* enjoyed some degree of decision-making autonomy.

Enterprise incumbents' voice, or self-determination, was even more pronounced in factories set up by 'serf entrepreneurs', who had been encouraged by landowners since the early nineteenth century to set up ventures and factories and move to the cities – the town of Ivanova was made up almost entirely of such ventures (Blackwell, 1970: 20). Together, serf entrepreneurs and *kustari* were responsible for over five million workers in 1914, more than double the number employed in conventional factories (Falkus, 1972: 12).

This self-determination by serfs must ultimately have had a strong influence on the Communist Revolution, and even on human relations in contemporary

Russian factories, but it was emphatically not a feature of state factories, whether administered directly by the state or handed over to private owners (see above). With fine understatement, Crisp observes that before 1860 (1976: 12) 'there [was] no evidence of state peasants or townspeople volunteering for factory work'. Rather there was a long tradition of Russian factories being manned by labourers dragooned and transported to factories in towns and cities. For example, according to Blackwell (1970: 10) 'it was far more difficult for Peter [the Great] to find workers and engineers than to attract capitalists. He scraped the bottom of an empty labour barrel, using orphans, criminals, prisoners of war and heretics. Ultimately, peasants owned by the state were consigned in perpetuity, or leased out, to factories. Slavery and industrialization thus went hand in hand in Russia's first attempt to modernize.' Indeed after 1721 merchants in the towns could buy whole villages of serfs and put them to work in factories (ibid.: 19). This pattern re-emerged under Stalin on an even larger scale, with the forced migration of national minorities from areas such as Chechnya and Crimea, and of course the forced labour sent to the GULAGs.

In addition to forced migration, which was of course the very antithesis of employee voice, labourers in Russian factories were long subjected to poor working conditions, and constant bullying to increase production. After the tsarist factories, where semi-feudal industrialists kept down costs by progressively exploiting labour (Gatrell, 1986: 148), Stalin implicitly but enthusiastically adopted Frederick Taylor's scientific management techniques for use in Soviet factories. Here, a fondness for the stopwatch on the shopfloor was augmented by Stakhonovite campaigns to ratchet-up work norms and productivity (Blackwell, 1970: 117).

The significant point for modern Russian business is that there has been a long tradition of cronyism and over-bureaucratization among state and private owners, and harsh, militaristic conditions for labourers. Taken together these traditions are quite unsuited to modern factories (Blackwell, 1968: 410), breeding as they do a defensive attitude among enterprise incumbents and a hostility and distrust towards outsiders that are likely to prove very costly to remove.

After 1965, and particularly in the 1980s under Gorbachev, successive economic reforms gave a stronger voice to incumbents in individual enterprises and associations of enterprises. The new influence granted to managers and other employees extended to strategic decisions on output and employment levels, and to the distribution of part of any financial surplus. This decentralization, coupled with the incumbents' hostile attitude towards outsiders in general and the state in particular, was a potent recipe for alienation and defensiveness. However the enterprise shares granted to incumbents after 1991 may eventually serve to soften these attitudes. Conversely ownership of the shares might give a degree of control to managers and employees that will lead to their entrenchment and the putting up of greater obstacles to industrial reform involving outside investors.

Following this consideration of the state and enterprise incumbents as stakeholders (and possibly shareholders) in Russian history, different categories of outside investors must now be considered. Of course the state itself is an existing stakeholder in industrial enterprises and a potential shareholder. It should also be noted that the attitudes of incumbents might interact with the attitudes of outsiders.

In general suppliers of capital on Russian markets have always been confronted with high contractual and external risks, or contractual and country risks in the case of foreign outsiders. These risks can mostly be attributed to the patrimonial Russian state and its willingness to seize or give away enterprise assets, as well as its failure to establish and enforce property rights to safeguard minority outside investors, for example through legislation on joint-stock companies and bankruptcy. In addition the absence of a legal framework has stalled the development of an effective banking sector.

High risks mean that domestic or outside investors will generally only consider investments with a low degree of commitment and thus of risk exposure (Anderson and Gatignon, 1988: 7). This effectively restricts foreign investors to primary industries based on natural resources (oil, gas, timber, metals and so on) that can be used as collateral for investment, and to short-term, portfolio investments that amount to speculation. While the period 1850–1914 was characterized by substantial foreign investment, it was mostly in the form of guaranteed, fixed-interest bonds and railway stock that gave a guaranteed return (Gatrell, 1986: 222).

Domestic investors were confronted with the same high risks. Consequently the Russian landed gentry, certainly before 1861, preferred to accumulate a regular income in the form of payments by their serfs, and the merchant class (like foreigners) preferred to concentrate on low-commitment trading activities rather than production. In a typically Russian vicious circle, industrial capitalists did not generally come forward to finance industrial enterprises, owing to risks created mostly by the state, and so the state (from Peter the Great's time onwards) had to force the gentry and traders to invest in and manage factories.

In general the Russian state has only been prepared to welcome foreign investors and to reduce their risks by protecting their investments during periods of perceived national emergency, for example following Peter the Great's recognition of Russia's military backwardness and after Russia's defeat in Crimea in 1856. Consequently, in an attempt to reduce their risks, capitalists in the early twentieth century formed syndicates that verged on being cartels. Similarly, in about 1710 banks (backed by German and French capital) formed industrial conglomerates that today would be called financial–industrial groups (FIGs). According to Gatrell (1986: 212),

> each bank was surrounded by affiliated companies, whose shares it marketed, whose bills it discounted and upon whose boards its directors had seats. A. I. Putilov, chairman of the Russo-Asiatic Bank (founded 1910) was also chairman of the engineering company that bore his name, a director of at least three oil companies, the Nikolaev Shipbuilding Co., the Lena Goldfields Co.

and the Moscow-Kazan Railway. The Russo-Asiatic Bank had interests in at least 46 industrial companies, and specialized in armaments, oil and tobacco.

The formation of conglomerates such as these amounted to an attempt to reduce and internalize risks through diversification. As with the syndicates, conglomerates faced with high country risks formed close allegiances with members of the government. Capitalists, mostly interested in short-term or guaranteed returns, chose to trade rather than manufacture, and openly sought political protection. In these circumstances enterprise incumbents, with their own history of exploitation and being bullied, understandably perceived outsiders equivalent to as horse-traders, asset strippers and portfolio speculators (Pipes, 1995: 206).

With this combination of foreign investors being reluctant to commit themselves to Russian factories and incumbents being hostile towards all but 'friendly' outsiders (Wright *et al.*, 1998), the consequences should come as no surprise. Despite rapid progress after 1880, Russia's industrial revolution was still incomplete by 1914, with low levels of industrial investment and a general inability to produce modern machinery. According to Pipes (1995: 219), 'It is noteworthy that in the historical evolution of Russian industry, native resources have always proved inadequate to the task of making the transition to more advanced methods of production', and that the State has been 'forced to rely on foreign capital and foreign technology, paying for both, as it had done throughout its history, with raw materials.' In 1914 manufactured goods accounted for 5.6 per cent of total exports (mostly raw materials) but 22 per cent of imports (Falkus, 1972: 20). It could be argued that, outside certain high technology industries related to military production, this situation still prevails into Russia today. Still in desperate need of foreign capital and know-how, Russia has consistently failed to attract large-scale outside (especially foreign) investment in manufacturing, and its aggregate inflow of foreign capital has been negligible compared with that, for example, of China. Despite Russia's extensive natural resources – oil, gas, timber, minerals and metals – it attracted only $3900 million in FDI during the period 1989–95 (equivalent to $1.10 per capita in 1995). During the same period China received $121700 million ($18.20 per capita), and consequently Chinese manufactured goods have been able to compete in world markets.

MODERN RUSSIA AND AMERICANIZATION

As we have seen, Russia experienced intensive state intervention in industry in the tsarist and communist periods, accompanied by underdeveloped financial institutions, weakly protected private property rights, high country risks for foreigners and a low degree of trust between enterprise incumbents and all investors, but particularly foreigners. In 1992 the Russian government, under pressure from foreign creditors, embarked on a series of economic reforms that were ostensibly designed to bring US-style capitalism to Russia (Blasi *et al.*,

1997: 29). With Russia having the least open and most relational CG in the world, the reforms were intended to promote company information disclosure and liquid capital markets as a means of controlling the actions of enterprise decision makers, rather than the voices of relational shareholders such as the state or enterprise incumbents. Other reforms were concerned with political democratization and the deregulation of product markets. The relative merits of market and voice-based CG have already been discussed above, and no preference for Americanization should be implied from what follows.

Rather than provide a chronological or unstructured description of the CG reforms, the method of stakeholder analysis used in the previous section – involving the state, enterprise incumbents and outside investors – will be employed again. A major obstacle is presented by the discrepancy between the actual economy and the 'virtual' economy (Maddy and Ickes, 1998) depicted in official statistics and company reports. As far as possible, this review will rely on independent, unofficial surveys and reports.

After 1991 the Russian government was ostensibly concerned with the state's withdrawal from ownership and control of industry, and the restructuring of industrial enterprises to permit Russian firms to compete in global product markets (Sachs and Warner, 1995). In the meantime creditor nations in the West were anxious to bring about political reforms, industrial privatization and product market reforms that would prove irreversible. A compromise was developed to promote each of these objectives. Since political democratization was given high priority, the survival of the government depended on the popularity of its economic reforms among the electorate, but the reforms were heavily influenced by the employees of state enterprises (in industry and agriculture) and their families. Incumbent managers and other employees exhibited a high degree of collective solidarity within their enterprises and great hostility towards outsiders, including little tolerance of the distant power of the state and a high degree of enterprise self-determination that had accumulated over time with the help of earlier reforms (Filatotchev *et al.*, 1999). It soon became clear that state employees had a virtual veto over the reforms.

Faced with these realities, the reforms had to be conducted rapidly in order to ensure irreversibility, but since enterprise incumbents could delay or even veto the reforms, the latter had to be acceptable to the incumbents. The outcome was a two-stage industrial privatization programme to facilitate the state's withdrawal from industry. The first stage (1992–94) involved the mass privatization of state-owned enterprises (SOEs) with a low stock-market value, that is, most manufacturing enterprises but excluding a number of 'strategic, defence-related firms. In this stage, a centralized privatization programme with vouchers gave citizens in general and enterprise incumbents in particular the opportunity to acquire controlling stakes in the SOEs. The thinking here was that if outsiders obtained stakes from incumbents and other citizens, the latter would at least be compensated and electoral popularity would be maintained.

The second stage (1995–96) comprised the piecemeal privatization of more highly valued firms engaged in the production of raw materials (oil, gas, metals and so on) and the supply of energy and telecommunications.

It is difficult to estimate the impact of the state's sudden withdrawal from industry. In the case of manufacturing firms, it is clear that the centralized privatization programme of 1992–94 enabled the state to reduce its ownership of large firms to a negligible level, from 100 per cent in 1991 to 8.5 per cent in 1996 and 5.7 per cent in 1997 (Filatotchev *et al.*, 1999: 483). Explicit product subsidies from the state also became insignificant.

However, it can be argued that this sector is, in global terms, less important than primary extractive firms, energy producers, financial services and telecommunications, which were all excluded from the first stage of the programme. When these industries are taken into account the state's disengagement from industry is not yet complete. In 1995, the Russian government, anxious to raise funds before a presidential election, arranged for Russian banks to hold large amounts of shares in 28 of Russia's 'blue chip' companies in a loans-for-shares arrangement (Blasi *et al.*, 1997: 74), to culminate in open auctions in 1996 to accommodate foreign bidders. In practice, however, only 12 companies were auctioned (some to the banks themselves) and the banks held on to the shares as security for loans that were never to be repaid. These holdings ultimately formed the basis of the Russian financial – industrial groups, which were not dissimilar from those of 1910.

The outcome of these auctions for some of Russia's best companies was very unsatisfactory, and the state continued to influence their activities through its personal contacts with industry and their links with the media and banks. For example Boris Berezovsky was in charge of LogoVAZ, a conglomerate based on car distribution, while he was deputy secretary of the Security Council and had access to files on politicians and businessmen. In many cases the state held on to a 'golden' share that guaranteed continued state control, and in the case of Surgutneftgaz, the company's pension fund (under the control of enterprise managers) was allowed to win the auction. In the case of Norilsk Nickel, the auction was organized by Oneximbank, which itself won the contest with a bid of $170.1 million – the reserve price was $170 million. Indeed the whole loans-for-shares scheme was designed by Minister of Finance Vladimir Potanin, who was also chairman of Oneximbank, though he had nominally resigned upon joining the government. The state held on to large packets of shares in Russian regional telecom monopolies through its Svyazinvest holding company, United Energy Systems is more or less the old Ministry of Power Generation in all but name, and in early 2000 the Russian State still held 38.4 per cent of the total shares in Gazprom. It can, therefore, be seen that the participation of foreigners was in practice seriously restricted.

In the commanding heights of the Russian economy it is difficult to quantify the state's continuing influence experienced by these blue chip companies, but many of the private owners have strong personal links with the government and many large groups of companies still incorporate the old ministerial structures they were supposed to replace. In quantitative terms, despite the privatization of most manufacturing (that is, loss-making) firms, 'the Ministry of State Property still remains a majority shareholder in over 12,000 SOEs and a minority share-holder in over 3,800 companies with no coherent set of goals to exercise ownership rights. Assets are managed mostly via state boards composed of 2,000 members of ministries and agencies' (OECD, 1999c: 5).

In the case of Gazprom – the Russian gas and oil company, valued at around 8 per cent of Russia's GDP – in 2000 the Russian Federation still held 38 per cent of shares. The chairman of Gazprom is Rem Vyakhirev, who was first deputy minister of the FSU for the gas industry in 1986–91, and the government's representative on the Gazprom board is a former Russian prime minister, Viktor Chernomyrdin.

Beyond formal state ownership and board representation, many of the old state structures survive. For example the crisis in early 2000 in the supply of the precious metal palladium has been attributed to the bureaucratic procedures for the exportation of palladium. The metal is produced by Norilsk Nickel, stocked by the Central Bank of Russia and Gokhram, the state's precious metals agency, and export quotas and licences are issued by the president's office and Almaz, the exporting arm of the Ministry of Finance.

The involvement of Russian enterprise incumbents as relational shareholders in former SOEs from 1992 onwards was based on voucher auctions – a process that was designed to put shares into the hands of citizens in general. The degree of control enjoyed by managers was magnified by a disproportionate number of board seats being awarded to senior managers, but employees were somewhat under-represented (Filatotchev *et al.*, 1999: 485). Although outside investors have gradually gained a high proportion of total equity (see below), they too have been under represented on company boards (ibid.: 48)

In 1991, Western creditors, including the World Bank and the IMF, acknowledged that voucher privatization would initially favour incumbents but that it could gradually evolve into US-style outside ownership. However, pessimists feared that incumbents would try to influence the privatization programme in order to acquire permanent power for themselves. Surveys conducted in 1997 confirmed the continuation of insider ownership and the hostile attitude of incumbents towards outside investors (ibid.: 487). Estimates of share ownership vary, but by 1997 the average stake of managers in manufacturing firms was around 15 per cent of voting shares, and 37 per cent in the case of employees (Estrin and Wright, 1996: 409). It seems that privatized manufacturing firms are still 'manager-controlled, employee-owned' companies (Earle and Estrin, 1996: 33). As with blue chip companies and state shares, however, there are problems with identifying so-called outsiders, since many offshore funds have been set up by managers as pocket companies to conceal holdings under their direct control (Blasi *et al.*, 1997: 66).

While insider control of firms by incumbents had fallen to 52 per cent by 1997, compared with around 65 per cent immediately after the centralized privatizations were completed in 1994, it seems unlikely that many of these shares found their way into the hands of genuinely unrelated outsiders. Former

SOEs used a range of devices to obstruct US style outsider control, including informal managerial pressure on employees not to sell their shares to outsiders and obstructive share registration procedures, despite the existence of a Federal Securities Commission and rules on independent share registers.

Even when genuine outsiders have succeeded in obtaining shares, their ownership rights have often been severely weakened by insiders (OECD, 1999c). Outsiders' stakes have been diluted by new holding structures (Maddy and Ickes, 1998) and by new share issues authorized at company meetings held at short notice. There have also been serious deficiencies in Russian accounting standards and in the disclosure of information to outsiders, and enterprises have often been stripped of their best assets by incumbents in a number of ways, including transfer pricing, which deflects value away from subsidiaries and their outside investors to a manager-controlled holding structure (OECD, 1999c).

The situation for genuine outside investors, therefore, is a capital market that is quite different from that in the US. Nevertheless, in 2000, the Russian Trading System (RTS) boasted 60 regularly traded stocks, and 27 of these had American Depository Receipt (ADR) quotations in New York, which was a means of 'escaping the weakness of their home country's institutions' (Black, 2000). Despite the barriers to free float in Russia, only four of these ADR stocks in early 2000 traded at a substantial premium on the US market, indicating lower shareholder risks and trading costs than on the Moscow RTS market. Among the firms privatized in the central programme, outside ownership gradually increased from around 20 per cent in 1994 to 39 per cent in 1997 (Estrin and Wright, 1999: 409).

Despite signs of a less hostile attitude towards outside investors, incumbents in Russian SOEs have been notoriously unwilling to accept foreign investors in 'cherry picking' joint-ventures, whereby parts of SOEs are left out of a joint-venture and consequently incur even bigger financial deficits, ultimately leading to savage downsizing. However, since the capital market collapse of mid 1998 there has been evidence that SOE incumbents have become more positive about joint-ventures, and are not insisting that foreigners adopt a fully committed entry mode, that is, accept that foreigners' full responsibility for an SOE's liabilities, especially social provisions. For example Fiat negotiated a joint-venture with GAZ (for 'kit assembly' by GAZ of Fiat models) after many years of the enterprise incumbents insisting on fully committed entry by foreign investors. Sadly this joint-venture was suspended in 1999 because of the capital market collapse of 1998. It appears that this collapse softened the attitude of incumbents towards outsiders, but it simultaneously made the Russian market less attractive to foreigners.

However other signs suggest that outsiders are still facing cultural and institutional barriers set up by enterprise incumbents. For example, in early 1998 more than 220 companies, regularly traded their shares on the RTS, but this number has since fallen to 60, only three of which are in the manufacturing sector. The bulk of traded companies are in primary extractive industries, telecommunications and electricity supply. Furthermore, it is rare for any company to have more than 20 per cent of its shares in 'free float' and available for purchase, and this is quite typical of countries characterized by relational shareholding, that is, most countries beyond the US and UK (Blasi *et al.*, 1997: 153). Although 27 companies had ADRs at the beginning of 2000, all of these were at level 1, involving just the same information disclosure as in Moscow. Two years earlier, two Russian companies had level 3 ADRs, involving full information disclosure to US GAAP standards. Since the collapse in Russian shares in August 1998 the prices of four of the Russian ADRs on the US market have fallen below ten cents and the ADRs are essentially dormant. Outsiders' minority shareholder rights continue to be abused. For example, in late 1999 British Petroleum was invited to tender for the purchase of Chernognyeft, a subsidiary oil company of Sidanco (TNK) that it already substantially owned.

Thus institutional arrangements and national culture have effectively obstructed attempts to Americanize corporate governance in Russia.

CONCLUSIONS

The very existence of a capital market in Russia with degree of openness reflects the considerable influence exerted by the post-1991 reforms, which in turn were strongly influenced by Western creditors. Nowadays the managers of quoted Russian companies, and particularly those with ADRs, must be feeling the discipline of share price movements. The increase in outside ownership in (mostly unquoted) manufacturing firms has been substantial, though this trend must be interpreted in light of the fact that 'top managers are known to hide their ownership by using outside shareholder fronts' (Blasi *et al.*, 1997: 67). Econometric studies of industrial firms in the FSU have shown that outside ownership has been positively associated with capacity downsizing (Buck *et al.*, 1999) and successful exporting strategies (Filatotchev *et al.*, 2000). It might, therefore, be argued that some Americanization of corporate governance in Russia is starting to have a cumulative effect on former SOEs. In addition, there are signs that enterprise incumbents' hostility towards foreign investors is waning: in a desperate economic situation where many former SOEs have enormous problems with unpaid wages, incumbents are now beginning to welcome joint ventures with only intermediate levels of foreign commitment. This does not imply, of course, that Americanization offers Russia an ideal form of CG

At the same time, outside ownership and US style capital markets might best be viewed as 'alien tissue', grafted on to an organism whose cultural and institutional mechanisms demand its rejection. Russian history demonstrates that relational CG has generally been the Russian 'default mode', with ownership and control generally lying in the hands of enterprise incumbents, banks and (especially) the state rather than outsider investors. This statement does not imply criticism, since different varieties of relational CG have led to successful industrial performance in Germany, Japan, France and Scandinavia. In the case of the post-1991 reforms in Russia, relational CG has been promoted by the flouting by enterprise incumbents of legislation aimed at protecting the rights of genuine outside shareholders. These laws have been weakly enforced by the legal and political authorities in Moscow, in what amounts to collusion to preserve the institutional *status quo*.

Doubts remain about whether Russia's unique (mostly relational) CG is capable of enhancing industrial performance. Reflection on Table 5.1 suggests that the necessary conditions for successful relational CG are not in place in Russia: there is little evidence of a culture of trust, the economic situation generally requires the contraction of manufacturing firms rather than expansion, and the technological levels in manufacturing are generally not high.

Successful relational CG in Germany and Japan involves a high degree of trust between enterprise stakeholders with a degree of ownership and control, but cultural studies in Russia have found that although collectivism within enterprises is strong, tolerance of power distance is weak. This suggests that relations between enterprises and the state may always be characterized by opportunistic behaviour at both the centre and the periphery. This opportunism (often amounting to tacit collusion) means that Russia will continue to present the high country risks that have prevailed for centuries, discouraging high-commitment foreign investments and reinforcing incumbents' view of foreign investors as speculators and asset strippers. In an attempt to reduce these risks, conglomerates, and particularly financial – industrial groups started to become fashionable governance vehicles in Russia, in a repetition of 1910. However this occurred just at the moment when *chaebol* in Korea and *keiretsu* in Japan were being discredited to some extent as weak forms of CG and as promoting industry – government cronyism (Hundley and Jacobson, 1998). By 1999 two of Russia's 'big seven' financial – industrial groups had already gone into liquidation.

On the somewhat heroic assumption that enhanced competition in global product markets has been the main purpose of the post-1991 economic reforms, then substantial investment and restructuring will be needed to improve product design and enhance overall quality in Russian manufacturing. The major shareholders in Russian manufacturing firms (managers, employees, banks and the state) lack the necessary financial resources for such restructuring, and Russia's high country risks and hostility by incumbents have prevented large inflows of foreign direct investment. There is a real danger, therefore, that Russian manufacturing firms will be 'stuck with insider domination and no private external finance at all' (Shleifer and Vishny, 1997: 773).

Any progress with the Americanization of CG in Russia, which will bring benefits as well as costs, has so far been mostly limited to firms in primary extractive industries, which by definition have no major problems with product design and quality. Ironically, therefore, corporate reform has been accomplished in sectors that do not really need it for long-term survival. Raw material export prices were buoyant in 2000, and memories of the national emergency of 1998, which prompted a more welcoming attitude towards foreign investors, are receding. Both these factors discourage governance reform. If US style capital markets are to make a substantial contribution to Russia's global competitiveness, it seems that this will be the result of the inexorable grind of Americanization in the very long term in the face of opposition from Russia's culture and institutions, and/or another period of acute and sustained national economic emergency.

Arguably, without some elements of Americanization and a restructured manufacturing sector, Russia will have to continue to export materials in return for manufactures and services. This will preserve the centuries-old and rather risky pattern of governance.

Part Three

The Strategic Development of Subsidiaries

6 Globalization, Corporate Restructuring and Influences on the MNC Subsidiary

Stephen Young, Neil Hood and John R. Firn

INTRODUCTION AND OBJECTIVES

There has been considerable interest in and research on the evolution and development of subsidiaries of multinational corporations (MNCs). It seems that the greatest influence on subsidiaries' operations is likely to continue to be exerted by their parent MNCs. Indeed, the widespread corporate restructuring that is currently taking place, associated chiefly with globalization and the information technology revolution, will strengthen MNC centralization and top-down influences. There have been relatively few studies of this issue to date, although it clearly has important implications for our understanding of the engines of subsidiary change and restructuring, and of the relationship between corporate and subsidiary strategies, and ultimately for host government policy. This chapter draws on in-depth interviews with representatives of a sample of manufacturing subsidiaries in Scotland in order to explore (1) the major influences on and features of MNC corporate restructuring in the recent past, (2) the relationship between parent and subsidiary-level restructuring and (3) the extent and characteristics of subsidiary restructuring.

GLOBALIZATION, THE KNOWLEDGE ECONOMY AND CORPORATE RESTRUCTURING

The importance of globalization and information technology (IT) in the emergence of the networked knowledge economy is widely discussed in both the popular and the academic literature. Features of this era include the following (Aggarwal, 1999; Young, 2000; Sheenan and Grewal, 2001): the crucial role played by human capital, with a requirement for higher skill sets and labour flexibility; the intensification of competition and changes in its characteristics; the need for a re-evaluation of core competences and business missions; the commoditization of manufactured products and stronger emphasis on the services component of manufacturing; the importance of backward and forward linkages with suppliers and customers; and reconsideration of the advantages of in-house activity versus collaborations or external supply.

Corporate restructuring is an inevitable outcome of the transformation of the external and internal environments. According to Bowman and Singh (1993), corporate restructuring involves the reconfiguration of a firm's activities along one or more of three dimensions, namely assets, capital structure and management. A distinction is thus made by these authors between financial restructuring (governance structures, relationships with shareholders and the capital market), portfolio restructuring (mergers, acquisitions and alliances [MAAs], divestments, core competences, outsourcing) and organizational restructuring (changes in company structures, processes or personnel).

Drawing on these definitions, Ruigrok *et al.* (1999) have identified nine restructuring variables[1] as possible features of the 'new organization', linked to changing structures, processes and boundaries. In an empirical investigation involving nearly 500 European firms, Ruigrek *et al.* found a trend towards flattened organizational hierarchies (but this was not a robust trend as some firms were adding layers), greater reliance on task forces and teams, a shift from 'command and control' to 'facilitate and empower' mechanisms. There was also a move away from single business and diversified firms towards dominant firms and related businesses. Missing from this study were the multinational and spatial dimensions of restructuring, which have implications for all MNC global operations.

Figure 6.1 highlights key features of the global knowledge economy. It adapts and extends Ruigrok *et al.*'s (1999) framework to include a number of restructuring dimensions of the MNC. The 'changing locations' dimension has been added to reflect multinational business issues. There have been a variety of studies on the engines of globalization, models of global strategy and strategic options. Corporate restructuring clearly emerges as an important issue as MNCs select among and balance global, regional and local strategies for different value chain activities Roth and Morrison, 1992; Rugman, 2000). However there has been rather little research on the spatial restructuring dimensions of strategic change.

The other elements in Figure 6.1 incorporate new managerial features of the global knowledge economy. In terms of impact, there is a need to distinguish between 'changing boundaries' and 'changing locations', on the one hand, and 'changing structures' and 'changing processes and practices' on the other. The former are more likely to have immediate and large-scale effects, while the effects of changing structures and processes may be longer term, although perhaps no less important. Some of the forms of restructuring shown in Figure 6.1 may be interrelated, for example corporate benchmarking may lead to a change in the configuration of global manufacturing activities.

RESTRUCTURING AND THE MNC SUBSIDIARY

Much of the research on MNC restructuring has focused on divestment and plant closures, with emphasis on the subsidiary level. Thus a number of studies in the 1970s and 1980s (see for example Boddewyn, 1979, 1983; Van Den Bulcke *et al.*, 1979; Wilson, 1980; ILO, 1981a, 1981b; Young *et al.*, 1985; Casson, 1986)

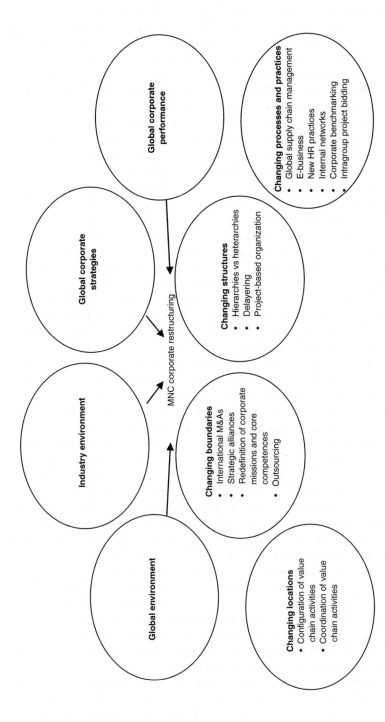

Figure 6.1 The global knowledge economy and characteristics of MNC corporate restructuring Global knowledge economy

Source: Adapted from Ruigvok *et al.* (1999).

were linked to concern about job losses in the subsidiaries of foreign-owned companies at a time of significant technology-induced restructuring. According to Boddewyn (1979), the 180 largest US MNCs added 4700 subsidiaries to their networks between 1967 and 1975, but also divested more than 2700 affiliates.

Interest in the subject has revived more recently with work by Padmanabhan (1993) on UK companies and Barkema *et al.* (1996) on large Dutch MNCs. The latter authors confirmed the multinationals' relatively high divestment rate of 225 foreign direct investments (FDIs) undertaken between 1966 and 1988, only 50 per cent or so were still in existence in 1988. Benito (1997) investigated the divestment of foreign production operations by Norwegian companies. His results showed that divestment was inversely related to host country economic growth, and was significantly higher for acquisitions than for greenfield ventures. In addition, related (horizontal) subsidiaries were less likely to be divested than unrelated (non-horizontal) subsidiaries.

A related topic is international relocation (Buckley and Mucchielli, 1997) or production switching. This commonly involves relocation from high to low wage countries in labour-intensive sectors, but it may also take place on an intra-regional basis between industrialized countries, or indeed involve relocation from a developing to a developed country, as part of the process of 'global shift' (Dicken, 1998). Linked research investigates the new international division of labour (NIDL) and the distinction between the economic 'core' and 'periphery' (for a review see McCallum, 1999).

Gray (1998) notes that globalization has caused trade and investment barriers to be lowered, and hence has increased the ability of firms that produce Schumpeter goods (S-goods) to relocate from industrialized to industrializing countries in order to reduce costs. Conceptually, Gray proposes that the larger the proportion of assets that are no longer location-bound, the greater the difference in costs between feasible locations, the lower the barriers to vertical integration of value adding activities in different regions, the faster the growth of management skills in subsidiary units in different locations and the faster the rate of increase in technologies that allow more efficient management of spatially-dispersed assets, the greater the extent of relocation. These conditions apply particularly strongly to labour-intensive assembly operations. In this regard Gray's ideas belong to the same genre as those presented by Vernon (1966) in his product cycle model.[2] However the determining forces are not simply those of costs and technology. Further crucial factors are the size and growth of markets in developing and emerging economies, and shifts in global and regional economic centres of gravity. Empirically, there is still only limited understanding of the context which and the process by which divestment and relocation occur. Furthermore, divestment and relocation should properly be seen in the wider context of corporate restructuring, which may encompass a wide range of firm-level activities, as noted earlier.

The other relevant body of literature addresses the roles and development of the MNC subsidiary (for reviews see Martínez and Jarillo, 1989; Birkinshaw, 1994; Young *et al.*, 1994). This includes research that attempts to identify typologies of MNE subsidiaries (White and Poynter, 1984; D'Cruz, 1986; Pearce, 1992; Roth and Morrison, 1992; Birkinshaw, 1996; Taggart, 1996a and b; Ferdows, 1997). This work has important policy implications for host counties because of the link between subsidiary type and economic impact. From the perspective of restructuring, the most vulnerable subsidiaries are, *inter alia*, those whose capabilities are limited to low-cost assembly, such as offshore or source factories (Ferdows, 1997).

Subsidiary evolution is a major theme in this strand of literature (Birkinshaw and Hood, 1998a, 1998b; Taggart, 1999), with a focus on the potential for and examples of subsidiary initiative and upgrading. Birkinshaw and Hood (1998a) identity, five recognized generic evolution processes, namely parent-driven investment, subsidiary-driven charter extension, subsidiary-driven charter reinforcement, parent-driven divestment and atrophy through subsidiary neglect. They imply that restructuring occurs as part of the investment or divestment process. Birkinshaw and Hood's emphasis of is primarily on the causes of subsidiary evolution and less on the forms of restructuring. The implication for the present chapter is that subsidiary-level factors (the affiliate's track record, subsidiary entrepreneurship and parent–subsidiary relations) and host country variables (innovative local clusters, the strategic importance of the local environment, host government support and the relative cost of factor inputs) could influence the form and extent of restructuring. In the Scottish context, however, the mediating effects of the local environment are less important than in more innovative milieux where strong regional clusters of technological activities exist. Similarly a feature of the multinational subsidiary sector in Scotland is its assembly/manufacturing focus, with low amounts of local R & D.[3]

METHODOLOGY

The above review of the literature highlights the importance of the topic being investigated have, with globalization and the knowledge economy having a profound impact on the nature of corporate activity. This chapter will explore a number of gaps in this literature in respect of the characteristics of MNC restructuring at the corporate and, especially, subsidiary levels. A number of preliminary inferences can be drawn from the above discussion. First, restructuring (as defined below) will be much more prevalent than divestment or international relocation. Second, there will numerous forms of restructuring, as set out in Figure 6.1, and it should be possible to identify parallel forms of restructuring at both the corporate and the subsidiary level. Third, restructuring will be strongly evident in Scotland because of the assembly/manufacturing emphasis in the FDI stock and the dominance of S-goods.

MNC corporate restructuring is defined as an activity that emanates from a decision by the corporate headquarters that has (often radical) implications for all or a number of the parts of a multinational group, leading to a reconfiguration of locations, boundaries, structures or processes and practices. In many cases a process will be set in motion whose effects extend over a number of years. Corporate restructuring thus excludes decisions that focus on one plant in isolation, and changes that take place as part of the normal evolution of an MNC, for example re-equipment and capacity or product line extensions. When viewed from the subsidiary level, restructuring can be either positive or negative in terms of its impact on employment, the value chain, managerial responsibilities and so on.

The empirical data for this study derive from a major policy-orientated evaluation of the quantitative and qualitative economic benefits provided by inward investment to the Scottish economy.[4] The qualitative research involved in-depth case studies of 28 key foreign-owned subsidiaries, of which 22 were in manufacturing and six in the service sector. These entailed confidential discussions with senior company executives in Scotland, and, when appropriate, key suppliers and development partners, supplemented by reviews of confidential company case files held by public sector bodies. Multiple interviews were normally undertaken at the subsidiaries, involving the plant manager/managing director and the heads of finance, purchasing, sales and marketing, and research and development (R & D), as appropriate. The total interview time at each subsidiary was approximately five to eight hours. The case studies were conducted over the period August 1998 to August 1999.

For the purposes of this chapter only foreign-owned manufacturing subsidiaries are included in the analysis. Two of these had only recently been established and were still in early start-up phase at the time of the study, and hence are excluded here, leaving a sample of 20 overseas-owned subsidiaries: nine American, six European (non-UK) and five Japanese. The sample was selected in conjunction with the sponsors so as to include the largest and most significant foreign investors (in terms of perceived autonomy and authority), and to ensure a mix of nationalities and manufacturing sectors. 'The names of the companies are suppressed to maintain confidentiality.

The restructuring cases analyzed took place during the 1990s and the first half of 2000, although most restructuring occurred post-1995. The interview guide used in the discussions did not include a specific section on corporate restructuring, but this issue was at the forefront of most executives' minds and therefore emerged clearly during the discussions. However, since MNC corporate restructuring was reviewed from the perspective of subsidiary executives, not all the influences highlighted in Figure 6.1 were assessed in detail.

FINDINGS: (1) INFLUENCES ON AND FEATURES OF CORPORATE RESTRUCTURING

Influences

It was apparent from the data that all the US and European-owned MNCs were involved in restructuring during the period analyzed. Among the Japanese

MNCs, however; with the exception of one company, which announced a closure at the very end of the period in question, there was much less evidence of major restructuring. In many Western countries, stock market pressures have led to short planning and performance horizons, and therefore rapid response to influences such as globalization. Japanese companies, in contrast have had a longer-term orientation and a stronger commitment to their regionalization strategies, with support being given to their manufacturing centres in the Triad areas. Arguably, Japanese MNCs gained 'latecomer advantages' in implementing these regional strategies, unlike American and European MNCs. On the negative side, structural rigidities and the prevailing social and economic paradigm have meant a delayed response by Japanese firms to the pressures of the global knowledge economy (Young, 2000). Among the sample Japanese subsidiaries, several had evolved according to very long-term plans, which on occasion had been delayed by adverse market conditions.

For all the US and European sample firms the *industry environment* (see Figure 6.1) had a significant influence on restructuring. In many cases this was expressed in terms of maturity of products, the competitive environment and price pressures. During this period, product, market and technological innovations had a major impact on the commoditization of manufacture, even affecting formerly high technology goods such as semiconductors. There were also industry-specific factors, such as the defence industry's need to restructure as spending cuts took effect, and environmental pressures on the chemicals industry. Cost cutting was a ubiquitous theme, and could be linked to the emergence of *regional and global strategies* in nine of the sample companies. Thus manufacturing standardization (using common components and platforms) and global sourcing were important constituents of global restructuring and consolidation. Weak *corporate performance*, consequent on global pressures (digitalization, globalization and regionalization) and industry forces, appeared to have a specific effect on six of the sample subsidiaries.

Features

With regard to forms of restructuring, the focus tended to be on *changing the boundaries* of the firm: nine of the sample were involved in international mergers and acquisitions during the period of the study; six MNCs redefined their company mission as a result of corporate break-up and the disposal of non-core products; and four introduced outsourcing programmes. Among the electronics companies, redefinition of the corporate mission tended to be associated with an emphasis on systems, software and services rather than manufacturing. As one interviewee explained: 'In the new corporate model, manufacturing is subservient. The role of manufacturing is to give competitive advantage, not to provide value in the market.'

Such restructuring programmes were associated in five MNCs with *changing structures*, mainly involving greater centralization and hierarchical organizational arrangements – this was surprising in the light of other evidence, but reflects the focus on global supply chain management and cost-cutting pressures in the sample MNCs. For half of the sample, restructuring took the form of *changing locations*, affecting both the configuration and the coordination of value chain activities.

Finally, *changing processes and practices* were evident in nearly all the MNCs studied. During the period of the study, therefore, none of the US and European MNCs were immune to the forces and pressures exerted by the global knowledge economy. By the start of the millennium, although outside the scope of this chapter, it was also becoming clear that Japanese MNCs were belatedly addressing similar restructuring issues.

FINDINGS: (2) CHARACTERISTICS OF SUBSIDIARY RESTRUCTURING

MNC restructuring through the lens of the evidence from Scotland; and Table 6.1 summarizes the restructuring characteristics observed in the sample MNCs and provides illustrative examples.

Impact on the Manufacturing Subsidiaries

The effects of restructuring were most profound in the 10 MNCs where manufacturing regionalization/globalization and, particularly, plant divestment or relocation occurred. Closure announcements were made for two plants during the period of the study. One of these, a subsidiary of a European MNC, had been engaged in assembly operations for 25 years, but its focus on the idiosyncratic requirements of the UK market, together with its small size and labour-intensive operations, meant that its operations were doomed when its parent began to restructure. The latter involved global product development, production and sales, plus, within Europe, a decision to concentrate on the growing markets and take advantage of the low labour costs in Central, Southern and Eastern Europe, with manufacture being centralized in Poland. The second closure was of a Japanese consumer electronics subsidiary, set up in Scotland in 1992. Its establishment had been designed to overcome tariff restrictions, but from the outset it had faced intense competition in its mature, price-sensitive product niche. Added to this was the allegation that its manufacturing efficiency and labour productivity were the poorest in the corporation. Markets would henceforth be supplied from existing facilities in continental Europe.

In the case of three other MNCs, the production of mature products was relocated to lower-cost manufacturing areas without divestment in Scotland. The beneficiary countries were the Czech Republic and Slovenia, China and mainland Europe respectively. Once again the reasons were chiefly cost- and market-related. In one interesting case, which highlights classic product cycle effects (Vernon, 1966), the manufacture of one line of products had shifted over time from the US to Scotland to China, with a further evolution from the company's

Table 6.1 Characteristics of subsidiary restructuring

Characteristics of restructuring	No. of cases[1]	Examples
Manufacturing:		
Manufacturing plant closure	2	Closure of loss-making operation. Closure and transfer to Poland and Northern Europe
Manufacturing relocation[2]	3	Relocation of mature products to Czech Republic and Slovakia. Transfer of mature products to China
Manufacturing regionalization/globalization[3]	5	Reorganization of multiplant European operations. Transfer in of new products as part of globalization. Manufacturing responsibility for operations in Korea and China.
Other value chain activities:		
Loss of activities	1	Loss of R&D
Regionalization/globalization of activities	8	Principally regionalization/globalization of procurement function
Gain of activities	7	Transfer in of R&D, European marketing, European call centre. Establishment of European HQ.
New subsidiary mission	1	R&D centre replacing assembly.
Structures and management:		
Structures, responsibilities and reporting lines	4	Establishment of global/European matrix structure. Reorganization of matrix. Changing UK structure and reporting lines
Processes and practices:		
Benchmarking	11	Primarily manufacturing benchmarking
Intragroup project bidding	8	Number and location of competitor plants vary
Subsidiary boundaries:		
Outsourcing	4	Outsourcing to Chinese-owned company in England, and to subcontractors around the world

Table 6.1 Characteristics of subsidiary restructuring   *cont.*

Characteristics of restructuring	No. of cases[1]	Examples
Spin-out from subsidiary	1	Services engineering and training consultancy company established

Notes:
1. Subsidiaries may be involved in more than one form of restructuring. In total 55 examples of restructuring were recorded among the 20 plants.
2. Transfer of particular products without plant closure.
3. Regionalization/globalization without Scottish plant closure or manufacturing relocation.

subsidiary in China to third party sourcing. In all three cases in the relocation category, new projects were launched in Scotland in order partly to compensate for the job losses associated with production transfer, and other forms of restructuring were in progress.

In five other cases the regionalization/globalization of manufacture had a variety of effects, some beneficial, on the Scottish subsidiaries. For example one escaped more or less intact from a global manufacturing rationalization programme involving the closure of nearly a quarter of the parent MNC's 160 manufacturing plants by late 2000. Perhaps the most interesting development, affecting three of the sample subsidiaries, was the allocation of manufacturing responsibility or manufacturing support for production operations outside the UK. In one instance the Scottish subsidiary was made responsible for the establishment of joint ventures in Korea and China, and, until further restructuring at the end of the 1990s, for the provision of technical leadership and engineering support for these plants, as well as supplying a board member for a joint venture in India. In the case of a US consumer electronics MNC, the Scottish subsidiary was made responsible for supervising and supporting manufacturing in China. These investments were chiefly market-driven, but clearly the issues of production relocation could arise at some point in the future. In fact the latter subsidiary had recently lost the major part of a project to Mexico, whose low labour costs and membership of the North American Free Trade Area (NAFTA) had acted in its favour American country.

Impacts on Other Value Chain Activities

As Table 6.1 shows, restructuring affected value chain activities other than manufacturing. The most common form of reorganization was the regionalization or, principally, globalization of procurement. This meant a trend towards centralized purchasing, with local procurement from approved suppliers. The site of centralization was most commonly the head manufacturing facility, although responsibility was sometimes shared between plants or a worldwide purchasing team structure was operated. The Scottish subsidiaries were rarely represented on these teams. In a small number of cases, such policies were associated with a single source; but in any event, approval of global suppliers was normal. Global sourcing mainly concerned 'key', 'sensitive' or 'strategic' production items, with subsidiaries often being restricted to non-strategic purchases. By the end of the study period, seven of the sample subsidiaries still had a reasonable degree of authority to purchase a range of production materials and services. However in most of these cases, cooperation between plants was being actively investigated, with attempts being made to take a regional or global view.

Impact on Processes and Practices

In respect of changing processes and practices, benchmarking was the most frequent form of restructuring. The activity focus of benchmarking was closely related to the nature of plant operations, with the emphasis on manufacturing. In manufacturing different measures of production efficiency were compared, for example yield, output and key quality parameters or manufacturing costs in terms of rate per hour. Sometimes more sophisticated measures were employed, such as manufacturing flexibility or overall costs as opposed to production costs, or total customer service capabilities. Company-specific measures such as inventory turnover were also used.

With regard to comparator plants, the Scottish subsidiary of one US MNC; was benchmarked against 15–20 factories worldwide; another was benchmarked against 10 group plants with similar technologies, raw materials and production tasks. Normally, one or a small number of best-performing units set the benchmark standards. These were commonly the largest facilities or those in the MNCs' home countries. However, Thailand set the production cost benchmark for the plants of one MNC; at another, where the US had historically set the benchmark, new plants in Mexico and China were to pilot innovative manufacturing systems and technologies and evolve as benchmarks.

There were criticisms of some of the benchmarking practices operated. For example mention was made of the need for simple, transparent measures to avoid manipulation. There was a call for 'benchtrending' rather than 'benchmarking', which was a static measure; and for the approach to be used flexibly to ensure that benchmarking did not stifle creativity. As benchmarking was becoming a global practice for one MNC, it was thought that it would eventually encompass the capability to rush forward the technological frontier. At another, subjective factors were incorporated into the benchmarking process, including problem-solving ability and total customer satisfaction.

The introduction of benchmarking had been a top-down initiative in all but one of the MNCs implementing this practice. The one exception was a highly decentralized MNCs where the technique had been introduced by a new manufacturing manager in Scotland and then taken up by the group as a whole.[5] At time of the interviews, nine of the sample MNCs did not have a formal benchmarking system. The reasons for this were the decentralized management style of some MNCs, the use of multiple-domestic strategies and differences in product mixes that made comparisons difficult. Some of these firms had reporting systems for production efficiency and other factors, but there were no formal comparisons among group facilities.

Benchmarking is included here as a form of restructuring since it is often introduced as part of a global strategy package and because of its potential as a global management control and evaluation system. It is particularly powerful as a tool to facilitate resource allocation, and this relates in part to another practice that was becoming more common among the sample MNCs: formal intragroup project bidding for projects. As Table 6.1 shows, eight of the sample had introduced a project bidding system. In the most sophisticated of these, the comparisons were not simply of intra-group mobile projects, the company also had to justify decisions on the basis of comparisons between internal supply, external supply and joint-ventures or partnerships, reflecting the commoditization of manufacture and the new global to focus on systems.

Impact on Structures and Firm Boundaries

At the subsidiary level there was less evidence of changing structures and management or changing enterprise boundaries, although as forms of restructuring their effects can be quite significant. For example the introduction of or amendments to matrix structures at two firms represented a significant increase in centralization at the corporate headquarters.

FINDINGS: (3) RESTRUCTURING PROCESSES

One objective of this chapter is to facilitate the understanding of multinational corporate restructuring processes, and particularly the link between corporate and subsidiary restructuring. Towards this end, Case Studies 6.1–6.3, are presented to illustrate the influences on and the nature and interrelated characteristics of restructuring at the corporate and subsidiary levels.

Case study 6.1 US consumer products manufacturer – global shift
Established in Scotland in the 1960s. Employment range: 500–1000.
Position in the global knowledge economy:
- Continuing group losses, partly associated with expansion into emerging markets.
- Intense competition as digitalization influences product design and performance, and introduces new competitors.
- Core products require labour-intensive assembly processes.
- Strategy of technological innovation; increased pace of new product introductions; cost reduction.

Corporate restructuring:
- Downsizing to cut costs.
- Cost reduction through international production relocation and rationalization; focus on Mexico and China at expense of UK and Netherlands.

Subsidiary restructuring in Scotland:
- Transfer of mature products to China; established by Scottish managers with continued technical support from Scotland.
- Loss of new project to Mexico but added responsibility for production for Europe; technical support for Mexico from Scotland.

Subsidiary management strategy:
- Continuous efforts to add value.
- Informal and now formal R & D (with financial incentives) to develop European product versions.
- Constant promotion of subsidiary capabilities and performance at parent HQ.

Case study 6.2 US electronics products manufacturer – new corporate mission
Established in Scotland in the 1960s. Employment range: >1000.
Position in the global knowledge economy:
- Strong global position in growing, but highly volatile and competitive product sector.
- Evidence of commoditization of manufacture.
- Weaker global position in major growth area of software and services.
- New corporate mission based on systems and solutions; manufacturing downgraded in importance.

Corporate restructuring:
- Centralization and globalization focus, including downgrading of former European HQ.
- Huge restructuring programme for domestic and international manufacturing, with closures, sell-offs and relocation of low tech activities.

Subsidiary restructuring in Scotland:
- Stronger control over subsidiary within new matrix structure.
- Transfer of low tech products to East European joint-venture (subsequently sold).
- Financial incentives to expand manufacture of high tech electronics, but sell-off possibilities.
- One new business area sold off, leading to loss of R & D.

Subsidiary management strategy:
- Minimize adverse effects on subsidiary through collaboration with public sector in Scotland.

Case study 6.3 European chemicals manufacturer – corporate spin-off
Established in Scotland prior to 1950. Employment range: 500–1000.
Position in the global knowledge economy:
- Corporate spin-off with new stock market listing; subsequent acquisition of related enterprise and creation of new divisional structure.
- Businesses mature, commodity with year-on-year price reductions.
- Strategy to maximize economies of scale in developed countries and exploit low labour costs in emerging markets (Korea, China and India, the former two of which were established by Scottish subsidiary managers).

Corporate restructuring:
- Recency of corporate spin-off means emphasis on reorganization of structure, management and reporting lines.
- Limited number of job losses to reduce cost base.

Subsidiary restructuring in Scotland:
- New matrix structure means wider European manufacturing and supply chain responsibilities for general manager in Scotland; but loss of authority for R&D and marketing in Scotland.
- Change from profit centre to cost centre.
- Management control over Korea, China and Indian ventures removed from Scotland to HQ; but management, technical and engineering support still provided.

Subsidiary management strategy:
- Short/medium-term future of facility secured with the establishment of a new plant in the late 1990s. Facility is the largest in the world for the product area, and was won in direct competition with the company's US subsidiary. Since the Asian operations manufacture similar products, they represent a longer-term threat.
- Strengthened leadership role of Scottish operation in its product area, but problematic because of changing managerial and organizational arrangements.

The three case studies highlight, respectively, the influence of global shift, a new corporate mission and corporate spin-off. These are classic illustrations of the types of corporate restructuring programme associated with the global knowledge economy. The most all-embracing and far-reaching example of restructuring is that in Case 6.2, where in effect, the MNC is largely withdrawing from manufacturing. This will affect all aspects of its global business operations. The changes are more tentative in Case 6.3, partly because of the recency of the establishment of the new enterprise by way of corporate spin-off. Case 6.1 highlights an ongoing global shift (relocation) from the US to Europe to Asia, with Mexico emerging as a new production base after the establishment of NAFTA.

While not the major focus of this chapter, the mediating effects of subsidiary level/host country influences on affiliate restructuring are apparent in the company cases. In Cases 6.2 and especially 6.3 the Scottish plant managers once had a degree of freedom to manoeuvre but this has been removed, with more centralized control being a feature of the restructuring. On the other hand the competences of both these subsidiaries and their long history has worked in their favour. Case 6.3 is interesting in that the general manager has been promoted to take a wider group role in the manufacturing and supply chain area, but the status of the Scottish plant has been downgraded and the general manager's responsibilities in Scotland have been reduced. With Case 6.1, a strong performance record, an entrepreneurial general manager and a broad-based managerial team have benefited the subsidiary. Recognizing the dynamics of innovation and global restructuring, the MNC in question has been alert to opportunities and effectively promoted a number of subsidiary initiatives. But this was facilitated by the fact that the restructuring programme has been less ubiquitous than in the other two cases, where corporate influence has been overwhelming.

DISCUSSION AND CONCLUSIONS

This chapter has extended the framework devised by Ruigrok *et al.* (1999) to analyze corporate restructuring in the global era; and tested this for a sample of MNC subsidiaries based in Scotland. Ruigrok *et al.*'s framework does not include the multinational and spatial dimensions of restructuring, which have been shown to be significant. Moreover, some of the present findings do not support those of Ruigrok *et al.*. For example the latter identified some flattening of organizational hierarchies and a shift towards facilitating and empowering mechanisms. In this study, by contrast, there are stronger indications of a move towards centralization and hierarchical organizational arrangements. These differences may be related to multinationality and the pressures of global supply chain management, but further work is clearly required on this topic.

The focus of this chapter is on restructuring generated by decisions taken at corporate headquarters, and this provides an interesting counterbalance to many of the previous studies of MNC subsidiaries, which have tended to emphasize subsidiary initiative and development (for example Birkinshaw and Hood, 1998a, 1998b; Taggart, 1999). It extends the literature on subsidiary divestment by exploring the underlying driving forces and processes; and it shows that restructuring has many interrelated facets rather than being restricted to divestment or relocation, which have been the focus of many earlier works (for example Benito, 1997; Buckley and Muchielli, 1997). Restructuring was quite widespread during the period under consideration, and this must reflect the influence of globalization and the IT revolution because the macro environment was very benign at the time.

Despite the diversity of experience among the sample MNCs, an issue that is common to many firms (and to all three companies in the case studies) is production relocation and global shift (Dicken, 1998). The sample, of course, comprised manufacturing facilities, but the plants were operating in increasingly mature, commodity-like sectors (one feature of the global knowledge economy). Hence they were S-good firms, in Gray's (1998) terms, and subject to relocation pressures on the basis of substantial cost differentials between locations (as well as strong market growth in emerging markets). Extending Gray's model, the narrow value chain in most enterprises meant there were few internal factors to support locational 'stickiness' (Markusen, 1996). Externally there was little if any evidence of innovative regional clusters that might encourage spatial immobility. Hence there were signs of a reduced association with 'place'. Replying to a question on technological and R & D impacts on the plant on Scotland, one interviewee replied: 'I don't think of it in these terms – we are part of a global business, serving global customers – we happen to be based in Scotland.'

The findings have important implications for different levels of policy. Historically the policy stance at the UK (including Scottish) host country level has involved maximizing investment flows rather than investment quality, and policy has failed to support foreign-owned plants by investing in complementary assets (Hood and Young, 1997). These policy choices are in part responsible for the restructuring observed in the sample firms, and in the future Scotland (and other UK regions) are unlikely to be competitive in terms of high-volume production and assembly operations. The mantra of 'moving up the value chain' needs to be converted into policy action. This will require radical changes in, for example, incentive policies and, obviously, investment in infrastructure and other public goods. But more fundamentally the following question must be asked: what can be achieved from cluster-based development strategies (Enright, 2000; Peters and Hood, 2000) when corporate influences appear to be so strong and restructuring so ubiquitous? Perhaps a major conclusion is that space is becoming even more 'slippery' (Markusen, 1996). There are important policy implications for other stakeholders too, particularly suppliers to MNC subsidiaries. Local suppliers are under great competitive pressure as MNCs globalize procurement. And their failure to achieve the status of a global supplier (the situation with the large majority of supplier firms in Scotland) in turn weakens the competitive position of the manufacturing plant.

At the regional (European Union) and multilateral levels, there clearly are significant policy concerns about production switching and divestment, which could be particularly problematic in a period of global recession (and might be associated with 'divide and rule' practices, as alleged by Peoples and Sugden, 2000). But this chapter has shown that a policy focus on divestment *per se* is inadequate when restructuring has many forms. In reality, the onus is on the MNCs themselves to develop 'internal programmes ... and management systems that underpin their commitment to good corporate citizenship, good practices and good business and employee conduct' (OECD, 2000).

Notes

1. The nine variables are delayering, project-based organization, decentralization (associated with changing structures), business diversification, outsourcing, strategic alliances (associated with changing boundaries), the use of IT, new human resources practices and horizontal/vertical linkages (associated with changing processes). See Ruigrok *et al.* (1999), p. 44.
2. Vernon (1966) notes that: 'The underdeveloped south of Italy and *the laggard north of Britain* and Ireland both seem to be attracting industry with standardized output and self-sufficient process' (emphasis in original).
3. There is an extensive body of literature on regional clusters (for example Porter, 1990; Enright, 2000) and associated concepts such as technology districts (Storper, 1995), innovation networks (Cooke and Morgan, 1994) and innovative milieux (Aydalot and Keeble, 1988). Peters and Hood (2000) provide illustrations of the cluster concept in the Scottish software and semiconductor industries. But the literature on FDI in Scotland in general shows very clearly that Scotland has primarily been a low-volume, low-cost assembly/manufacturing base for MNCs, and the study on *Inward Investment Benefits to the Scottish Economy*, from which the material in this chapter is derived, confirms this conclusion.
4. *Inward Investment Benefits for the Scottish Economy*, an evaluation report for Scottish enterprise and the Scottish Executive, January 2000.
5. In this company the manufacturing manager was part of the global corporate manufacturing team, and hence the benchmarking initiative is legitimately included as part of 'corporate headquarters decision making'.

7 Product Mandate Subsidiaries and High Value-Added Scope in MNEs' Operations in the UK: an EU-based Comparative Investigation

Ana Teresa Tavares and Robert Pearce

INTRODUCTION

A number of earlier studies of the UK operations of multinational enterprises (MNEs) (Hood and Young, 1988; Young *et al.*, 1989; Hood *et al.*, 1994; Taggart, 1996a, 1997a; Papanastassiou and Pearce, 1999) have used variants of the scope typology (White and Poynter, 1984) to support the view that there has been substantial emergence of product mandate (PM) subsidiaries. Where the evolution of the roles/strategies of individual subsidiaries has been investigated (Hood *et al.*, 1994; Taggart, 1996a, 1997a; Papanastassiou and Pearce, 1999) there is evidence that the dominant impetus is towards subsidiary PM-type operations. Some of the above – mentioned studies also indicate extra functional scope on the part of PM subsidiaries as exemplified by their propensity to possess research and development (R & D) units.

Another influential typology (Prahalad and Doz, 1987; Jarillo and Martínez, 1990; Taggart, 1997b) categorizes subsidiaries according to their degree of integration with other group operations (*I*) and their responsiveness to local conditions (*R*). Analyses of operations in the UK (Taggart, 1996b, 1997b, 1997c) demonstrate a strong and growing presence of 'active' subsidiaries that possess both high *I* (extensive interdependence with wider group strategies) and high *R* (locally derived individualized competences). Such operations have considerable commonality with mandate-type operations (considered later in this chapter), as underlined by Taggart's finding that 'actives' possess a significant R & D capacity and a distinct propensity to develop products that are responsive to the market needs of sister subsidiaries (Taggart, 1996b; 1997b, 1997c).

A number of studies that focus specifically on the product development aspect emphasize that such activity is frequently undertaken by UK subsidiaries (Pearce, 1999a, 1999b; Cantwell and Mudambi, 2000). This will receive detailed consideration later in the chapter, and the parallel between subsidiary scope and R & D complexity (Taggart, 1997d) will be explicitly addressed. This aspect is crucial from a host country perspective given that, as Cantwell and Mudambi (2000) note, the R & D investments of subsidiaries with mandates are qualitatively distinct from those without them. Based on previous empirical evidence and common expectations about the nature of MNEs' operations in the UK, this chapter will investigate two related propositions:

- *Proposition 1:* mandate-type subsidiaries are more common in the UK than in other European Union [EU] economies.
- *Proposition 2:* subsidiaries in the UK tend to have higher value-added scope and conduct more sophisticated technological activities than their counter-parts in other EU countries.

THE STUDY AND PRELIMINARY EVIDENCE

This chapter draws on the results of a questionnaire survey (conducted in 1999) of the largest multinational subsidiaries in the UK. Only manufacturing firms were targeted in this survey. A total of 328 firms were contacted, and 61 replies were received (a 19 per cent response rate). The present analysis uses data on 58 of these subsidiaries (the other three responses were either not complete or invalid, that is, the firms had been wrongly classified as MNEs or manufacturing operations). The questionnaire was also sent to 769 MNE subsidiaries in three other EU countries: Portugal, Spain and Ireland. Where appropriate the results from the latter will be used for comparative purposes. The statistical details of the surveys are provided in Table 7.1.

One of the salient features of UK subsidiaries is that on average they are older than those in the other three countries considered, reflecting the pioneering character of the UK as a host country to MNEs (1998; Hood *et al.*, 1999). This fact is quite relevant to the context of this chapter as it allows us to invoke the temporal dimension of subsidiary evolution. Thus a 'vintage effect' may have contributed to the fact that subsidiaries in the UK have tended to develop higher value-added activities than those in the other countries studied. Another pertinent factor is the relatively large size (in EU terms) of the UK market (for a review of the reasons underlying MNEs' investment in the UK, see Papanastassiou and Pearce, 1999). The results of our survey indicate that the main reasons for investment are local-market competitiveness and the UK workforce's considerable qualifications/skills in the MNEs' areas of activity, followed by low input costs. these motivations (a mixture of market seeking,

Table 7.1   The sample

	No. of firms surveyed	Replies	Valid replies	Response rate (%)
Portugal	419	118	95	28.2
Spain	145	37	34	25.5
Ireland	200	49	46	24.5
UK	328	61	58	18.6
Total	1092	265	233	24.3

strategic asset seeking and efficiency seeking) help us to understand the coexistence of distinct roles in MNE subsidiaries in the UK, which will be the focus of analysis in the following section.

SUBSIDIARY ROLES/STRATEGIES AND SUBSIDIARY EVOLUTION

The roles or strategies characterizing the subsidiaries surveyed in the UK are the core subject matter of this chapter. While static contemporary evidence on the relative prevalence of roles is included in this analysis, of more fundamental concern is the firms' evolution and dynamics (Birkinshaw and Hood, 1998a and b; Taggart, 1998; Luostarinen and Marschan-Piekkari, 2001). Without a full understanding of the nature of the operations conducted by MNE subsidiaries, a country's policies cannot be formulated in a manner that reflects the country's real needs and addresses its developmental potential (Young *et al.*, 1994; Hood and Taggart, 1997; Hood *et al.*, 1999; Tavares and Pearce, 1999; Pearce, 2001). This section uses as a conceptual instrument a tripartite version of the 'scope' typology of subsidiary roles/strategies (White and Poynter, 1984; Hood and Young, 1988; Taggart, 1996a; Papanastassiou and Pearce, 1999), whereby respondents are asked to situate their activities according to the relative importance to their operations of three roles/strategies (explained in Tables 7.2 and 7.3), *viz.* the role/strategy of the autarkic subsidiary (AS), the rationalized subsidiary (RS) and the product mandate subsidiary (PM). A broad concept of PMs is used here, encompassing both product specialists and strategic independents (in the terminology of White and Poynter, 1984), which are very difficult to distinguish empirically (Hood *et al.*, 1999).

This rating of the relative importance of distinct roles/strategies acknowledges that at any point in time a particular subsidiary may embody differing degrees of commitment to more than one role, and this in turn reflects the potential presence of evolutionary role changes. Table 7.2 provides details of the three roles in UK-based subsidiaries by industry and country of origin, and Table 7.3 summarizes the data on the three other EU host countries surveyed. The latter is included to enrich the analysis by emphasizing the comparative dimensions of evolutionary processes, since the other countries differ from the UK in various respects, notably industrial development (all three countries), timing of entry into the EU (Portugal and Spain) and the importance of the local market (especially Portugal and Ireland).

In order to capture the dynamics of subsidiary activity and the nature (and perhaps origins) of their development processes, three moments in time were considered in the survey. The year 1986 is treated as the benchmark for EU integration, as it was considered that 1973 (the year of UK accession) was too long ago for respondents to have an accurate idea of the role they then performed. For the UK subsidiaries, 1986 was the year in which the adjustments required to bring about the Single Market started to be seriously implemented, with the con-

Table 7.2 Questionnaire survey: relative importance of distinct subsidiary roles/strategies in the UK by MNE home country and industry

	Roles of subsidiaries[1] (average response)[2]								
	AS[3]			RS[4]			PM[5]		
	1986	*1999*	*2009*	*1986*	*1999*	*2009*	*1986*	*1999*	*2009*
Home country:									
EU	2.07	2.00	1.87	1.47	1.82	1.88	2.64	2.44	2.53
Other European countries	2.80	2.30	2.20	1.20	1.50	1.50	2.20	2.40	2.70
USA	2.32	1.80	1.55	2.05	2.33	2.39	2.42	2.70	2.80
Japan and SE Asia	2.25	2.29	2.14	2.00	2.57	2.29	2.25	2.14	2.57
Total	2.29	2.02	1.85	1.76	2.07	2.07	2.45	2.49	2.67
Industry:									
Cars and car components	1.75	1.75	2.00	2.25	2.75	3.00	2.00	1.50	1.50
Chemicals and plastics	2.45	1.83	1.67	1.55	1.85	2.00	2.45	2.54	2.67
Electrical and electronics	2.40	2.33	2.17	2.67	3.14	2.71	1.80	1.83	2.17
Machinery, engineering and instruments	1.88	1.75	1.58	1.78	2.00	1.92	3.25	2.92	3.08
Metal products	1.00	1.00	1.00	2.00	2.00	2.00	4.00	4.00	4.00
Pharmaceuticals	2.67	2.33	1.67	2.00	2.33	2.67	2.33	2.33	2.00
Other manufacturing	2.60	2.36	2.14	1.18	1.60	1.60	2.20	2.57	2.93
Total	2.29	2.02	1.85	1.76	2.07	2.07	2.45	2.49	2.67

Notes:
1. Respondents were asked to evaluate each role/strategy as (1) our only role/strategy, (2) our main role/strategy, (3) a secondary role/strategy and (4) not a part of our role/strategy.
2. The average response was calculated by allocating 'only role' a value of 4, 'main role' a value of 3, 'secondary role' a value of 2 and 'not a part of our role' a coefficient of 1.
3. Autarkic subsidiary – the UK subsidiary produces some of the parent's product lines (or related product lines) for the UK market.
4. Rationalized subsidiary – the UK subsidiary produces a set of component parts or finished products for a multicountry or global market.
5. Product mandate – the UK subsidiary has the autonomy and creative resources to develop, produce and market a restricted product range (totally innovative products) for multicountry (regional or global) markets.

comitant emphasis on free trade within the EU. Crucially, 1986 was also the year of accession of two of the other host countries surveyed (Portugal and Spain). The other two years are 1999 (the year of the survey) and 2009. Clearly the projections for 2009 should be treated with caution, but scepticism they embody valuable attempts by contemporary decision makers to predict the evolution of subsidiary scope, and they provide informative perceptions of the nature of adaptation to changing environmental forces.

Table 7.3 Questionnaire survey: relative importance of distinct subsidiary roles/strategies in four EU host countries

| | Roles of subsidiaries[1] (average response[2]) | | | | | | | | |
| | AS[3] | | | RS[4] | | | PM[5] | | |
	1986	*1999*	*2009*	*1986*	*1999*	*2009*	*1986*	*1999*	*2009*
Portugal	2.10	1.73	1.64	2.55	2.85	2.83	1.39	1.74	2.03
Spain	2.19	1.65	1.70	2.11	2.72	2.68	1.54	1.77	1.65
Ireland	1.51	1.14	1.14	2.91	2.95	2.83	1.54	2.00	2.25
UK	2.29	2.02	1.85	1.76	2.07	2.07	2.45	2.49	2.67

Notes:

1. Respondents were asked to evaluate each role/strategy as (1) our only role/strategy, (2) our main role/strategy, (3) a secondary role/strategy and (4) not a part of our role/strategy.
2. The average response was calculated by allocating 'only role' a value of 4, 'main role' a value of 3, 'secondary role' a value of 2 and 'not a part of our role' a coefficient of 1.
3. Autarkic subsidiary – the subsidiary produces some of the parent's product lines (or related product lines) for the host country market only.
4. Rationalized subsidiary – the subsidiary produces a set of component parts or finished products for a multicountry or global market.
5. Product mandate – the subsidiary has the autonomy and creative resources to develop, produce and market a restricted product range (totally innovative products) for multicountry (regional or global) markets.

As would be expected from generalized perceptions of MNEs' strategic reformulation (and more specifically from a deepening commitment to European integration), Table 7.2 shows a notable decline in autarkic operations in the UK, with this clearly predicted to be the least prevalent role by 2009. For the mainly mature US and European subsidiaries in particular, the presumption was of a rise in autarkically oriented entry. By 1999, however, it was Japanese and other European (non-EU) subsidiaries that retained the strongest elements of autarkic local-market responsiveness, with US operations exhibiting the most decisive move away from this role. In sectoral terms, electrical and electronics, pharmaceuticals and healthcare and the residual 'other manufacturing' category were the most local-market oriented.

Despite the relative decline shown in Table 7.2, the comparative evidence in Table 7.3 makes clear that the UK has consistently been the most significant host to autarkic subsidiaries (the importance of local-market-oriented subsidiaries in the UK has been pointed out by Hood *et al.*, 1999; Papanastassiou and Pearce, 1999). In addition to the obvious influence excerted by the UK's market size and income levels, it may be that the learning opportunities provided by the autarkic role (as a supportive adjunct to the more outward-looking PM) are perceived as being of greater value in that economy. By notable contrast the autarkic role has been considerably less important in MNE operations in Ireland, indeed it has become virtually irrelevant (Tavares, 2001). In both Portugal and

Spain the autarkic role seems to have been quite significant in the initial positioning of early (pre-1986) subsidiaries, but was decisively usurped by new strategic priorities once these countries entered the EU.

RS operations increased in importance in the UK between 1986 and 1999. This is consistent with the findings of Hood and Young (1998), Papanastassiou and Pearce (1999) and Hood *et al.* (1999). That this was mainly at the expense of autarkic operations is in line with the expectation of a reorientation of subsidiary activities relating to the production of established products in the MNEs' range. This seems to have been a 'one-off' re-focusing, however, with no further movement towards the predicted rationalized role. Asian firms are the most rationalized in the UK (Hood *et al.*, 1994; Papanastassiou and Pearce, 1999), followed by US firms. For European subsidiaries (both EU and non-EU) the RS role has never transcendend the autarkic. Electrical and electronics, cars and car components, and pharmaceuticals and healthcare are sectors in which the rationalized aspect of strategic positioning is most pronounced in the UK. In Ireland (Table 7.3) the RS role has more commonly been the initiating one than elsewhere, and it has retained its position at the core of MNE strategic positioning in that economy. In both Portugal and Spain the RS role was already pervasive before 1986 (albeit only modestly behind the autarkic role in the case of Spain), and had risen to dominance by 1999. The PM role was the most prevalent one in UK subsidiaries throughout the period (Table 7.2), and is clearly perceived as embodying the most decisive growth potential (confirming the finding of Papanastassiou and Pearce, 1999). The empirical evidence hence supports the first of the proposition presented at the start of this chapter.

While EU subsidiaries emphasized PM operations in the UK before 1986 (probably due to the need to 'tap into' the UK's established knowledge base in certain sectors – see Pearce, 1999a, 1999b; Cantwell and Mudambi, 2000) they have shown little propensity to develop them further. This may reflect a strong desire to concentrate their European market product development activities in their home countries. In contrast non-EU European subsidiaries in the UK were not committed to PM activities before 1986, but thereafter there was a persistent (and pervasive) move towards them. PMs asserted a strong and growing status amongst US subsidiaries throughout the period. This corroborates Dunning's (1958, 1998) claim that US MNEs are seeking to augment rather than exploit their comparative advantages. In the case of Asian subsidiaries, PM is expected to become the strongest role by 2009, mainly at the expense of rationalized positioning. The strongest sectoral emphasis of PMs is on metal products, chemicals, machinery and other manufacturing.

Throughout the period covered, PMs were most well established in the UK (Table 7.3). This may indicate the presence of two evolutionary forces deriving from distinctive characteristics of the UK economy. First, the intuitive learning processes that are essential to an effective autarkic subsidiary's locally responsive operations may derive a particular richness from the UK market, with this generating a strong internal impetus towards PM-type ambitions. Second, when a subsidiary begins to nurture PM ambitions the extra knowledge and skills it has to acquire externally may be relatively more available in the UK than in the other countries covered. For both Ireland and Portugal there are signs of more steady movement towards PM strategies over time (Tavares, 2001; Tavares and Pearce, 2001), and this has been consistently stronger in the former country than in the latter. Though PM activity has grown modestly in Spain, it is expected to decline in the future (uniquely amongst the four host countries). For Spain, PMs are not only predicted to become considerably less important than elsewhere by 2009, but will also (again uniquely) become the least important role. This is because there is strong evidence that rationalization processes are taking place in Spanish subsidiaries, which are usually large operations that are very tightly integrated into and controlled by their MNE group.

Our results so far give credence to proposition 1. They also confirm the contention by Hood and Young (1998) that subsidiaries in the UK have undergone considerable change when adjusting to EU integration. Yet, as already noted, the magnitude of the phenomenon is not as great as in other (smaller and more peripheral) EU economies, probably because the UK stands more on its own as a market, and has more consolidated multinational activities and an older industrial tradition.

DECISION MAKING AND AUTONOMY OF SUBSIDIARIES

The evidence reviewed in the previous section clearly indicates the presence in MNE subsidiaries of evolutionary processes, as manifested by the existence of roles that are differentiated by various dimensions of scope. Another factor investigated in the (reported in Table 7.4) was the way in which the presence of these roles, and their change, is reflected in the decision-making autonomy of subsidiaries. The persistently high level of decision-making autonomy enjoyed by UK-based subsidiaries in all four of the areas reported in Table 7.4 can be attributed to the considerable and sustained presence of the PM role (testifying to the higher value-added scope of mandate-type operations – of which greater decision-making autonomy is a sign). The increased autonomy in 'broad strategic direction' that is predicted to take place between 1999 and 2009 may be associated with the growth in PM status that is also expected during that period (Tables 7.2 and 7.3), but it might also derive from extra in-house discretion over technology secured before 1999.

The most pronounced and wide-ranging autonomy has been obtained by subsidiaries in Ireland, and this again appears to be related to their move into the PM role (Tavares, 2001). Perhaps building on the very significant growth of decision-making discretion over technology to date (and predicted to continue modestly in the future), Irish subsidiaries have gained ever more control over their strategic direction (to a degree that is expected to exceed that of UK subsidiaries by 2009) in respect of both markets and products. Since this has occurred in a situation where RS (rather than AS) was the initial status, this evolution probably

Table 7.4 Questionnaire survey: degree of decision-making autonomy of subsidiary (mean values)

	Portugal			Spain			Ireland			UK		
	1986	1999	2009	1986	1999	2009	1986	1999	2009	1986	1999	2009
Market area supplied	2.22	2.22	2.24	2.59	2.41	2.33	1.59	2.11	2.36	2.53	2.55	2.49
Product range supplied	2.14	2.23	2.28	2.44	2.42	2.37	1.71	2.24	2.38	2.77	2.79	2.68
Broad strategic direction	2.07	2.19	2.32	2.33	2.38	2.26	1.62	2.29	2.49	2.32	2.33	2.42
Technology used	2.18	2.31	2.41	2.26	2.15	2.15	1.82	2.60	2.76	2.45	2.59	2.61

Notes: When calculating the respective means the following values were applied:- (1) decisions taken mainly by parent/regional HQ *without* consulting with or seeking advice from subsidiary; (2) decisions taken mainly by parent/regional HQ *after* consulting with or seeking advice from subsidiary; (3) decisions taken mainly by subsidiary *after* consulting with or seeking advice from parent/regional HQ; (4) decisions taken mainly by subsidiary *without* consulting with or seeking advice from parent/regional HQ.

reflects a very conscious effort by managers and government planners to bring about new functional scope. These findings are consistent with those in a comparative study of German subsidiaries in the UK and Ireland by Hood and Taggart (1997), who found that the degrees of decision-making autonomy enjoyed by subsidiaries in these two countries were not significantly different.

In Portugal the steady rise in mandating (Table 7.3) could be related to increased discretion over technology and broad strategic decision making (Table 7.4). Bearing in mind that RS operations dominate in Portugal, the rise in RSs is compatible with increased mandating. For Spain, subsidiary evolution is mainly from AS to RS (Table 7.3). While this does result in some loss of autonomy over market choice, the latter remains comparatively high. The main impression gained from the Spanish sample is that there has been a tendency for subsidiaries' decision-making autonomy to decline, which is consistent with domination by RSs. The relative unimportance of mandating is reflected in subsidiaries' limited technological autonomy.

TECHNOLOGICAL ACTIVITIES IN SUBSIDIARIES

Earlier sections have indicated that technological positioning is central both to the role of subsidiaries and to their evolution. This section briefly reviews activities carried out by the sample subsidiaries that relate to the application or generation of technology (Table 7.5).

About three quarters of the sample provide customer and technical services, which are strongly associated with local market supply. Around two thirds adapt products to the host-country/regional market. This type of activity, which may encompass learning processes that support or lead towards PM operations, has been consistent among UK subsidiaries and has grown in Portugal and Ireland. However, it has declined in Spain, where As have they tended to be replaced by RSs and there is no strong trend towards mandating. The adaptation of manufacturing processes (for example in order to take advantage of local factor conditions)' is of most concern to RSs. Its growth between 1986 and 1999 is compatible with this proposition, as is its predicted persistence in Spain and Ireland.

Two of the activities reported in Table 7.5 relate mainly to the strategic aims of PMs: the development of new and improved products for host country/EU markets is a key responsibility of regional product mandate (RPM) subsidiaries, whilst the development of new and improved products for world markets is a focus of world product mandate (WPM) operations. By 2009, almost two thirds of subsidiaries are expected to develop regional products (although this represents only a modest rise from the current level) and half are expected to develop products for the global market (representing large size in growth). Given the very low propensity of Spanish subsidiaries to engage in the full range of PM operations (Table 7.3), a surprisingly large number of them are occupied with both variants of product development (Table 7.5). In contrast, the rise in man-

Table 7.5 Technological activities carried out by subsidiaries (percentage of respondents engaging in such activities)

	Total			Portugal			Spain			Ireland			UK		
	1986	1999	2009	1986	1999	2009	1986	1999	2009	1986	1999	2009	1986	1999	2009
Customer and technical services	72	74	74	55	58	60	89	88	90	55	76	71	89	91	88
Adaptation of products to host country/regional market	61	66	65	44	60	59	70	59	62	55	65	67	74	81	73
Adaptation of manufacturing technology or processes (e.g. to take advantage of local factor conditions)	64	78	76	53	77	72	81	79	83	52	85	82	72	75	71
Development of new and improved products for host country/EU markets	45	60	64	28	47	47	52	62	64	26	61	67	70	81	84
Development of new and improved products for world markets	30	38	50	14	26	35	33	47	57	23	52	67	47	42	52
Generation of new technology for the parent company (basic and applied research)	14	21	27	18	2	1	22	26	31	16	33	44	19	32	36
None of the above	2	12	12	12	5	2	0	12	0	1	15	0	6	0	0

dating in Ireland and Portugal is reflected in the growth of product development responsibilities, with the WPM variant being particularly strong in Ireland. Table 7.4 confirms the persistently strong mandate orientation of UK subsidiaries, especially in the case of the RPM variant (that is, the targeting of European markets). Finally, the generation of new technology for the parent company (basic and applied research) is expected to rise, with just over a quarter of subsidiaries engaging in such activities by 2009. While technology generation is usually the task of an R & D unit in a PM, it is quite likely that where a country offers suitable potentials an MNE may decide to set up a stand-alone laboratory as a separate strand in its technology network.

These results highlight the differential technological content of the activities developed by MNE subsidiaries in the four host countries surveyed. In particular they confirm the superior technological sophistication of most UK-based subsidiaries *vis-à-vis* their European counterparts (preposition 2), especially in respect of product development and the generation of new technology.

CONCLUSIONS AND POLICY IMPLICATIONS

This chapter has investigated the strategic roles undertaken by and evolution of MNEs in the UK. A comparative approach has been used, situating the UK case in the EU context with the use of findings from a cross-country survey of MNE operations in four EU economies. Two research propositions have been addressed that mandate-type subsidiaries are more common in the UK than in other EU countries, and that technological activities are more sophisticated and value-added scope is higher in UK-based subsidiaries. Both propositions receive strong support from our empirical analysis.

The case of the UK is particularly interesting in the EU scenario given the observable co-existence of roles. On the one hand, local-market-focused operations (reflecting the importance of the domestic market, which was one of the reasons for the UK's pioneering host-country status) remain important, despite the freedom of trade brought about by EU integration and the Single Market programme. On the other hand, and more interestingly for our purposes, the prevalence of mandate-type subsidiaries and their greater functional scope endorses the fact that MNE strategies have been aimed at co-opting creative capabilities from established UK industrial sectors. Last, but not least, the rationalized role is much less prevalent in other EU countries, reflecting the more positive evolutionary processes that have occurred in the UK and the far greater technological content of UK-based subsidiaries, as discussed at length in this chapter.

In terms of UK policies towards MNE operations, our findings have two implications. First, the relatively limited presence of RS operations should be welcomed, not feared. This cost-based activity is one that has to be transcended if MNE subsidiaries are to play a supportive role the pursuit of sustainable development (Pearce, 2001). Second, the strong presence of autarkic subsidiaries can be seen as a positive factor in the (highly desirable) growth of internationally competitive (That is, more outward-looking) PMs. Their strength in the UK can be seen as reflecting the need for competitive individualization (initially targeting locational markets), the effective pursuit of which is likely to generate subsidiary-level creative capabilities that can ultimately be leveraged for PM (external market) status. Thus policies should not be dominated by low-cost (RS) priorities, but be more supportive of knowledge-related, scope-enhancing (PM) investment at the subsidiary level. MNEs global strategies need these types of operation and our evidence suggests that the UK can accommodate them.

8 Knowledge Transfer Between Parent and Developing Country Subsidiaries: A Conceptual Framework

Paul N. Gooderham and Svein Ulset

INTRODUCTION

The purpose of this chapter is to develop a conceptual framework that captures the crucial components involved in transferring knowledge between the home country operations of multinationals located in developed countries and their subsidiaries in developing countries. Traditionally the scope of knowledge transfer between multinational parent and developing country subsidiary has been limited. Beyond gaining access to raw materials or markets, foreign direct investment has been confined to utilizing low-cost, unskilled or semiskilled labour based on established technologies involving limited training. However, rising educational standards and government-led aspirations have increasingly made at least some technology and knowledge transfer mandatory.

The transfer process is affected by the out-transfer capacity of the transferor, and the in-transfer capacity of the recipient, as well as factors such as the cultural distance and local environment of the recipient (Leonard-Barton, 1995; Martin and Salomon, 1999). Also significant is the degree of tacitness involved in the knowledge to be transferred. Tacit knowledge involves 'causal ambiguity' (Lippman and Rumelt, 1982; Reed and DeFillippi, 1990) – that is, there is a basic difficulty with comprehending the precise nature of the causal connections between actions and results, which is vital when attempting to replicate a capability in a new setting.

For Nonaka (1994), tacit knowledge is deeply embedded in action in idiosyncratic contexts. It involves knowledge that is complex, difficult to codify and therefore 'sticky' (von Hippel, 1994; Szulanski, 1996). Thus while explicit knowledge consists of easily codifiable information that can be transmitted 'without loss of integrity once the syntactical rules required for deciphering it are known' (Kogut and Zander, 1992: 386), tacit knowledge comprises recipes that can be difficult to articulate in precise terms because they involve experiential insights that may only be transferable via the exchange of employees (Bresman *et al*, 1999). Thus, whereas explicit knowledge can be extracted from the person who developed it, independent of that person and reused for other purposes, tacit knowledge can generally only be transferred through some form of social interaction (Nonaka and Takeuchi, 1995). In general, the more tacit the knowledge the more expensive it is to transfer it across national borders (Teece, 1977, 1981). Moreover, trying to turn inherently tacit knowledge into explicit knowledge can lead to serious problems if inappropriate transfer mechanisms are used (Hansen *et al.*, 1999).

Clearly, attention should be paid to developing and selecting the most appropriate mechanisms for knowledge transfer. The aim of this chapter is to provide a conceptual framework that distinguishes between the challenges involved in transferring explicit 'know-what' knowledge and those involved in the transfer of tacit, 'know-how' knowledge (Polanyi, 1962; Kogut and Zander, 1992). This issue is addressed with a particular focus on knowledge transfer between high-knowledge parents and low-knowledge subsidiaries in developing countries. Our starting point is the distinction between the out-transfer capacity of the transferor and the in-transfer capacity of the subsidiary.

OUT-TRANSFER CAPACITY

Out-transfer capacity can be subdivided into the transferor's ability to transfer explicit knowledge and its ability to transfer idiosyncratic, tacit knowledge. The former involves the ability to codify and disseminate information through operating manuals, routines, procedures and physical systems that enable the user to know what to do. Just as some manufacturers of consumer products are more able than others to produce clearly articulated operating manuals and user-friendly end products, so some firms are more efficient than others at communicating explicit knowledge to their subsidiaries.

There are a number of factors that make the out-transfer of tacit knowledge relatively problematic. First, the generation of tacit knowledge is the product of organizational routines (Nelson and Winter, 1982) that have evolved as a consequence of individuals interacting with one another, face-to-face, over an extended period of time. As a result there will be a strong sense of collective identity. Strongly tied, multilateral social relationships are not easily duplicated. Pathways between the out-transferor and the recipient have to be deliberately created to facilitate the social ties that make tacit knowledge flows possible (Dyer and Nobeoka, 2000). One increasingly common type of pathway consists of intranet systems that enable employees to pinpoint relevant experts within the firm together with e-mails, the phone and video-conferencing systems. However, many multinational companies consider that over-reliance on Web-based systems for competence networking can lead to loss of continuity and responsiveness in knowledge building and competence sharing (Hellström *et al.*, 2000). While not abandoning web-based tools, they also make extensive use of face-to-face dialogue, not only on a one-to-one basis but also by transferring people between offices for brain-storming sessions.

Another constraint on the out-transfer of tacit knowledge is that individuals or groups of individuals have to be motivated to share their valuable knowledge, despite the fact that their income and their status in the firm are invariably linked to their know-how. This problem is particularly acute when there is no prospect of receiving an immediate payback in equally valuable knowledge, or when there is fear that proprietary knowledge may be leaked to competitors (Porter, 1985). For intra firm knowledge transfer to take place a motivation system must be designed to provide the sources of knowledge with sufficient incentive to engage in transfer (ibid.)

Last but by no means least is the initial strategic aim of the out-transferor. As we noted above, it is often the case that multinationals establish foreign subsidiaries in order to benefit from inexpensive labour or achieve market access. In knowledge terms, not only is the subsidiary totally dependent on the parent company, but also the parent company has a restricted view of what knowledge should be transferred. This is often limited to technical know-what information rather than tacit know-how knowledge.

IN-TRANSFER CAPACITY

Going beyond a knowledge dependency relationship is a theme that Leonard-Barton (1995) focuses on in the context of the in-transfer capacity of subsidiaries located in developing countries. Szulanski's (1996) research on intra firm knowledge transfer confirms the salience of in-transfer capacity, which he refers to as absorptive capacity (Cohen and Levinthal, 1990). Likewise Lyles and Salk (2000) demonstrate the importance of absorptive capacity as a determinant of knowledge acquisition from foreign parents the context of international joint ventures.

Leonard-Barton (1995) identifies four levels of in-transfer capacity at the subsidiary level:

- *Level 1*: the capacity to operate assembly or turnkey equipment.
- *Level 2*: the capacity to adapt and localize components.
- *Level 3*: the capacity to redesign products.
- *Level 4*: the capacity independently to design products.

Moving from one level to the next is not only dependent on the transferor's out-transfer capacity, it is also heavily influenced by the subsidiary's in-transfer capacity. In developing countries, lack of education and relevant experience can mean that a level 1 mode of operation is the only practical possibility. Level 1 operations are characterized by the construction of a complete working plant (a turnkey factory) or an assembly plant. This usually involves older technology that has been tried, tested and successfully debugged, so that it is 'foolproof'. Beyond the advantage of ease of use, older equipment means that proprietary knowledge is not revealed.

At level 1 there is little or no capacity for the receipt of tacit knowledge. Knowledge transfer is limited to explicit knowledge that is either embodied in the equipment, software or other physical systems, recorded in manuals, or communicable through instructions and demonstrations. The only skill required by the recipients is the ability to use the equipment and perform routine maintenance.

However even the vertical, formal transfer of explicit knowledge can be subject to severe constraints. One major problem is finding a match between the functioning of the equipment and the existing infrastructure in developing countries. Another challenge is to ensure that there is a clear understanding among employees of what is required of them in terms not only of output but also quality.

Moving a subsidiary from level 1 to level 2 requires the recipient to develop the ability to adapt the product to local tastes and to produce it using a substantial proportion of local components. For the recipient to be able to fine-tune the technology and make use of opportunities to procure locally produced components, the explicit knowledge transferred must be upgraded to include the basic engineering principles needed for the successful operation of the transferred technology. This is in turn dependent on the efficacy of the explicit knowledge transfer mechanisms between parent and in-transferor.

A basic problem with the move to level 2 is obtaining local managers of sufficient calibre. More than half the firms questioned in a survey of multinational companies with operations in China (*Economist*, 21 June 1997) admitted they were disappointed with their performance in China. Many complained about difficulties with their joint-venture partners, but nearly all said that the greatest problem was obtaining good local managers. As a result many factories were still heavily dependent on expensive expatriate managers.

One particular shortcoming of local Chinese managers is that few have any experience of working with suppliers outside their own vertical chain. Thus one critical in-put of explicit knowledge involves the training local managers in logistics and working with a network of suppliers.

Adapting the product to take local conditions into account depends on being able to go beyond the mechanistic order-taking approach at level 1. It means developing a workforce that is capable of assuming responsibility, cooperating with other employees and contributing to the development of local knowledge building. The discipline and quality consciousness needed for this move may be lacking in substantial numbers of employees, indeed their presence may hinder such a move. However, large-scale dismissals may be politically unacceptable, thereby blocking the move from level 1. Institutional factors of this kind are as much a part of the local infrastructure as the reliability of the local power supply.

Finally, it should be noted that these explicit-knowledge transfer mechanisms have to embrace not only the subsidiary but also the entire network of local suppliers. In China, the local sourcing of components has commonly been problematic because of the amount of training suppliers need in order to meet the necessary quality standards. This has acted as yet another constraint on the move from level 1 to level 2.

At level 3, rather than adapting components, the required in-transfer capacities include the ability to redesign all facets of a product in order to produces a superior product. This capability requires both a strong theoretical grounding and a great deal of practical experience. Because of the more advanced Japanese infrastructure it took Fuji Xerox less than 10 years to reach this level (Leonard-Barton, 1995), whereas Hewlett-Packard's Singapore facility took 20 years (Thill and Leonard-Barton, 1993). Although recipients at this level are still dependent on the transferor for the scientific knowledge underlying the product, there is a move from know-what to know-how, or from explicit to tacit knowledge.

One factor determining the move from level 2 to level 3 is the recipient's degree of initiative at all levels. This may have to be developed in purposively by implementing mechanisms that permit informal social interaction and thereby the communication of values and norms. At Hewlett-Packard the successful transfer of tacit knowledge was contingent on the development of substantial opportunities for interaction, between recipient engineers and managers and their transferor counterparts including physical co-location.

Ultimately, though, the move from level 2 to level 3 will be a product of interactions between parent and subsidiary over and above the mechanical transfer of technical know-how. Nonaka and Takeuchi (1995) use the notions of socialization and internalization for such interactions. The former refers to the acquisition of culturally embedded knowledge through exposure to the foreign parent, while the latter refers to the conversion of explicit knowledge into routines as a product of experience.

Iveco, the truck-making subsidiary of Fiat, was focusing particularly on parent – subsidiary interaction mechanisms when it introduced a management-training programme at its Chinese subsidiary. In the late 1980s, it selected nearly 400 Chinese engineers and workers, taught them Italian and transferred them to Italian factories (*Financial Times*, 2 February 1999).

What characterizes level 4 in-transfer capacity is the ability of subsidiary to design products independently of the knowledge transferor. The move from level 3 to level 4 is dependent on a substantial bi-directional knowledge flow, which implies acceptance of the subsidiary as a potential equal. Roles and relationships have to be redefined if synergies are to be created. Pathways for knowledge exchange have to be established, coupled with incentives to encourage the sharing of knowledge. In the case of Fuji Xerox, it took about eight years to develop an in-transfer capacity that enabled it to produce its first copier based on its own design concept (Leonard-Barton, 1995).

The possession of level 4 subsidiaries, either through subsidiary development or acquisition, means that an MNC's sources of innovation are geographically dispersed. The hierarchical relationship between headquarters and the subsidiary is replaced by a network of equals, in which the foreign subsidiary is a member of a set of interdependent knowledge-generating subunits. Bartlett and Ghoshal (1989) have labelled this organizational form the transnational, whereas Hedlund (1994) refers to it as a hetarchy. Specialized knowledge about the product or product line resides in the subsidiary, with the subsidiary managing research and development activities on a global basis.

The next matter to address is the role and development of the knowledge-exchange mechanisms involved in upgrading the in-transfer capacity of subsidiaries from level 2, through level 3 to level 4.

BEYOND FORMAL VERTICAL MECHANISMS

While knowledge transfer is challenging, at levels 1 and 2 when the local infrastructure is taken into account, to a large extent headquarters can exert unilateral control over the process. This means that while distance proximity makes it difficult for headquarters to directly supervise the behaviour of foreign subsidiary managers, it can nevertheless monitor them through rules, programmes and procedures, as well as via expatriates staff (O'Donnell, 2000). In other words it can determine the flow of knowledge from headquarters to subsidiary as well as its application through formal, vertical mechanisms. The decision to move beyond level 2 entails a substantial increase in subsidiary autonomy. To some extent the intention at level 3, but much more so at level 4, is that – through the synergistic transfer of tacit knowledge – the subsidiary should have knowledge assets equivalent to but different from those of headquarters, such that it can take on global responsibility for a set of value activities. In order to achieve this the use headquarters makes of supervision and monitoring mechanisms (that is, formal, vertical mechanisms), should decrease as increased effort is invested in generating the cooperative behaviour and trust needed for bidirectional knowledge transfer (O'Donnell, 2000). A perceived lack of trust may lead to opportunistic behaviour on the part of the subsidiary in the sense that knowledge is surreptitiously withheld from other parts of the network (De Meyer, 1995; Ghoshal and Moran, 1996).

In order to create the conditions for the tacit knowledge exchange that enables movement towards level 3 vertical knowledge transfer mechanisms of an increasingly interpersonal type are necessary.

Informal Vertical Mechanisms

Reger's (1997) research and De Meyer's (1995) interviews with 14 large multinational companies with international R & D operations indicate that the majority of multinationals expend a considerable amount of effort on developing mechanisms to facilitate social interaction. The function of these mechanisms is to create what Kogut and Zander (1992) call a 'social community', that is, a set of shared values and beliefs across subsidiaries. Gupta and Govindarajan (2000: 479) refer to this as 'interpersonal familiarity, personal affinity, and convergence in cognitive maps . . . between the interacting parties.' O'Donnell (2000) lists a variety of informal vertical mechanisms that are used to facilitate the interaction needed to increase subsidiaries' identification with the organization as a whole, including the assignment of subsidiary managers to corporate headquarters, headquarters-based training programmes and the use of parent company personnel as mentors for the managers of foreign subsidiaries.

As subsidiaries move from level 3 to level 4 the intention is that the firm should move away from operating on the basis of hierarchy to that of hetarchy – that is, the balance of power, or at least in knowledge terms, within the corporation undergoes radical change. This implies the development of knowledge exchange mechanisms that permit and enable either partner to initiate knowledge exchange. Although many of these lateral mechanisms are formal, their aim is to facilitate informal corporate socialization processes by increasing the opportunity for more open and richer communication.

Lateral Mechanisms

Strategic committees, generally consisting of the head of central research and the heads of development at the subsidiaries, are widely used as formal lateral mechanisms, as are planning departments, which are changed with developing and coordinating R & D and technology portfolios (Reger, 1997). Both of these mechanisms provide relatively durable structures for lateral knowledge exchange. Other lateral mechanisms are temporary in character. These include temporary inter-unit committees that are set up to allow managers from different international locations to engage in joint decision-making on a project-by-project basis, temporary task forces for the co-ordination and facilitation of international collaboration between subsidiaries on a specific project, expatriate assignments between subsidiaries, and training programmes that involve participants from several international locations.

A further lateral mechanism is the executive development programme which brings together participants from headquarters and the subsidiaries. In some cases these programmes develop into corporate universities. For example in 1999 Asea Brown Boveri (ABB) founded its own academy not because it was disappointed with the products of the world's business schools but because an arena for both lateral and vertical interaction was deemed necessary. As Arne Olsson, head of management resources, explained, ABB initiated its academy because it was felt that business schools

cannot deliver information on where we are going, what the issues, problems and challenges are. People told us they want to get straight messages directly from the top, to build networks with peers, to get a better understanding of ABB's culture and values, and to get specific tools, ideas, and project management techniques to help them manage better. This is a large and very decentralised company. It may sound like a paradox but the more decentralised you are, the more you need some kind of mechanism to build that organisational glue. To manage a company of this size cannot only be done by instructions and memos. You have to have that glue of people contact and trust (*Financial Times*, 3 April 2000).

Another widely utilized lateral mechanism is the use of central staff members as liaison personnel (De Meyer, 1995). Their specific job is to coordinate the efforts of international functional areas, and many of them have to travel around constantly to follow up the evolution of technology. Part of their mandate is to actively trigger contact between different individuals and groups across the company. Other tasks are involvement in coaching, guiding and monitoring R & D activities, and bringing to the attention of corporate head quarters potentially significant developments the network. De Meyer (ibid) notes that the success of such people is dependent on, at the minimum, a combination of technological credibility, and social and integrating skills. Another dependent factor is acquaintanceship with the decision makers at corporate headquarters.

CULTURAL DISTANCE

In this section we consider the impact of cultural distance on knowledge transfer. Hofstede's (1980) research suggests that even when linguistic difficulties are reduced by the employment of a common business language, cultural differences can impede the ability of people to interact successfully and to interpret the subtleties of meaning involved in tacit knowledge transfer. For instance Nonaka (1994: 22) notes that 'Japanese firms encourage the use of judgement and knowledge formed through interaction with customers – and by personal bodily experience rather than by "objective," scientific conceptualisation.' This is a fundamentally different epistemological tradition from that in the West and it can contribute to causal ambiguity. It is reasonable to suppose that the degree of cultural distance is a particularly salient factor at levels 1 and 2, but beyond these initial stages, given that the appropriate knowledge transfer mechanisms are in place, it would seem that the impact of cultural distance is of less significance. Research by Simonin (1999) on the transfer of marketing know-how in international strategic alliances indicates that there is a significant reduction of cultural distance as the degree of collaborative experience increases. This is consistent with Meschi's (1997: 218) finding that 'all cultural differences in an international joint-venture, regardless of their nature or intensity, will ultimately recede over time.' It might be supposed that the same applies to integrated MNCs. Certainly research by Bresman *et al.* (1999) on post-acquisition knowledge transfer by Swedish MNCs indicates that communication processes improve with time, to the point where cultural differences have no significance. In other words effective, informal, vertical and lateral mechanisms mitigate the effects of cultural distance.

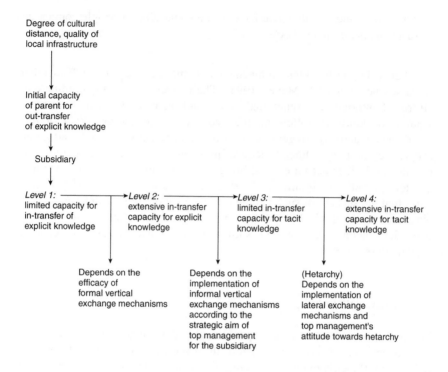

Figure 8.1   Factors determining the move from level 1 to level 4 knowledge in-transfer capacity

SUMMARY AND DISCUSSION

Figure 8.1 summarizes the factors that determine the moves from level 1 to level 4 knowledge in-transfer capacity. First, the cultural distance between the parties and the quality of the local infrastructure will affect the parent's initial capacity to out-transfer explicit knowledge and the subsidiary's in-transfer capacity. The efficacy of the formal exchange mechanisms that are established will determine the move to level 2, signalled by an extensive capacity for the in-transfer of explicit knowledge. Both cultural distance and the quality of local infrastructure will affect the efficacy of formal exchange mechanisms. The move to level 3 requires the subsidiary to have some capacity to in-transfer tacit knowledge and is dependent on the parent establishing effective informal vertical exchange mechanisms to promote social interaction. The implementation of the latter depends on the parent's strategic aim for the subsidiary. The move to level 4, which requires a substantial capacity for the in-transfer of tacit knowledge, will be determined by the implementation and efficacy of social exchange mechanisms of a more lateral type. Again, their implementation will be a consequence of the strategic intent of the parent, that is, whether it regards the development of a hetarchical organization as advantageous. Once a subsidiary is positioned at level 4 it is no longer a subsidiary in the conventional sense, but a corporate technology and/or production centre that transfers technology and/or intermediate products to other production or assembly facilities.

Although this sequence has been given a linear form, here in practice the appearance of the various exchange mechanisms may be less orderly, not least in the case of informal vertical exchange mechanisms. For example level 1 subsidiaries that are managed or co-managed by Western-educated locals may readily develop such mechanisms without any impetus from the parent company. However it is less certain whether on this basis such mechanisms can comprehensively embrace the subsidiary, as Michailova and Anisimova's (1999) case study of the Russian subsidiary of a Danish company reveals.

The knowledge exchange mechanisms we have listed are well documented. Further research will undoubtedly reveal other examples and rank them according to their knowledge transfer efficacy. The tendency, however, has invariably been to present knowledge transfer mechanisms with only scant regard to the context in which they evolve. This chapter has attempted to provide this context. We have argued that it is largely determined by the interaction between the out-transfer capacity of the parent company and the subsidiary's in-transfer capacity, and that the development of this interaction is primarily contingent on the ability and willingness of the parent to develop appropriate knowledge exchange mechanisms.

This is particularly the case with the development of lateral exchange mechanisms, not least because they depend on the parent company being prepared to redefine its relationship with its subsidiaries. Hence we emphasize that the role of top management in defining the self-identity of the company is critical if organizations are to go beyond the use of vertical knowledge transfer mechanisms.

Although this chapter has been framed in the context of subsidiaries' progression from low knowledge content to high knowledge content, the model we have proposed is also applicable to high-knowledge-content mergers and acquisitions. Successful knowledge exchange depends on the development of informal vertical mechanisms combined with lateral exchange mechanisms. Without regard to these mechanisms the synergies that are so often claimed as the *raison d'être* for mergers and acquisitions will simply not materialize.

9 Autonomy and Procedural Justice: Validating and Extending the Framework

James H. Taggart and Jennifer M. Taggart

Some studies of the multinational corporation (MNC), despite adoptings a headquarters (HQ) orientation, have attempted to identify the kinds of role that subsidiaries may suitably assume in international networks. Bartlett and Ghoshal's (1986) model of national subsidiary roles was developed from a study of major MNCs in global industries. They identify two main HQ views of the world: the 'UN model assumption', whereby all foreign subsidiaries are treated in a very uniform manner, and the 'headquarters hierarchy syndrome', which deems that all strategy and resource control activities belong naturally at the centre. While these views, either singly or in combination, may well be appropriate in some circumstances, general application would lead to a multitude of demotivated subsidiary managers. As an alternative, Bartlett and Ghoshal propose a model based on two dimensions: the competence of the local subsidiary and the strategic importance of the local environment to the MNC's global aspirations. Subsidiary roles developed from the model (strategic leader, contributor, implementer, black hole) recognize that within any particular MNC there will be a wide variation in the overall ability of management teams at the subsidiary level, and that these teams are organic entities and are therefore likely to develop in competence over time. By means of a skilful mingling of the authorities and responsibilities of corporate and subsidiary managers they may each become more aware of, and more sensitive to, the nature of the problems faced by the other. Practitioners will readily recognize that this is a more empathetic perspective than the rather mechanical and deterministic approach of, for example, the configuration–coordination paradigm (Porter, 1986a; Taggart, 1997c).

This anthropocentric element also appears in the integration-responsiveness grid, particularly in emphasizing the need for locally responsive subsidiaries that have a good relationship with their HQ (Prahalad and Doz, 1987: 270). It is a substantial factor in White and Poynter's (1984) paradigm of subsidiary strategy, built on three measures of subsidiary scope (market, product and value added). It also informs other overviews of affiliate roles (Jarillo and Martínez, 1990; Beechler and Zhuang, 1994; Birkinshaw and Morrison, 1995; Liouville and Nanopoulos, 1996; Taggart, 1997a). Another common factor that appears, explicitly or otherwise, in these perspectives is the question of subsidiary autonomy; this may be an explanatory factor in local responsiveness or localization, it may underlie concepts such as scope or organizational fit, or it may be a constraint on local management practices.

Recently these elements have been brought together as axes for a model that provides an alternative evaluation of subsidiary strategy (Taggart, 1997b); the particular dimensions are autonomy and procedural justice. The first has been used in many surveys of subsidiary activity (Picard, 1977; Hedlund, 1981; Kagono, 1981; Rugman and Bennett, 1982; Garnier, 1982; Gates and Egelhoff, 1986; Ghoshal and Bartlett, 1988; Young *et al.*, 1989; Martínez and Jarillo, 1991; Moon, 1994; Gnan and Songini, 1995) and is now widely accepted as an essential measure for evaluating subsidiary characteristics. The importance of management philosophy as a second general determinant has been emphasized by Bartlett (1981), Quelch and Hoff (1986) and Ghoshal and Bartlett (1988), among others, but the specific concept of procedural justice was introduced to the international management literature by Kim and Mauborgne (1991, 1993). While this subjective concept may be applied to a wide range of organizational decision making, these writers used it as a measure of the 'fairness' perceived by subsidiary managers in their dealings with corporate staff over the strategy-making process. The rigorous empirical studies by Kim and Mauborgne confirm that this is an important measure when considering subsidiary activity. The autonomy–procedural justice (A–PJ) model proposed by Taggart (1997b) gives a four-quadrant typology of subsidiary strategy that appears to be internally and externally valid, and it has some explanatory power when considering a subsidiary's shift from one strategy state to another (Figure 9.1).

The A–PJ model was derived from exploratory research that proceeded on the basis of general research questions rather than specific propositions. The purpose of this chapter is to carry out further empirical testing of the model by means of a number of discrete propositions. In the next section the A–PJ model is described briefly and set in context with other approaches to subsidiary strategy. Based on this, a number of research hypotheses are then set out and the research methodology is described. Following a presentation of survey results, the model is evaluated and interpreted, and its implications are discussed. Finally, some indications for future research are outlined.

BACKGROUND

The further a company internationalizes its operations in the drive to create and sustain competitive advantage, the more it confronts the problem of effectively managing geographically dispersed units. There are two conceptually different ways of doing this, as implied by Bartlett and Ghoshal (1986). The first is to consider a network as metaphor for the spider and its web. The web is passive, while the nodes are there to support the network's physical structure and send messages back to 'headquarters', which plays the only truly active strategic role. This was perhaps the basic standpoint taken by Ouchi (1978) and Jaeger (1983) in organizational studies, and later taken up by Cray (1984), Martínez and Jarillo (1991), Kobrin (1991) and Axel (1995) in specific studies of a variety of control functions within MNCs. Indeed, it was also utilized in functional studies by Brandt

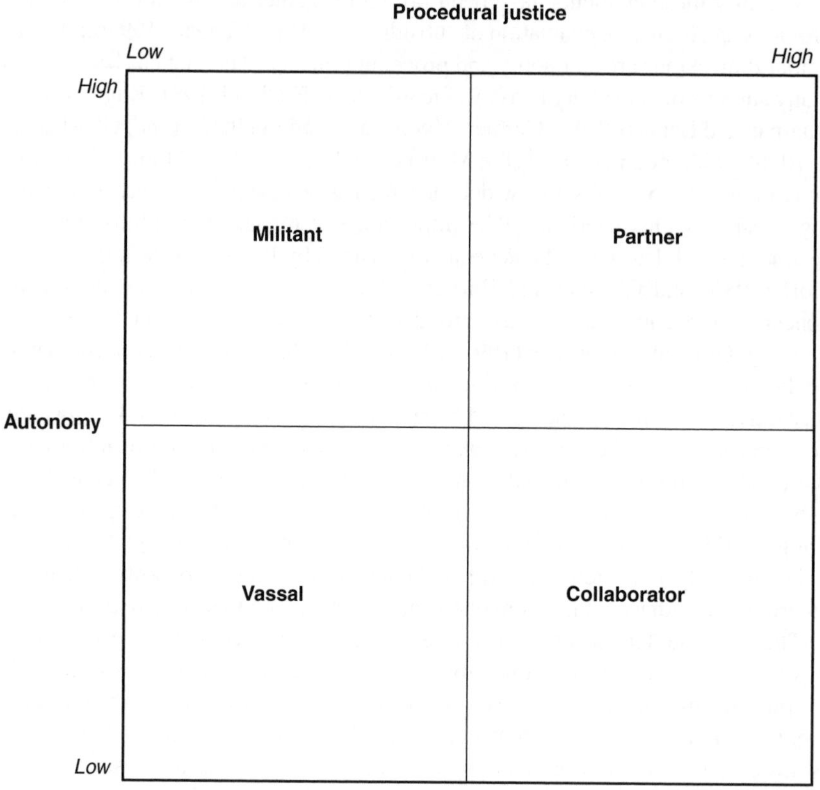

Procedural justice

Figure 9.1   Autonomy–procedural justice framework

and Hulbert (1977) and Takeuchi and Porter (1986) (marketing); and by Erickson (1990), De Meyer (1993) and Cheng and Bolon (1993) (technology). There is of course nothing deprecatory about this methodological approach, as it has been adopted in practice with varying degrees of success by a large number of MNCs.

The second approach to managing geographically dispersed subsidiaries sees the network as an example of biological symbiosis, where different types of element that exist for quite different purposes have a high degree of mutual interdependence. Here the host is undoubtedly dominant in many ways, though this is unlikely to be recognized by a symbiotic partner, whose crucial role must be not only tolerated but also actively encouraged. This appears to be the philosophical perspective adopted by a number of researchers on MNC subsidiary strategy (Bartlett, 1981; Boyacigiller, 1990; Doz and Prahalad, 1991; Roth and Morrison, 1992; Kobrin, 1994; Birkinshaw and Morrison, 1995). A second parallel line of research, starting with the concept of the heterarchical MNC, has developed rapidly towards considering subsidiaries within certain types of network as 'centres of excellence'. Here the normal dependency relationship *vis-à-vis* the HQ is substantially reversed (Hedlund, 1986; Hedlund and Rolander, 1990; Forsgren *et al.*, 1992; Surlemont, 1996; Taggart and Berry, 1997). While this approach is not intrinsically superior, conceptually or practically, to the more hierarchical and centripetal perspective described earlier, it does explicitly place considerably more emphasis on motivational aspects of managing a network of subsidiaries.

The A–PJ model quite clearly falls into this category, and will be briefly described using characteristics derived from a previous empirical investigation (Taggart, 1997b). The *vassal* subsidiary is characterized by low levels of autonomy (A) and procedural justice (PJ) (that is, low A, low PJ), and seems to be a most unattractive strategy locus for local managers. There will always be friction at the HQ–affiliate interface, and in some cases this will be characterized by lack of trust and dissent. Disagreements will virtually always be resolved in the HQ's direction, since the vassal subsidiary usually has a very specific function allocated to it within the parent's international network. In keeping with its low degree of autonomy, this type of subsidiary generally has little scope for adjusting the range of markets it serves, the products it offers, or the nature and extent of added value. While it has some similarities to White and Poynter's (1984) miniature replica (adapter type), and may in some cases fit reasonably well with Porter's (1986a) export-oriented strategy or the integrated strategy of Prahalad and Doz (1987), it is difficult to understand why the subsidiary comes to terms with its situation, or why the corporate management team is be prepared to tolerate such a problem in its network. We tentatively suggest that this behaviour pattern will lead to relatively poor performance at the subsidiary level and an unsatisfactory contribution to overall network success. Taggart (1997b) suggests that it may be essentially a transition type; it may also be the temporary crystallization of a number of motivational problems that are in the process of being cleared up, at the behest of either affiliate or HQ.

The *collaborator* affiliate (low A, high PJ) shows much more trust in the way the HQ sets about the strategy-making process, and the higher degree of cooperation thus engendered may well prompt the subsidiary to be more flexible when carrying out the diktats of the HQ. Unless its management is highly aggressive and/or proactive, this is likely to result in an unstressed operational environment for the subsidiary; corporate strategic decisions will be implemented wholeheartedly and without bickering. The strength of the local management team will lie in interpersonal skills rather than leadership or entrepreneurial ability, and this type of affiliate will not have a significant exemplary role to play *vis-à-vis* its more purposeful sister subsidiaries. This type resembles the receptive subsidiary of Jarillo and Martínez (1990) and would operate smoothly within the corporate umbrella of Porter's purest global strategy. From the HQ's perspective, the collaborator may well be the most desirable subsidiary type, particularly in the short run, as it will most readily accommodate and implement the corporate strategic thrust. In the longer term this level of docility may well turn out to be a poor bargain for corporate managers if it is accompanied by lack of drive, creativity and direction at the subsidiary level. We conjecture a substantial contribution by the collaborator to network performance, sometimes at the cost of short-term subsidiary results.

The high A, low PJ quadrant is occupied by the *militant* subsidiary, which presents a particular problem for the HQ. The high degree of autonomy coupled with a poor procedural justice scenario will lead to a degree of strident disagreement, even hostility, at the HQ–subsidiary interface. Disagreements will often be resolved in the subsidiary's favour, especially where there is a strong requirement for local responsiveness. It may be that this role works quite well when there is little need for the subsidiary to integrate closely with other elements of the parent's network, or when there is a pressing need to have a strong presence in a strategically important market. In this respect militant subsidiaries clearly have something in common with Bartlett and Ghoshal's (1986) strategic leader. On the basis of its high degree of autonomy, however, it may also be compared to White and Poynter's (1984) miniature replica (innovation type), operating within Prahalad and Doz's (1987) multifocal (area emphasis) strategy. The performance of the militant subsidiary may occasionally be excellent, but perhaps not sustainable in the long run; its contribution to overall network utility is likely to be erratic. Subsidiary managers may be well advised not to carry militancy too far, as this type of affiliate may become a prime candidate for closure in times of network rationalization.

The *partner* subsidiary (high A, high PJ) is likely to be run by a proactive management team that builds and maintains an excellent relationship with the HQ, particularly in matters of strategy development. In many ways this is the ideal combination of model dimensions for a vigorous and self-confident affiliate; it may also be the first choice of a positive and audacious corporate management team with extensive experience of managing at the subsidiary level. It is likely to demonstrate good long-term performance, and it will make a considerable contribution to the overall network. In contrast to the vassal subsidiary, the partner subsidiary is marked by extensive market, product and value-added scope (accordingly it has many operational similarities with White and Poynter's strategic independent). In extreme cases this may diminish the value of network linkages, but well-developed leadership and management skills in the partner subsidiary mean that it could operate very effectively within Porter's high coordination corporate strategy. Perhaps the obvious question is: why are not all subsidiaries partners? Undoubtedly the answer lies in the allocation of scarce resources; establishing and maintaining a high degree of autonomy, and especially of procedural justice, often requires substantial and continuing investment in high-quality management staff and extensive, ongoing management development. However, in some cases a positive perception of procedural justice among the top management team as a whole may reflect little more than the team's view that it is being fairly treated by the HQ.

HYPOTHESES

The original exploratory research that led to the A–PJ model was based on general research questions. Following on from the previous discussion, a number of specific research hypotheses can now be framed that constitute a methodological advance as well as a further attempt to validate the model and interpret its implications. However, since some indeterminate issues remain, two general research questions are introduced below to complete the analytical inter-rogation of the model. Since underlying concepts are so firmly rooted in corporate and subsidiary strategy, it seems appropriate to test the model against variations in how subsidiaries approach the question of strategic decisions. Six decision types are identified and explored below, relating to long-term strategy, short-term strategy, the impact of risk, the effect of government regulation, elements of creative thinking and aspects of product differentiation.

In validating a four-quadrant model it is useful to concentrate on the separation of (differences between) diagonally opposite subsidiary types (that is, partners and vassals, or collaborators and militants) as this more closely focuses on possible interactions between the dimensions. Comparisons, for example, between militants and partners suggest strategic differences that are linked to movement on only one of the model's dimensions. Perhaps the greatest contrast in Figure 9.1 is between partners (high A, high PJ) and vassals (low A, low PJ). From the earlier discussion on the nature of the dimensions and their impact on subsidiary types, it follows that partners will put more stress than vassals on certain types of strategy decision. In particular, the combination of substantial local decision-making capability coupled with strong mutual trust between HQ and subsidiary is likely to give the partner a stronger locus in terms of long- and short-term strategy matters, greater confidence with regard to evaluating a range of strategic alternatives and a substantially less risk-averse approach to these matters. The subsidiary with lower PJ than the partner (the militant) may be less likely to explore these areas without the tacit support of the HQ; and with less autonomy than the partner, the collaborator may not have control over sufficient local resources to make such positive moves. However, in light of the current state of development of the A–PJ model, it is not yet appropriate to postulate a particular rank order in these areas between militants and collaborators. Therefore, the following research propositions may now be advanced.

- *Hypothesis 1*: partner subsidiaries will put greater emphasis on long-term strategic decisions than vassals.
- *Hypothesis 2*: partner subsidiaries will put greater emphasis on short-term strategic decisions than vassals.
- *Hypothesis 3*: partner subsidiaries will put greater emphasis on the risk content of strategic decisions than vassals.
- *Hypothesis 4*: partner subsidiaries will put greater emphasis on evaluating alternative strategic decisions than vassals.

However it is possible to suggest tentatively that both militants and collaborators will have less scope for action in these four areas of strategy than partners, and correspondingly more scope than vassals. Hence, we have the first general research question:

- *Research question 1*:
  With respect to the emphasis put on long- and short-term strategic decisions and the risk and creative content of strategic decisions, collaborators and militants will occupy a position intermediate between partners and vassals.

We now turn to aspects of government regulation in the host market. It can be argued that collaborator subsidiaries will demonstrate substantially more sensitivity than militants. This is because they have less decision-making scope to explore aggressive alternatives, and because they will be much more anxious to keep the repercussions of poor subsidiary–government relations away from corporate managers. They will thus maintain the otherwise excellent level of empathy at the HQ–affiliate interface. Thus we have:

- *Hypothesis 5*: collaborator subsidiaries will put greater emphasis on the government regulations aspect of strategic decisions than militants.

While we might expect partners to be active in terms of increased penetration of existing markets and entry into new markets, the more likely market development route for collaborator affiliates is to introduce new products and brands into the existing market. Many of these may be network sourced, coming either directly from the HQ or from sister subsidiaries. Conversely, the very nature of the militant will often be an obstacle to this kind of network-supported activity. Hence:

- *Hypothesis 6*: collaborator subsidiaries will put greater emphasis on product differentiation decisions than militants.

Again, we suggest (tentatively, due to the early stage of development of the A–PJ model) that the vassal (with less independence than the militant) and the partner (with more network orientation than the militant) will assume a broadly intermediate position. This gives us the second general research question:

- *Research question 2*:
  With respect to the emphasis put on the government regulation aspect of strategic decisions and product differentiation decisions, partners and vassals will occupy a position intermediate between collaborators and militants.

RESEARCH METHOD

Sample

The original exploratory research for this model (Taggart, 1997b) was carried out on a sample of MNC manufacturing subsidiaries in the UK. Of the 171 respondents to that survey, 165 were based in England (recognized as the dominant and core constituent of the UK economy). Since the present research is, among other things, a validation test, it is appropriate to use a completely different sample of subsidiaries. Accordingly, official listings of manufacturing subsidiaries located in the peripheral countries of the UK – Scotland, Wales and Ulster – were obtained, as well as a similar listing for the Republic of Ireland, which is also regarded as a peripheral economy in terms of both England and the European Union. In addition, the Irish affiliates lent a cross-border dimension to the already strong cross-cultural element due to the inclusion of Scotland, Wales and Ulster.

From the four constituent countries, a total of 1000 subsidiaries were randomly selected from the appropriate listings: 350 from Ireland, 300 from Scotland, 250 from Wales and 100 from Ulster. A separate sample of ten subsidiaries was used to pretest the measures for validity and reliability. A postal survey was deemed the most appropriate data collection method for reasons of resource constraint and generalizability of results. The pretested and appropriately amended research instrument was mailed to the chief executive of each subsidiary, and a follow-up mailing was undertaken when necessary. Responses were received from 265 subsidiaries (26.5 per cent): 92 from Scotland (30.7 per cent), 37 from Wales (14.8 per cent), 16 from Ulster (16.0 per cent) and 120 from Ireland (34.3 per cent). Chief executives completed 63 (23.8 per cent) of the questionnaires, other directors 115 (43.4 per cent) and other executives 87 (32.8 per cent). The letter that accompanied the questionnaire specifically requested that if the chief executive was not in a position to respond, the instrument be passed to another executive involved in the annual strategy-making round with the HQ. Due to the high strategic content of the research instrument the fact that one third of the responses were made by non-directors may introduce an element of measurement error, and this should be remembered when interpreting the results. A summary of the basic characteristics of the respondent firms is presented in Table 9.1.

Measures of Autonomy and Procedural Justice

Seven measures of autonomy at the subsidiary level were used (see Appendix 9.1): decisions about markets supplied, product range, advertising and promotion, R & D, production, product pricing, and product design. The first five of

Table 9.1   Characteristics of respondent subsidiaries (mean values)

	Scotland	*Wales*	*Ulster*	*Ireland*
Age (years)	13.5	11.2	11.1	13.0
Number employed	410	161	281	211
Sales (£ million)	135.7	43.2	42.0	42.7
Exports (per cent)	47.4	38.0	43.2	81.2

these were used in the original study by Taggart (1997b); the remaining two were utilized to determine the robustness of this dimension when constituent changes are made. After the pretest some minor alterations were made to these items before including them in the final instrument. The correlations between these seven items were all high ($p < 0.001$) and the Cronbach alpha was 0.89, a very satisfactory level indeed. Thus, the measures contributing to the autonomy dimension were accepted as both valid and reliable.

Measuring procedural justice is a delicate matter, and a number of precautions have to be taken (summarized in Taggart, 1997b). Basically, the researcher must ensure that an executive who participated in the most recent strategy-formulating exercise completes the research instrument, and that questions are answered with specific reference to that exercise. This procedure was used rigorously in the present research with five standard measures (Kim and Mauborgne, 1991, 1993a, 1993b; Taggart, 1997b). Note, however, that Kim and Mauborgne used these measures at the individual level; in the present research the respondents were asked to assess the top management teams' perceptions of procedural justice (see Appendix 9.1). Pretesting indicated that these could be included in the final research instrument without change. Again the correlations between the five measures were high ($p < 0.001$) and the Cronbach alpha was 0.82, a satisfactory level for validating research. Thus, the measures for the procedural justice dimension were accepted as valid and reliable.

Measures of Emphasis in Strategic Decision Making

These measures were largely drawn from a research instrument developed, tested and used by Tan and Litschert (1994) in an empirical study of the Chinese electronics industry. After adapting them to the purposes of the present research, 16 measures were pretested, after which four were excluded from the final instrument and a number of minor amendments were made. The strategic decision variables were measured on a seven-point Likert scale (1 = strongly disagree, 7 = strongly agree) and the correlations are shown in Table 9.2. Three variables relating to future anticipated conditions (*STRAT*), the development of competitive edge (*EDGE*) and the use of planning techniques (*PLAN*) measured emphasis on long-term strategy decisions. Short-term decisions involved two variables: the priority given to short-term profitability (*SHORT*), and speed of response to market opportunity (*RESPON*). Aspects of risk were covered by type of opportunities favoured (*RISK*), balance of risk and return (*FOCUS*), and propensity to favour major opportunity areas over a larger number of small ones (*MAJOR*). Government regulatory matters were covered by two variables: attitude towards and ambiguity in regulations (*GOVREG*), and attitude towards compliance (*ALLOW*). The creative and product differentiation aspects of strategic decisions were covered by one variable each: thorough scanning of alternatives (*ALT*), and propensity to introduce new brands (*BRAND*). Note that both the independent variables and one dimension of the dependent variables measure different aspects

Table 9.2 Strategic decision variables (means, standard deviations and Pearson correlation coefficients)

	Mean	S.D.	STRAT	EDGE	PLAN	SHORT	RESPON	RISK	FOCUS	MAJOR	GOVREG	ALLOW	ALT
STRAT	5.51	1.14											
EDGE	5.45	1.12	0.38										
PLAN	4.70	1.30	0.28	0.40									
SHORT	4.53	1.58	0.27	0.32	0.16								
RESPON	4.82	1.29	0.17	0.29	0.46	0.15							
RISK	4.50	1.20	0.22	0.35	0.20	0.16	0.31						
FOCUS	3.58	1.33	0.12	0.18	0.08	0.15	0.13	0.36					
MAJOR	3.32	1.44	0.03	0.19	0.06	0.14	0.19	0.43	0.49				
GOVREG	3.95	1.49	0.18	0.16	0.25	0.10	0.26	0.19	0.18	0.19			
ALLOW	4.40	1.43	0.15	0.21	0.26	0.16	0.17	0.19	0.04	0.21	0.35		
ALT	4.82	1.24	0.38	0.37	0.48	0.13	0.37	0.27	0.05	0.09	0.23	0.34	
BRAND	4.54	1.62	0.17	0.24	0.15	0.18	0.23	0.25	0.21	0.20	0.32	0.16	0.08

of decisions. However the latter is strictly a measure of how much autonomy resides with the subsidiary in respect of certain functional decision areas, while the independent variables measure the degree of emphasis the subsidiary places on a range of strategic aspects. It is thus infeasible that 'autonomy' and 'strategic decisions' are measuring some common underlying factor. This was confirmed in both the pretest and the post-test interviews.

Data Analysis

The analysis of the postal survey data was completed in five stages. A preliminary factor analysis was carried out on the seven-variable autonomy dimension and the five-variable procedural justice dimension to ratify their mutual orthogonality, and to make certain that both groups of variables loaded significantly and uniquely onto their respective dimensions. The twelve strategic decision variables were then added to this analysis to ensure that the previous two-dimension solution was robust (that is, not broken down by the addition of new variables) and that none of the twelve loaded significantly or uniquely onto either dimension of the model.

Second, since the Cronbach alphas and intradimension correlations were high, the respective groups of variables were aggregated and mean values calculated for each (Ghoshal and Bartlett, 1988). These served as inputs for cluster analysis, with hierarchical and non-hierarchical methods being used in combination (Dess and Davis, 1984; Johnson, 1995). Third, an analysis of variance was conducted to detect whether significant differences existed between strategic decision variables across clusters of subsidiaries identified in the previous stage. This would give a broad indication of systematic variation, but would be insufficient to accept or reject hypotheses.

The fourth stage of the analysis was specifically related to the research hypotheses. Since these related to prior expectations, the appropriate method here was either contrast analysis (Sharma, 1996: 356) or planned comparisons. This would allow a significance test of predicted specific differences between different clusters, which would in turn allow acceptance or rejection of hypotheses 1–6. Finally, since research questions 1 and 2 address relationships in an indeterminate manner, depending on systematic variation, a *post hoc* method was the appropriate technique here. Thus Duncan's multiple range test (Roth and Morrison, 1990) was selected to determine whether positive responses to research questions 1 and 2 were forthcoming.

RESULTS

With a sample size of 265, a power level of 80 per cent, and standard errors assumed to be twice those of conventional correlation coefficients, a significant factor loading (based on $p \leqslant 0.05$) would be 0.34 or above (Hair *et al.*, 1998:

385). Principal components analysis, carried out with seven autonomy and five procedural justice variables, led to a two-factor solution in which the autonomy variables all loaded onto one factor (loadings of 0.75 to 0.87) and the procedural justice variables all loaded onto the other (loadings of 0.65 to 0.82). In addition, the highest autonomy loading onto the procedural justice factor was 0.18, with 0.16 being the highest procedural justice loading on the autonomy factor. Thus, we may conclude that the dimensions were orthogonal and that all variables loaded significantly and uniquely on their respective dimensions. When the 12 strategic decision variables were added to the principal components analysis, a five-factor solution was obtained. Two of these represented autonomy and procedural justice and, as before, all the variables had a loading of 0.62 or above on the appropriate dimension; the highest loading for a strategic decision variable on the autonomy factor was –0.27, and on procedural justice it was 0.22. The A–PJ factor solution thus seemed robustly orthogonal with significant and unique loadings, and the strategic decision variables did not seem to be functionally related to either model dimension.

Cluster analysis was carried out using aggregated measures of autonomy and procedural justice. The hierarchical clustering algorithm used (unweighted pair-group average) could handle a maximum of 100 cases, so five separate random samples of 100 cases were drawn from the 265 cases available and clustered. Four of these indicated that there were four groups of companies in the underlying structure; the fifth was less determinate, showing a possibility of four or six groups. As a precaution, non-hierarchical clustering was used to produce 2, 3, 4, 5, 6 and 7 clusters, and between-groups variance as a proportion of total variance was examined for each solution. Again, it emerged that the four-group solution appeared to be most effective and stable, with between-groups variance accounting for 72.6 per cent of the total (Taggart, 1997b). This four-group solution lay beyond the minimum acceptable range of $n/50$ to $n/30$, and thus appeared to be highly robust (Roth and Morrison, 1990). The means of the autonomy and procedural justice variables are presented in Table 9.3. The usual caution should be shown when interpreting the F-test as the clustering technique ensured that groups of subsidiaries would be effectively and significantly separated.

The four-group solution was also assessed at this stage for evidence of other effects that might dilute the model's robustness, and a number of cross-tabulations were carried out across clusters (chi-square test for difference among k-proportions, $p \leqslant 0.05$). No linkage was found between cluster membership and subsidiary location (Scotland, Wales, Ulster, Ireland), home country of parent (US, Europe, Japan, other), industry (engineering, chemical, other) or job title of respondent (chief executive, other director, other executive). Despite lack of significance in the last of these, it should be noted that 'other directors' had a slight tendency to underestimate the vassal effect and overestimate the militant effect, while 'other managers' had a slight tendency in the opposite direction. While this confirmed earlier fear about a possible measurement error related to the respondent's hierarchical position, it also suggests that the scope of the

Table 9.3 Cluster analysis: means of four-cluster solution

Variable	Cluster 1: vassal subsidiaries (n = 49)	Cluster 2: collaborator subsidiaries (n = 85)	Cluster 3: militant subsidiaries (n = 67)	Cluster 4: partner subsidiaries (n = 64)	F-statistic
Autonomy:					
Decisions about markets supplied	1.61	2.16	3.90	3.55	77.08
Decisions about product range	1.92	2.34	4.12	3.67	101.10
Decisions about advertising and promotion	2.08	2.29	4.36	4.08	64.01
Decisions about R & D	1.73	1.94	3.57	3.31	45.95
Decisions about production	3.45	3.21	4.67	4.41	37.58
Decisions about product pricing	2.59	2.46	4.57	4.17	72.31
Decisions about product design	1.80	2.19	4.03	3.77	81.75
Procedural justice:					
Communication with HQ	2.08	4.41	3.18	5.84	96.93
Challenging HQ views	1.94	4.16	2.99	5.69	85.15
HQ has local knowledge	3.37	5.15	4.54	5.88	44.74
HQ accounts for decisions	3.00	5.68	3.87	6.16	75.68
HQ makes consistent decisions	3.37	5.09	3.93	5.97	52.27

Notes: For autonomy, higher scores signify greater autonomy. For procedural justice, higher scores signify more procedural justice. All *F*-statistics are significant at $p < 0.001$

potential error was fairly low. We may conclude from this analysis that differences between clusters represent differences in autonomy and procedural justice, and are not related to industry, home or host country, or (subject to the marginal qualification above) the respondent's position in the subsidiary hierarchy.

An analysis of variance was carried out across the four-group solution using three structural variables as a final test for the presence of extraneous effects. This indicated that there was no systematic variation across clusters in terms of age ($F = 1.21$, $p = 0.31$), employment level ($F = 1.22$, $p = 0.30$), or annual sales ($F = 0.28$, $p = 0.84$). The results of a second analysis of variance of the 12 strategic decision variables across the four clusters is shown in Table 9.4. Overall the design shows distinct separation of the clusters (Rao's $R = 2.80$, $p < 0.001$), and the contrast analysis columns show the differences between vassals and partners, and between collaborators and militants where these variables refer to hypotheses 1–6. There are significant differences between vassals and partners in respect of the emphasis put on long-term (*STRAT, EDGE, PLAN*) and short-term (*SHORT, RESPON*) strategic decisions, so hypotheses 1 and 2 can be accepted. Similarly, major differences exist with respect to aspects of risk (*RISK, FOCUS*), though the variable related to a firm's propensity to favour major opportunity areas over a larger number of small ones (*MAJOR*) is not significant. Hence, there is substantial, but not complete, support for hypothesis 3. For creative aspects of strategic decision making (*ALT*), substantial differences exist between vassals and partners, and so we can accept hypothesis 4. Turning now to differences in emphasis between militants and collaborators, the latter have significantly higher scores with respect to government regulation (*GOVREG, ALLOW*) and product differentiation (*BRAND*); we can therefore accept hypotheses 5 and 6.

The final column of Table 9.4 shows the results of Duncan multiple range tests (*post hoc*) for differences between clusters (excluding 1–4 and 2–3). It is clear that each pair of clusters is significantly separated; that collaborators and militants occupy intermediate positions between vassals and partners for long- and short-term decisions, risk, and creative aspects; and that vassals and partners occupy intermediate positions for government regulation and product differentiation. We thus have positive responses to both research questions 1 and 2.

DISCUSSION

The results for hypotheses 1–4 show that vassals and partners are significantly separated in the strategy space described in Figure 9.1. Partner subsidiaries put much greater emphasis than vassals on both long- and short-term strategic decisions. They appear to be much more concerned about the degree of risk involved in these decisions. They also put more stress on the need for creative strategic thinking in terms of examining a wider range of options before deciding on the subsidiary's future strategic direction. Collaborators and militants are also

Table 9.4 Means of strategic decision making

Variable	Cluster 1: vassal subsidiaries (n = 49)	Cluster 2: collaborator subsidiaries (n = 85)	Cluster 3: militant subsidiaries (n = 67)	Cluster 4: partner subsidiaries (n = 64)	Contrast analysis: clusters 1–4 (p-level)	Contrast analysis: clusters 2–3 (p-level)	Difference between clusters
STRAT	5.02	5.49	5.55	5.84	0.000	–	1 < 2,3
EDGE	5.20	5.39	5.43	5.75	0.010	–	–
PLAN	4.27	4.79	4.78	5.14	0.000	–	1 < 2; 3 < 4
SHORT	4.10	4.61	4.45	4.86	0.011	–	
RESPON	4.41	4.65	4.87	5.31	0.000	–	1 < 3; 4 > 2, 3
RISK	3.90	4.60	4.43	4.89	0.000	–	1 < 2,3; 3 < 4
FOCUS	3.14	3.73	3.25	4.05	0.000	–	2 > 1,3; 3 < 4
MAJOR	3.16	3.29	3.13	3.64	0.081	–	
GOVREG	4.10	4.12	3.57	4.02	–	0.024	3 < 1
ALLOW	4.43	4.66	3.91	4.53	–	0.001	3 < 1,4
ALT	4.12	5.00	4.79	5.11	0.000	–	1 < 2,3
BRAND	4.31	4.84	4.19	4.70	–	0.016	–

Notes: Higher scores signify higher levels of emphasis for all variables. The final column shows the results of the Duncan's multiple range tests (p ≤ 0.05).

significantly separated by the results for hypotheses 5 and 6; the former appear to be much more sensitive to government requirements when considering strategic decisions, and they put more weight on the need to consider strategic aspects of product differentiation.

Furthermore, the results flowing from the two broad research questions serve to separate the remaining pairs of subsidiary types in the strategy space. Vassal subsidiaries put significantly less emphasis than collaborators on five aspects of strategic decisions: anticipating future conditions (*STRAT*), use of planning techniques and information systems (*PLAN*), acceptance of higher risk when balanced by higher potential returns (*RISK*), tendency actively to seek out such high risk-high return investment (*FOCUS*) and thorough evaluation of strategic alternatives (*ALT*). Vassals also put significantly less emphasis than militant subsidiaries on four facets of strategic decisions: anticipating future conditions (*STRAT*), acceptance of higher risk when balanced by higher potential returns (*RISK*), thorough evaluation of strategic alternatives (*ALT*) and tendency to respond quickly to signals of opportunity (*RESPON*). Conversely, vassals put more emphasis than militants on both aspects of government regulation: tendency to be proactive when regulations seem ambiguous (*GOVREG*) and moving carefully with relation to regulatory changes that are specifically permitted (*ALLOW*). Collaborator subsidiaries show significantly lower values than partners on only one variable (*RESPON*), though the difference is nearly significant for use of planning techniques and information systems (*PLAN*) and tendency to favour ambitious initiatives with somewhat uncertain outcomes (*MAJOR*). Collaborators and partners are thus less well separated by strategic decision measures than any other pair in the strategy space. Militants and partners are, however, well separated by five variables: use of planning techniques and information systems (*PLAN*), tendency to respond quickly to signals of opportunity (*RESPON*), acceptance of higher risk when balanced by higher potential returns (*RISK*), tendency actively to seek out such high risk-high return investment (*FOCUS*) and moving carefully with relation to regulatory changes that are specifically permitted (*ALLOW*). Militants have a significantly lower value in each case.

Tables 9.3 and 9.4 indicate that the four types of subsidiary are significantly separated in the strategy space, and the validating analysis above supports this assessment. Strategic decision variables are most effective in separating vassals and partners (eight variables), followed by vassals and militants (six variables), then vassals and collaborators, and militants and partners (five variables each), then collaborators and militants (two variables), with collaborators and partners (one variable) showing least effective separation (see final column of Table 9.4). However, subsidiary types may also be described with reference to a number of operating variables that were also included in the postal questionnaire.

The typical vassal subsidiary has been established for 13.6 years, employs 170 people (the lowest of any subsidiary type), of whom only three are R & D staff (again the lowest). It has the highest level of sales (£93 million) of any of the four subsidiary types. It also has the highest level of exports – 71 per cent of sales, of which about a third goes to other group plants for further processing and/or final assembly. It draws the highest proportion (38 per cent) of material inputs from sister subsidiaries and a further 35 per cent comes from local suppliers. As the number of R & D staff would suggest, vassal subsidiaries are involved in the lowest levels of R & D, with most firms engaging in nothing more elaborate than the provision of customer technical services. Perhaps reflecting high export propensity, vassal subsidiaries also have the greatest market scope, with a substantial proportion of firms serving selected world markets. Though the vassal classification is the smallest (49 members), it still represents a substantial proportion of the overall sample. The research was not aimed at why this may be so. However MNC parents may regard Scotland, Wales, Ulster and the Republic of Ireland as strategically as well as geographically peripheral. Accordingly they may be more prepared to tolerate this type of subsidiary.

The typical collaborator affiliate is 14.4 years old, making it the longest established of all four groups; perhaps because of this and other factors it also has the largest number of employees (325), of whom 16 are R & D staff. Its sales, at some £89.5 million, are almost as high as those of vassals. About two thirds of sales are exported, with 37.5 per cent of these being transferred to other group affiliates for further processing. Just under a third of its material inputs come from this source, and a further third are derived from local suppliers. The collaborator subsidiary's market scope is almost as wide as that of the vassal, but it has more complex in-house R & D operations; many are involved in adapting manufacturing technology, and a few also develop new or improved products for the home and European markets.

The archetypal militant subsidiary is the youngest, being established for just over 11 years. It employs 265, the second lowest among the four subsidiary types. Its in-house technical operations are broad, more than half being new product development; however this activity is supported by an average of just over four R & D staff. We can infer from this either that R & D activity is highly specialized and requires few scientists for its implementation; or that it is an irregular or unofficial activity not knowingly sanctioned by the HQ. Due to the nature of their relationship with their HQs, we speculate that the latter is the more likely explanation for militant subsidiaries. Corresponding to its relative youthfulness and low employment, this type of subsidiary also has the lowest sales figure (£55 million per annum) and the lowest export propensity (52 per cent). Again, around one third of exports are partly finished goods shipped to other group subsidiaries for additional processing. The return flow of material inputs from these sister subsidiaries accounts for just over 20 per cent of all inputs, by far the lowest figure for any group of affiliates. In contrast, it derives the highest proportion of material inputs from indigenous suppliers, and in this regard is the most locally responsive subsidiary type. Unsurprisingly, militants also have narrowest market scope in the sample, with only 14 of the 67 subsidiaries selling in world markets.

The typical partner subsidiary has been established for 12 years and employs 293, 19 of whom are R & D staff (the highest number in our sample). It has sales of some £65 million per annum, of which 55 per cent are exports. Approximately 29 per cent of exports are accounted for by shipments of partly finished goods to other group plants for further processing, the lowest proportion of all four groups of subsidiaries. Sister subsidiaries supply just over a quarter of the material inputs, and almost half come from local suppliers. The partner's market scope is only a little broader than the militant's. However it has the most complex in-house R & D operations in the sample, with one third of the 64 firms being involved in high-level product development for world markets and generating new technology to meet the parent corporation's needs.

An earlier analysis indicated that collaborators and partners were significantly separated by only one strategic decision variable (quick response to signals of opportunity, *RESPON*). However, a Duncan multiple range test on the operating variables used in the present analysis shows that these two groups of affiliates are also significantly differentiated in terms of the proportion of outputs going to other group plants for further processing, the proportion of material inputs sourced locally, and in-house R & D complexity (all at $p \leq 0.05$). Similarly, collaborators and militants were differentiated in the earlier analysis by only two strategic decision variables – proactivity on government regulation (*GOVREG*) and remaining within the limits of regulation changes (*ALLOW*). Here, they are also significantly separated by export propensity, proportion of material inputs coming from other group plants, and proportion of material inputs sourced locally. Thus, taking the strategic decision and operating variables together, each pair of subsidiary types is significantly differentiated by at least four variables.

IMPLICATIONS

This research has implications for the autonomy–procedural justice model as a behavioural model of MNC subsidiary management. First, the significant separation of collaborator and militant subsidiaries is hardly surprising, given their dimensional profile and diametric positioning in Figure 9.1. The collaborator is confirmed as the type of affiliate most likely to appeal to harried corporate managers. It is cooperative, constructive without being overtly innovative, will work hard to maintain smooth subsidiary – HQ relations and puts sufficient stress on strategic decision making without allowing internal confrontations to develop. Most of all it puts much more emphasis than any other type of subsidiary on the question of government regulation in the host country. It ensures not only that it stays out of trouble itself, but also that the parent corporation is spared the time and resources needed to cope with hostile host government responses. While it is a substantial employer in its host country (with all the relationship benefits involved), it is also the subsidiary type most integrated into the parent's global network. Most MNCs are likely to want a fairly large proportion of collaborator subsidiaries in a stable international configuration, and all the more so in mature industries.

Conversely the militant subsidiary is likely to be lowest on the wish list of the parent company's CEO. It is prickly and pushy, and probably welcomes the inherent instability caused by difficulties at the subsidiary – HQ interface. In many cases militant subsidiaries have been acquired, or are involved in non-core activity and/or using differentiated technology. While it accounts for the least sales, the militant is most closely linked to its local economy and has many attributes of the locally responsive subsidiary (Prahalad and Doz, 1987; Jarillo and Martínez, 1990). It is not unreasonable to speculate that such an affiliate, operating with a relationship of some hostility *vis-à-vis* the HQ, is likely to have a very effective management team; it is also likely to be operating in a market of some strategic significance to the parent. In these circumstances the corporate aim must be to move the subsidiary gently into the partner quadrant by investing in the relationship. This will of course require effective management at the corporate level; if this is not in place or forthcoming, the more likely trajectory for the militant subsidiary is a longer-term slide into the vassal posture, accompanied (or perhaps impelled) by a loss of local management quality. Ultimately, the militant subsidiary may represent an unsustainable set of organizational relationships, and the implied instability may well depress further perceptions of procedural justice and tempt the management to seize even more autonomy for itself. Failing the kind of proactive strategy shift indicated above, the alternative might be depressed performance and ultimate divestment.

In similar vein, the import of Figure 9.1 is that significant differences between vassal and partner subsidiaries are not unexpected. The vassal is likely to contribute least to corporate requirements or the utility of its international network. Overall the vassal puts far less emphasis on strategic decision making than any other affiliate type, perhaps because it feels so alienated from the corporate body and so powerless to influence its own future. It is particularly risk-averse (Table 9.4) and shows little creativity in respect of strategic issues. It is relatively unimportant to its host economy in terms of employment, local sales and local linkages, and its ability to develop and transfer technology (either locally or intranetwork) is highly limited. At this stage we can only speculate why these subsidiaries exist in such numbers. They may result from poor acquisitions, they may (as suggested above) be the end-point of poor corporate management of former militants, or they may develop within disjointed networks where the proportion of militants is sufficiently high to absorb a large proportion of network management resources. Whatever their origin, it is difficult to accept that vassal subsidiaries contribute significantly to shareholder value, and they may be viewed as prominent candidates for closure. However, as noted previously, MNC parents may tolerate this type of subsidiary in countries of lower strategic importance.

It is likely that the partner subsidiary contributes most to long-term shareholder value. While an MNC with a large proportion of this type of subsidiary would undoubtedly constitute some form of heterarchy (Hedlund, 1986; Hedlund and Rolander, 1990), most international corporations arguably need a sprinkling of them, especially where strategic country markets and/or rapidly advancing technologies are involved. The partner can be a true centre of excellence within the MNC (Forsgren *et al.*, 1992), a role that is well supported by its extensive resource control and its excellent relations with the HQ. Overall, it puts the greatest emphasis on strategic decisions, probably because it has more of them to make. It is an important player in its local economy, but is not highly integrated into its internal network. It has the broadest market scope of any type of subsidiary, and the same is true of its in-house R & D. This supports the speculation that, while integration is fairly low in terms of material inputs to and outputs from other group subsidiaries, it may be much higher in terms of co-operative market development and intranetwork sharing of new technology (Birkinshaw, 1996; Ghoshal and Bartlett, 1988).

CONCLUSIONS

This research set out to validate the A–PJ model of subsidiary strategy using a new sample of affiliates, and to extend the understanding of the model by examining its classifications across a range of strategic issues. While the autonomy variables differ somewhat, the model emerges as clearly and robustly as in Taggart's (1997b) original research. Vassal and partner subsidiaries are significantly differentiated in the predicted ways by short-term, long-term and risk-associated issues of strategic decision making. Government regulation and product differentiation issues similarly separate collaborator and militant affiliates. In addition, all other pairs of subsidiary types are significantly and robustly separated by the strategic and operating variables used in this research.

The discussion of the model suggests that it may have a useful part to play in understanding the behavioural dynamics of strategy development and implementation across the subsidiary – HQ interface. It could be argued, for example, that A–PJ considerations play a significant role when the subsidiary is required to become more or less integrated and/or coordinated with its network, when corporate strategy demands shifts in market/product/value-added scope, or when the balance of host country and network pressures calls for a change in local responsiveness. However, two caveats should be entered. First, as well as the normal sources of measurement error present in a survey of this kind, specific attention has been drawn to the question of non-CEO respondents. There is some evidence to suggest that this is not a serious source of measurement error, but this evidence is fairly weak. It is now intended, as an additional stage to the research project, to interview a number of such respondents with a view to assessing the likelihood and magnitude of measurement error from this source. Second, it is clear from the discussion that this research raises many more questions about vassal subsidiaries than it manages to answer. While detailed investigation of this type of affiliate is clearly a matter of high sensitivity, further fine-grained research is necessary, and perhaps should concentrate on ways of moving such a subsidiary to a more positive locus in the strategy space.

APPENDIX 9.1 POSTAL QUESTIONNAIRE ABSTRACT, AUTONOMY AND PRO-
CEDURAL JUSTICE

The following categories of decision-making have been identified:

1. Decided mainly by the parent company or regional headquarters *without* consulting with or seeking the advice of this subsidiary.
2. Decided mainly by the parent company or regional headquarters *after* consulting with or seeking the advice of this subsidiary.
3. Decided jointly with *equal weight* being given to the views of this subsidiary
   and the HQ.
4. Decided mainly by this subsidiary *after* consulting with or seeking the advice
   of the parent company or regional headquarters.
5. Decided mainly by this subsidiary *without* consulting with or seeking the
   advice of the parent company or regional headquarters.

Referring to the above, please indicate below which category (i.e. 1, 2, 3, 4 or 5
above) best describes the decision-making authority that this subsidiary has in
terms of the eight functional areas listed on the right-hand side of the table.
Please mark 1, 2, 3, 4 or 5 against each function as appropriate.

Market area supplied by subsidiary	
Product range supplied by subsidiary	
Pricing of subsidiary's products	
Design of subsidiary's products	
Advertising and promotion of subsidiary's products	
R & D at subsidiary	
Production operations at subsidiary	

Procedural justice refers to how the HQ strategy-making process for its subsidiary
units are judged to be fair by subsidiary top management. In the following 5 questions, please circle the appropriate number to indicate your perception between
either end of the scales in terms of how you feel the top management team views
each of these aspects.

Effective two-way communication exists between this subsidiary and corporate
or regional HQ during the process of formulating the parent company's strategy.
    This does not apply at all   1   2   3   4   5   6   7   *This applies fully*

This subsidiary has adequate and legitimate opportunity to challenge the strategic views of corporate or regional HQ during the process of formulating the parent company's strategy.

This does not apply at all   1   2   3   4   5   6   7   *This applies fully*

Corporate or regional HQ is knowledgeable about the local situation of this subsidiary.

This does not apply at all   1   2   3   4   5   6   7   *This applies fully*

This subsidiary is provided with an account of the final strategic decisions of corporate or regional headquarters.

This does not apply at all   1   2   3   4   5   6   7   *This applies fully*

Corporate or regional HQ is fairly consistent in making decisions across all subsidiary units within this multinational corporation.

This does not apply at all   1   2   3   4   5   6   7   *This applies fully*

10 The Development of Pan-European Industrial Structures and the Strategic Development of Subsidiaries

Frank McDonald, Heinz Tüselmann and Arne Heise

INTRODUCTION

The integration programmes of the European Union (EU), such as the Single Market and European Monetary Union programmes, have reduced the trading costs of engaging in intra-EU trade. These developments have provided incentives to rationalize production and distribution systems so as to reap economies of scale and develop markets. The integration programmes are also inducing changes to industrial structures, with nationally based structures being broken down and replaced by pan-EU systems, albeit with significant variations according to industry and member state (European Commission, 1996; Dunning, 1997). Geographical concentration is most pronounced in industries that have strong economies of scale, and these industries tend to be located near to large markets (Brülhart, 1996a, Amiti, 1998). However geographical concentration is not as pronounced in Europe as it is in the US (Brülhart, 1996b). The operations of MNCs are crucial to the process of industrial restructuring as their DFI flows, both extra- and intra-EU, play a vital role in the creation and evolution of EU industrial structures.

However studies of European MNCs suggest that they are less likely than non-European MNCs to develop core competences in subsidiaries located in Europe (Schmidt, 1999; Chesnais *et al.*, 2000). A study of Irish foreign direct investment (FDI) found that subsidiaries of non-European MNCs (American, Australian, Canadian and Japanese) and from smaller European countries are more likely to supply the rest of Europe than MNCs from large European countries and the Netherlands. MNCs based in the latter countries tend to focus on sales to the domestic market, with FDI flows strongly linked to export-enhancing activities by parent companies. The study also found that subsidiaries of non-European MNCs and those from small European countries are more likely to source their Irish subsidiaries from the rest of Europe. However those from large European countries and the Netherlands primarily source from the home country (Egelhoff *et al.*, 2000). This home-based tendency of European MNCs is also evident in a survey of 452 foreign-owned subsidiaries in the UK, which revealed that European MNCs are less likely to make significant purchases in the UK than North American or Asian firms, and that many European MNCs make no or only very small purchases in the UK (Williams, 1999). Studies of German FDI in the UK and Ireland have found that German-owned subsidiaries tend to focus on sales to the domestic market, and there is little evidence that their subsidiaries are evolving into more diversified operations that embrace high value-added operations in the host countries (Hood and Taggart, 1997; McDonald *et al.*, 2000).

These studies indicate that the European subsidiaries of MNCs from the large countries of Europe often resemble outposts of their parent company. In contrast, non-European MNCs, especially US firms, are more likely to make more purchases in the host country and to develop their European subsidiaries into integrated European networks covering a wide variety of activities. These subsidiaries often have considerable autonomy to develop products and to specialize in particular operations, such as R & D, in which they have advantages. These types of network lead to high levels of intra-industry and intra-firm EU trade that stimulate pan-European operating systems (Chesnais and Soilleau, 2000). This implies that the European subsidiaries of non-European MNCs are likely to be involved in more technologically advanced and higher value-added activities than subsidiaries with parents in large European countries. This is because they are mandated to develop products and to specialize in activities such as R & D.

There is growing interest in policies that encourage the development of clusters based on local networks of firms, governmental and research agencies and other types of support service (OECD, 1999a). The literature in this area tends to focus on the role of public sector bodies or public–private partnerships that facilitate the development of local networks and encourage the growth of clusters (Steiner, 1998; Lagendijk, 1999; Enright, 2000). However, this literature does not explicitly consider country-specific effects on subsidiary development and the implications of these for the evolution of clusters.

This chapter examines the effects of European integration on the process of regional development in the light of factors that influence FDI flows and the strategic development of subsidiaries. In particular, a model is developed to explain why the European subsidiaries of MNCs based in the large economies of Europe are generally involved in lower-level operations than non-European subsidiaries and those from the smaller economies of Europe. Finally, some of the policy implications of the model are explored.

EXPLANATIONS OF FDI AND REGIONAL SPECIALIZATION

Traditional theories of FDI suggest that FDI flows arise from the desire to develop international markets and sources of supply while retaining control over ownership rights using the lowest transaction cost methods of securing these objectives. Location-specific advantages such as labour costs, taxation and subsi-

dies also influence FDI flows (Dunning, 1992). Stage theories of internationalization indicate that FDI flows evolve from simple international operations such as
exporting to more complex activities such as product development and R & D
activities (Johanson and Vahlne, 1977). However these models are rather mechanistic and suggest that MNCs follow a rigid linear pattern of internationalization
that is not verified by empirical evidence (Andersen, 1993). Theories based on
the development of networks (Nordstrom, 1990), contingency theories (Reid,
1983) and the accumulation of knowledge (Kogut and Zander, 1993) have sought
to clarify the complex factors that appear to determine the internationalization
path of MNCs. Most of these theories and empirical evidence provide support for
the view that FDI flows follow an evolutionary process, but that the time path and
major characteristics of this process seem to be influenced by a variety of
complex factors (Young, 1987).

These traditional theories suggest that MNCs develop high-value-added operations their subsidiaries in industries and locations that provide high ownership
and location benefits (including the accumulation of useful knowledge), and that
this process evolves as MNCs gain experience of operating in host regions.
Modern theories of FDI focus on spillover effects and technological and geographical factors.

Spillover benefits to domestic firms and industries from FDI activities arise
from demonstration effects and the transfer of knowledge to suppliers and other
supporting firms and organizations connected to foreign subsidiaries. Some
studies suggest that FDI provides spillover benefits that improve the general
level of productivity in host countries (Engelbrecht, 1997; Blomstrom and
Kokko, 1998). In the UK there is mixed evidence on the extent and significance
of spillovers. Driffield (1999) has found that they benefits are small and
restricted to areas near centres of FDI, and that they do not benefit industries that
have experienced large FDI inflows. However other studies have found that the
spillover effects are large and benefit both industries with large FDI flows and
other industries (Hubert and Pain, 1999). Beneficial spillover effects generate
desirable conditions in regions that may encourage further investment to take
advantage of the enhanced productivity potential, thereby creating a virtuous
cycle of FDI inflows and begetting more investment, both foreign and domestic.

Technology-based theories are founded on the premise that firms seek to
transfer technology to locations that offer improved benefits from exploiting the
technical expertise of MNCs (Narula, 1996). In order to successfully transfer
technical knowledge, host countries must have the capability to use such technology effectively. The technological capability of a country is determined by
the assets of its firms (Nelson and Winter, 1982), its institutional structure
(North, 1990) and the ability of the infrastructure to support technological developments (Freeman and Soete, 1997). The more amenable the internal resources
of subsidiaries, institutional frameworks and the infrastructure to the effective
utilization of technological systems, the greater the depth and level of technological transfer to host countries. Therefore, subsidiaries in locations that have the

management and other resources needed to use transferred technology effectively, and where the institutional system and infrastructure of the host region are supportive of new technology, are likely to receive high-level technology transfer. The proviso that host countries must be able to assimilate new technology effectively implies that the bulk of FDI flows that embody significant technology transfer is between countries with similar but slightly different technological capabilities

New international economics explains the reasons for trade based on internal and external economies of scale (Helpman and Krugman, 1985). It is argued that trade opportunities between countries with similar economic structures is largely based on the ability of firms to reap increasing returns from economies of scale in the design, production and distribution of goods and services. Therefore, firms located in areas that confer internal and in some cases external economies of scale will have advantages over firms that are not located in such places. New international economics considers that FDI flows are partly a consequence of the attempts by firms to secure advantages by locating in different areas and supplying a number of national markets from these locations. Models using this approach focus on the proximity benefits of geographical concentration (clustering) that arise from internal and external economies of scale to achieve low transport costs to large markets (Krugman and Venables, 1990; Krugman, 1991). The availability of proximity benefits encourages clustering, as the lower trade costs brought about by European integration have led to the development of pan-European industrial structures, enabling the European market to be supplied by a small number of clusters or perhaps just one cluster.

The insights into the importance of geographical factors that emanated from new international economics led to greater focus on what became known as new economic geography (Ottavianno and Puga, 1998). Models based on new economic geography focus on factor mobility and availability and congestion costs as limiting factors in the incentive to cluster (Ricci, 1999). According to these models the process of clustering initially leads to cost advantages from internal and external economies of scale, from low-cost access to essential resources that lower costs and/or increase quality, and from the growth of the market as concentration raises the income of the population within the cluster. The advantages of clustering induce suppliers of inputs to migrate to clusters, thereby creating a cycle where success breeds further success.

However, as clusters develop the incentive to disperse operations increases because factor prices rise for inputs that are characterized by immobility or inelasticity of supply. Congestion costs also increase as clusters develop and grow. In these circumstances, FDI decisions are influenced by the desire to find locations that confer the best possible supply of immobile factors of production and provide a more elastic supply of factors that are undergoing large price increases in existing clusters. A trade-off emerges between the economies of scale and scope and the market size advantages of clusters on the one hand, and the rising production costs associated with input supply and congestion on the other. A differentiation of operations emerges, with core activities that benefit from geographical proximity being located in clusters, and operations with low proximity benefits being consigned to peripheral locations. The main effects of FDI inflows on regional specialization and integration into pan-European industrial systems are illustrated in Figure 10.1.

These factors can explain the development of pan-European industrial structures in response to reductions in trade costs that enable high-level subsidiary development in regions that are able to provide a pool of desirable resources. Firms located in such regions tend to source a large part of their operations from their host region, and supply a large part of the operations of the MNC as a whole from its key subsidiaries. Consequently, regions that attract such investment become integrated into pan-European trade and business networks. Regions without such benefits are likely to attract subsidiaries with low-level mandates, such as sales and distribution or low value-added manufacturing, mainly for the domestic market. Such regions are unlikely to become strongly integrated into pan-European trade and business networks. However these factors cannot explain why MNCs subsidiaries based in the large economies of Europe tend to be engaged in low-level operations.

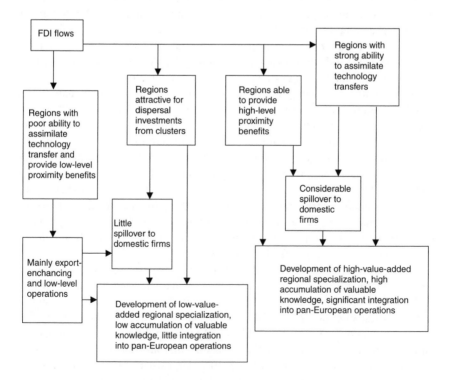

Figure 10.1 FDI flows and pan-European specialization

THE STRATEGIC DEVELOPMENT OF SUBSIDIARIES

Resource-based theories regard differentiated networks of subsidiaries as a major means of developing competitive advantage (Bartlett and Ghoshal, 1989). MNCs that develop differentiated networks transform some of their subsidiaries into centres of competence. These centres develop core activities that play an important part in the operations of all or significant parts of the MNC. Therefore locating these centres in economically favourable areas is a central objective of MNCs (Birkinshaw and Hood, 1998a). However, centres of competence located in the periphery of economic activity can play an important role in the development of regions that are not part of the heartland of the EU (Taggart and Taggart, 1997b).

Subsidiaries that are chosen to be centres of competence have desirable resources based on local networks. These networks are founded on trust and access to inputs that are useful in achieving the goals of MNCs. Areas that offer pools of skilled labour, access to high-quality products and local networks of organizations and agencies that can help the parent company to achieve its strategic objectives are attractive locations for MNCs. If these desirable resources cannot readily be transferred to other parts of the firm, it is beneficial to develop subsidiaries into centres of competence and to use the output from these centres to satisfy the demands of all or large parts of the firm's operations. On the other hand, if desirable resources can be easily transferred to other parts of the firm, these resources will move to locations that offer the greatest benefits to the parent company. The goal of MNCs' resource-based strategies is to blend their network of subsidiaries into a more effective unit. Therefore, MNCs take advantage of the different cultures and business environments in which their subsidiaries operate to develop intra-firm networks that make the best use of the resources available to them (Birkinshaw, 2000).

The development of subsidiaries into centres of competence is an evolutionary process connected to the development of mandates. Subsidiaries can be given a variety of mandates ranging from basic, which involve little more than sales and distribution with limited 'screwdriver' type production, to top-level strategic autonomy that permits the development of main lines of business for regional or even global markets. Movement up the mandate hierarchy depends on the ability of subsidiary managers to develop good managerial competences and relationship assets with other parts of the MNC and with local networks of firms, government agencies and other types of organization (Birkinshaw and Hood, 1998b; Foss and Pedersen, 2000). Managerial competences include the ability to add significant value to the operations of the subsidiary by developing and transferring internally created knowledge, and to convince senior managers in the parent company that the subsidiary is capable of developing mandates. Relationship assets help subsidiaries to deliver desirable outcomes by providing them with resources and information that is not available (or can only be secured at high cost) to the parent company. Relationship assets include membership of beneficial local networks and contact with useful information sources such as R & D centres, governmental agencies and so on (Zander and Kogut, 1996; Spender, 1998). The accumulation of relationship assets combined with the development of managerial competences enables subsidiaries to acquire higher-level mandates. This process is illustrated in Figure 10.2.

If there is no significant accumulation of managerial competence and relationship assets, subsidiary development will stop at the appropriate mandate level. In cases where there is a deterioration of managerial competences or relationship assets, or when subsidiaries fail to keep up with developments elsewhere, mandates may be withdrawn, leading to a move down the mandate hierarchy. The initial point of entry to the hierarchy need not be at the basic mandate level. For example an international financial services firm entering a well-established cluster may well enter with a mid- or even top-level mandate by acquiring a firm that already has strong relationship assets and managerial competences (Andersson *et al.*, 1997; Mattson, 1998).

Analysis of the development of mandates centres on the internal resources of subsidiaries. However, external factors relating to regional specialization (ability to assimilate technology transfers, proximity benefits and spillovers) are important to the development of subsidiaries because they affect their ability to accumulate relationship assets and acquire useful knowledge (Spender, 1998). In addition, the labour market conditions in host regions affect the development of managerial competences in that regions with high value-added specialization are more likely to possess a pool of labour with the attributes and skills necessary

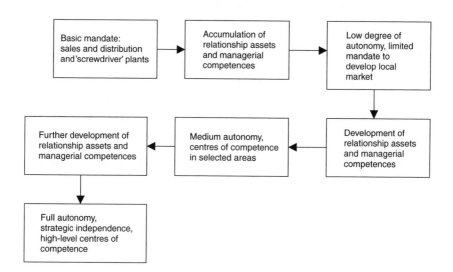

Figure 10.2   The development of mandates

for the effective management of subsidiaries with high-level mandates (Porter, 1990b; Porter and Sölvell, 1999).

REGIONAL SPECIALIZATION AND SUBSIDIARY MANDATES

Subsidiaries that manage to accumulate and develop relationship assets and managerial competencies but that are located in regions with a poor ability to assimilate technology transfers and/or low-level proximity benefits are not able to move up the mandate hierarchy shown in Figure 10.2 as the former are of limited value without the latter.

The observed tendency among MNCs from large European countries to retain core operations in their home countries may be connected to the long-term accumulation of relationship assets and managerial competences embedded in their home base. For MNCs based in countries with large markets and access to extensive national or regional networks and desirable assets there may be little incentive to develop the mandates of their European subsidiaries. However, MNCs based in small European countries may not have these advantages, or at least not to the same extent, so the development of high-level mandates among their European subsidiaries is attractive. Non-European MNCs have a strong incentive to develop the mandates of their European subsidiaries because the parents companies are less embedded in local networks that can help them secure desirable assets in Europe. Furthermore, they are geographically and culturally distant from European markets and face trade and regulatory obstacles that hamper exportation from the home base. In addition, Europe is a major area of economic activity with substantial technical and market developments, knowledge of which is attractive to many MNCs. Developing pan-European networks may be attractive for non-European MNCs because many of the newer entrants are not embedded in the existing national networks in Europe and they therefore have the opportunity to develop differentiated networks among their European subsidiaries to create optimal access to desirable markets and resources. The extensive pan-European operations of US MNCs that have operated in Europe for many years indicates that American firms in Europe are more 'European' than German, French or British firms (Chesnais *et al.*, 2000). This provides some support for the view that access to effective networks in European countries at least partly explains the parent country effect on mandate development (Figure 10.3).

Host regions with the characteristics shown in Figure 10.4 enter into a virtuous cycle where by the desirable conditions they offer are developed and expanded as firms invest in the regions, thereby adding to the stock of attractive assets. Obstacles to the continuing success of successful regions include increased input prices in response to high demand (this is particularly acute if movement of appropriate resources is limited) and rising congestion costs. Failure to adjust to technical changes and market developments can also undermine the continuing development of such regions. In these circumstances,

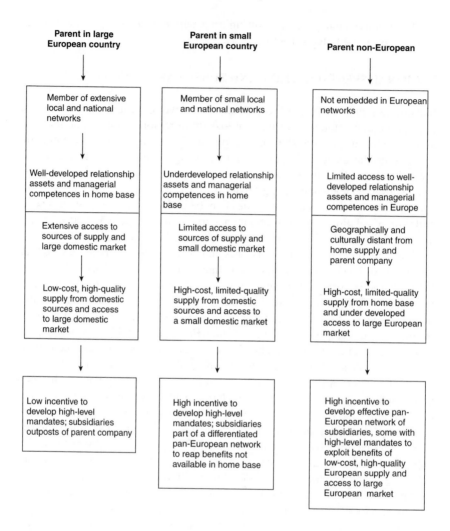

Figure 10.3   Parent country effects

MNCs are likely to remove mandates from their subsidiaries. These factors may also explain the rise of new 'successful' regions. The development of desirable conditions in the face of changing technical changes and/or market developments and the availability of low-cost, high-quality resources with low congestion costs can stimulate the process of regional specialization and thereby stimulate the development of high-level mandates.

Regions that are well integrated into pan-European industrial structures are likely to be successful if they are host to significant numbers of subsidiaries that

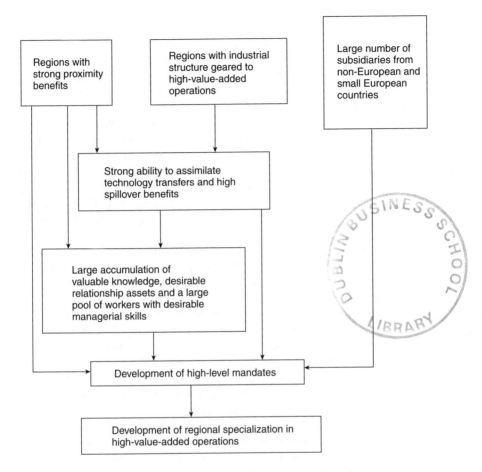

Figure 10.4   Characteristics of host regions and development of mandates

are crucial to the overall European operations of MNCs. These subsidiaries are likely to have high-level mandates that enable them to take advantage of favourable local conditions. These mandates induce large-scale intra-industry and intra-firm trade because subsidiaries with such mandates are often key providers of major inputs and outputs. Given this central role in European operations it is unlikely that MNCs will downgrade the subsidiaries' mandates unless very unfavourable conditions arise in the host region. Regions that are host to a large number of subsidiaries of non-European MNCs and MNCs from small European countries are likely to be better integrated into pan-European operations than those with a large number of subsidiaries of MNCs based in large European countries.

POLICY IMPLICATIONS

Some tentative policy implications can be gleaned from the above analysis. Consideration of the factors that determine the development of subsidiaries' mandates and that influence FDI flows indicates that regional specialization emerges from the interaction of these forces. The attractiveness of regions for FDI flows depends on factors such as low labour costs, taxation and subsidy benefits, proximity to large markets, ability to assimilate technology transfers and the existence of well-developed local networks. Subsidiaries located in regions with such features are more likely to be able to accumulate relationship assets and develop managerial competences that are conducive to the evolution of high-level mandates. These regions are also more likely to be integrated into the emerging pan-European industrial structures because the high-mandate subsidiaries located in these regions often provide key inputs and outputs for the European operations of MNCs.

Regions with low proximity benefits and a poor ability to assimilate technology transfers do not offer an environment that is conducive to the granting of high-level mandates. These regions will mainly attract FDI that is prompted by low-cost inputs and tax/subsidy benefits or the development of domestic markets. Subsidiaries located in such regions are unlikely to develop high-level mandates because the accumulation of relationship assets and managerial competences are not sufficient to support their strategic development. Such regions tend to be poorly integrated into pan-European operations as they offer little more than low production costs and sales and distribution outlets. Moreover low-production cost subsidiaries are subject to transfer to other European regions or parts of the world if cost conditions become more favourable elsewhere.

The analysis in this chapter suggests that regions that are likely to develop high value-added specialization are already successful in the sense that they possess good proximity benefits and a strong ability to assimilate technology transfers. These regions provide a favourable environment for subsidiaries to develop high-level mandates. The development of such mandates helps, by way of spillover effects, to increase the ability of subsidiaries to accumulate relationship assets and managerial competences. This creates a virtuous cycle where success begets further success.

Regions that are not in this fortunate position may escape from their dependence on low-value-added operations if they can create the conditions needed for the accumulation of desirable relationship assets and managerial competences. This will be enhanced if they can also provide low-cost but high-quality assets and low congestion costs. The latter requires them to respond to new technical and market conditions more efficiently than regions that are currently host to successful high-value-added operations. Attracting non-European MNCs and MNCs from the smaller countries of Europe may be the best way to develop high-value-added operations because the subsidiaries of these companies appear to be more inclined to strive for high-mandate status.

CONCLUSIONS

Regional specialization along similar lines to that evident in the US is beginning to emerge in Europe. However, the existing nationally based industrial structures continue to be important in the large countries of Europe. This appears to have encouraged MNCs based in these countries to confer only low-level mandates on their European subsidiaries. In contrast, the European subsidiaries of non-European MNCs and MNCs from small European countries are likely to have mandates that permit greater autonomy in order to facilitate the development of a pan-European operational network of differentiated subsidiaries by taking advantage of local benefits.

The attractiveness of regions for the development of clusters that are strongly integrated into the pan-European system is linked to their ability to provide proximity benefits, assimilate technology transfers and confer useful knowledge. However, these features are not sufficient in themselves and it is also necessary for MNCs to grant their subsidiaries high-level mandates. European MNCs that are firmly embedded in advantageous networks in their home base may not be attracted by the benefits offered by other European regions.

Obviously research is necessary to validate this view. This will require investigation of the strength of country-specific and industry-specific effects. Verification of the views expressed in this chapter could have significant implications for the policy debate on the encouragement of clusters.

11 Cluster Development Policy and New Forms of Public–Private Partnership

Philip Raines

INTRODUCTION

Since the early 1980s considerable academic attention has been paid to the progressive blurring of the boundary between public and private spheres of economic activity (OECD, 1998). Against a background of longer-term reform of the tasks of government and the approach to its conduct, the balance of responsibility between the private and public sectors has shifted, particularly with respect to government functions in the economy (Farnham and Horton, 1996). Indeed, a significant 'crossover' has taken place in the management of activities that overlap private and public, with an ever-increasing variety of joint public–private endeavours being developed.

The field where this has perhaps been most evident is economic development, where a partnership model has become common in a range of policy areas (Bailey, 1994). However, while research has focused on the use of joint public–private partnerships in areas such as urban and spatial policy, their common use in cluster development has been less publicized. Interest in the cluster concept has transformed the government's approach to improving the competitiveness of local/national industrial sectors. In this context clusters can be defined as networks of firms, research providers (such as universities) and public bodies that are located in relatively close geographical proximity and whose linkages create local competitive advantages. Popularized by the work of Porter (1998) and others, there is widespread recognition that clusters can support technological innovation, produce economies of scale and enhance self-sustaining development within regionally and nationally based industrial sectors. The popularity of the concept can be seen in the proliferation of policies designed to promote such networks between firms, examples of which can be found at the national and subnational levels in virtually every European country (OECD, 1999a).

Public sector organizations have taken the lead in developing policies to support clusters. Their role has been central in identifying both the most promising clusters and the market failures that may be preventing these clusters from developing into self-sustaining groups of economic activity. At the same time, active involvement by and partnership with the private sector in designing and implementing support programmes has been an important feature of these policies (Steiner, 1998). In order to understand the resulting policy interactions between the private and public sectors, this chapter examines how public–private partnership models of policy making have been applied to the development of clusters. It contends that the unique features of cluster policy have made the sharing of policy responsibilities more extensive than in many other policy areas where similar partnerships have been introduced. The chapter focuses on the development of cluster policies in three regions – Östergötland (Sweden), Scotland (the UK) and Tampere (Finland), all of which have made cluster support an important part of economic development – and is based on original case-study research carried out by a team based at the University of Strathclyde (Raines, 2000).

MODELS OF PUBLIC–PRIVATE RESPONSIBILITIES IN POLICY ACTIVITIES

Although no sharp boundary has ever existed between the public and private spheres of economic activity, there has been a marked shift in the division of responsibilities in recent years (Osborne and Gaebler, 1992). While this is often characterized as a contraction of the governmental sphere, it should perhaps be more accurately depicted as increased intermingling of the private and public sectors (Weintraub, 1997). In terms of public service provision, these changes have been closely associated with the rise of the 'managerialist' approach to government, prompted by the pressure to reduce the scope and costs of government activity and introduce a more market-led approach to public sector administration. Rather than leading to a simple assertion of *a priori* market primacy when reassessing the government's economic functions, this has resulted in a more subtle approach to determining where the responsibility for different tasks should lie. In some cases it resulted in 'mixed' forms of responsibility being jointly held by the private and public sectors.

In this context it is useful to distinguish between the 'strategy' and 'service' elements of government policy towards the economy. In this study *strategy* refers to the overall determination of government policy in a particular functional area and has three key components: strategy sets the limits on the *scope* of policy activity; it defines the *content and design* of policy; and it determines the mechanisms by which policies are to be delivered in broad terms. In contrast *service* is concerned with the actual administration of policy, and deals with the technicalities of matching policy requirements to the resources needed for their achievement. Hence, for example, government intervention to support a particular industry contains both strategy and service elements: strategy includes the definition of the sector to be addressed, the policy instruments to be used in its support and the organizational arrangements for implementing those instruments; while the service aspects cover the actual implementation of the policy measures.

The distinction between the two elements is crucial as either (and in some cases both) the private or the public sector can be responsible for strategy or service activities. By separating the two elements it is possible to elaborate a series of models to examine how the responsibilities for government functions have changed and have been distributed in more complex ways during the restructuring of the public sector's relationship with the economy. No one model is paramount and the extent to which a policy area follows one or other model is determined by a complex series of policy-specific variables. However, as a whole the models trace a general shift of policy responsibility from the public to the private sector. Extending the geographical metaphor of private and public 'sectors', three types of model can be presented that describe this shift of responsibilities: 'territorial shifts' 'territorial leasing' and 'shared ownership'.

First, definite *territorial shifts* of the boundaries separating public and private economic tasks have taken place. Most commonly this has occurred through the privatization of public enterprises, where the government has withdrawn from certain economic activities to allow them greater exposure to market competition and enable more effective, private-sector-based managerial methods to be brought to bear. Privatization normally involves the unequivocal transfer of both the strategy and the service elements to the private sector, though in many cases government regulation of the newly privatized enterprise restricts the private sector's ability to exercise its strategy powers to the full.

Second, many economic tasks have undergone what is called *territorial leasing* from the public sector, where by partial control over a range of public sector activities is transfered to the private sector. In this model the service elements tend to pass unequivocally to the private sector, but strategy responsibilities are retained by the government. Many public sector activities have been outsourced to the private sector, where they can be undertaken more cost effectively, notably local government services such as waste removal and urban transport, but this does not involve the full transfer of responsibilities. Whereas improvements can be made to the efficiency of these services by subjecting them to market pressure, policy making and the setting of service specifications are kept within the public sector to prevent individual businesses from underly benefiting from what are effectively public goods.

Finally, a new model has emerged in recent years where there is no clearly defined change in responsibilities, but a kind of *shared ownership*. This has been most apparent in government activities where public and private bodies jointly manage certain tasks. In recent years, shared ownership has taken the form of public–private partnerships set up to develop areas of traditional governmental activity (Rosenau, 1999). For example, such partnerships have been made part of UK urban policy, in that joint public–private 'development corporations' have been formed to address urban development problems more effectively (Bailey, 1994). Similar organizations have been set up to promote industrial R & D, especially where technologies can benefit from collective private sector development that would not occur without government involvement (Stiglitz and Wallsten, 1999).

In the shared ownership model, theoretically all aspects of policy can be shared between the two sectors, but in practice it mainly involves service rather than strategy functions. As in the territorial leasing model, the private sector brings additional resources and ways of utilizing resources that are absent in the public sector, but in this model the service functions tend to be a joint responsibility. They are not wholly outsourced by the public sector because they usually encompass areas of activity where market incentives are partial or there are strong 'public good' issues. For example, spatial policy can benefit from private sector participation in its implementation. In many cases semi-autonomous organizations have been specially set up to develop localities, with personnel being drawn from both government and business, and delivery mechanisms and performance criteria being determined by the organizations in collaboration with the sponsoring part of the public sector (Halkier and Danson, 1997). Yet responsibility is not wholly transferred to the private sector because of the importance of non-market considerations in the conduct of policy. However, with respect to the strategic functions of policy, the public sector has a more commanding role: whether as a limited single project (for example, infrastructure development) or a more wide-ranging programme (for example, urban regeneration). The policy decision to act in the first place and the main form that the policy will take is usually made by government agencies outside the partnership.

PUBLIC–PRIVATE RESPONSIBILITIES IN CLUSTER POLICY DEVELOPMENT

Before discussing how the partnership model can be applied to cluster policy it is important to define the area of policy activity, although this is not an easy task. The diversity of ways in which the cluster concept has been interpreted has resulted in a profusion of policy practices worldwide. Indeed, cluster programmes and their constituent measures apply to a shifting set of instruments and approaches and usually comprise a never-the-same-twice portfolio of analytical tools and policy instruments, often 'borrowed' from other policy areas (Feser, 1998). Indeed, some cluster policies consist more of novel combinations of existing policy measures than of newly developed instruments. Nonetheless, cluster policies are distinguished by a number of differences in approach that separate them from earlier, sector-based policies.

First, cluster policies reflect a greater awareness of the role of knowledge and innovation in sustaining the competitive advantage of sectors and, more importantly, the structures already in place to ensure that such knowledge can be generated on an ongoing basis, diffused throughout a particular sector/region and transformed into products and services that will enhance individual business's competitiveness (OECD, 1999a). There has been renewed interest not only in the sources of innovation – with increased attention to innovation occurring *between* businesses (and other organizations) rather than simply within them –

but also in its transfer within (and between) sectors. Unlike traditional sectoral policies, cluster policies proceed from an understanding that such knowledge and innovation are localized processes, made possible by the geographical proximity of a range of innovative institutions (including businesses, universities and policy organizations) (Storper, 1997). Cluster policies are less focused on end-product sectors, and involve government action with a wider number of private sector actors drawn from related industrial value chains (Porter, 1998).

Second, and consequently, instead of the relationship between government and business being dominated by hierarchical economic interventions such as subsidies and protective measures, cluster policy requires a more holistic approach in which the government–business dialogue is more wide-ranging and programmatic in nature. Having identified a need for government intervention in the first place, public sector responsibility is usually cast as a series of specific interventions designed to stimulate a potential or dormant cluster or rejuvenate activity in a mature one (see Enright, 2000). In contrast, with sector-based policies, the government aims to avoid an open-ended, semi-permanent relationship with the industries in question, as this runs the risk of their developing a degree of dependency. Rather the cluster approach involves the identification of key areas where highly bounded government action can catalyze the longer-term development of a self-sustaining cluster through a series of time-limited measures (Lagendijk, 1999).

The resulting overlap of public and private responsibilities in cluster development is evident in both strategy and service functions. Turning first to the strategic aspects of policy, there is the responsibility for defining the *scope* of the policy. This involves not only selecting which clusters should be targeted, but also identifying the main gaps requiring policy attention within those clusters, (for example, missing links in an industrial value chain, or deficiencies in key inputs such as training or finance). Cluster policies demand greater information on industrial activities than has often been the case with previous industrial policy interventions, and potentially require the extensive involvement of participating businesses. Second, the strategic *design* of cluster policy may require contributions from both the public and the private sector, particularly when it is intented to use public sector resources to obtain private sector funding for key projects that are necessary for the cluster's development, or so instil a longer-term collective responsibility in the private sector for sustaining the cluster. Finally, as cluster actions often involve active collaboration between cluster members (such as networking and cooperation projects), the service (or policy implementation) side of cluster development must involve the private sector to a significant degree.

PUBLIC–PRIVATE PARTNERSHIPS AND CLUSTER POLICY: EVIDENCE FROM THREE REGIONS

Examination of actual cases of public–private partnership in cluster development reveals a diversity of experiences. At one end of the spectrum, the public sector has played a key role in underpinning the ability of a cluster to take action, as for example in some Italian industrial districts where the local authorities have been central to the organization of cluster activity (Becattini, 1990). At the other end of the spectrum of the regional government País Vasco in Spain has effectively farmed out the running of cluster policy to a series of largely independent associations situated clearly in the private sector (Taylor and Raines, 2001).

In order to examine how cluster policy responsibilities are distributed between the private and public sectors, case studies were made of three regions that had recently begun to implement cluster development policies at the local level. In each case, interviews were held with the main agencies responsible for developing and putting the policies into practice. The policies of the three regions – Östergötland in the east of Sweden, Tampere in central southern Finland and Scotland in the UK – are discussed briefly below; a fuller summary can be found elsewhere (Raines, 2000).

- Östergötland was the first Swedish region to consider a cluster-based regional development strategy. As part of the regional growth development strategy of 1999, support for the region's main clusters was identified as a key priority. Four areas of activity were to be targeted: information/communications technology, software development, medical technology, food, and wood products. The main policy actions would consist of the identification and promotion of networking opportunities, especially between the private and university research sectors.
- In the 1990s, the government of Finland initiated a centrally funded scheme to develop local competitive advantage at the regional level by encouraging networking within clusters. As a participant in the scheme the Tampere region has operated several 'Centre of Expertise' programmes for the region's main clusters since 1995 (Valtonen, 1999). As with Östergötland, the policy has largely consisted of measures to encourage greater cooperation within the clusters and more effective use of the region's research institutions by the private sector. At present Tampere has five cluster areas, comparising mechanical engineering and automation, information and communications technology, medical technology, multimedia, and knowledge-intensive businesses.
- The Scottish experience of cluster development policy is one of the best known in Europe (Danson and Whittam, 1998). Since the early 1990s the main development agency in the region, Scottish Enterprise, has been using the cluster approach to produce a series of specific programmes to develop clusters and to refine its more generic policy activities (for example the attraction of inward investment, and export promotion). Seven cluster activities are currently being targeted by these programmes: semiconductors, food/drink, biotechnology, opto-electronics, wood products, tourism, and creative industries. The scale of the programme is considerably larger than in the other two regions, allowing a wider range of measures to be supported,

including projects based on networking within the cluster, infrastructure development, financing, skills training and R & D.

To understand the role of the public and private sectors in cluster policy making, the three elements noted earlier were examined for each region, that is, policy scope, policy design and policy implementation.

Policy Scope

In all three regions, policy scope largely remained in the public sphere. In each case the cluster concept was championed by a public sector agency – in other words the shift in policy took place because of pressure within the public sector, not because of private sector lobbying of government authorities.

In Östergötland the principal agency supporting cluster development was initially the East Sweden Development Agency (ESDA), a public sector intermediary jointly funded by the municipal authorities, the main regional body (the County Administrative Board, which oversees national government expenditure in the region) and regional representatives of national government agencies (ALMI, which supports the development of small and medium-sized enterprises). The ESDA played a key part in persuading other important public sector bodies in the region to adopt the cluster approach when designing their development strategies.

Scottish Enterprise was both the initial proponent and the main instigator of the cluster approach in Scotland. Its original interest was in cluster analysis as a way of understanding the workings of the Scottish economy in the early 1990s, but it came to realize that the cluster approach offered several operational attractions and would agency allow its varies functional activities – including financial help for small and medium-sized enterprises, training support, property development, and export and FDI promotion – to be integrated more effectively by targeting specific sectors.

Similarly the public sector was the instigator of cluster development in Tampere, first at the national level, with the decision by the Ministry of Interior to launch the Centre of Expertise programme, and then at the regional level, where the main regional body, the Tampere Regional Council, and the most significant municipal authority, Tampere City Council, made award applications under the programme.

The pursuit of cluster-based policy in these regions largely proceeded without any private sector influence – indeed in all three cases the initial task for the public sector was to engage the interest of a reluctant private sector and persuade businesses of the virtues of the cluster approach. Moreover, the choice of which clusters should be the focus of policy was made almost exclusively by the public sector as there was little private sector input.

In Östergötland, the choice of which clusters should receive funding was made within the context of the Regional Growth Agreement. Put together under the direction of the County Administrative Board at the behest of the national government, this three-year regional development strategy was intended to pool the existing expenditure funds for the region to bring about improved cooperation between the various bodies charged with promoting growth and employment at the regional level. The choice of clusters was based on independent analyses of the regional economy, and the final decision was made after consultations between the public sector bodies involved in the agreement.

In Scotland, cluster selection was also undertaken by the public sector, though primarily by a single agency, Scottish Enterprise, as it principally affected that agency's activities. The selection was made on the basis of each cluster's actual and potential economic significance (externally as well as domestically) and the extent to which it could be influenced by policy interventions, together with the extent to which the proposed clusters were broadly complementary and representative of the Scottish economy.

Finally, Tampere's clusters were chosen by public sector bodies as part of the Centre of Expertise programme. Here too there was little input from the private sector.

Policy Design

Unlike policy scope, the design of the policy framework for cluster development was shared by the public and private sectors, though to varying degrees in the three regions. The most extensive form of policy partnership was in Scotland, where the key members of the target clusters were closely involved in drafting the programmes for each of the seven cluster areas. Such close links with the private sector largely characterized the overall activities of Scottish Enterprise, which was set up in 1991 to facilitate a strong private sector voice in matters of policy priority (Danson and Whittam, 1998). When developing the cluster programmes, the goals and actions were defined with the help of the private sector through extensive consultation exercises, whereby businesses and other cluster participants were invited to take part in a series of meetings to discuss the main challenges affecting their industries and to develop a 'vision' for their development over the next five to ten years. Specific groups were set up for each of the clusters, led by Scottish Enterprise officials but containing representatives from the private sector. These groups were responsible for setting strategic priorities, deciding policy measures and defining the anticipated outcomes for each cluster. The resulting strategic plans were widely circulated and commented upon by private sector participants in the consultation process before being authorized by the Scottish Enterprise management board.

Similar activities took place in Tampere. Strategic plans outlining the focus of policy action, the main measures to be used and the anticipated outcomes for each cluster were set out for each of the Centres of Expertise. As in Scotland, these strategies were drawn up with the participation of significant private sector actors, in strategy-making groups (though less widely drawn than in Scotland).

In contrast, strategy design in Östergötland did not involve a significant input by the private sector as the cluster strand of the Regional Growth Agreement was produced largely within the public sector. However, the agreement did not specify the precise actions to be taken in each cluster area. Rather a series of 'cluster catalysts' were to be set up, and these intermediary bodies were to determine relevant actions to improve networking within their clusters, theoretically in consultation with private sector actors in the cluster.

Policy Implementation

Whereas the strategy aspects of cluster policy involved varying degrees of private sector participation, shared existence of responsibilities was most evident in the service aspects of policy. Whilst the financing of the cluster policies overwhelmingly fell to the public sector (often as part of levering-in private sector funding for continuing projects), management of the programmes involved various forms of public–private partnership. Organizations straddling the private and public sectors were often set up to facilitate the contracting out of the tasks involved in implementing the relevant strategies in the various sectors. Indeed, successful implementation of the cluster policy was often due to the appointment or in some cases, creation of agencies with close ties to the sectors in question. Such strong links were essential if the agencies were to be seen as credible by the private sector members of the clusters.

In Tampere, intermediaries were selected to carry out the service aspects of cluster policy. The Centres of Expertise programmes were largely overseen and implemented by agencies that already had close links with the cluster. For example, the Tampere Technology Centre (responsible for managing the Hermia Science Park, where the bulk of the two clusters were located) was put in charge of the mechanical engineering and communication technology programmes. For the medical technology cluster a new organization was set up, Finn-Medi, which would not only manage a new science park dedicated to biotechnology firms but also promote networking between and among businesses and university research providers. Both agencies were funded by a mixture of public sector funds for specific policy tasks and private sector fees for services provided (such as administration of the science parks).

In Östergötland, the intermediary organizations had less clear links with the private sector, though they performed the same functions. The Regional Growth Agreement included the appointment of a public sector organization – the Technology Bridge Foundation, which provided public financing for R & D projects – to oversee the selection of the 'cluster catalyst' agencies. These agencies were drawn from the university/research sector, rather than the private sector, although the principle of choosing agencies embedded in the cluster prevailed here too.

Different arrangements were made to carry out the cluster programmes in Scotland, where partnership between the public and private sectors was more evident. The cluster groups responsible for producing the strategies for each cluster tended later to be charged with overseeing their implementation. These *ad hoc* groups were often responsible for different parts of the strategy – including individual projects – and were led by or had a substantial number of private sector members.

DISCUSSION

The 'shared ownership' model can clearly be applied to the cluster policies of the three regions, though the different versions show an overlap with other policy partnership models. As can be seen in Table 11.1, for each of the three regions there is a slant in the shared ownership approach in respect of 'territorial shift' (more private sector involvement) or 'territorial leasing' (more public sector involvement), depending on whether the strategy or service aspects of policy are being considered.

Responsibility for implementing the cluster policies was often shared between the private and public sectors. In the case of Tampere and Östergötland, intermediary organizations outside the public sector were appointed to undertake the service aspects of the policies (that is, these regions towards the 'territorial leasing' model). In Scotland, the responsibilities were more obviously overlapping, with joint public–private sector groups being charged with overseeing both the cluster programmes as a whole and the individual projects.

Where the organizational forms of policy making for cluster policy are distinct from the public–private policy partnership model is with respect to the strategic aspects of policy. In the case of Scotland and Tampere, private sector involvement in the design of policy was pronounced, especially in Scotland, where diligent efforts were made to engage with as many businesses within each cluster as possible (this is more characteristic of the 'territorial shift' model). While the decision about which parts of the economy should be targeted lay firmly with government, joint public–private groups representing the clusters played a significant part in shaping and authorizing the programmes of policy support. In Östergötland, the details of policy design were the joint responsibility of the intermediaries, which were largely drawn from research institutes rather than the private sector.

What is important here is the extent of participation by the private sector in the 'higher' aspects of policy, more than has been traditional in industrial policy

Table 11.1 Public–private partnership, policy orientation

	Strategy	Service
Östergötland	Shared ownership	Shared ownership → territorial leasing
Scotland	Shared ownership → territorial shift	Shared ownership
Tampere	Shared ownership → territorial shift	Shared ownership → territorial leasing

and more than is commonly found in other forms of public–private policy part-nership. This level of involvement proceeds directly from the requirements of the government when developing a cluster policy. The private sector has an important part to play in the provision of policy intelligence. Given the policy importance of identifying gaps in the value chain or business environment that will prevent the full development of clusters, substantial consultation with private sector agents is essential. Consequently, the private sector tends to have considerable involvement in the development of cluster policy. While cluster policy often involves extensive participation in service delivery, either in the joint financing of cluster-based projects and measures or in assisting with their implementation, it is the private sector's contribution to the development of the policy's direction and priorities that is most important. In a sense, such a policy enables the principal actors in a cluster to take responsibility for maintaining its competitiveness over time. This requires the businesses within a cluster to act more collectively than is often the case with traditional sectoral policy, placing emphasis on their ability to enter policy partnerships with each other and the public sector.

In effect, what the public sector did in the three regions studied was partially to outsource not just the service aspects but also the strategic aspects of cluster policy making. In all three cases, by introducing 'bottom-up' elements into its policy the public sector was encouraging the participants in the targeted clusters to develop a sense of ownership over the cluster's development. At the heart of cluster policy making is the need to promote the ultimate self-sufficiency of the cluster, in terms of its capacity both to diagnose its actual or potential weak-nesses and to address those weaknesses. To do this the public sector has to gal-vanize a large number of agents within the cluster, or at least its dominant agents, such as large enterprises or key research providers. Indeed, the ability of such partnerships positively to influence cluster development depends on the extent to which the targeted cluster is cohesive in terms of existing networks among the participants or the existence of readily identifiable common chal-lenges that could catalyze such networks. Without the presence of a substructure for policy cooperation within the private sector it will be difficult for the public sector to establish a public–private partnership, and hence to create an effective policy framework for cluster support.

The capacity of clusters to become self-governing, then, is crucial to success-ful cluster policy and the development of strong, self-sustaining clusters. As the three cluster policies discussed here are still in their infancy it is too early to comment on their performance. However, conclusions can be drawn about the public sector's success in engaging private sector communities that are cohesive and willing to cooperate with other cluster participants in the policy partnership.

Overall, partnerships where private sector members have been drawn either from small but growing clusters – such as medical technology in Östergötland, biotechnology in Scotland and multimedia in Tampere – or from niches within larger clusters – such as ICT in Östergötland (where mobile telephony is the *de facto* focus), creative industries in Scotland (where it tends to be software development) and mechanical engineering in Tampere (automation) – appear to have been more productive in terms of the public–private partnership contributing to the strategic and service elements of policy. The small number of actors and ease of definition are the main factors behind the success of these policy partnerships. Policy success depends on how easily cluster commonality can be demonstrated between the various agents.

Given the significance of self-governance as a goal of policy, it is often difficult to make a distinction between strategy and service in cluster policy making. The problem of demarcating policy functions and distributing responsibilities between the public and private sectors is the main reason why the responsibilities of both are so strongly intertwined. Public and private interests in policy making are closely aligned, but while this can make cluster policies better informed and targeted, it does carry risks. The identification of the public sector with the development of a particular sector can lead to institutional capture, where either the cluster begins to display cartel characteristics or the more active private sector participants in the partnership exploit their influence for individual gain at the collective expense. Lovering (1999) has commented on how the fusion of interests between policy officials and a select group of companies in foreign investment promotion can lead to the calcification of policy. What is damaging is when both public and private sector bodies develop political (in the case of government officials) and economic (in the case of businesses) incentives to maintain a policy of support regardless of its wider efficacy. This can produce a form of institutional arthritis in policy making, whereby a region becomes locked into a particular policy direction and dependence on vulnerable clusters, and the government loses its ability recalibrate policy (Grabher, 1993). Thus, while the partnership approach to industrial development has led to success in the design and implementation of policy, questions remain about the longer-term capacity of the public sector to retain its independence in respect of when and how to intervene in the economy. This highlights the need for researchers to monitor the performance of such partnerships over time and study their impact on other aspects of policy design and delivery.

Part Four

Assessing the Performance of International Business Operations

12 Export Behaviour Research in the UK: A Review

Colin Wheeler and Kevin Ibeh

INTRODUCTION

Serious academic inquiry into the export behaviour of UK firms dates back to the 1960s, marked by the publication of Tookey's (1964) research on export success factors. Yet no attempt has been made, as far as the present authors are aware, to appraise the state of this research field, or to understand the crucial influences on firms' export behaviour in the UK context. The Bolton Committee's (1971) report was a good effort in this direction, but its general focus on small and medium-sized enterprises (SMEs) meant that not enough attention was paid to firms' export behaviour. This chapter intends to redress this situation as part of the wider focus, in Part Four of this book, on the performance of international business operations. It will follow in the tradition of the Bolton Committee's report to seek some understanding of UK SMEs' need for, usage of and perceptions of government export promotion programmes.

This leads to another compelling reason for this review: the vital importance of the export sector to the health of the UK economy, including the role of SMEs within it. There is no doubt that exporting remains the preferred and, for the vast majority of SMEs, the most feasible internationalization route. Greater insights into the crucial influences and determinants of firms' involvement and success in this important activity could therefore help improve their overall contribution to the UK economy. This is particularly necessary given the widely reported underperformance of UK SMEs in exporting. In the early 1980s Cannon and Willis (1981), for example, observed that while small firms accounted for nearly 25 per cent of the UK's gross national product, they contributed less than 10 per cent of all manufactured exports. More recently Morgan and Katsikeas (1998) have also commented on the relatively modest export performance of UK SMEs and highlighted Germany and Italy's successful implementation of SME-anchored export growth policies.

Another justification for this UK-focused review lies in the increasing appearance of country-specific, integrative reviews of export behaviour studies. These include the reviews by Bonarccosi (1993) of Italian and Brazilian export behaviour studies, respectively; and Valos and Baker's (1996) attempt to model Australian export performance. Two interrelated factors may account for this trend. One is the widespread recognition that differences between country environments – culture, economic climate, government support and so on – could affect research findings (Sullivan and Bauerschmidt, 1990; Das, 1994; Morgan and Katsikeas, 1998; Whitelock and Jobber, 1999). The other is the dawning realization that the nature of export behaviour in individual countries apart from the US is not clear; this is because US-focused studies still dominate in the major integrative reviews of export behaviour research.

It is important to highlight that the present review covers only empirical export behaviour research published in the UK during the period 1990–2000. This is because the more recent research has a greater likelihood of capturing the probable effects of recent developments in the UK exporter's environment, such as the emergence of new markets in Eastern Europe and South-East Asia and the growth of the Internet. More recent research may also provide useful empirical insights into topical issues confronting policy makers, such as the amount of resources that should be committed to cluster development programmes, and for academics, information on the usefulness of resource-based and network theories in explaining international business success. It is also arguable that reviewing more current research will highlight those aspects of export behaviour which are being investigated and those which are receiving little or no attention. This knowledge may be useful in determining the direction of future export research in the UK.

The chapter is organized into four sections. Sections one and two present the need for and scope of the review, respectively. This is followed in section three with a presentation and discussion of the key findings of UK export behaviour research. The chapter ends in section four with a discussion of the implications of the study's conclusions for managers, policy makers and researchers.

THE REVIEW'S SCOPE AND APPROACH

Scope

This review covers 64 research papers drawn from 41 research projects investigating one or more aspects firm export behaviour in the UK, using quantitative or qualitative data. Only one paper (Wakelin, 1998) based primarily on secondary data is included (see Appendix 12.1).

The first step in the search process was to draw on a number of Internet-based resources, including the ABI / INFORM and MCB Emerald electronic databases. Search terms included exporting, export performance, export marketing strategy, export channels and export networks. In some instances the full text of articles was only available from 1994, so copies of the articles were obtained elsewhere. The search also extended to journal and publishers' web sites, and physical searches were made for the books and other references mentioned in the articles collected. The analysis of the articles was carried out by both authors and the results were agreed by both.

Two thirds of the articles were published between 1996 and 2000. There is no obvious reason for this surge in publication, apart perhaps from the influence of the Research Assessment Exercise (RAE) in the UK.

The studies cover a wide range of sectors, including food and beverages, agriculture, clothing, machinery, metal and paper, but the preponderance of studies focus on industrial goods. There are also a number of studies on the export behaviour of high-technology firms (for example Oakley, 1996; Jones, 1999; Crick and Jones, 2000; Burgel and Murray, 2000) and service firms (O'Farrell *et al.*, 1996, 1998a, 1998b; Eyre and Smallman, 1998; Mazzarol, 1998), including export intermediaries (Balabanis, 2000).

The primary study unit in the majority of the studies is the exporter – defined as a firm selling at least part of its products abroad. Only three studies have export ventures as the data unit. The majority of studies involve SMEs, with only four exclusively using a large firm sample. This reflects the widespread notion of a characteristic fit between SMEs and the earlier stages of internationalization, especially exporting (Miesenbock, 1988).

A very high proportion of the export studies are cross-sectional, time-specific studies, involving the use of postal surveys and quantitative analytical tools. Indeed mail survey was the sole source of data in 33 studies, but an additional four studies complemented this with personal interviews. It would appear that some of the more recent research efforts were conducted in response to earlier observations about the methodological limitations of export research, as well as calls for richer, in-depth, qualitative research and 'paradigmatic pluralism' (Kamath *et al.*, 1987; Bell and Young, 1998). For example four studies employed only personal interview data.

Analytical Approach

Overall the relevant UK studies can be categorized into three groups: those which merely describe or profile UK exporters; those which compare UK exporters with their international counterparts or considered their relationships with international suppliers or distributors; and those which investigate the determinants of specific measures of export performance. Obviously the findings of the first two types of study generally include fewer export performance implications than studies in which export performance effects are specifically investigated. This presents a major challenge in respect of integrating the evidence emerging from the present review, a challenge that has arguably thwarted researchers' attempts to heed Aaby and Slater's (1989: 23) rousing call to establish 'what is known' and to broaden the range of 'solid conclusions' about firm export behaviour (and hence rid the field of its fragmentary label).

One way of getting round this challenge would be to exclude the first two categories of studies, and restrict the review to those which measure firms' position on some dimension of export performance (Aaby and Slater, 1989). Doing so would be to join the relatively few integrative reviews (Madsen, 1987; Gemunden, 1991; Zou and Stan, 1998) that have not lumped together studies of firms at different levels of the export development process (Leonidou and Katsikeas, 1996). There is, however, one important reason why this approach would not be the right one. Given that most of the studies in which aspects of UK firms' exporting practices are described (for example Crick and Chaudhry, 1995, 1996, 1997a, 1997b, 2000a, 2000b) or compared with those of their foreign counterparts/partners (for example Moore, 1990, 1991, 1992) mainly involve firms at the initial (including pre-) exporting stages, this exclusion could lead to the loss of valuable knowledge about this crucial phase of UK firms' export development.

The approach taken in the present study, therefore, is to present and review the findings reported in all the relevant UK studies, but to specify where possible whether or not the evidence obtained is explicitly linked to export performance. Hence this review will not take a quantitative, meta-analysis approach (Madsen, 1987; Gemunden, 1991) or a vote-counting approach (Chetty and Hamilton, 1993), but will adopt the narrative style employed to such good effect by Aaby and Slater (1989).

Independent Factors Investigated

Another major problem associated with reviewing export behaviour research is the diversity of independent variables investigated. Indeed there is no better reason for the reluctance of export behaviour researchers to build on previous efforts (that is, 'a mosaic of autonomous endeavours' – Aaby and Slater, 1989: 7) than having to deal with the selection of independent variables, and the lack of consistency in the way in which these variables have been measured. A major contributory factor in this is the disparate nature, or complete absence in some studies, of an underlying theory to guide the choice of independent variables (Zou and Stan, 1998).

In line with the calls in the literature for researchers to build on previous efforts (Aaby and Slater, 1989) and explore the complementarities among relevant theoretical perspectives (Bell and Young, 1998), the present review bases its selection and categorization of independent factors on the frameworks proposed in three previous review works: Aaby and Slater (1989), Styles and Ambler (1994) and Zou and Stan (1998). This is because, between them, these three studies incorporate the key theoretical perspectives that have been employed most beneficially to illuminate firm export behaviour: the resource-based view of the firm/organizational capability/strategic management; the network theory; and the industrial organization theory.

FINDINGS

The review that follows is therefore organized around the following major categories of factors: management-related attributes and resources; firm characteristics and resource base; firm competences and strategies (including relational and export marketing strategies); industry/market characteristics; domestic market characteristics; and foreign market characteristics. The first three of those factors relate to the internal environment of the firm, the last three pertain to the firm's external environment. Because of space limitations the commentary focuses on the major categories of factors, with only occasional remarks about specific variables within the categories. This is to allow for some discussion of other issues that arise from the overall analysis of the UK export research findings.

Internal Environment

Management-Related Attributes and Resources

There is a considerable body of evidence in the reviewed UK studies to suggest that top management attributes such as international orientation, previous relevant experience and positive perception are essential to internationalization and good export performance. Diamantopoulos and Schlegelmilch (1994), for example, conclude that export managers' perceptions of the importance of exporting, their specialized export training and overall exporting commitment have a positive influence on export performance. Westhead (1995) have found that owner-managers of exporting firms have significantly better human capital skills and experience of establishing a new venture than their counterparts in non-exporting firms. Similar evidence is reported by Crick and Jones (2000): several of the international firms in their study were started by managers with previous international market experience, acquired from previous employment.

It would also appear that international outlook, experience and commitment among top management staff significantly influence companies' perception of export-related barriers and problems. As Lowe and Doole (1997) report, 'the variation in perception of export market risks appeared to depend primarily on the experience of, and commitment to, exporting by top managers as a vehicle for market growth'. Bennett (1998) apparently agrees – this author attributes the significantly more positive perception of export barriers exhibited by German Internet-using firms (relative to their UK counterparts) to their more internationalist outlook.

Firm Characteristics and Resource Base

The firm resource base seems to have a particularly important influence on export behaviour among UK firms. High-performing exporting firms were found by Piercy *et al.* (1998) to be considerably superior in terms of physical, experiential and financial resources. Likewise Lowe and Doole (1997) conclude that firms' resources and capabilities are a very strong predictor of their performance and progress in international market development. Mazzarol (1998), whose study includes UK service (educational) organizations, equally emphasized the importance of 'image and resources' (including financial and brand related resources) as crucial success factors for the surveyed institutions.

The majority of UK studies that have examined the effect of firm size conclude that this is positively associated with export behaviour, particularly in terms of increased export propensity (McAuley, 1993; Westhead, 1995; Bennett, 1997; Wakelin, 1998). This supports the assertion in previous export behaviour literature that organizational size may be more important at the time of export entry than when extending export involvement. It should be noted that a number of UK studies have concluded that the relationship between firm size and export performance is not significant (Morgan and Katsikeas, 1997a; Piercy *et al.*, 1998; Eyre and Smallman, 1998). This suggests that firm size may be more useful in predicting propensity to export than export performance, thus reinforcing the view that beyond a certain point, size ceases to be important (Withey, 1980; Reid, 1981).

Firm Competences and Strategies

The reviewed UK research appears to provide strong support for the importance of firm-specific competences or advantages in encouraging positive export behaviour. Crick and Jones (2000) also highlight the importance of organizational competences, including proprietary technological know-how, in underpinning and triggering rapid and successful internationalization. The specific firm competences for which consistently positive conclusions have been reported include marketing research (Crick *et al.*, 1994; Hart *et al.*, 1994; Styles and Ambler, 1994; Hart and Tzokas, 1999; Souchon and Diamantopoulos, 1997), web usage (Bennett, 1997), innovativeness, including product innovation (Oakley, 1996; Wakelin, 1998), and marketing mix factors (DTI, 1997; Piercy *et al.*, 1998).

Piercy *et al.* (1998), for example, have found significant differences between high- and low-performing exporting firms with respect to four key areas of competitiveness: product development, customer relationships and service, information provision, and supply chain links. Styles and Ambler (1994) highlight the importance of similar competitive competences, that is, consistent quality, overall company reputation, meeting delivery dates, and matching customer specifications. Oakley (1996) reports that the most successful firms, relative to the least successful, demonstrate a much greater commitment to their product launches. Morgan and Katsikeas (1997a) found that competences related to export market knowledge and communication separated the exporting from the non-exporting groups in their study sample. Further supportive evidence is reported by Lowe and Doole (1997), who state that possession of products with significant technological competitive advantage explains the differences in the market entry approach adopted by the 'born internationals' in their sample.

It is perhaps useful to draw attention to the strength of the UK evidence on the relationship between marketing research and export behaviour. Given that export behaviour research is so often marked by contradictory findings (Aaby and Slater, 1989), it is remarkable that none of the studies that have examined this factor has found a negative effect. Indeed all the studies report a positive impact, with only one (Souchon and Diamantopolous, 1997) reporting a 'not significant' result. Among the supportive findings are those by Crick *et al.* (1994), who conclude that better-performing firms pay more attention to marketing research, and Hart and Tzokas (1999), who suggest that the use of export marketing information is related to export success. Likewise Whitelock and Jobber (1999) have found that the systematic use and analysis of information on market attractiveness, including the structure and nature of competition, has a strong influence on firms' export entry decision and success. Additional evidence is reported by Crick and Bradshaw (1999), to the effect that the majority of successful exporting firms conducted some research before their market entry.

Export Marketing Strategy

The findings on the effectiveness of the strategic planning approach to exporting are mixed. Whitelock and Jobber (1999), for example, conclude that international market entry and success is positively associated with the adoption of a business strategy approach (involving a systematic analysis of all relevant information on the target market, including the structure and nature of the competition). Tzokas *et al.* (2000a) have found that for firms with a strong strategic pricing orientation, on average a larger proportion of their turnover is accounted for by exports than is the case with other groups. Further useful, albeit descriptive, evidence is reported in a number of other studies. For example Crick and Jones (2000) conclude that choice of market and mode of entry are on the whole planned rather than *ad hoc*; Burgel and Murray (2000) find that strategic considerations and the exploitation of new opportunities rather than psychic/economic distance are more likely to account for entry mode decisions; and Schlegelmilch *et al.* (1991) observed a strategic planning orientation among the UK firms they studied prior to the introduction of the Single European Market in 1992.

Among the studies that find against the importance of the strategic planning approach are Brown and Cook (1990), Lowe and Doole (1997), O'Farrell *et al.* (1998b), McAuley (1999) and Crick and Chaudhry (1999). McAuley (1999), for example, concludes from a study of small craft firms in the UK that international market opportunities are taken when they arise, with little emphasis on systematically planned and targeted sales growth in export markets. O'Farrell *et al.* (1998b) report that foreign market entry is also a relatively casual process for business service firms, indicating that market selection is fundamentally unsystematic and *ad hoc*.

In the main, UK studies have not linked the use of an adaptation strategy to better export performance (Styles and Ambler, 1994; Crick and Katsikeas, 1995; Crick and Chaudhry, 1995; DTI, 1997). The DTI (1997) could find no significant difference between better- and poorer-performing exporting firms in terms of adaptations, including adaptation of product quality. Styles and Ambler (1994) conclude that if a firm offers a high-quality product that meets customers' needs, country-specific adaptation of either product or advertising is not necessary for success. This finding reflects the conclusion reached in other UK studies that adaptation is not widespread (Crick and Katsikeas, 1995), and that firms are not likely extensively to adapt marketing mix elements (Crick and Chaudhry, 1995). Some contrary evidence is, however, reported by Crick and Bradshaw (1999), whose survey of Queen's Export Award winners revealed that most had adopted an adaptation strategy to meet the local requirements of particular export markets.

Other firm-specific competences that UK research has consistently found to be essential to positive export performance are the management of channel relationships and the leveraging of external network resources. Styles and Ambler (1994, 2000) strongly underline the importance of channel relationships to successful exporting. The key variables identified include establishing and maintaining close, trusting, long-term relationships with customers and overseas distributors, including personal visits by directors. According to Piercy *et al.* (1998), superior export performance is underpinned by the ability to manage a complex network of relationships that can be used to develop an appropriate skills and resources base to act as the foundation of sustainable competitive advantage. This reflects Katsikeas *et al.*'s (1997) finding that manufacturing firms with higher exporting levels have a better understanding of the important variables driving the import decisions of overseas distributors than do their counterparts with lower levels of exporting.

There is also some indication by Westhead (1995) that exporting firms pursue efficiency gains through conscious management of their supply links. A related finding, this time pertaining to customer links, is reported by O'Farrell *et al.* (1998a). They observe that entry often occurs when a new contact is made or a domestic client internationalizes. Supporting evidence comes from Crick and Bradshaw (1999), who found that most of the successful exporting firms they surveyed had developed good relationships by means of regular visits to their export markets. Other studies that highlight the importance of relationship factors include McGuinness *et al.* (1991), Crick and Katsikeas (1995) and Crick and Jones (2000). The last mentioned authors point to the influence of 'relations in networks' on the market selection decisions of UK high technology firms, adding that in some cases this factor encourages market entry strategies other than exporting, for example alliances to exploit R & D technology.

External Environment

Three categories of factors in the external environment have been reported in the export behaviour literature as impinging firms' export behaviour: industry or market characteristics, domestic environmental factors, and the foreign market environment.

The balance of relevant UK evidence appears to suggest that *industry/market characteristics* have a strong influence on export behaviour. Researchers such as

Westhead (1995), Oakley (1996), Wakelin (1998), Burgel and Murray (2000), Crick and Chaudhry (2000a), and O'Farrell *et al.* (1996, 1998a, 1998b) have found significant sectoral differences in export performance/international market behaviour among firms. Wakelin (1998), for example, concludes that the higher the level of innovation in a sector, the greater the probability that all firms in the sector will export, be they innovative or non-innovative. Oakley's (1996) study of high technology firms associates this sector with greater international market activity, indicating that the more successful new high technology products are generally launched sooner in overseas markets. A study of high technology start-up companies by Burgel and Murray (2000) has produced similar evidence. The young firms in this study had typically initiated their international activities two years after formation, established a market presence in ten countries and averaged 38 per cent of foreign sales, with 33 per cent of the firms generating more turnover from the international than the domestic market. Crick and Chaudhry (2000a) report that groups of firms in particular trade sectors have significantly different perceptions of export barriers and assistance requirements.

It should be noted, however, that Piercy *et al.* (1998) could find no significant relationship between export performance and type of market, be this industrial or consumer. This supports Eyre and Smallman's (1998) conclusion that sector is not a good indicator of export activity.

A relatively small number of UK studies have looked at the effects of *foreign market characteristics* on the export behaviour of UK firms. However, although the evidence is less than clear-cut it would seem that the export behaviour of UK firms is influenced by factors associated with prospective export markets. Whilst market opportunities (that is, foreign market attractiveness) are reported to have drawn UK firms in certain industries into particular foreign markets (O' Farrell *et al.*, 1998a; Crick and Jones, 2000), intense competition in other foreign markets (that is, foreign market competitiveness) appears to have had the contrary effect (O'Farrell *et al.*, 1998a). The factors for which no significant export performance effects could be found are foreign market infrastructure and macro environmental variables. For example, although Styles and Ambler (1994) have observed a number of marked differences between industrialized and less developed country markets, they could find no significant correlation between macro environmental variables and export performance. Likewise the DTI (1997) could find no significant difference between poor and good export performers with regard to their perception of the quality of export market infrastructure (roads, telecommunications and so on) across various foreign markets.

The balance of the UK evidence suggests that factors in the firm's *domestic environment* also influence export behaviour. These factors may serve to impede as well as to promote or push export activities. Westhead (1995), for example, has found that UK firms may be pushed into exporting by their perception of conditions in the domestic environment. Another indication that domestic environmental factors affect export behaviour is provided by Morgan and Katsikeas (1997a, 1997b), who found that exporting firms perceive significantly less difficulty regarding government assistance programmes than firms that did not export.

CONCLUSIONS AND IMPLICATIONS

This review of UK export behaviour studies has highlighted a number of issues that will be briefly discussed in this section. The first is that the characteristics and resources associated with top management appear to be a major factor in positive exporting (and internationalization) behaviour among UK firms. Indeed the empirical evidence reviewed in the present study provides overwhelming support for such variables as managers' international orientation, favourable perceptions of and commitment to exporting, and relevant international experience (through education, travel, residence or prior employment in companies operating internationally). This suggests that all UK parties seeking to achieve a better export performance – the government and its agencies, private sector organizations (for example, the Confederation of British Industries, The Federation of Small Businesses and the British Chamber of Commerce) – should intensify their efforts to improve the international orientation and readiness of UK managers.

Two other factors with an important influence on firm export behaviour are the resources and competences embodied in firms. It is worth stressing that the crucial issue is not how large or entrenched the firm is, but the extent to which it possesses, or can leverage, the key resources it needs to compete in or effectively serve its target market(s). This suggests the need to update the Bolton Committee's (1971) conclusion that size is an insuperable barrier to exporting, with the more positive message that firms, whatever their size, should be encouraged to acquire or gain access to the key resources and competences – managerial, organizational and technological – they need to be internationally competitive in their given product markets.

Indeed factors related to firms' product/service competences, relationship-making skills and export-market knowledge acquisition and management appear to be particularly strong indicators of positive export behaviour. The link between these three variables are worth noting: there is strong UK evidence that export market (research) knowledge is most effectively obtained experientially, through interactive, interpersonal contact with partners and actors based in foreign markets (for example through regular overseas and trade fair visits) (Styles and Ambler, 1994, 2000; DTI, 1997). It can be argued that regular, face-to-face contact with key target market actors, and the knowledge accumulation arising therefrom, are likely to result in better product/service offerings. These essential competences are transferable, and it behoves the appropriate organizations charged with furthering export development in the UK to pay greater attention to these skills in the curriculum for small firm international business training. This is particularly necessary given that small-business education in the UK is underdeveloped (Eyre and Smallman, 1998).

Another reason why capacity enhancement must be urgently addressed is the consistent finding that UK firms are relatively weak in a number of competences: channel relationships (Tuncalp, 1990; Moore, 1991; McGuiness *et al.*, 1991; Beamish *et al.*, 1993; Katsikeas *et al.*, 1997), product/service quality

(Tuncalp, 1990; McGuinness *et al.*, 1991), Internet management and usage (Bennett, 1998) and export performance (McGuiness *et al.*, 1991; Diamantopoulos and Schlegelmilch, 1994). These studies compared UK firms with their counterparts in other developed countries and found the former to be generally less competitive. Particularly telling are McGuinness *et al.*'s (1991) findings, based on their study of customers' perceptions of Western hardware companies operating in the Chinese market: German and Swiss firms are beginning to supplant Japan at the quality end of the market, while the Italians are moving strongly into the sizeable lower-quality, lower-priced equipment niche. British firms are perceived to be worst placed in medium-quality goods with rather high prices and weak promotional and service activities. These competence gaps must be addressed in order to improve the international competitiveness of UK firms and boost the UK's overall export performance.

It should perhaps be emphasized to UK managers that it is not necessary for all the resources and competencies required for export success to be available within the firm itself – some can be accessed or leveraged through meaningful links with network partners. This raises a number of relevant policy issues, including the extent to which firms, particularly SMEs, can be expected to establish resource-seeking network links on their own. What kinds of training could assist them in this task? What roles could public and private sector organizations play in activating such networks?

The present review has also highlighted a number of issues of interest to export behaviour researchers. The first is that while over 60 papers were published in the UK between 1990 and 2000, only 24 involved some measurement of export performance, with the remainder generally providing descriptive insights into aspects of the export behaviour of UK firms. While not down playing the importance of the latter strand of research, there are significant grounds to argue that UK export research and its many stakeholders – including exporters (actual and potential), policy makers and other researchers – would benefit from studies with explicit export performance implications.

One area in which such guidance is still largely unavailable is the impact of Internet usage on export performance. Although a number of UK studies (for example Hamill and Gregory, 1997; Bennett, 1997, 1998) have reported empirical findings on Internet usage among UK firms, none, to the best of our knowledge, has reported on the relationship between Internet usage and export performance. It is acknowledged that the Internet revolution is relatively recent and that journal articles are often not published until a year or two after their acceptance, but it seems reasonable to expect some performance-based research articles to have appeared.

Finally, given the strength of empirical evidence that UK firms have a poor overall awareness of government export assistance programmes (Crick and Czinkota, 1995; Westhead, 1995), (including external information sources – Chaudhry and Crick, 1998), make little use of them (Crick and Chaudhry, 2000a, 2000b) or have low regard for them, (Crick and Chaudhry, 1997a), greater effort should be made by the relevant agencies to improve the marketing of both their organizations and their support programmes, and to address the concerns identified in previous research for example the perceived difficulty of gaining access to some programmes and the limited usefulness of others . A particular policy challenge is highlighted in the series of studies undertaken by Crick and Chaudhry (1997a, 1997b, 2000a) on the influence of ethnicity on export behaviour. These studies, which compared Asian and 'indigenously owned' UK firms, revealed that Asian SMEs have a lower awareness of sources of government assistance and a generally negative attitude towards organizations outside their ethnic grouping. These findings, have obvious implications for developing and targeting export support policies for different categories of exporters. Future research should investigate the extent to which these findings can be generalized across other cross-cultural ontexts.

APPENDIX 12.1   UK EXPORT BEHAVIOUR STUDIES, 1990–2000

Author	Sample	Study type	Dependent variable	Topic
Balabanis (1998)	135 international intermediaries (all sizes)	Multi-industry survey, quantitative analysis	Unspecified	Channel cooperation, conflicts, relationships
Balabanis (2000)	135 Export intermediaries (all sizes)	Multi-industry survey, quantitative analysis	Unspecified – extent of intermediary service mix	Service offerings characteristics, decisions, product markets.
Beamish et al. (1993)	197 exporters (106 UK and 91 Canadian SMEs)	Cross-national, multi-industry survey, quantitative analysis	Export performance (sales, profit)	Firm characteristics, marketing strategy
Bennett (1997)	358 firms (all sizes)	Multi-industry survey, quantitative analysis	Internet usage	Internet usage, firm size, export barriers
Bennett (1998)	148 exporters (and German counterparts)	Multi-industry survey, quantitative analysis	UK versus German exporters	Internet usage and perceptions of barriers, firm characteristics
Brown and Cook (1990)	214 small exporters; Queen's Export Award (QEA) winners	Multi-industry (manufacturing services) survey, quantitative analysis	Export performance (composite measure)	Strategy
Burgel and Murray (2000)	246 small young firms	Multi-industry (high technology) surveys, quantitative analysis	Foreign market servicing modes	Determinants of foreign market entry and servicing modes
Chaudhry and Crick (1998)	342 Asian and 906 indigenous SMEs	Multi-industry (manufacturing) survey, quantitative analysis	Unspecified	Perceived usefulness of export information sources/assistance, ethnicity
Clark and Mallory (1997)	23 large manufacturing organizations	Multi-industry structured interviews, qualitative analysis	Entry modes	Internationalization strategies, strategic choice perspective

APPENDIX 12.1   UK EXPORT BEHAVIOUR STUDIES, 1990–2000   cont.

Author	Sample	Study type	Dependent variable	Topic
Crick (1992)	422 exporting and 98 non-exporting SMEs	Multi-industry survey, quantitative analysis	Unspecified	Export assistance, internationalization stages
Crick (1995)	422 exporters and 98, non-exporting, (SMEs)	Multi-industry survey, quantitative analysis	Stage of internationalization	Export assistance, internationalization
Crick (1999)	185 SMEs	Multi-industry survey and interviews, quantitative analysis	Unspecified	Use of language: benefits, barriers, recruitment and training
Crick and Bradshaw (1999)	180 firms, mainly SMEs (QEA winners)	Multi-industry (manufacturing services) survey, quantitative analysis	Export performance (composite)	Adaptation, marketing research
Crick and Chaudhry (1995)	25 exporting and 9 non-exporting Asian SMEs	Clothing industry survey, quantitative analysis	Unspecified	Export practices: planning, information, adaptation, export markets
Crick and Chaudhry (1996)	59 Asian and indigenous exporters	Clothing industry survey, quantitative analysis	Unspecified	Export behaviour tactics: organizational, planning and operational
Crick and Chaudhry (1997a)	342 Asian and 906 indigenous exporters	Multi-industry (manufacturing) survey, quantitative analysis	Unspecified	Ethnicity, perception of problems and government assistance
Crick and Chaudhry (1997b)	342 Asian and 906 indigenous SMEs	Multi-industry (manufacturing) survey, quantitative analysis	Unspecified	Export motives and internationalization stages, ethnicity
Crick and Chaudhry (1999)	1242 SMEs (Asian and indigenous)	Multi-industry (manufacturing) survey, quantitative analysis	Unspecified	Cultural diversity and exporting motives

APPENDIX 12.1   UK EXPORT BEHAVIOUR STUDIES, 1990–2000   *cont.*

Author	Sample	Study type	Dependent variable	Topic
Crick and Chaudhry (2000a)	342 Asian and 906 indigenous SMEs	Multi-industry (manufacturing) survey, quantitative analysis,	Unspecified	Awareness, perception and usage of export assistance, ethnicity
Crick and Chaudhry (2000b)	101 exporting firms	Multi-industry (agricultural products) survey, quantitative analysis	Unspecified	Export barriers, government assistance
Crick, Chaudhry and Batstone (2000)	101 exporting firms	Agricultural products; survey; interviews; quantitative	Objective achieved and competitive advantage	Concentration and spreading strategies
Crick and Czinkota (1995)	422 SME exporters	Multi-industry (manufacturing) survey, quantitative analysis	Stage of internationalization	Export assistance, exporters' need
Crick and Jones (1999)	88 QEA winners and 88 SMEs (non-winners)	Multi-industry (high tech) survey, quantitative analysis	Technological success	Technology, design strategies, firm tactics and perceptions
Crick and Jones (2000)	10 small, relatively young international firms	Multi-manufacturing, indepth interviews, quantitative analysis	International performance (composite)	Internationalization, firm characteristics
Crick, *et al.* (1994)	50 small exporting firms	Multi-industry (manufacturing) survey, quantitative analysis	Export performance (sales, profit)	Marketing research, firm size
Crick and Katsikeas (1995)	55 exporting SMEs	clothing and knitwear survey, quantitative analysis	Unspecified	Exporter profile: planning, organizational and operational tactics
Department of Trade and Industry (1997)	434 export projects (202 UK and 232 Australia)	multi-industry (manufacturing) survey, quantitative analysis	Export performance (composite)	Export success factors, relationships

APPENDIX 12.1   UK EXPORT BEHAVIOUR STUDIES, 1990–2000   *cont.*

Author	Sample	Study type	Dependent variable	Topic
Diamantopoulos and Schlegelmilch (1994)	133 UK firms plus 96 German, 67 US	Cross-national, single industry (manufacturing) survey, quantitative analysis	Export performance (sales)	Managerial tactics/resources, firm export experience
Diamantopoulos and Souchon (1996)	11 exporting firms (all sizes)	Manufacturing and services, interviews, qualitative analysis	Export information usage, decision making	Export information use
Eyre and Smallman (1998)	32 UK exporting SME and 50 French SMEs	Multi-industry (manufacturing services) survey, quantitative analysis	Export performance (sales)	Euromanagement competences, language use, firm characteristics
Hamill and Gregory (1997)	103 exporting and non-exporting SMEs	Multi-industry (manufacturing services/distribution) survey, quantitative analysis	Unspecified	Internet marketing usage
Hart and Tzokas (1999)	50 exporting SMEs	Multi-industry (manufacturing) survey, quantitative analysis	Export performance (sales, profit)	Marketing research utilization
Hart *et al.* (1994)	50 industrial SME exporters	Multi-industry (manufacturing) survey, quantitative analysis	Unspecified	Export marketing research and experience
Jones (1999)	196 small firms	Multi-industry (high technology) survey, quantitative analysis	Internationalization patterns	Internationalization patterns
Katsikeas *et al.* (1997)	66 exporters and 35 Bahrain importing firms	Cross-national, multi-industry survey, quantitative analysis	Export involvement intensity	Channel relationships, export involvement
Lowe and Doole (1997)	35 South Yorkshire exporting firms	Cross-sectional (manufacturing services) interviews, qualitative analysis	Internationalization	Internationalization process, market selection and entry
Mazzarol (1998)	315 large (including UK) institutions	Single service industry (education) survey, quantitative analysis	International Market success (composite)	Services (education) exporting, critical success factors

APPENDIX 12.1   UK EXPORT BEHAVIOUR STUDIES, 1990–2000   *cont.*

Author	Sample	Study type	Dependent variable	Topic
McAuley (1993)	77 firms (all sizes) QEA winners	Multi-industry survey, quantitative analysis	Type of information source used	Export information sources, influence of firm characteristics
McAuley (1999)	15 small entrepreneurial firms	Cross-sectional (manufacturing services) interviews, qualitative analysis	Speed of internationalization	Entrepreneurship, influences on internationalization
McGuinness *et al.* (1991)	19 large UK firms and 217 Chinese buyers	Comparative, multi-industry industry (manufacturing) interviews, quantitative analysis	Export performance (success)	Customer relationships (China), strategies, success factors
Moore (1990)	80 UK exporters and 56 German agents/distributors)	Cross-national, multi-industry industry survey, quantitative analysis	Unspecified	Conflicts, channel relationships
Moore (1991)	80 UK exporters and 56 German agents/distributors	Cross-national, multi-industry industry survey, quantitative analysis	Relationship states	Channel relationships: number of products/annuals visits
Moore (1992)	81 UK exporters and 59 German agents/distributors	Cross-national, multi-industry survey, quantitative analysis	UK versus German firms	Channel relationships: motivation, perceptions, satisfaction
Morgan and Katsikeas (1997a)	258 exporting and 191 non-exporting SMEs	Multi-industry (manufacturing) survey, quantitative analysis	Export intention/involvement	Export stimuli: intention versus activity
Morgan and Katsikeas (1997b)	258 exporting and 191 non-exporting SMEs	Multi-industry (manufacturing) survey, quantitative analysis	Export intention	Export initiation and expansion: obstacles
Morgan and Katsikeas (1998)	254 exporting SMEs	Multi-industry (manufacturing) survey, quantitative analysis	Export versus non-exporting	Exporting problems

APPENDIX 12.1   UK EXPORT BEHAVIOUR STUDIES, 1990–2000   *cont.*

Author	Sample	Study type	Dependent variable	Topic
Neale and Schmidt (1991)	43 UK and 27 German firms	Multi-industry (manufacturing) survey, quantitative analysis (simple)	UK versus German firms	Export credit policy: attitudes, relationships official aid schemes
Oakley (1996)	30 medium-sized sized high-tech firms	One manufacturing industry, interviews, quantitative analysis	Export performance (composite)	Speed of export entry, NPD success
O'Farrell *et al.* (1996)	856 offices (417 Scottish and 439 English)	Multi-industry (business services) survey, interviews, quantitative analysis	Inter-regional comparison	Internationalization process; timing, initial market selection, entry mode choice
O'Farrell *et al.* (1998a)	413 SMEs (135 Scottish, 238 English, 40 Dutch)	Multi-industry (business services) survey and interviews, quantitative analysis	Internationalization modes, Inter-regional comparison	Internationalization process; timing, initial market selection, entry mode choice
O'Farrell *et al.* (1998b)	370 offices (135 Scottish and 235 English)	Multi-industry (business services) survey, interviews, quantitative analysis	Inter-regional comparison	Internationalization process; timing, initial market selection, entry mode choice
Pfeiffer *et al.* (1998)	62 UK firms and 91 German firms	Multi-industry survey, interviews, observations, quantitative analysis	UK versus German exhibitors	Trade fairs: importance, objectives
Piercy *et al.* (1998)	312 ventures (SMEs)	Multi-industry (manufacturing) survey, quantitative analysis	Export performance (sales, profit, composite)	Competitive advantage, resource base, export performance
Schlegelmilch *et al.* (1991)	20 producers marketers (all sizes)	Single industry (Scottish whisky) survey, quantitative analysis	Export strategy changes	Single European market (1992), strategic planning

APPENDIX 12.1   UK EXPORT BEHAVIOUR STUDIES, 1990–2000   *cont.*

Author	Sample	Study type	Dependent variable	Topic
Souchon and Diamantopoulos (1997)	39 exporting firms	Cross-sectional survey, quantitative analysis	Export performance (composite)	Export information: awareness, acquisition modes
Stewart and McAuley (1990)	160 SMEs	Multi-industry (manufacturing) survey, quantitative analysis	Export performance	Export stimuli and export strategy
Styles and Ambler (1994)	67 exporters	Multi-industry (manufacturing) survey, quantitative analysis	Export performance (composite)	Export success factors, relational factors
Styles and Ambler (2000)	434 export projects (202 UK 232 Australia)	Multi-industry (manufacturing) survey, quantitative analysis	Export performance (composite)	Relational variables, export commitment, interactive research
Tzokas *et al.* (2000a)	178 manufacturing firms	Multi-industry (manufacturing) survey, quantitative analysis	Strategic export pricing (SEP)	Strategic pricing considerations
Tzokas *et al.* (2000b)	178 firms	Multi-industry (manufacturing) survey, quantitative analysis	Export pricing competence	Industrial export pricing
Wakelin (1998)	320 small manufacturers	multi-industry (manufacturing) survey, secondary data, quantitative analysis	Export propensity (exporter/non-exporter)	Firm characteristics (including size) and innovation experience
Westhead (1995)	267 small firms (203 exporting, 64 non-exporting)	multi-industry (manufacturing producer services)survey, quantitative analysis	Exporting versus non-exporting	Exporter profile: firm/founder tactics and perceptions
Whitelock and Jobber (1999)	64 large industrial marketing firms	Multi-industry interviews, quantitative analysis	Market entry	Strategic approach, competitor analysis, information and market entry
Winklhofer and Diamantopoulos (1996)	11 small, medium and large firms	Manufacturing and (one) service interviews, qualitative analysis	Export sales forecasting practice and performance	Exporter profile and company-specific characteristics

13 Understanding International Strategy in the Professional Services Industry: The Case of the International Marketing Communications Sector

Dev K. Boojihawon and Stephen Young

INTRODUCTION

The professional services industry is one of the fastest growing economic sectors in most Western and European economies, expanding at an annual rate of 20 per cent. The companies in this sector now account for 18 per cent of jobs in the West, with revenues of over £600 billion a year (GATS, 2000). Along with other professional services the importance of international marketing communications has grown significantly since the early 1980s and has led to the emergence of multinational advertising agencies. These agencies are capable of serving foreign clients in multiple markets and further penetrating these markets to generate new business activities. While little is understood of the modes of the international expansion by advertising agencies, it is apparant that cross-border activities have become increasingly important as a strategy for growth.

The objective of this chapter is to contribute to the understanding of international strategy and development in the professional services industry by studying the advertising and communications sector, and specifically the case of a multi-national advertising agency. The chapter is organized as follows. The first section reviews the definitions of and studies on management and strategy in professional services. In the second section a conceptual framework is presented to identify the key issues in this area. The third section evaluates the case study on the basis of this framework. In the final section a number of key propositions are discussed.

PROFESSIONAL SERVICES

Although there is little consensus about which services should be regarded as 'professional services', there is some agreement on the characteristics of professional service firms (PSFs). This chapter concentrates on knowledge/information-intensive enterprises that rely primarily, and in many cases exclusively, on the provision of professional expertise for their value-creation activities. These are firms whose growth and evolution is driven by the effort, competence and personal relationships of individuals with the ability to convince potential clients of their problem-solving capabilities in specific areas. Nachum (1998) identifies two distinct characteristics of such firms: (1) knowledge is their core resource, and (2) the clients of these firms are other institutions and organizations, and their output is used as inputs in the production processes of other businesses. Examples include management consultancy, market research, tax planning, public relations, advertising and marketing communications, law, auditing, information technology, architectural and engineering services. Marketing communication services (or advertising – the terms are used interchangeably in this chapter) include the preparation of advertisements and their placement in various media. The former encompasses the development of advertising plans and the creation of advertisements, and the latter involves the purchase of space or time in print, broadcast or interactive media. Broadly speaking the marketing communications sector consists of three parties: *advertisers*, who produce branded products or services; the *media*, through which such products and services are advertised; and *advertising firms*.

INTERNATIONALIZATION AND THE INTERNATIONAL STRATEGY OF PROFESSIONAL SERVICE FIRMS

Data on the international activities and trade of multinational professional service firms (PSFs) is very limited, except in the case of the US. Furthermore, the studies conducted so far, mainly by international bodies such as the United Nations Centre on Transnational Corporations (UNCTC), suggest that this data should be carefully interpreted given the lack of consensus on what constitutes 'professional services' (UNCTAD, 1989). US PSFs have moved rapidly into foreign markets in order to capitalize on the growing opportunities available there. During 1990–97, US exports of professional services rose by an average annual rate of more than 17 per cent to reach $21.3 billion. Imports of professional services, on the other hand, grew by 19.5 per cent to reach $6.6 billion. During this period, therefore, the US trade surplus in professional services increased at an average annual rate of 16.5 per cent. Overall, trade in professional services accounted for more than 18 per cent of the total US service trade surplus in 1997 (US Department of Commons, 1998).

The US advertising industry accounts for nearly 48 per cent of all expenditure on advertising services worldwide. US firms are widely considered to be the most competitive participants in the international advertising market, given the breadth and calibre of their creative skills, media relations expertise and ability to tailor advertising campaigns to targeted audiences. Trade in this sector consists of cross-border trade and affiliate transactions, with the latter predominating. This is because agencies with a local presence cultivate knowledge that is vital to the successful administration of advertising services, including an understanding of the local media environment, as well as familiarity with local consumer tastes, language and culture. Consequently, affiliate firms tend to develop a competitive advantage over agencies that export advertising services from their home country. In 1996, sales by US-owned advertising affiliates abroad amounted to $5 billion, compared with the $551 million earned from cross-border exports of advertising services. For the UK, the value of advertising services sold overseas was £774 million in 1999, with advertising services valued at £545 million being bought by UK companies, yielding net exports of £229 million (ONS, 2000). The UK is ranked as having the fourth largest concentration of professional service providers in the world (Nachum, 2000).

Regarding PSFs' modes of international expansion, the General Agreement on Trade and Services (GATS) identifies four narrower channels or 'modes' of supplying professional services to foreign consumers. Figure 13.1 shows the relationship between these modes.

The forces behind the transformation of the international competitive scene for PSFs are deregulation, technological advances, growing global competition and, especially, the increasing globalization of client firms. Insurance, advertising, law and consultancy firms have all responded to clients' demand that they invest in cross-border operations and provide a consistent and coordinated cross-border service. Smith (2000) notes, however, that consultants working globally

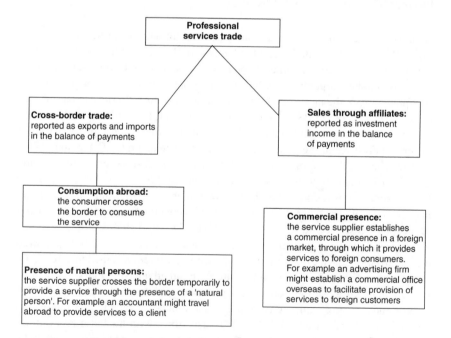

Figure 13.1   PSFs and modes of supply

Source: Adapted from GATS (2000).

are faced by the challenges that national cultural differences pose on their business practices as they attempt to build co-ordinated global services.

In respect of the international marketing communications industry, Ko (1995) postulates that multinational advertising agencies are primarily motivated by market factors, with conglomerate agencies dominating the global industry through their integrated networks, capital and research capabilities. Grein and Ducoffe (1998) point to the need for advertising agencies simultaneously to integrate and to respond internationally as their markets and clients become more global. But as the examples below illustrate, the motivating factors are more than just markets, they also include the globalization and fragmentation of the media industry, the digital revolution and the consolidation of multinational advertising conglomerates.

BBH (Bartle Bogle Hegarty) has disregarded the traditional strategies for setting up international offices and refused to participate in the time-consuming and expensive exercise of producing speculative work on a worldwide basis. It has instead chosen to work for like-minded clients, and to position itself as a single source of creativity for all of Europe (Cooper, 1994). Bigger multinational advertising conglomerates such as WPP, Interpublic and Publicis are expanding through worldwide horizontal and/or vertical acquisitions and diversifications, but are faced with the challenge of generating profits, cost and knowledge synergies and economies of scale through cross-fertilization among businesses (Turnbull and Doherty-Wilson, 1990). For Japanese advertising conglomerates such as Dentsu, the driving force for outward internationalization is foreign competition within Japan, but they are faced with major cultural barriers, especially outside Asia (Kilburn, 1999). Another Japanese advertising giant, Asatsu, has concentrated on penetrating China and South-East Asia via joint-ventures and tie-ups with local enterprises.

While studies on the international strategies and development of PSFs are limited, three relevant groups of literature have been identified. The first comprise studies that have borrowed significantly from the marketing and management literature on manufacturing companies, for example Winch and Schneider (1993), O'Farrell (1995) and Majkgard and Sharma (1998). The second consists of studies, that treat professional services as a distinct industry, and have sought to provide specific managerial knowledge applicable to professional services, for example Nachum (1996), Brush and Artz (1999), and Alon and McKee (1999). Some of the studies in this category also include strategic management issues, but the focus is more on the domestic than the international. Among the latter are Heischmidt and Hekmat (1991), Bhat *et al.* (1993), Ghose (1994), Panitz (1995), Lowendhal (1997) and Bagchi-Sen and Kuechler (2000). The third category stems largely from the efforts of institutions such as the World Trade Organization (WTO)/GATS, the Organization for Economic Co-operation and Development (OECD) and the UNCTC to further the understanding and assess the implications of regulations or international codes of ethics on the global conduct of PSFs.

The above review has highlighted a number of key issues that are common to the strategy of multinational PSFs and are central to the conceptual framework that forms the core of this study:

- *Internal factors*: firms' strong reliance on their people (professionals), firm-specific experience and accumulated knowledge for strategy development; and issues relating to the assessment and management of corporate performance with increasing international expansion.
- *External factors*: the underpinning changes in the industry's environment (chiefly associated with globalization), and the increasing ability of PSFs to serve foreign markets through foreign affiliates, acquisitions, joint-ventures and integrated international partnerships and networks.

These key variables and other strategic constructs are drawn from studies of international strategy by authors such as Doz (1980), Ohmae (1985), Porter (1986a), Bartlett and Ghoshal (1987, 1994), Yip (1992), and Hamel and Prahalad (1993), and have been integrated into the conceptual framework presented in Figure 13.1. The latter reflects three theoretical strands that underpin much of the international strategic management literature, namely the resource-based view, the network-based view and the industrial organization view.

We argue that the key internal strategic factors in multinational PSFs are associated with the resource-based view, as explained by Wernerfelt (1984), Grant (1999) and Peteraf (1992), as PSFs are heterogeneous in terms of both their reliance on the expertise of their professionals and their accumulated knowledge base, and their idiosyncratic service provision and corporate performance. The resource-based view provides important insights for analyzing the dynamics of the interactions among the key internal forces and their relation to strategy development. The theoretical insights from the industrial organization view of Caves (1974, 1996), Venkatraman and Prescott (1990), Bartlett and Ghoshal (1989) and Yip (1989, 1992) are linked to external industry forces that underlie the changes in the global industry and PSFs' strategic responses. Finally, the network-based view – as hypothesized by Welch and Luostarinen (1988), Welch and Welch (1996) and Rugman and D'Cruz (1997) – permits an understanding of the two-way implications for strategy development emerging from agencies' interactions with their external environments, and the key internal issues that are central to firms' strategies and performance.

THE CONCEPTUAL FRAMEWORK: A DYNAMIC VIEW OF
MULTINATIONAL CORPORATE STRATEGIES IN PSFs

The conceptual framework (Figure 13.2) has been developed from a review and understanding of the relevant literature and associated theoretical analyses. The far left of the framework shows the theoretical background underlying the set of internal and external/industry influences that are assumed to form the basis of sustain-

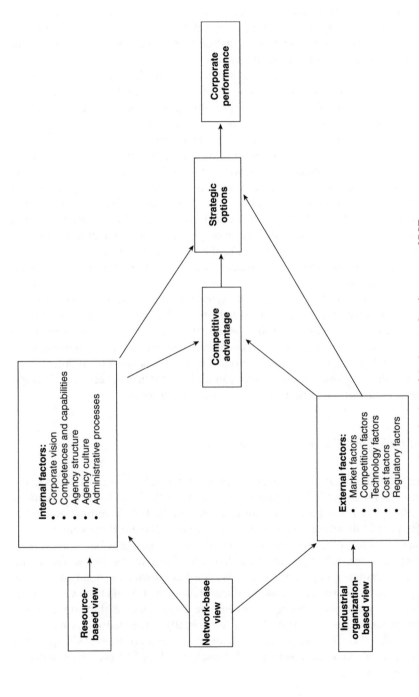

Figure 13.2 The conceptual framework: a dynamic view of the international strategy of PSFs

able competitive advantage and strategic options in multinational PSFs. Internal factors such as strategic intent, the core resource base, organizational/corporate structure, corporate culture and management processes are among the interrelated influences that emerge from the organizational dynamics and value-creation activities of PSFs. The heterogeneity of this industry and its various sub-sectors calls for careful examination of these internal influences.

At first sight the framework may not seem too dissimilar from a model devised for a traditional manufacturing firm. The main difference lies in the underlying assumptions. For example, taking a resource-based view, it is argued that the idiosyncratic resources and capabilities of these firms (described here as their core resource base) are the principal sources of competitive advantage, with PSFs relying on individual professionals and their knowledge base for their value creation. It is further assumed that other internal factors support the core resource base, as part of the organizational dynamics of the firm, to form the basis of PSFs' competitive advantage, strategy and performance. Network theoretical insights are also considered, as it is assumed that a number of influences emerging from the inter-office(s) organizational structure of companies and/or the personal contacts of professionals, or again the external environment, can be of importance to firms' international strategy.

It is also asserted that a number of external or industry factors, emerging primarily from the globalization of the industry, influence the competitive advantage and strategic options of PSFs. Such factors are best described using Yip's (1992) model of globalization 'drivers', namely market, cost, competition, technology and government factors. As argued by Lovelock and Yip (1996), most of these industry globalization drivers can also be applied to services, although their impact varies according to service type and by sector.

CASE EVIDENCE: THE WAVE AGENCY

This section presents and evaluates evidence relating to the key variables in the conceptual framework.[1] The case-study company – the WAVE Agency, founded in 1981 – is a leading direct marketing agency in the UK. Its billings amount to more than £140 million and it employs in excess of 280 direct marketing professionals. It is part of a larger group that is Europe's biggest provider of direct marketing services, which in turn is a division of one of the largest marketing communications groups in the world. WAVE has grown consistently during the 20 years of its existence. It owns six offices (four in the UK and two overseas) and deals with a number of clients across Europe through partnership arrangements with its sister agencies. WAVE is a horizontally integrated direct marketing agency that owns its own supply chain and manages a portfolio of six specialist service areas within the direct marketing discipline. Box 13.1 presents a profile of the company.

Box 13.1 Characteristics of the WAVE Agency, 1998–99
- Billings (main media services):£43 340 000
- Annual turnover: £57 970 000
- Income: £4 600 000
- Top markets: UK, Netherlands, France.
- Mode of servicing: Netherlands (three years) – partnership arrangement; France (two years) – joint-venture.
- Percentage of contribution to total billings by market: Netherlands, 1%; France, 5%.
- Proportion of billings/fee income: UK, 94%; international, 6%.
- Proportion of total employment: UK, 94%; international 6%.
- Proportion of client base: UK, 60%; international, 40%.
- Offices: London, North of England, West of England, Scotland, Netherlands, France
- Service areas: Database management, list broking and management, media, digital, direct marketing, strategic communications consultancy, others from global agency network

(Source: Company documents.)

Internal Factors

The WAVE Agency attributes its consistent record to a number of internal and external factors that have directly or indirectly influenced its strategic development. With regard to internal factors, management ambition to expand the agency, the ability to develop personal relationships with sister agencies in the network and shareholder returns have been prime influences. However, taking a resource-based view the expertise of and quality of work by the direct marketing professionals can be seen as the core resources in the strategic development of the agency. Four internal variables have played an important albeit supporting role in developing these core resources: a clear vision for the agency (strategic intent), a company environment that nurtures value-creation activities by the professionals (culture), an appropriate support structure, that attracts new business developments from parent and sister networks (corporate structure), and policies and procedures to manage the internal workings of the firm (management processes). The combination of these elements appears to have facilitated a heterogeneous service delivery and created difficult-to-copy qualities in the work produced by the agency's professionals. Some of the network influences emerging from the support provided by the parent network seem to have been double-edged, facilitating as well as constraining the agency's international strategic development. But there is little evidence of the nature of this influence or interference.

Corporate Vision

Four essential concepts are at the heart of the agency's strategic vision and its value-creation activities, namely accountability, passion, challenge and partnership; these are embedded in the agency's 'DNA' and, according to the firm, are the values that make 'the firm unique, defining the way it does business, its standards of service and its quality of thinking'.

Competences and Capabilities

Central to the agency's strategic development and value-creation activities are its professionals, and the key to the agency's evolution from a 'conservative' culture to an 'entrepreneurial' culture has been its ability to retain its professionals:

> We have a very strong individual entrepreneurial staff with a feudal heritage. Our strength is in our people . . . in the ability to track and retain and develop the skills set of key individual talents . . . that's our heritage . . . and we are adding on to that the ability to make those key individual stars work together towards a common good.

WAVE employs 280-plus experienced staff with expertise in a variety of relevant tasks – from the effective use of data and strategic consultancy to direct-response advertising and e-marketing. WAVE is very committed to maintaining and updating the skill levels and abilities of its professionals. While most of its professionals are graduates and are all trained in-house, the company also seems to profit extensively from a number of programmes conducted by the parent network.

Agency Culture

The corporate culture of WAVE strongly promotes the core values of the agency. But at the same time the management has to nurture an environment that sustains this culture and enables the professionals to work towards the common good of the agency. As the agency notes:

> We focus on things we can and we are delivery focused . . . we are known as people who deliver what the client needs; hence our position in the marketplace is accountable marketing. We only do direct marketing and our culture is all about being on time, on budget, on brief.

In order to extend and promote that culture across the agency WAVE has created an incubation-type environment with what are known as 'centres of excellence'. These small incubators, structured around the services portfolio, provide a 'safe haven' in which its professionals can develop their skills and 'germinate their seeds of innovation and creativity' for quality service delivery and new market development.

Agency Structure

As noted earlier, WAVE is a direct marketing subsidiary of a global marketing communications group. The majority of the company's services are focused on the domestic market, through various regional offices. Outside the UK, the Netherlands office specializes in charity businesses while the French office provides general direct marketing and media services – together they account for 6 per cent of total billings. However, 40 per cent of the firm's client base is international and the agency profits significantly from international business generated through network interactions.

Administrative Processes

Despite an apparently creative and supportive culture, WAVE has no internal management processes or integrated management systems to allow the adequate co-ordination of its various service structures or to benefit from the workings and knowledge of its professionals:

> We are now beginning to get the chief execs to consider operating in conjunction with one another. We believe the strength of our competitive advantage is getting our people to talk to one another, to work towards a cooperative culture; but we can't get them all to communicate at the moment.

External Factors

As well as internal factors, a number of industry variables have both positively and negatively shaped the strategic orientation of WAVE's expansion and market development over the past twenty years. While growth and expansion has been principally client-driven, a closer analysis of the data reveals a number of other industry factors that have indirectly affected the strategy of the firm, as follows:

- Clients' need for strategic cost control and consistency of message across international territories.
- Availability of global solutions (local solutions are increasingly able to be adapted to international markets).
- Availability of global media, horizontal commonalities among consumers across markets in terms of activities and attitudes.
- Global information and communication technologies and presentation of global brand identity.
- Competitive pressures from emerging multinational advertising conglomerates, and from other professional service firms (for example management consultancies) encroaching into the communications market.
- Regulatory factors that limit the ability to collect data and access markets in a systematic way.

Hence, as assumed when taking an industrial organization view, external factors have directly or indirectly affected the strategic development of the agency. The market variables seem to be of prime importance, although the overall influences involve a mixture of factors, including technology, competition and regulation.

Competitive Advantage

The WAVE Agency acknowledges that its competitive advantage is substantially due to the 'hearts and minds' of its professionals, so its key challenge is to retain those people who have provided the impetus for business growth in an industry where there are relatively low barriers to entry. WAVE does not have a clear-cut means of doing to this, but believes that a strong corporate culture is crucial:

> We have a very strong corporate culture which is essential if you want your professionals to keep believing in you. We believe that retaining them is a mix of partially corporate culture, partially personnel development, and partially remuneration. And I would say that it's probably 40 per cent corporate culture, 40 per cent personnel development, and 20 per cent remuneration. However, remuneration is becoming more and more important, ironically, as we transit from a start-up culture to a team culture where we are calling upon staff to work together.

The above evidence clearly illustrates how the idiosyncratic characteristics of the core resource base and the integral contribution of the other key internal variables affect the agency's ability to sustain its competitive advantage. The conceptual framework assumes that some influences on competitive advantage arise from the agency's interaction with its external environment, but the case study provides no evidence to support this assumption.

Strategic Options

Underlying WAVE's growth and expansion is the twin strategy of focusing on what it does best as an agency while ensuring that it is innovative and responsive to the changes and imperatives of the industry's environment. On the one hand the agency feels fully equipped and determined to accommodate further expansion: 'we want to expand ourselves in a new market space with new services, and we are . . . looking at new geographical locations'. On the other hand it is facing the pressure of being locked into the global politics of its conglomerate parent network and maintaining co-operative teamwork, common standards and a global culture.

International Expansion

WAVE is committed to furthering its international expansion. It took a big step towards this by selling itself to the US group six years ago, but so far its international operations have been restricted to two countries – the Netherlands and France, through a joint-venture and a partnership arrangement respectively. Both of these international initiatives and some of the agency's domestic expansion were the result of *ad hoc* collaborations with key individuals in the two countries:

There are a lot of bright guys in the industry with whom you spent a lot of time and enjoy working with [and] forming personal professional relationships ... the Netherlands office, for instance, was set up on the back of a specific individual we have a strong relationship with and whom we met at a global convention in Amsterdam.

But along with this focus, WAVE has systematically concentrated on rationalizing its strategy to strengthen the portfolio of services and direct marketing businesses it covers in order better to control its supply chain. Hence, a number of diversifications have been undertaken in related service areas, and a number of companies established within its own supply chain: 'we've been big players in data for a long time, and now we've taken that a stage further with the launch of a strategic consultancy company called Zalpha; and to keep up with the digital/media revolution we launched WAVE Digital'.

WAVE considers that two factors are currently hampering its further internationalization. The first relates to the erosion of expertise and individual competences:

Cash is not the real issue ... the constraint is more in terms expertise erosion ... you have to make sure that you ... start any overseas office with the right people in place ... so the risk is always linked to whether we have found somebody we can do business with or whom are we going to transfer from our local base.

Second, its international development is closely tied up with group politics: 'we looked around for something that could be based on the consensus of New York policies but more than directly competitive to its strategies'. Ironically, however, a number of international business opportunities were unlocked by tying WAVE to its parent multinational: 'a vast majority of business we do is not with [divisional] offices but instead with direct marketing agencies that were acquired by [our parent company] along the way'.

Network Influences

The above statements clearly illustrate the influence that the parent company has on WAVE's strategic development, providing support for network influences and the network-based view:

We sold [the agency] to [our parent company] six years ago for two reasons – for cash and to get into the European network. On the other side, our clients were increasingly looking for global marketing opportunities in order to have the lowest common denominator control in terms of image and quality of service delivery ... but at the same time it's a factor of fear and uncertainty. It's very simple for us because effectively what we are doing is copying the business models of accountants and ... management consultants.

Coordination

Associated with the interesting challenges of network dynamics and the drive for internationalization is the coordination of value-creating activities. Analysis of WAVE's case (and others) suggests that co-ordination is a crucial element in the success of an international strategy. For instance, WAVE recognizes that with international network interaction and integration comes the need to bring in teams of professionals to work together with a 'common heart and mind' and on the basis of 'common methodologies':

> We are effectively getting co-operation at a senior management level when it comes to co-ordination with the mother ship, but . . . [we] control our operations in a very autonomous fashion . . . so far, co-ordination is very centralized . . . we have managing directors in the overseas offices who effectively [undertake] sales by liaison, and everything else is done from here; so we approach the agency as one business and migrate our services and expertise to suit the local context.

Overall, three international growth and expansion strategies can be observed in this case. The first was the agency's decision to open up offices in countries where it might have a strategic advantage with respect to its expertise and the quality of work it produced. The second strategy is basically diversification-related, and again depends largely on the agency's own initiative to expand into related or unrelated service areas. To a greater or lesser extent, this is closely related to the agency's desire to gain greater control over its own supply chain and to collaborate further across its own networks. The third strategy relates to the company's ability to profit from its relationships with its parent and sister networks, within the framework of top-down coordination.

Corporate Performance

The indicators of WAVE's corporate performance are principally revenue growth and margin growth, with the latter becoming increasingly important in evaluating international expansion. It seems to be doing well on both these counts, but parent-company control is reflected in its greater reliance on a number of in-house measurement tools to regulate its operations and value-creation activities, such as measures of creativity, staff retention and turnover, and client and staff satisfaction. These measures are derived from surveys conducted on an annual or biannual basis.

CONCLUSIONS

This chapter has reviewed the literature on professional services and international strategic management and proposed a conceptual framework for understanding the nature of international strategies among multinational PSFs. A case study of a multinational advertising agency (The WAVE Agency) was presented to illustrate the key constructs and variables in the framework.

The finding is that PSFs are different from traditional manufacturing and consumer service companies. The international development of PSFs is centred on effective client servicing in foreign markets, the generation of new business activities through established networks, and the development and nurturing of their professionals' expertise and skills to provide local solutions within a global framework. The external environment introduces factors that have specific influences on the formulation and implementation of international strategy. On this basis, four key propositions are suggested for future research:

1. Internal and external factors influence the choice, development and implementation of PSFs' strategic options.
2. Internal and external factors affect PSFs' ability to develop and sustain competitive advantage(s).
3. A PSF's choice of strategic options is strongly related to its ability to develop and maintain (sustainable) competitive advantage(s).
4. The PSF's choice of strategic options has an impact on the its corporate performance.

Further, it is expected that multinational PSFs will respond to their industry's globalization potential in an integrated fashion according to a number of key globalization indicators, namely: managerial vision/mindset (strategic intent), client base, value creation, growth mode, network nodes, geographical spread and co-ordination. It is assumed that setting an international strategy involves decisions about these strategic dimensions, which are directly or indirectly a function of chiefly internal but also external influences. These dimensions and choices determine whether a strategy lies towards the multilocal or global end of the strategy continuum.

One key issue raised by the case study relates to the ownership structure of PSFs and its implications for international strategy. As the case study revealed, WAVE continues to identify itself as an independent agency even though it sold itself to a conglomerate – this was done mainly to reap the benefits of size and acquire new business and markets. For its part, the parent conglomerate was keen to gain access to the entrepreneurial flair and skills of the agency. Altogether, ownership and subsidiary issues seem to take on a different definition and significance in this industry, as smaller firms appear to be more keen to ally themselves with big international conglomerates that can assist them in their effort to expand across borders and gain access to new markets and business opportunities. This raises a number of questions that demand further examination with respect to the model presented in this chapter. Questions of interest relate to the differences between informal networks, strategic alliances and wholly owned subsidiaries in this sector; whether the relatively informal relationship between parents and subsidiaries tend to be short term, to be followed later by closer integration; whether and how the conceptual framework and propositions need to be adapted to incorporate ownership factors, and so on.

The present research focuses on exploration and theory building, and is designed to contribute to the limited literature on the international strategic management of PSFs. The issues and concepts discussed here are part of a more extensive study currents being undertaken across UK. The model presented in this chapter has been analyzed with the help of a single case study – a larger sample must be considered at a future stage to substantiate the preliminary findings discussed here.

Note

1. The data in this study are derived from a major international-strategy-oriented study conducted across the UK. The qualitative research consisted of in-depth interviews at 19 advertising agencies engaged in international business activities. Senior managers of these agencies were interviewed on a confidential basis for two hours. When appropriate and available, secondary data on the various companies were used to support the interview data. The agency chosen for study in this chapter has been given a fictitious name (WAVE) to maintain anonymity. The managing director was interviewed for two hours in November 2000 on various issues relating to our conceptual framework, and the main findings are discussed in this chapter.

14 Modelling the Export Marketing Strategy–Performance Relationship: A Replication

Colin Wheeler, Steven Tagg and James H. Taggart

INTRODUCTION

Relatively few tests have been carried out on the links between export marketing strategy and export performance in different country environments (Diamantopoulos and Schlegelmilch, 1994; Styles, 1998). In this chapter an attempt is made to replicate a US model of export performance to determine the extent to which the elements of the model pertain in a different country environment, namely Scotland. Because much of our knowledge about export performance is based on American findings, the study by Cavusgil and Zou (1994) was chosen to test an American study in a non-American context. Cavusgil and Zou use a comprehensive set of variables (including variables relating to the external environment), posit direct and indirect effects on export performance and use appropriate statistical techniques to handle this complexity.

THE RESEARCH DESIGN

The export marketing strategy–performance link is conceptualized in the following way. Both internal forces (firm and product characteristics) and external forces (industry and export market characteristics) influence export marketing strategy. In turn export marketing strategy influences export performance, which is the attainment of a firm's strategic and economic goals. Firm characteristics also directly affect export performance. Cavusgil and Zou (1994) argue that there is neither a well-defined conceptualization of the topic nor any measures of the appropriate constructs, but they identify potentially significant variables. These variables (shown in Table 14.1 below) relate to export marketing strategy and firm, product, industry and market characteristics. By means of personal interviews they gathered data on 202 product market/ventures by 79 manufacturing firms in 16 industries. When data was collected on multiple product ventures by a single company, different export managers were interviewed for each venture. The sample was split into two and exploratory factor analysis was carried out on one subsample. Factors and items were checked for consistency before deriving a testable model. The other subsample was used for confirmatory factor analysis, and path analysis was used to test the model.

THE CURRENT STUDY

Using items from the survey instrument tested in the original research, a mail questionnaire was developed and piloted with academics and experts in international business. Changes were made to three of the 44 items to take account of local conditions. The sample was drawn from a database of Scottish exporters maintained by the Scottish Council Development and Industry. The questionnaire was mailed to 330 Scottish exporters in 1998 and a reminder was sent two weeks later. Twenty-four uncompleted questionnaires were returned because the companies in question had ceased trading, changed address or did not export. These were duly eliminated from the sample. One hundred and fifty one firms responded, giving a response rate of 49 per cent. Three firms supplied data on two product/market ventures, each completed by different executives for different markets. In total, data was collected on 154 product/market ventures. A telephone follow-up was used to check the accuracy of the data. Approximately 90 per cent of the product/market ventures in the Scottish sample were by firms with fewer than 500 employees, compared with 50 per cent in the American sample. In both studies approximately 30 per cent of the product/market ventures were rated as unsuccessful and most of the ventures had been in place for at least five years, permitting a long-term measure of export performance.

TESTING THE CAVUSGIL AND ZOU MODEL

The Cavusgil and Zou (C & Z) model was tested in two stages (see Hair *et al.*, 1998, for details): in the first stage, constrained factor analysis and reliability analysis was used to check whether the items in the scales related to each other in the same way at the 'measurement model' level. The second stage involved checking whether the measures related to each other in the expected way: this involved structural equation modelling. The expectation was that the empirical links in export market ventures would be consistent across country environments, and that with a questionnaire designed to measure the same concepts with the same types of scale, the C & Z model of the marketing strategy–export performance relationship would be applicable in Scotland.

Plan of the Analysis

There were two reasons why we did not follow the precise methods employed by C & Z. The first was that the procedures used were not available to us so instead we chose to use AMOS, a more widely used structural equation modelling package available with SPSS. There follows an explanation of the decisions we made when faced with the data analysis, in some respects comparing our methods with those of C & Z, and in other respects describing procedures not mentioned by them. The second reason why the C & Z methods were not appropriate was that we were attempting a replication. In a replication study (Byrne, 1994) it is not appropriate to duplicate the exploratory factor analysis and scale construction process used in the original study – especially in the stage using the second subsample or hold-out, as effectively a replication study is a repeat of the hold-out stage. A simple replication of C & Z's analysis steps was likely to fail to fit because the empirical links between measures were not expected to be identical, as the original replications were seen as independent samples of the same multivariate normal distribution. Therefore we relaxed the constraints in a logical pattern derived from Byrne (ibid.), but without any theoretical constraints.

Non-normality

C & Z do not mention the use of corrections for non-normality, but they did use a correction for attenuation. This can deal with non-normality in categorical data, as it increases the correlations between pairs of variables to compensate for unreliability. However the precise method used was not available to the present authors, who also believe that combining correction for attenuation and factor analysis increases the risk of misinterpreting chance patterns of correlation. Polychoric correlations for categorical variables (Dunn *et al.*, 1993) were available in some structural equation modelling packages (EQS, but not AMOS). This can be seen as equivalent to a combination of correction for attenuation and correction for non-normality. However it requires an extremely large sample, much larger than in this study. Not using a correction for attenuation meant that our correlations would be lower than those of C & Z. However if the variables were acting in the same way this would make little difference to our confirmatory factor analyses – except perhaps to reduce the levels of fit. Some of the variables (employment and unit price) were measured in actual values rather than categorical scales. They were generally positively skewed and required corrections for non-normality. We used the SPSS Rank procedure's Blom option (SPSS, 1998): this gives near normal distributions from a skewed continuous variable such as employment, while maintaining the rank order of the cases on that variable. This may increase some correlations but it is likely to reduce spuriously large correlations produced by outliers. This was more of a risk with our Scottish sample, which included fewer large firms.

Missing Data

There is a possibility of logical missing data in the series of related questions in C & Z's survey. For example, answering a question on the training provided for the sales force of a foreign distributor/subsidiary requires the respondent to have a foreign distributor/subsidiary. Nowhere do C & Z describe what happens with logical missing data in their data analysis. We took an open approach to missing data, including cases with several items of missing data. In the data analysis we used list-wise deletion, but when we came to overall analysis that included lots of variables, our total number of cases was considerably reduced. So we recoded the missing values as appropriate valid values. In the above example this would mean coding the answer to the training question as no training for respondents with no foreign distributor or subsidiary. The effect of our approach to missing data was to keep the number of cases at around 150 for all analyses. This approach may be the same as that used by C & Z, but if they discarded incomplete cases and we included them, this may be another reason for differences between the results. Such discarding of incomplete cases would bias the sample towards companies with more complete internationalization, for whom all items would be relevant.

The First Stage of the Replication

Scale Reliability
The first stage of the replication analysis was to check whether the response patterns for our items achieved acceptable reliability coefficients with our sample. We could have simply checked the coefficients alpha, but it was appropriate also to use constrained factor analysis to check whether the pattern of exploratory factor analysis results found by C & Z fitted our Scottish data. The results are shown in Table 14.1. As in some cases the reliability coefficients were not acceptable, we used the same approach as C & Z in respect of item deletion; this usually meant deleting the items with the lowest factor loading on our analysis (shown in Table 14.1).

The alphas for export marketing strategy were good for factors one and four, once the asterisked variable was dropped. The alpha for promotion adaptation was only marginally acceptable, and those for distribution strategy and price competitiveness were not at all acceptable. This caused one to suspect that these groups of factors would not work well alone. For firm characteristics the reliabilities were all acceptable or good. Clear factors that worked well for both country samples were used for firm characteristics. The reliability results showed that for this sample these were not very good factors. The first two factors were marginally acceptable, but scale 3 was not. The alpha for industry characteristics was 0.103 and the correlation between the items was not in the expected direction. The alphas for export market characteristics were not satisfactory.

C & Z only showed alphas for the purified measurement model used in their path analysis. The alphas for these are presented after the constrained factor analysis.

Constrained Factor Analysis

To check whether C & Z's factors fitted the Scottish data, AMOS was used for constrained factor analysis. As C & Z used 13 factors and over 40 variables

Table 14.1   Initial measurement model

	Coefficient alpha (Scotland)	Coefficient alpha after a variable was dropped
Export marketing strategy		
1.1 Support to foreign distributor	0.870	–
Overall support to foreign distributor/subsidiary		
Training provided to sales force of foreign distributor/subsidiary		
Promotion support to foreign distributor/subsidiary		
1.2 Promotion adaptation	0.529	0.576
Degree of adaptation of product positioning		
Degree of adaptation of packaging		
Degree of adaptation of promotional approach		
Degree of market coverage		
1.3 Distributor strategy	0.169	0.347
Number of export customers of the venture		
Sales goal of the export venture		
Type of export distribution channel*		
1.4 Product adaptation	0.402	0.846
Degree of initial product adaptation		
Degree of product adaptation subsequent to entry		
Extent of product labelling in local language*		
1.5 Pricing strategy	0.157	–
Degree of price competitiveness in export market		
Degree of target market specification		
Firm Characteristics		
2.1 International competence	0.792	–
Number of full-time employees		
Annual sales volume of firm		
Amount of firm's international experience		
Years of IB involvement of firm		
Number of foreign markets operated		
Resources for export development		
2.2 Commitment to venture	0.877	–
Extent of careful entry planning		
Extent of management commitment		
Extent of resource commitment		
2.3 International business intensity	0.668	0.871
Firm's relative position in industry*		
Percentage of sales from IB		
Percentage of profit from IB		
Product characteristics		
3.1 Firm's experience with product	0.610	–
Age of Product		
Extent of establishment with firm		

Table 14.1   Initial measurement model   *cont.*

	Coefficient alpha (Scotland)	*Coefficient alpha after a variable was dropped*
3.2 Product's technical complexity	0.511	0.529
Training needs of sales force		
Service/maintenance requirement		
Strength of product patent*		
3.3 Product features	–0.006	–
Product's unit price		
Degree of product uniqueness		
3.4 Cultural specificity of product		
Degree of culture-specificity		
Industry characteristics		
4 Industry characteristics	0.103	–
Degree of technological orientation of industry		
Intensity of price competition		
Export Market Characteristics		
5.1 Export market attractiveness	0.295	–
Demand potential of export market		
Sophistication of marketing infrastructure		
5.2 Cultural/legal similarity of markets	0.306	–
Cultural similarity of markets		
Extent of legal/regulatory barriers		
5.3 Export market competitiveness	0.289	–
Competitive intensity		
Product exposure in export market		
5.4 Brand familiarity of export customers	0.352	–
Degree of brand familiarity in export market**		

  * Dropped variable.
** This was a single item in the C & Z study.

there were insufficient cases to generate a stable analysis. However with separate analysis for each group it made the comparison more focused. Formally the
null hypothesis was that the same population (with population covariance structure) was the origin of both C & Z's and this study's sample. Independent
samples from a population can produce different results with precisely the same
measuring instrument. However the differences should typically vary within
margins, so that the chi-square tests of difference of fit will not be significant. In
this research some adaptation of the measuring instrument was used. The low
reliabilities for the majority of C & Z's scales suggest that the content domains
were not sampled properly. It is possible, although unlikely, that the same inter-
concept covariance structure could apply to both samples, allowing for the fact

that the concepts were not identically measured. The constrained factor analysis allowed this to be checked. C & Z did an exploratory factor analysis with all variables, extracting 17 factors. They grouped these factors into five groups. We used these groups to simplify the confirmatory factor analysis process. The strategy for fitting the factor model outlined in Table 14.2 follows Byrne (1994).

Applying the strategies for fitting the factor model for the export marketing strategy variables produced an almost acceptable fit (CFI = 0.983, RMSEA = 0.031, chi-square 75.635, df 66). A large number of factor cross-loadings were introduced into the model and the error covariances in this study suggest that an analysis of our data independently of C & Z's might produce different results. With a fair degree of flexibility the C & Z structure might just fit the Scottish data for export marketing strategy, but there was a considerable drift from tight fit and it is likely that an independent analysis would reveal a different structure.

For firm characteristics various cross-loadings had to be allowed, but a fit of CFI 0.968 and RMSEA 0.065 was obtained, which approached acceptability. In general this group (which had better alphas too) showed a better fit. Problems with identification and inadmissible factor covariances were difficult to overcome for product characteristics and it was not possible to achieve a good fit even with all the permitted changes. The best fit was CFI = 0.933 and RMSEA = 0.064. Industry characteristics had one factor with two items. The correlation between the two variables was not significantly different from zero, which suggests that this factor was not expressed in our study. Export market characteristics fitted, with CFI = 0.969 and RMSEA = 0.039. Only a few adjustments were made.

So by following our procedures we found an acceptable fit for export market characteristics, marginally acceptable figures for export marketing strategy and firm characteristics, and unacceptable figures for product characteristics.

Table 14.2   Fitting the factor model

Step	Objective	Strategy
1	Starting position	Take the variable loadings on each factor from C & Z table; set other loadings to zero and require covariance between factors (an oblique solution)
2	Acceptable solution	This must be identified and there must be no inadmissible values
3	Add loadings	This is done if the modification indices are greater than 4
4	Add error covariance	This is done if the modification indices are greater than 4
5	Factor quality	Either force independence between factors, or fix variance to unity, or delete the factor if there are unacceptable solutions

However a large number of adjustments were necessary, and in fact none of the models showed any sign of fitting with precisely the same factor model. What might be the reasons for this lack of fit? It is possible that the C & Z model did not apply. However it could be that the content domains were not properly sampled – this is indicated by poor reliabilities, although these might be due to our decision not to use the correction for attenuation. It is possible that with unlimited resources applied to measurement construction we could generate reliable measures of the same concepts. However if we continue with the purified model it is possible that something of the relationship between variables may still be apparent.

The Second Stage of the Replication

Purified model

Cavusgil and Zou (1994) reported reliabilities for a purified measurement model. This model only included factors with more than one item – as a measurement model was not appropriate for single item factors. They also used a structural equation model to check the measurement model for the predictor factors of export performance only. Table 14.3 shows the reliabilities from the Scottish data for C & Z's purified measurement model.

For export market performance it was very difficult to produce a reliable collection of items. Only when the sales growth figures for each year were disaggregated did we get an alpha even approaching 0.5, and to drop the variable extent to which strategic goals were achieved would have been rather difficult to contemplate from a theoretical perspective. This made the prospect of path analysis of an overall model a little unpromising. However the alphas for all the other purified models were acceptable. All but two factors had alphas greater than 0.7 and the others were around 0.6. So at this level our study showed reasonable agreement with C & Z's purified measurement model.

SEM for the Purified Measurement Model

C & Z's purified measurement model was used to generate a constrained factor analysis and attempts were made to fit the model. This was done without including export marketing performance. However in the absence of adjustments there was no approach to good fit. Making quite a large number of adjustments produced CFI = 0.964 and RMSEA = 0.0467. To validate the operational model (Figure 14.1), summary variables were generated for each aspect of the model and the overall paths were estimated in another AMOS run. The fit for the model was extremely unsatisfactory (CFI = 0.380, RMSEA = 0.171) and in some cases the fit of the parameters was not in the same direction. Obviously the reliability of these results was suspect as the fit was so poor. The replication of the path model did not involve a revision of the item–factor groupings to take into account the suggestions of ways

Table 14.3 Purified measurement model reliability for the Scottish and US samples

	Coefficient alpha (Scotland)	Variable dropped	Coefficient alpha (Scotland)	Coefficient alpha (US)
Export market performance	0.467	Extent to which strategic goals are achieved	0.677	0.781
Extent to which strategic goals are achieved				
Perceived success of the venture				
Average sales growth over the first five years				
Average profitability over the first five years				
Product adaptation	0.402	Extent of product labelling in local language	0.846	0.559
Degree of initial product adaptation				
Degree of product adaptation subsequent to entry				
Extent of product labelling in local language				
Promotion adaptation	0.576	No improvement	–	0.857
Degree of adaptation of product positioning				
Degree of adaptation of packaging				
Degree of adaptation of promotional approach				
Support to foreign distributor/subsidiary	0.870	No improvement	–	0.853
Overall support to foreign distributor/subsidiary				
Training provided to sales force of foreign distributor/subsidiary				
Promotion support to sales force of foreign distributor/subsidiary				

Table 14.3   Purified measurement model reliability for the Scottish and US samples   *cont.*

	Coefficient alpha (Scotland)	Variable dropped	Coefficient alpha (Scotland)	Coefficient alpha (US)
International competence	0.792	No improvement	–	0.930
Number of full-time employees				
Annual sales volume of firm				
Amount of firm's international experience				
Years of IB involvement of firm				
Number of foreign markets operated				
Resources for export development				
Commitment to venture	0.877	No improvement	–	0.884
Extent of careful entry planning				
Extent of management commitment				
Extent of resource commitment				
Firm's experience with product	0.610	Only 2 items	–	0.592
Extent to which product is established the firm				
Age of product since commercialization				

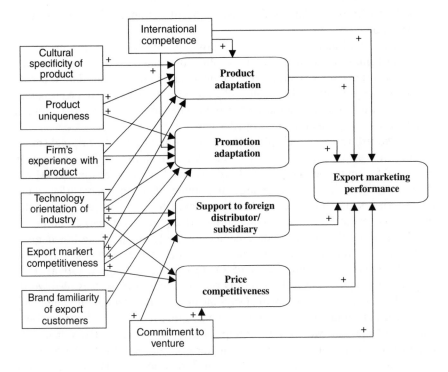

Figure 14.1   Operational model of export marketing strategy and performance

Source: Reprinted with permission from *Journal of Marketing*, published by the American Marketing Association – S. T. Cavusgil and S. Zou, 'Marketing Strategy–Performance Relationship', 58 (January 1994), pp. 1–21: 12.

to improve the examination of the measurement models refered to above. It is possible that if the revised versions of the factors derived in the previous constrained factor analyses had been used, a new path model with better fit may have ensued. However this would no longer have been a replication study.

DISCUSSION

There are some similarities between the two studies, with firm characteristics having much in common with the original study. It is consistent with other studies in that firm characteristics such as international competence, commitment to the venture and the relative business intensity of the firm are linked to export performance (Zou and Stan, 1998). Overall, however, the fit was not good.

One possible explanation of this is that, on the whole the firms in the Scottish study were smaller and arguably had fewer resources than the US sample. It also seems reasonable that the nature of the two samples' export marketing strategies may have differed. It is possible that a more formal marketing strategy process in the larger firms may have influenced the results, although this needs further investigation.

Cavusgil and Zou drew data from 79 firms for 202 cases, an average of 2.5 cases per firm. Using a mail survey to collect the data on product/market ventures meant that over 151 firms were sampled, and in three cases data was collected on two product/market ventures by one firm. It may be that the corporate culture of firms produced some similarity between the cases collected within a firm that was not present in the Scottish study.

The Scottish research took place four years or more after the original study, and this may be one reason why the model was difficult to fit, although many of the variables might be expected to have remained stable over time. However there were differences in the economic environment that would have affected the characteristics of export markets. When the Scottish survey was undertaken the pound was very strong, making competitive pricing in export markets problematic. In addition the UK was not a member of the Exchange Rate Mechanism (ERM) and therefore could not benefit from the stable exchange rates that existed between the members of the ERM (Taggart and Taggart, 1997a). This may help to explain the lack of results on the pricing factor. It is also worth asking if contextual variables will always mean we will be looking for commonalties and not replication. It seems reasonable that if we carried out our own analysis of the data we would develop a different model of determinants of export performance. But in the Scottish study we did not do this because we wanted to test the American model in a different context. The exercise was confirmatory, not exploratory. Gemunden (1991) and Zou and Stan (1998) have explored the difficulty of making meaningful comparisons of the results of export performance studies from the mass of export research endeavours, and our attempt to build on previous research highlights the problems involved. In our study, even when there was a similarity in the methodology used, the results were in many respects divergent.

There is also the issue of the purification process, where judgements are made about which items and factors should go forward to the final structural equation model. In what is ostensibly a highly quantitative, objective methodology, individual judgement is a key factor. With so many conflicting findings in the literature it is perfectly possible to propose alternative interpretations based on empirical evidence and theoretical reasoning from the evidence.

CONCLUSIONS AND RECOMMENDATIONS

This chapter set out to replicate a model of export performance developed from data drawn from the American market. Some commonalities were evident, with management competence, support for individual export market ventures, and relative business intensity being similar. The nature of export marketing strategy, product characteristics and export market characteristics had far less in common. There are many possible reasons for the differences, some of which relate to the research methodology employed and others which may relate to the nature of the firms sampled. It seems quite likely that if a model of export marketing performance was developed for our sample of Scottish firms, it would be significantly different from that developed in the original study.

The implications for academics are several. There have been calls in the literature for more extensive replication of studies from different contexts. The questions raised in this chapter lend support to this view. The results of our replication may also support the position of Coviello and McAuley (1999), who argue that commonalities are to be found across studies in different environments, rather than identical results. Gemunden (1991), Ford and Leonidou (1991) and Zou and Stan (1998), among others, have asked for more attention to be paid to the research methodology used in studies and for the publication of comprehensive details on the statistical results. We would support this call as the methodologies used need to be made more transparent. There is also reason to make more explicit the role of culture in cross-national studies. In our study the data collection instrument was piloted with academics and international business experts, but no other assessment of culture was used.

Decisions also have to be made about the future direction of export performance research. One school of thought effectively, argues for measures of export performance, that depend on what the purpose of the measurement is. Buckley, *et al.* (1990, 1994) argue that the measures used should depend partly on the export process in the firm. In other words, the measures should relate to what the firm is trying to achieve. Others, who wish to adopt a narrower view of performance, argue for a single, standardized but comprehensive measure of export performance (Zou, *et al.*, 1998). It seems that the implication of this for academics is that they should set out the conceptualization of and the theoretical justification for the export measures used. For managers, the implication seems to be that the influence of context on export performance is paramount. This study has identified the importance of firm characteristics such as management commitment to export success. This holds in the US and in Scotland, and there is a good deal of other evidence to support this view. For policy makers, the importance of management characteristics is again underlined in both the US and the Scottish context. A firm's competence, commitment to product/market ventures and involvement with exports are all key influences. Government-sponsored export promotion programmes aimed at increasing the competences of individuals and firms are clearly of importance.

As noted by Zou and Stan (1998), the export performance literature needs to build upon and develop existing research. One aspect of this is carrying out similar research in other countries. In this chapter we have attempted to replicate a model of the determinants of export performance, but we could only reproduce some of the components of Cavusgil and Zou's (1994) model. This suggests that a reduced model could be replicated elsewhere, but the problem of measuring performance remains.

15 Does International Entry Mode Choice Influence Firm Performance?

Keith D. Brouthers and Lance Eliot Brouthers

INTRODUCTION

Research on international entry modes has concentrated on transaction cost explanations of mode selection (Anderson and Gatignon, 1986; Gatignon and Anderson, 1988; Hennart, 1991a; Erramilli and Rao, 1993; Taylor *et al.*, 1998) and has given little consideration to the performance implications of foreign market entry (Woodcock, *et al.*, 1994; Brouthers, *et al.*, 1999). Several studies have examined performance differences between wholly owned modes (either acquisitions or greenfield start-ups) and joint-ventures (both equity and non-equity) (Simmonds 1990; Woodcock *et al.*, 1994; Nitsch *et al.*, 1996; Pan *et al.*, 1999). However, these studies tend to (1) rely exclusively on financial performance measures, (2) examine only wholly owned and joint venture modes, and (3) ignore other factors that may affect performance such as transaction costs, while targeting market, institutional and cultural factors.

The purpose of this chapter is to extend the work of Woodcock *et al.*, (1994), Nitsch *et al.*, (1996) and Pan *et al.*, (1999) in three ways. First, it extends previous scholarship by examining financial and non-financial performance measures. Second, it examines a broader range of mode choices: wholly owned modes of entry, joint-ventures, licensing agreements and exporting modes. Third, it controls for the impact of transaction cost variables as well as target markets institutional context and cultural context variables.

TRANSACTION COSTS

Most entry mode research relies exclusively on transaction cost theory to explain mode choice decisions (for example Anderson and Gatignon, 1986; Gatignon and Anderson, 1988; Hennart, 1991a; Erramilli and Rao, 1993; Taylor *et al.*, 1998). Transaction cost variables are concerned with the costs of integrating an operation within the firm compared with the costs of using an external party (the market) to act for the firm in a foreign market (Hennart, 1991a; Agarwal and Ramaswami, 1992; Erramilli and Rao, 1993). Transaction costs are composed of the costs of finding and maintaining an appropriate partner to perform the firm's functions in the international market, the cost/risk of disseminating proprietary knowledge, and the cost/risk of deterioration of the quality of the product or service.

Transaction costs can vary between markets because of differing levels of firm expertise, competition (market concentration), technology or economic development. The ability of a firm to work with another firm in the host country directly affects the perception of transaction costs. In markets with low transaction costs, firms may find a large number of potential partners with the skill level and ability needed to deliver the product or service in an effective manner. In markets with high transaction costs there may be few if any qualified potential partners, and trade, culture or business practices may mean an increased risk of technology dissemination.

Scholars have found that when transaction costs are low, firms tend to rely on the market to deliver their products or services. However as transaction costs increase, firms tend to switch their preference to more hierarchical modes, such as wholly owned subsidiaries. Hence we propose:

- *Hypothesis 1:* firms entering high transaction cost markets tend to use more integrated entry modes and perform better than firms entering lower transaction cost markets.

INSTITUTIONAL CONTEXT

Madhok (1997) and others (for example Brouthers and Brouthers, 2000; Delios and Beamish, 1999) suggest that transaction cost solutions examine only the exploitation of existing capabilities and fail to take into account the enhancement potential of foreign market entry. Foreign entry may enhance firm capabilities by providing access to new technologies or additional managerial and financial resources. Capability enhancement can also occur through access to unique resources or marketing channels. In these cases, mode selection may be motivated not only by transaction cost considerations but also by the value added through capability enhancement. Madhok (1997) and Delios and Beamish (1999) suggest that the institutional context includes tangible and intangible assets as well as legal restrictions.

Tangible assets include the level of financial and managerial resources available to the firm. Greater size allows firms to engage in more extensive international activities because larger firms generally have more financial and managerial resources to devote to international expansion. Smaller firms, by contrast, have fewer resources and may benefit from sharing foreign entry with target market firms that possess additional assets that can be deployed in the target market. Hence:

- *Hypothesis 2:* firms with more tangible assets utilize more integrated entry modes and perform better than firms with fewer tangible assets.

Madhok (1997) suggests that intangible assets are also important sources of firm advantage that may be enhanced by international entry. Intangible assets include international experience and technological capability. International experience can provide firms with a set of routines and systems that enhance the exploitation of existing capabilities in foreign markets (Delios and Beamish, 1999). Firms with such experience tend to use more integrated (wholly owned) modes of entry (ibid.)

Contrary to this, firms with little international experience have not developed these systems and may find it quite difficult to transfer firm-specific capabilities across international borders (Madhok, 1997). Such firms may use market-based modes to enhance their existing capabilities and improve their access to market specific know how. Thus we propose:

- *Hypothesis 3:* firms with more international experience tend to use more integrated modes of entry and perform better than firms with less experience.

The level of firm-specific technology can also influence mode choice since firms with advanced technology do not need to access target market technology, but may incur higher transaction costs when safeguarding their technology from misappropriation.[1] Firms with advanced technology tend to prefer more integrated (wholly owned) modes of entry to international markets (Madhok, 1997). To safeguard their proprietary knowledge less technologically advanced firms may pursue capability enhancement through less integrated modes of entry that give them access to the technological capabilities of partner firms in foreign markets. Hence from an institutional perspective:

- *Hypothesis 4:* firms with more advanced products/services tend to prefer more integrated modes of entry and perform better than firms with less advanced products/services.

Finally, Delios and Beamish (1999) suggest that the institutional context includes host country restrictions on ownership. Basically, governments may restrict mode choice so that choices based on transaction-cost-predictions might not be available to firms. Where legal restrictions exist, firms tend to utilize less integrated modes of entry (Gatignon and Anderson, 1988; Delios and Beamish, 1999). Hence we propose:

- *Hypothesis 5:* firms entering countries with fewer legal restrictions tend to prefer more integrated modes of entry and perform better than firms entering markets with greater restrictions.

CULTURAL CONTEXT

Brouthers and Brouthers (2000: 91) suggest that the 'cultural context helps to define profit potential and/or the risks associated with a specific market entry'.

Cultural context includes the investment risks associated with different host countries economic, legal, political and cultural systems, as well as market attractiveness. Firms tend to be selective and prefer to enter more attractive, less risky markets (that is, similar countries with stable economic, social and political conditions). Strategically, firms enter these markets by means of wholly owned modes in order to obtain a high return. Firms that perceive the possibility of high investment risk may prefer less integrated modes that will reduce their exposure to such risk by reducing their resource commitment (Erramilli and Rao, 1993). Based on these predictive responses to the investment risk component of cultural context, we would expect that:

- *Hypothesis 6:* firms entering markets characterized by low investment risk tend to utilize more integrated modes of entry and perform better than firms entering higher investment risk markets.

The market potential component of cultural context can also influence mode choice. For example, in high-growth markets firms tend to prefer highly integrated (wholly owned) modes of entry so that they can reap the full rewards of the growing marketplace (Agarwal and Ramaswami, 1992). In slow-growth markets firms may find that less integrated modes provide better opportunities because (1) they do not increase the capacity in the market and hence do not affect prices as severely, or (2) They provide a better return on investment by minimizing the resource investment based on lower expected returns. We therefore propose:

- *Hypothesis 7:* firms entering high-growth markets tend to prefer more integrated modes of entry and perform better than firms entering less rapidly growing markets.

MODE CHOICE AND PERFORMANCE

Entry mode theory assumes that firms will select the mode that provides the best return on investment (Brouthers *et al.*, 1999). Our extended transaction cost model considers not only mode control costs (transaction costs), but also location-specific costs (investment risk), and it considers revenue potential in both a cultural context (market potential) and an institutional context (exploitation of firm-specific resources, including firm size, experience and technology). Hence we propose:

- *Hypothesis 8:* firms whose entry mode is based on transaction costs and institutional and cultural characteristics perform better than firms whose mode choice cannot be predicted by these variables.

METHODOLOGY

Dependent Variable

The dependent variable – performance – was captured using subjective performance measures. Subjective measures (management evaluations) of performance are preferred when non-financial performance is involved or when financial measures are not available (Dess and Robinson, 1984; Geringer and Hebert, 1991). Subjective measures can be used to measure performance against multiple financial and non-financial criteria (Dess and Robinson, 1984). Respondents were requested to rate three financial measures of performance (sales level, profitability and sales growth) and four non-financial measures (market share, marketing, reputation and market access), all of which were adopted from previous studies (ibid. Geringer and Hebert, 1991). The respondents evaluated performance on a scale of 1 'does not meet expectations at all' to 10 'meets expectations completely'. Factor analysis confirmed the existence of two performance factors: financial (Cronbach alpha = 0.82) and non financial (alpha = 0.87).

Independent Variables

Transaction Costs

Transaction costs were measured using a set of two Likert-type questions, which measured the cost of making and enforcing contracts in the target market (compared with the home market) and the cost of searching for and negotiating with a potential partner (Cronbach alpha = 0.73).

Institutional Context

Four institutional context variables were included in the study: firm size, international experience, technology level and legal restrictions. Firm size was measured as the number of employees worldwide. International experience was measured as the number of years of experience business outside the home country. Technology level was measured as the percentage of sales spent on R & D. Finally, legal restrictions were measured using one Likert-type question.

Cultural Context

Two cultural context variables were included: market potential and investment risk. Market potential was measured using a single Likert-type question about the market potential of the target market. Investment risk was measured with a set of four Likert-type questions on the risk of converting and repatriating profits, nationalization risks, dissemination risks and the stability of political, social and economic conditions (alpha = 0.72).

Entry Mode

Four mode types were included in the study: (1) wholly owned, (2) equity joint-ventures, (3) licensing and (4) exporting. A number of researchers have suggested that entry mode structure should be considered as a continuous variable for analytical purposes (Chu and Anderson, 1992; Brouthers, 1995; Tse *et al.*, 1997). This suggestion is based on the fact that entry mode is a measure of control and resource commitment (Anderson and Gatignon 1986; Agarwal and Ramaswami, 1992), and that a continuum of control and resource commitment exists. Integrated (wholly owned) entry modes represent the highest level of control and resource commitment, while exporting represents the lowest level of both these measures (Erramilli and Rao, 1990). According to Gatignon and Anderson (1988: 305) 'the continuum from market contracting to unified governance is accompanied by an increased degree to which resources are placed at hazard'.

Data Source

To test the hypotheses presented above, a sample of the 1000 largest European Union (EU) firms was selected with the assistance of a CD ROM database (AMADEUS). The AMADEUS database contains firm and financial information on more than 100 000 EU companies, private and public, manufacturing and service. The largest EU firms were determined for the twelve member nations (pre-1995 expansion) by examining annual sales for 1993.

Data Collection

A questionnaire was used for data collection. Two native-speaking individuals translated the questionnaire into French and German. Two other individuals then translated the questionnaires back into English. This process was continued until the meaning of the questions in French and German was the same as their meaning in English.

French-language questionnaires were sent to companies in France, Belgium and Luxembourg. German-language questionnaires were sent to companies in Germany. English-language questionnaires were sent to companies in all other EU countries. The questionnaires were addressed to the managing director of international operations at the home office of the organization. Three mailings were sent to each non responding firm, one month apart. The mailings included a covering letter in the appropriate language explaining the purpose of the study and requesting assistance.

Each firm was asked to complete the questionnaire in respect of the country they had most recently entered. In some cases the responding firms had only established a production, a sales/marketing or an R & D centre in the latest country. In other cases, all three units had been established in the country in question. In the latter case, the firms furnished multiple entry mode responses.

A total of 213 questionnaires were returned (21 per cent), covering 178 entries into foreign markets. Thirty-five firms returned blank questionnaires along with a letter stating that it was not their policy to participate in question-naire research. Of the remaining 178 questionnaires, 121 were from manufactur-ing firms and 57 from service firms. One hundred and nine (61 per cent) of the new entrants were wholly owned, 47 (26 per cent) were joint-ventures, 10 (6 per cent) were by license agreement and 12 (7 per cent) utilized export modes.

The responding firms appeared to be highly international with long interna-tional experience, averaging about 46 years. On average they had 42 foreign country locations, and foreign sales as a percentage of total sales averaged about 54 per cent.

FINDINGS

To investigate the connection between foreign market performance and our independent variables, we prepared two regression tests, one each for the financial performance and the non-financial performance measures (Hair *et al.*, 1995). Before running the regression analyses the variables were examined for potential multicollinearity problems. As can be seen in Table 15.1, there are numerous statistically significant relationships. However none of the correlations appears large enough to warrant concern for multicollinearity (Hair *et al.*, 1995).

Financial Performance

Studies of entry mode and performance have tended to find that financial perfor-mance measures and mode choice are related for firms that use wholly owned and joint venture modes of entry (Woodcock *et al.*, 1994; Pan *et al.*, 1999; Nitsch *et al.*, 1996). Regression Model 1 (Table 15.2) reveals that financial per-formance is significantly related to transaction costs, institutional context and cultural context ($p < 0.00$, $r^2 = 0.33$), but not to entry mode type.

In particular, firms reported better performance in markets with higher invest-ment risks ($p < 0.01$) and greater legal restrictions ($p < 0.01$). A poorer financial performance was reported for larger firms ($p < 0.07$) and target markets with higher transaction costs ($p < 0.02$). Hence, it appears that transaction costs, cul-tural context (investment risk) and institutional context (firm size and legal restrictions) all helped to explain firms' degree of satisfaction with financial per-formance. Mode choice, while signed correctly, does not significantly influence financial performance.

Table 15.1 Correlation matrix PRIVATE

Variable	1	2	3	4	5	6	7	8	9	10
Mean	25.9	45.9	2.4	6.1	4.0	4.6	8.6	1.6	19.0	27.1
S.D.	29.3	29.2	1.4	1.7	1.0	3.9	3.2	0.9	5.4	7.0
Variables:										
1. Firm size	–									
2. Firm experience	0.02	–								
3. Legal restrictions	-0.19	-0.06	–							
4. Transaction costs	-0.14	-0.32*	-0.14	–						
5. Market potential	0.12	0.23	-0.08	-0.22	–					
6. Technology level	0.19	-0.03	0.06	-0.26	0.14	–				
7. Investment risk	0.08	0.22	-0.54*	-0.10	-0.09	0.18	–			
8. Entry mode	-0.14	-0.15	0.37*	-0.18	-0.04	0.11	-0.10	–		
9. Financial performance	-0.15	0.18	0.10	-0.32*	0.04	0.15	0.34*	0.01	–	
10. Non-financial performance	-0.14	0.16	-0.03	-0.29*	0.09	0.23	0.42*	-0.01	0.71*	–

* $p < 0.01$.

Table 15.2   Regression analysis for performance

	Financial performance	Non-financial performance
Transaction costs	−0.27*	−0.20*
	(0.11)	(0.10)
Institutional context:		
Firm size	−0.22	−0.23*
	(0.12)	(0.11)
International experience	−0.03	−0.04
	(0.11)	(0.09)
Technology level	0.00	0.08
	(0.10)	(0.09)
Legal restrictions	0.39**	0.22
	(0.13)	(0.12)
Cultural context:		
Market potential	0.08	0.11
	(0.10)	(0.09)
Investment risk	0.54***	0.48***
	(0.13)	(0.11)
Entry mode	−0.17	−0.12
	(0.12)	(0.10)
Constant	0.24	0.39**
n	105	105
F	0.0001	0.0001
R^2	0.3302	0.3371

Notes:
***$p < 0.01$; **$p < 0.05$; *$p < 0.10$; standard errors in parentheses.

Non-Financial Performance

Several scholars argue that foreign market entry may be driven by non-financial considerations (Anderson, 1990; Kim and Hwang, 1992). They suggest that improved financial performance may not occur for a number of years after initial foreign market entry (if at all), but that other measures of performance may help determine the effectiveness of foreign entry (Anderson, 1990; Geringer and Hebert, 1991). Model 2 (Table 15.2) examined the impact of transaction costs, institutional context, cultural context and entry mode variables on non-financial performance. The result, were significant ($p < 0.00$), with a slightly higher r^2 (0.34).

Firms reported significantly greater satisfaction with non-financial performance measures when investment risk was high ($p < 0.01$) and legal restrictions were greater ($p < 0.06$). They reported less satisfaction with non-financial performance when transaction costs were high ($p < 0.04$) and firm size was large ($p < 0.03$). Again, mode choice was correctly signed but was not significantly related to non-financial performance.

DISCUSSION

Does entry mode affect the performance of a firm? The few studies that have attempted to investigate firm performance and mode choice have been limited to wholly owned and joint-venture entry modes, have not included licensing agreements or exporting modes, and have examined mainly financial performance measures. Our study addresses each of these issues and attempts to extend the understanding of firm performance and entry mode use.

Our preliminary analysis revealed that entry mode type is less important in determining foreign subsidiary performance than the level of transaction costs, the cultural context and the institutional context of the target market. We found that firms' financial and non-financial performance is better when they enter markets characterized by low transaction costs, greater legal restrictions and high investment risk. We also found that smaller firms tend to report greater performance satisfaction in these new markets.

We can offer several explanations for our findings. First, markets with greater legal restrictions and high investment risks may offer greater potential returns to firms that are willing to invest in these markets. Government protection of a market may mean that excess profits can be achieved and that the select firms that enter this market may achieve greater penetration.

Second, markets characterized by lower transaction costs may also enable better performance since foreign firms do not incur excessive costs for monitoring the activities of target-market-based operations. When transaction costs are high, additional expenses may be incurred to safeguard organizational advantage, which in turn may lend to poorer performance. Finally, smaller firms may perform better because the new markets being entered are not as mature and may offer niche markets that smaller firms can service more profitably than can larger firms. Of course these are only potential explanations for our findings, and additional research is required to verify the accuracy of our projections.

LIMITATIONS, IMPLICATIONS AND CONCLUSIONS

Our study suffers from a number of limitations. First, since it involved only very large EU firms the findings may not be applicable to firms outside the EU or to smaller firms. Future research should include firms of various sizes and be carried out in other countries to increase the applicability of the findings.

Second, because our sample consists solely of large, highly international firms the results may be biased by the target countries being entered and may not reflect performance in the more developed, larger markets of the world. Future studies should include information on developed market entries and firm performance for comparative purposes.

In addition, we have only examined the most recent entry mode for each firm and have not distinguished between types of operation, that is, whether the firms were establishing a manufacturing operation, a marketing operation or a service operation. It may be that firms differ in their degree of satisfaction with performance in respect of of different types of entry. Future research using more precise data on type of entry may clarify these matters.

Another methodological limitation was the time taken to gather the data. While the most recent entry mode was studied to minimize the time between the establishment and completion of the survey instrument, in many cases the time spread was a year or more. Because of this our study may suffer from the recall and memory biases that are typical of retrospective reviews. Future studies would benefit from by examining entry mode decisions as they are made, thus reducing time-based biases.

Finally, a shortcoming of our performance measurement technique is that different firms may have different norms for measuring performance. A performance measure of 'four' given by one firm may be completely different from the 'four' allotted by another firm. Future studies could adjust for this potential difference by standardizing respondent scales (assigning numerical performance levels to each potential response).

If the type of entry mode a firm uses in a new foreign market is not important from a performance point of view, how should managers go about achieving a superior international performance? While the results of this study are limited, the implications for managing the internationalization process should still be considered.

First, in general our study indicates that superior firm performance is associated with higher-risk markets, markets characterized by greater legal restrictions on ownership and high investment risks. This suggests that firms need to seek out less developed markets for their products and services, markets that hold out the promise of better performance by firms that are willing to face the additional risks.

Finally, if mode selection is not an important determinant of firm performance, then researchers should refocus their efforts on determining how firms can achieve a better international performance, and ignore the question of entry mode selection. Our research indicates that certain institutional, cultural and transaction cost factors are important elements in strong international performance. Future research could focus on these factors in an attempt to develop a more parsimonious explanation of foreign market performance, and research in this area should provide managers with useful insights.

Note

The authors would like to thank Patricia Plugge and Alfonso Dozzi for their research assistance. They would also like to thank Bureau van Dijk for providing access to the AMADEUS database.

16 International Price Competition on the Internet: A Clinical Study of the On-Line Book Industry

Rajesh Chakrabarti and Barry Scholnick

'Are we charging too little for our books?'
Question to the CEO of Chapters Online at its 2000 AGM (Shaw, 2000).

INTRODUCTION

While the emergence of e-commerce and the Internet has received huge attention in the business press, to date it has received scant attention in the academic international business literature, although some international business textbooks (for example Wild *et al.*, 2001) have been published as 'e-business editions'. Clearly, research is required on the many areas in which e-business will affect the conduct of international business.

Such issues have started to generate significant interest at both the business and the policy level. For example, a recent study by the OECD (Coppel, 2000) examines in detail how e-commerce can affect or hinder international trade. The World Trade Organization has also begun to examine the impact of e-commerce on the regulation of international trade (www.wto.org). The consensus is that e-commerce will 'blur the notion of geographical boundaries' (Coppel, 2000: 18) and necessitate significant regulatory and policy changes. Before such policy changes can be implemented, however, it is important to understand more fully the nature of international e-commerce. This chapter attempts to address this issue.

Has the advent of on-line retailing of consumer products affected the nature of international competition for such products? With transborder shopping becoming a matter of point-and-click, the Internet potentially has the power to bring about fundamental changes in international competition. Companies now can attract consumers around the world without making any foreign direct investment. Protectionist policies aimed at preventing the entry of foreign sellers into domestic markets cannot prevent domestic consumers from purchasing foreign goods on-line. Does this mean that the national border is losing its relevance in the international market place for consumer goods? Have transaction costs, and particularly search costs, become outdated? What about the impact of shipping costs? Have the old relationships and puzzles of international business ceased to exist in the virtual world?

In order to investigate these questions we conducted a clinical study of the pricing behaviour of two competitors in two countries (Canada and the US), each a leader of e-commerce in its own country and both selling the same commodity (books). The companies were Amazon.com, a world leader in e-commerce from the US, and Chapters Online, the leading on-line vendor in Canada. Amazon.com is a one of the world's largest and most successful Internet retailers and its name has become almost synonymous with the idea of buying books on-line. Chapters Online is the leading on-line retailer in Canada across all product categories.

Using an innovative data collection methodology, we built a unique data set, drawing the data directly from the websites of the two companies. We constructed a time-series cross-section panel of the listed prices from each company for more than 5000 books, collected weekly from March to August 2000. All books have a unique ISBN (International Standard Book Number), so we were able to compare the prices of identical products offered on two different websites, in two different countries in two different currencies. We were also able to obtain data on the time taken to despatch book to a consumer so as well as on the relative popularity of each book in our sample, as measured by its 'sales rank'.

Using this data set and information provided by the companies on shipping costs, we were able to examine in detail the pricing strategies of these two competitors and how they relate to each other. These price comparisons have given us important insights into the nature of international competition, the differences that a national border makes in the new economy, and how the old rules of international competition are being rewritten in the virtual marketplace.

The book industry is a natural choice for this type of study because of the popularity and growing importance of book retailing on the Internet.[1] This chapter examines the extent to which the Internet has opened up the Canadian market to US competition. Our international price comparison provides a measure of the degree of cross-border integration between the two countries on the Internet.

The following section outlines on-line book retailing in Canada and examines the two companies in question. The third section connects this study to the various branches of literature that are germane to our research. Our data collection technique is detailed in the fourth section. The fifth section analyzes aspects of non-price competition between the two companies, and the sixth section provides a detailed analysis of price competition. The final section provides pointers for future research.

CHAPTERS ONLINE, AMAZON.COM AND BOOK RETAILING IN CANADA

Large US book retailing chains have always been perceived as a major threat to the Canadian book retailing industry. In 1996, the Canadian government blocked the planned entry into Canada of large American booksellers such as Borders and Barnes & Noble by invoking the 'cultural exemption' clause of the North American Free Trade Agreement. The emergence of on-line retailing, however, has the potential of completely altering the nature of international competition among retailers. On-line retailing facilitates cross-border shopping by significantly reducing transaction costs, and it is less affected by protectionist measures. This is particularly true of on-line book retailing, which is the largest sector in on-line retailing (US Internet Council, 2000).

Chapters Online, the on-line counterpart of the leading Canadian book chain Chapters Inc., dominates on-line book retailing in Canada. Founded in April 1999, it has a customer base of over half a million consumers (Chapters Online, 2000) and offers over 2.5 million titles (Shaw, 2000). It is also by far the largest on-line Canadian vendor across all product categories (Chapters Online, 2000). One of its major competitors is the American firm Amazon.com. Founded in 1994, Amazon is by far the world's largest on-line bookseller. It has more than 3.1 million titles on offer, which is approximately 15 times more than any conventional bookshop (Hof, 1998), and its revenues from book sales are far in excess of those of its nearest competitor, Barnes & Noble.com (various SEC filings [10-K] available at www.edgar-online.com).

Chapters Online may be the smaller and newer entrant into the on-line book market, Nevertheless, it is well able to compete with Amazon, particularly in the case of Canadian consumers. According to a recent Internet survey of Canadian on-line shoppers, 26 per cent bought from Chapters but only 5 per cent bought from Amazon (Pollara, 2000).

While the effects of international competition in on-line retailing may be the same on both sides of the border, given the smaller size of Chapters, its exclusively Canadian name recognition and the powerful brand name of Amazon on the Internet, it is more likely that Canadian shoppers will compare the prices of the two outlets than American consumers. This is indeed reflected in the fact that Amazon is among the most visited e-commerce sites in Canada while Chapters has attracted few visitors from the US (Mediametrix, 2000). Therefore, this study focuses on price competition in the Canadian market.

RELATIONSHIP TO PREVIOUS RESEARCH

On-line international competition among retailers is a recent phenomenon, as are most other e-commerce activities. This chapter is, to the best of our knowledge, the first to offer research in this particular field. However, the topic stands at the intersection of at least three broader topics, each of which has been widely researched in the past: international price and trade comparisons, particularly in the US–Canada context; the internationalization of retailing; and on-line retailing and e-commerce.

International price comparisons and purchasing power parity have a long and rich history in international economics research (Rogoff, 1996, provides an excellent survey of this literature). Isard (1977) finds that the 'law of one price', one of the most important totems of international economics, is 'flagrantly and systematically violated by empirical data'. More often than not transaction costs, which prevent international arbitrage, are at the root of these deviations from the textbook approach to international trade. Obstfeld and Rogoff (2000) consider that transaction costs may hold the key to several major puzzles of international economics. In this chapter we examine both of these issues – the validity of the law of one price and the nature of cross-border transaction costs – in the context of e-commerce.

US–Canada comparisons of price and trade volume have been widely under taken in international economics. McCallum (1995) has compared trade flows across the US–Canada border with those within Canada and found that the border acts as a significant barrier to trade, in spite of the North American Free Trade Agreement and the close cultural ties between the countries. Engel and Rogers (1996) have found higher cross-border variation than within-country variation in price levels for identical categories of goods, implying a significant border effect in the determination of prices. Helliwell (1998) corroborates these US–Canada 'border effect' findings using a much more extensive database of trade, prices, capital market linkages and labour flows. In particular, he concludes that 'there are effectively no short-run price-equalizing pressures across national borders, even at the shortest distances' (ibid.: 68). We shall investigate whether this US–Canada border effect pertains in the e-commerce environment.

The retailing sector has traditionally been one of the most non-traded of industries because of the nature of its activity. Selling to customers in foreign countries has been, as Salmon and Tordman (1989) point out, 'partial and marginal'. Before the advent of the Internet, all attempts at international expansion by a retailer necessarily involved either an alliance with a retailing chain abroad or heavy foreign direct investment. Nevertheless, Akehurst and Alexander (1995) find that there has been a rising trend in international retailing. Simpson and Thorpe (1995) and Williams (1992) provide surveys of recent literature in the area. The most important reasons for the limited internationalization of retailing are the large transaction costs, particularly search costs and shipping costs. This chapter examines the nature of cross-border retailing in the on-line environment, where search costs are significantly lower.

The arrival of the Internet and the increasing popularity of e-commerce has generated a rapidly growing body of literature on on-line retailing, particularly book retailing. Kotha (1998) and Kotha and Rindova (1999) have studied Amazon's business strategy and its reputation-building efforts. Bailey (1998) has compared conventional and Internet prices for books, CDs and software and found a greater range of prices for homogeneous goods on the Internet than in traditional stores. Brynjolfsson and Smith (2000) have studied the price of books and CDs at conventional stores and on the Internet, Bakos and Brynjolfsson (1999) have looked at optimal bundling strategies for selling information goods on the Internet, and Lynch and Ariely (2000) have focused on the on-line wine market to study the effect of reduced information search cost in on-line shopping for a differentiated product. Most of the research in this new area has concentrated on on-line retailing in a domestic setting – the present chapter is among the first to take this line of inquiry to the international context.

The question of whether e-business will enhance internationalization has been discussed by Hamill (1997), Hamill and Gregory (1997) and Quelch and Klein (1996). A key issue in this research is the distinction between business-to-business (B2B) and business-to-consumer (B2C). Most commentator consider that B2B is likely to have a greater impact on internationalization than B2C. However, if it is shown that B2C has become internationalized, then it is even more likely that B2B and the Internet generally will have a significant impact on internationalization.

DATA AND DATA COLLECTION

The data set used in this chapter consists of weekly observations on the price, availability and popularity of more than 5000 books from the two companies for a period of 21 weeks. This is probably one of the largest data sets used to study issues relating to on-line retailing in the academic literature. Previous e-commerce research (Bailey, 1998; Brynjolfsson and Smith, 2000) has used much smaller databases to study on-line price competition. Our larger data set, however, has come at a cost. Given the difficulty of obtaining corresponding data from bricks and mortar book shops for such a large sample and time period, we had to focus exclusively on on-line competition. All the data used here are freely available on the Internet. The data collection technique is outlined below.

One of the reasons for selecting books for our study of on-line competition was the fact that the specifications of the product (that is, the physical characteristics of books) are perfectly captured by what is known as the International Standard Book Number or ISBN of each book. Thus, in order to construct our dataset of books we began by building a sample of ISBNs obtained from an on-line book-selling site – even better.com[2] – a source independent of the two companies studied here. From the list of books available at this site we generated a large sample of ISBNs of books in different categories[3] using proportionate random sampling.

Next, using a web-based program designed specifically for this purpose, we recorded the price and promised despatch time[4] by both companies for every ISBN in our list. In the case of Amazon, we also recorded the 'sales rank' of the book, which serves as a proxy for the popularity of the book (the closer the sales rank to 1, the more popular the book). In the absence of data on quantities sold, the sales rank provides us with the best available measure of the popularity of a particular title. This process generated our weekly data. We collected the data every Monday night between 20 March 2000 and 7 August 2000. We then selected the 5125 books for which data was available for all variables over the entire 21-week period.

The prices at Amazon and Chapters could not be compared without converting them to a common currency. We therefore obtained the weekly Canadian dollar–US dollar exchange rate from OANDA (www.oanda.com) and used this to convert Amazon's prices to Canadian dollars. The descriptive statistics of the constructed data set in Canadian dollars are reported in Table 16.1. Speed of despatch is clearly an important competitive element in on-line retailing. Table 16.2 lists the various despatch times of Amazon and Chapters. Since the despatch time categories differ between the two companies, for better comparison we developed a common schedule, shown in the last column of Table 16.2.

ELEMENTS OF NON-PRICE COMPETITION IN THE ON-LINE BOOK INDUSTRY

Given the uniformity of product quality and ease of price comparison on the Internet, it is likely that price competition is even more crucial in the on-line environment than it is for traditional retailers. However, prices are not the only

Table 16.1 Descriptive statistics of panel data (Canadian dollars)

Variable	No. of books	No. of weeks	Mean	SD	Min.	Max.
Amazon price	5125	21	35.50	39.63	1.16	601.12
Chapters price	5125	21	35.36	37.84	1.00	583.50
Price differential						
(Chapters price – Amazon price)	5125	21	−0.14	10.00	−186.01	96.25
Exchange rate (C$/US$)	n/a	21	1.48	0.01	1.45	1.50

Table 16.2 Despatch/availability categories

Amazon	Chapters	Common schedule
24 hours	24 hours	24 hours
2–3 days	7 business days	2–3 days
1–2 weeks	3–5 weeks	1–2 weeks
4–6 weeks	6–10 weeks	3–5 weeks
Not released yet	Unconfirmed	4–6 weeks
Not published yet	Unavailable	6 weeks or more
Not available yet	Publication cancelled	Currently unavailable*
Back order	Out of stock indefinitely	
	Out of stock	
	Out of print	
	Not yet released	

* Includes the last four categories for Amazon and last seven categories for Chapters.

dimension of competition. On-line book retailers such as Amazon and Chapters presumably compete on several other criteria, as do their traditional counterparts. These are likely to include effective cost to the consumer, despatch time and book availability, brand name or reputation, and quality of service, including such diverse features as the attractiveness and functionality of the web-page design, the effectiveness of search engines, suggestions and feedback from fellow shoppers, and so on. This section compares the two companies in respect of the various non-price dimensions of competition.

Shipping Costs and Speed of Delivery

Important considerations when purchasing a book on-line are the shipping cost, which is not reflected in the quoted price, and speed of delivery. Our key finding in this respect is that purely in terms of shipping costs it is significantly cheaper and quicker to purchase a book from a retailer your own country than to make a purchase that requires transborder shipment. For example, for a Canadian living in an urban area, to purchase a book from Chapters in Canada the cheapest option is C$2.75 per shipment plus C$0.75 per book for despatch in 1–3 days. The same book from Amazon in the US would cost approximately C$6 (US$4) per shipment and C$2.92 (US$1.95) per book for despatch in 2–4 weeks (assuming that US$1 = C$1.5). Thus, with Amazon the consumer would pay 2.5 times more for shipping costs (roughly a differential of C$5.50) for a single book and wait 1.5 to 3.5 weeks longer for delivery. In order to receive the book in roughly the same time as from Chapters the consumer would have to pay over C$50.00 to buy it from Amazon. In order to keep these figures in perspective, we should note that the average book price for our entire sample is less than C$36.00 (Table 16.1). Thus, the seemingly innocuous shipping charges drive a sizable wedge between the book prices that the two vendors can charge to make the ultimate cost to the consumer comparable. There is absolutely no arrangement whereby Amazon can beat Chapters at delivering the book to the urban Canadian buyer. Thus, for such a buyer, Chapters is always the fastest and cheapest source of books in terms of shipping only. Of course the exact shipping cost differential will depend on how many books we ordered at a time.[5]

In addition to this shipping cost difference, there are often other fees and taxes associated with buying books from the US. These additional costs serve to increase the price that the domestic seller can charge, so in terms of the all inclusive final cost to the Canadian buyer, Chapters enjoys 'protection' from its foreign competitor simply because of the shipping cost differentials. This may be thought of as a type of 'rent' that Chapters could possibly extract – a rent that arises from market imperfection in the form of shipping cost differentials. In other words it allows opportunity for Chapters to charge a higher price than Amazon – a 'Chapters premium' – while still keeping the final cost of the book lower for the Canadian buyer. The upper limit of this premium is, of course, determined by the shipping cost differential. How much of this potential price premium Chapters actually exploits is an important part of our study.

Product Availability

Another important element of competition in any retailing business is product availability, and for any distance delivery retailer the question of despatch time is also of crucial importance. Table 16.2 lists the despatch availability categories at each of the two websites, and Figure 16.1 plots the books in the sample against these categories. The median delivery time for each of the 5125 books over the 21-week period has been used to construct this figure. Note firstly that these despatch times were those promised by the companies on their websites, and both warned that the promised times could change without notice. Secondly, the time taken for a book to reach a customer after placing an order is the sum of the despatch time and the shipping time.

When examining Figure 16.1 it is important to remember that our sample consists of books for which we could find a price quotation for each of the 21 weeks at both websites. Consequently, our statistics do not reflect those which would be obtained from a random sample of all titles in print. It is fair to assume that with such a sample the proportion of books 'currently unavailable' would be significantly higher at both companies. Figure 16.1 shows that the largest proportion of books in our sample were available within 24 hours at both Amazon and Chapters – over 45 per cent for Amazon and more than 53 per cent for Chapters. However, while Chapters dominated in the 'within a day' segment, Amazon had a much larger proportion available for despatch in less than a week. The proportion of books currently unavailable at Amazon (1.9 per cent) was about half of that at Chapters (3.7 per cent).

Other Elements of Competition

While price and availability are probably the two most important aspects of competition in on-line retailing, there are several other factors on which firms compete, many of which are based on consumer behaviour. Branding and reputation are clearly of great importance in ensuring the success of any business-to-consumer firm. Kotha and Rindova (1999) provide a detailed the account of brand development strategy used by Amazon. In addition, the significant attention Amazon has received from the press owing to its pioneering role in the rise of e-commerce has helped it to become one of the most familiar brand names among on-line consumers. On the other hand, Chapters, though a new company, may have derived some benefit from having a brick-and-mortar presence in most major Canadian cities. In terms of web page characteristics, a recent study has ranked both Chapters and Amazon among the top five e-commerce websites (Devlin, 2000). The two companies are also comparable in respect of the extra

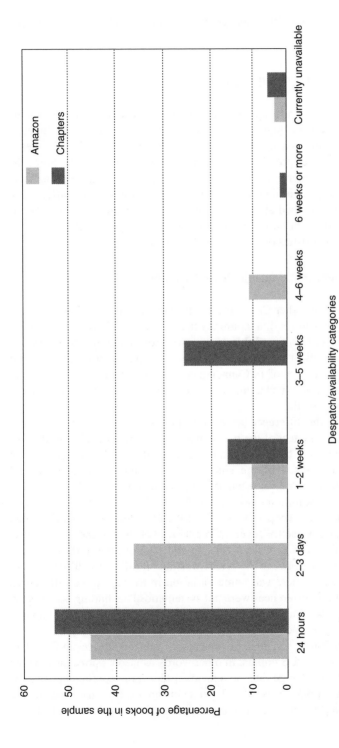

Figure 16.1 Percentage of books in each despatch/availability category (median over 21 weeks)

services they provide to on-line shoppers in terms of e-mail alerts, book reviews and so on.

ANALYSIS OF PRICE COMPETITION

As noted in the section on shipping costs, Chapters enjoys a natural advantage over Amazon in the Canadian market in terms of shipping costs. If Chapters were to compete with Amazon only on a 'total cost to consumer' basis, then it would be able to levy a 'premium' over Amazon on the listed price. Since the total cost to the consumer is the sum of the listed price and the shipping cost, this premium would be limited to the extent of the shipping cost differential. Using the dataset described above, this section explores and analyses various aspects of price competition between Amazon and Chapters, particularly the existence and characteristics of this potential price premium.

Does Chapters Levy the Available Price Premium?

In order to examine whether Chapters actually take advantage of the potential price premium, this sub-section examines the relationship between the prices charged by the two companies. Table 16.1 above showed that the mean price of all 5125 books over all 21 weeks at Amazon was C$35.50, while at Chapters it was C$35.36 – a difference of 14 Canadian cents or less than half of 1 per cent. Thus, Chapters was actually charging less than Amazon on average, though the difference was very small.

Figure 16.2 plots the difference between the prices (Chapters minus Amazon) and the t-statistic of the test of the null hypothesis of price equality in the two stores for each week. The critical values for rejecting the null hypothesis are also shown. During the period of the study the maximum value of Chapters' premium (Chapters price minus Amazon price, averaged over 5125 books) was 45 cents and the minimum was minus $1.10. The Chapters price was significantly higher than Amazon's for five of the 21 weeks, while Amazon had a significantly higher price for seven weeks. However, five of the seven weeks occurred in a straight run between weeks 15 and 19. For nine of the 21 weeks studied, the difference between the prices was not significantly different from zero. Therefore, while there was some variation in average price differences between weeks, these differences were not systematic. This finding is of importance because it shows that Chapters was not appropriating the rent available to it from the shipping cost advantage discussed above.

It appears from Figure 16.2 that movements in Amazon's prices in Canadian dollars reflected those in US dollars. In other words Amazon's price movements were dominated by exchange rate movements. Indeed, the coefficient of variation for Amazon's prices was, at 1.2 per cent, about 1.5 times that in the exchange rate (0.8 per cent) and three times that of Chapters (0.4 per cent). The

215

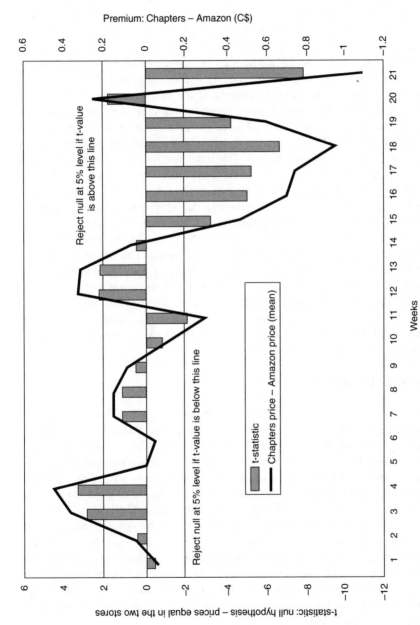

Figure 16.2 Chapters' premium: value and statistical significance by week (average for 5125 books each week)

role that exchange rate variations play in determining the price premium can be examined by comparing the actual exchange rate movements with movements in the 'implied exchange rate'. The implied exchange rate is defined as the ratio of average book prices over one week, measured in their original currencies. Thus, the average book price at Chapters in Canadian dollars divided by that at Amazon in US dollars gives us an implied exchange rate for the two currencies. A comparison between actual and implied exchange rates is presented in Figure 16.3. If the law of one price held perfectly during the period of the study, the two lines in Figure 16.3 would coincide. If the two rates were different but moved in step, this would imply constant price premium when measured in the same currency. As is evident from Figure 16.3, there was no such constancy in the price premium. However, in the first half of the study period the two rates moved in the same general direction. This indicates that the relative book prices were responding to exchange rate movements. However, after week 15 the two rates diverged significantly, indicating a change in relative prices in the opposite direction from the much smaller exchange rate movement. Almost the entire movement during this period was caused by changes in book prices at Amazon.

Figure 16.4 provides a different view of the price data by considering the median price of each individual book over 21 weeks. The Chapters price for each of the 5125 books is plotted against the Amazon price. The scatter plot data clusters around the (dotted) 45° line, indicating that there was a close relationship between Amazon's and Chapters' price for each of the books. This is confirmed by an OLS regression of the Amazon prices against the Chapters prices (the results are reported in Figure 16.4), which produced an estimated coefficient of 0.926 and an R^2 of 0.94.

Possible Explanations

This section provides possible explanations for the finding that even though Amazon's shipping costs were significant, the quoted prices for Amazon and Chapters were similar. One possible explanation of this lies in consumer behaviour. Morwitz *et al.* (1998) provide experimental evidence that consumers tend to underestimate the total price when the shipping cost is presented separately from the price of the product. According to their study the majority of decision makers make heuristic rather than precise mathematical calculations to arrive at the all-inclusive final cost. In such situations consumers typically 'anchor' their perception on the first piece of information (the price) and adjust later, generally insufficiently, for new information (the shipping cost). Hence, it is possible that on-line shoppers fail to factor in the shipping cost properly in their mental calculations. This is particularly likely given that the websites of most on-line retailers prominently display the price of the product early in buying process and the shipping cost usually comes up much later.

According to this explanation, if Chapters was to raise its book prices to incorporate most of the shipping cost advantage, it could lose customers to

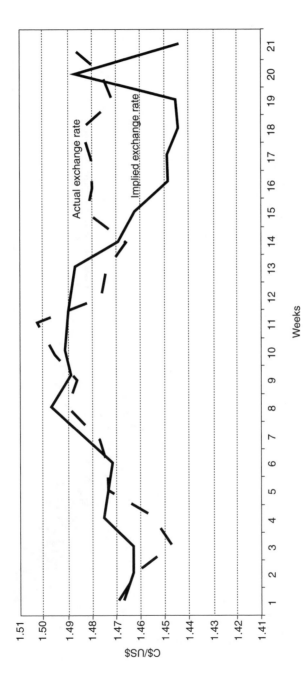

Figure 16.3   Actual exchange rate and implied exchange rates (ratio of average book prices in own currency: Chapters/Amazon)

218

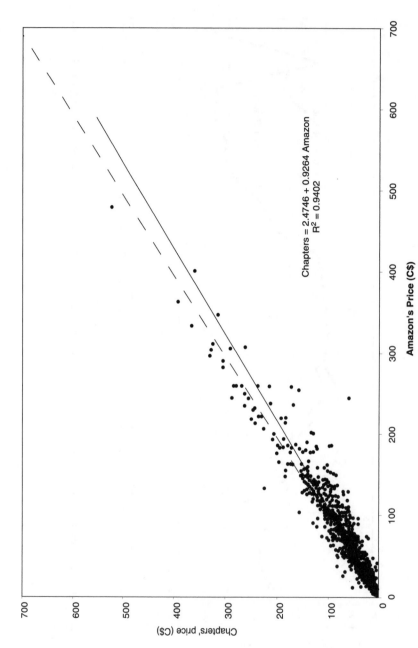

Chapters = 2.4746 + 0.9264 Amazon
$R^2 = 0.9402$

Amazon's Price (C$)

Chapters' price (C$)

Figure 16.4 Scatter plot of Amazon's and Chapters' prices for 5125 Books (C$, average prices over 21 weeks)

Amazon early in the selection process unless it could somehow convince them of the shipping cost advantage early on. It is important to note that for the above explanation to work, when setting its prices Chapters would have to believe that consumers behave in the way described by Morwitz *et al.* (1998). Clearly, the subject of on-line consumer behaviour requires further research before definite conclusions can be reached on this explanation.

Another possible explanation of rent foregone is that Chapters, being a comparatively late entrant into the business, may be keeping its prices low in order to gain a larger market share. If this hypothesis is correct, we would expect Chapters' prices to rise when their market share stabilizes at a higher level. Other strategic considerations or competition with bricks-and-mortar bookshops in Canada could also be behind this phenomenon.

CONCLUSIONS AND FUTURE RESEARCH

While e-commerce has the potential to change the dynamics of international business by significantly reducing cross-border transaction costs, the impact of the Internet on international business remains relatively unexplored. In order to evaluate the effects of international borders on the Internet this chapter has focused on two on-line booksellers selling identical products in Canada and the US. We constructed an innovative database of over 5000 price observations and other retailing characteristics of the two companies over 21 weeks using only data that was publicly available on the web. We then used this data set to analyze the nature and dynamics of on-line price competition across borders.

We found that cross-border shipping costs afforded significant protection to the Canadian on-line bookseller. However, we also found that the average price at Chapters was remarkably close to that at Amazon, measured in Canadian dollars. In other words, it appears that Chapters was not fully appropriating the rent available to it.

Probing further into the issue of the 'Chapters premium', we found a significant variation in the price differential between the two stores over time and across different categories of books. Chapters charged more for books that both companies could despatch quickly, for the more popular books and for cheaper books. Nevertheless, in no segment did Chapters fully appropriate its shipping cost advantage. Possible reasons for this are that on-line consumers failed to account properly for shipping costs, or that Chapters engaged in aggressive price competition as an entry strategy.

This chapter is among the first to study on-line competition in the international business context. It also contributes to the large literature on the law of one price and the literature on the effects of the US–Canada border by studying these issues in the context of the Internet. Furthermore, the approach to data collection used here is readily applicable to research on other areas of e-commerce as well as traditional commerce. The vast amount of real-time and constantly changing data freely available on the Internet may facilitate answers to several important research questions.

In terms of future research, several areas of international business are being transformed by the Internet. While this chapter has focused specifically on the business-to-consumer (B2C) sector of e-commerce, the current trend indicates that the present dominance of the business-to-business (B2B) sector is likely to continue. The international element is probably even more important in the B2B sector than in the B2C sector, because of the relative ease with which B2B goods can cross international boundaries compared with B2C ones. However, the results of this chapter, showing the close relationship between US and Canadian B2C prices, indicates that B2B markets may be even more integrated across international borders. These topics will remain important areas for international business research.

Notes

1. A Boston Consulting Group report predicts that on-line book sales will account for as much as 20–30 per cent of all book sales by 2004 (Green, 1999).
2. The original address of this site was www.evenbetter.com. However, during our study it was acquired by a more general comparison shopping site, DealTime.com (www.dealtime.com).
3. These categories are provided by the site itself.
4. The time it takes the company to despatch the book – the time it takes for the item to reach the customer after despatch is not included in this.
5. As is apparent from Table 16.1, Amazon enjoys a similar but smaller advantage over Chapters in selling to US consumers.

17 New Strategic Group Concepts in the Transition to a Changing Global Environment: A Dynamic Analysis of Strategic Group Behaviour in the World-Wide Spirits Industry

Benedikt Schwittay and Chris Carr

INTRODUCTION

'Strategic groups' (SGs) have been a popular concept in strategic management since the early 1970s. However, no researchers have yet looked at their relationship or interplay with the globalizing business environment. Many researchers, working primarily from a strategic management perspective, are only marginally aware that their original concepts need to be reshaped in light of globalization. Others, concerned primarily with international business, are often oblivious of the power and implications of the techniques that have been developed by strategists. Is this yet another fad, and not even a particularly popular or successful one at that? Surprisingly, as we shall show, it is only by combining these two perspectives that we can develop techniques that are both interesting and reasonably robust.

The concept of SGs was not originally developed to serve the purpose of strategists or of those concerned with international business. Industrial economists were simply concerned to extend their understanding of which sectors were more or less profitable. Bain's (1956) work on entry barriers took this work forward as it provided key determinants of what might allow one sector to become more profitable than another (for any given state of market concentration). Hunt's (1972) study of the US domestic appliance sector used similar entry barrier ideas to prise open the 'black box'. A sector's behaviour and profitability could not be fully understood, Hunt recognized, without taking into account the various strategies of the major players in that sector. Common entry barriers protected certain groups of companies within a sector, discouraging strategic imitation. Hence, these groups acted instinctively and were potentially more profitable than others. Porter (1980) adapted the same analytical tool to the purpose of competitive analysis, eliciting implications for industry analysis and prising out implications for companies' individual strategies. Hunt's (1972) sector was purely domestic, while Porter also illustrated or 'mapped' internationally orientated industries, using degree of international orientation as a key variable to distinguish particular strategic groups. The tool's significance was thus extended to international strategies.

The initial excitement soon faded into somewhat inconclusive, esoteric debates among strategists whose research sites were often domestic. SGs were criticized as purely descriptive, almost atheoretical categorizations; the suggested measures often proved impractical or subjective; economics-based techniques were considered out of touch with managers' actual perceptions and approaches; and study after study proved relatively inconclusive. More recently, however, SG studies have, gradually become more international, subtler and, potentially more useful concepts have emerged. This chapter presents the results of a new approach that draws on this academic heritage but is applied more globally than has so far been the case. The interrelationship between globalization and SGs is analyzed carefully. We apply our new framework to one particular industry – the spirits industry, which has recently entered into global competition. Suggestions are made about a more dynamic SG concept for global industries than those used to date by strategy academics. With regard to the inter relationship between SGs and globalization, the four major factors/issues to be looked at are country of origin, instability of membership within SGs, rivalry/strategy imitation and performance.

DEFINITIONS, LITERATURE REVIEW AND THEORY BUILDING

Hunt (1972) analyzed the US domestic appliance industry between 1960 and 1970 and found that even though concentration within the industry was high the industry's overall profitability was low. This stands in sharp contrast to Bain's (1956) hypothesis that barriers to entry and degree of concentration (market structure) are directly related to profitability (industry performance). Hence, the higher the barriers to entry and the fewer the market players, the higher the rate of profitability. This hypothesis is based on the assumption that all firms in a given industry are the same or symmetrical, with the exception of the firms' individual size. Hunt (1972) challenges the assumption that firms are generally similar in a given market and argues that there are industries where incumbent firms face different basic conditions. Hunt mentions three types of difference or asymmetry:

- *Economic asymmetry*: differences in cost structures, product differentiation and vertical integration.
- *Organizational asymmetry*: differences in formal organization, control systems and management rewards.
- *Discretionary asymmetry*: managers have different perceptions about suitable market strategies (for example some prefer lower and safer growth to higher but riskier growth, or they prefer increased market share to an increase in the profitability).

Hunt uses his SG model to apply Bain's (1956) market structure–performance relationship to asymmetrical industries. He defines SGs as a number of 'group(s) of firms within the industry that are highly symmetric' (Hunt, 1972: 81). Caves and Porter (1997: 251) extend the definition of strategic groups and describe them as 'firms within a group [that] resemble one another closely and recognise their mutual dependence most sensitively'. Since Hunt (1972) conducted his study of the US white goods industry, SG researchers have mainly chosen regional or national markets as their geographical sample frames. The focus on these markets might have been appropriate for the majority of industries during the 1960s and 1970s, but because of the increasing globalization of markets, since the 1980s, most of the researched industries have undergone dramatic structural change. For example, Hunt's sample industry, the US white goods industry, is no longer the exclusive realm of US firms – a powerful European competitor, Electrolux, has since entered the US market. At the same time the US firms Whirlpool and Maytag have entered foreign markets.

Because of the increasing internationalization of industries, Thomas and Venkatraman (1988: 550) consider that 'future research should evaluate the appropriateness of defining the sample frame to include multiple nations within one study'. Such a direction would lead to the isolation of strategic differences across different countries as well as shedding light on multi-point competition along a global scale'. Bogner (1991) makes a similar suggestion in respect of the US pharmaceutical industry. Although Bogner does concentrate on a national market (the US), because of their international importance and weight he includes foreign competitors with a relatively marginal and insignificant US market share. This stands in contrast to studies such as Cool and Schendel's (1987) analysis of the same industry at roughly the same time, which excludes non-US competitors because of problems with data access. Mascarenhas and Aaker (1989) were the first researchers to apply the SG model to an international industry: international offshore drilling during the period 1966–84. As the term 'offshore drilling' implies, it is impossible to limit such studies to national boundaries. However, it is not clear from their article whether Mascarenhas and Aaker concentrate just on US players in this industry or whether they include all US and non-US players in their analysis. As a result it is unclear whether their work is a truly 'global' study that includes a multitude of geographical markets as well as the most important market players – be these US or non-US companies.

Duysters and Hagedorn's (1995) study of three international high-tech industries was one of the first multinational SG studies to deal with 'international markets in order to address multi-point competition at a global scale'. However, their company sample was based on 'leading [US, European and Japanese] companies' (ibid.: 364), and no details are provided on the significance of the companies in terms of size or market share, or on the concentration rates of the industries in question. Second, the time frame differed between sample industry and sample industry, 'depending on the availability of consistent statistical material' (ibid.). Consequently, it is questionable whether theirs is a truly global SG study based on robust empirical data.

The study presented in this chapter offers a new definition of SG and applies the SG model to a global industry, the spirits industry. It proposes that SGs exist in global industries in the statistical, quantitative and qualitative sense, although the 'old' SG model has to be adapted to fit the new and turbulent global business environment. Hunt's (1972) definition of SG is updated by extending his three types of company difference (economic, organizational and discretionary asymmetries) to include a fourth one: geographical differences/asymmetries, that is, companies' geographical orientation or geographical spread of sales (whether this is of a national, international or global character). Hence:

- *Proposition 1:* SGs differ from each other not only because of economic, organizational and/or discretionary asymmetries but also because of geographical asymmetries. This means that SGs are not only a national phenomenon on but also exist at the global level.

COUNTRY OF ORIGIN

As a result of the geographically extended and thus more international character of markets and companies the question arises of whether any significant relationship exists between SG membership and country of origin (Duysters and Hagedorn, 1995; Bogner *et al.*, 1996). Peteraf and Shanley (1997) describe, in their concept of 'SG identity', how SG formation and behaviour is strongly influenced by economic, historical and institutional forces. They suggest that because companies of the same country of origin are subject to more of the same economic, historical and institutional forces than companies from different countries, country of origin has a significant effect on the formation of SGs in the national and global context. In this chapter we suggest that companies are strongly influenced by and interested in the strategy choice of national rather than international competitors because of their shared knowledge of each other. In addition, for the first time a direct link between SG membership and country of origin is not only suggested but also empirically tested.

- *Proposition 2:* Companies with the same country of origin are more likely to design similar strategies or imitate each other's strategies than companies with different countries of origin. Consequently, membership of an SG tends to be dominated by companies from one particular country. This means that there is a direct correlation between SG membership and companies' country of origin.

TURBULENCE/INSTABILITY

Hunt's (1972) study of the US white goods industry was conducted over a period of ten years. He took a static approach and treated the whole ten-year period as one point in time. Thus, he assumed that the companies were pursuing the same strategies over time, that SG membership remained the same and that the character of the entire industry was essentially stable over time. Hatten *et al.* (1977) were the first to point out the importance of time and the influence that time might have on changes to competitive strategies. In their study of the US brewing industry they split the overall time period of the study into shorter periods. This they argue, was made necessary by major changes in their sample's strategic dimensions (the manufacturing, financial and marketing strategies of the sample firms) between the time periods. They question Hunt's (1972) assumption that SGs are, *per se*, a stable phenomenon, although they do not elaborate on the stability/instability of SGs in detail.

Cool and Schendel (1987), Fiegenbaum *et al.* (1987) and Fiegenbaum and Thomas (1993a, 1993b) have built on Hatten *et al.*'s (1977) instability thesis and tried to develop a methodology to identify different periods of SG stability by statistical means. Separately they established the construct of strategic stable time periods (SSTPs). Fiegenbaum *et al.* (1987: 140) define these as periods in which '1) the variances and co-variances of the strategic variables remain relatively unchanged; and/or 2) the average (mean) behaviour of the firms remains relatively unchanged; and/or 3) the underlying competitive strategic variables are more or less the same'. If different SSTPs can be identified, this means that a change in group formation has taken place, either in the total number of SGs or in the number of members of the various groups. Cool and Schendel (1987), Fiegenbaum *et al.* (1987) and Fiegenbaum and Thomas (1993a) respectively identify four SSTPs in the drugs industry during a 20-year period and nine SSTPs in the insurance industry during a 15-year period. Fiegenbaum *et al.* (1987) suggest that the shorter the SSTPs within an industry the more turbulent the character or environment of that industry. They admit that the methodology of identifying SSTPs is merely statistical/quantitative and that it cannot identify factors that cause the evolution of SSTPs. Cool and Schendel (1987) and Fiegenbaum *et al.* (1987) concentrate on the development of a statistical means of breaking up longitudinal studies into 'appropriate' time periods rather than hypothesizing about the major factors that necessitate this break-up.

In this chapter we present a new model that is both quantitative/statistical and qualitative in character: the 'four phases' framework (Table 17.1). This framework, which is based on Vernon's (1966) 'international product life cycle', addresses the character of an industry and its players in terms of concentration and maturity. The regional orientation of companies and the industry's level of

Table 17.1　The 'four-phases' framework

	First phase	*Second phase*	*Third phase*	*Fourth phase*
Concentration Geography	Prenational consolidation	National concentration	Preglobal consolidation	Global concentration
Competition	Atomistic	Concentrated	Atomistic	Concentrated
Strategic orientation	Regional	National	International/ transnational	Global

competitiveness are included as additional factors. The obvious advantage of the 'four phases' framework compared with Cool and Schendel's (1987) and Fiegenbaum *et al.*'s (1987) SSTPs is that it does not treat these time periods (the potential periods of instability) in a purely descriptive way but includes both qualitative and quantitative explanations of the causes of instability. This might be of lesser importance for national, fragmented industries, but the more that industries become concentrated and the more they internationalize the greater the chance that combined company and industry statistics will produce coincidental, inconclusive results. Fiegenbaum *et al.*'s identification of nine SSTPs in the insurance industry during 15-years period is a good example of this. As the average SSTP lasts less than two years, is the break-up into SSTPs of any help to the analysis of the industry, or does it indirectly put the whole strategic group concept into question (Tang and Thomas, 1992)?

A proposed characteristic included in the 'four phases' framework is a high degree of instability and changes in SG membership between the four phases. With a changing business environment and the emergence of new strategies by competitor companies, companies have to reexamine and redesign their own strategies. This often results in the break-up of old SGs and the formation of new ones. Hence:

- *Proposition 3:* changing business environments (that is, the characteristics of industries in terms of concentration, competition and companies' geographical orientation) lead to the break-up of old and the formation of new SG formations.

STRATEGIC GROUP INTERACTION

Past SG research has mainly looked at the interaction between companies in the same or different SGs in terms of rivalry that is by speculating whether rivalry between members of the same SG is greater or lesser than that between members of different SGs. Both sides have put forward sound theoretical arguments supported by empirical evidence, thus the overall results have been inconclusive (Caves and Porter, 1997; Porter, 1980; Hatten and Hatten, 1987; Cool and Dierickx, 1993; Peteraf, 1993) and this has caused doubts about 'rivalry' being an appropriate factor to analyze in respect of SG interaction. One factor that has so far not been explicitly discussed (by Schwittay *et al.*, 1999) is 'strategy imitation'. Strategy imitation is to do with how closely SG co-members know and watch each other in order, according to Schwittay *et al.*, to predict strategic moves. It stands above friendly or hostile rivalry in the way that companies imitate each other's strategy for friendly, collusive or hostile competitive reasons. In a changing business environment, strategy imitation is becoming an increasingly important factor in SG interaction because it can serve as a defensive or offensive trigger for the national, international or global consolidation of an industry. Hence:

- *Proposition 4:* strategy imitation is the most important factor in and trigger of SG interaction in an industrial environment where there is national, international or global consolidation. Whether strategy imitation within an SG is based on friendly/cooperative or hostile relations is of less importance.

PERFORMANCE DIFFERENCES BETWEEN SGs IN GLOBAL MARKETS

As already mentioned, it was the differences between the financial performance of different groups of US white goods companies that prompted Hunt (1972) to establish the concept of SGs. Since then several SG researchers have found a statistically significant correlation between SG membership and financial performance (that is, differences in terms of financial performance within a SG are statistically insignificant compared with the statistically significant differences between members of different SGs). However, most of the research efforts in this area have failed to produce conclusive results. Either difference have been revealed for some performance variables but not all of them (Cool and Dierickx, 1993), or the financial performance–SG linkage can only be applied to certain time periods (Cool and Schendel, 1987; Fiegenbaum *et al.*, 1987). Other studies have found no statistically significant differences at all (Lewis and Thomas, 1990; Fiegenbaum and Thomas, 1993a). Consequently, we still await clear confirmation of the SG–performance linkage. So what are the performance results for SGs at the global level? Do SGs pursuing a global strategy outperform SGs pursuing an international or national strategy, or *vice versa*?

- *Proposition 5:* SG membership is correlated with financial performance at a statistically significant level. This means that membership of one SG can lead to a significantly higher performance level compared with membership of another SG.

METHODOLOGY

To test and apply the altered and extended SGs concept, a single-industry, longitudinal analysis of the spirits industry was conducted during the period 1982–1995. The spirits industry was chosen because it was changing from a multidomestic to a global industry during the period in question. Thus, it could be described as a evolving industry with highly dynamic players. Another reason for choosing the spirits industry was that one of the authors had extensive knowledge of the industry. As several researchers have pointed out, intimate industry knowledge enables relevant information to be found more quickly and easily (McGee and Thomas, 1986; Barney and Hoskisson, 1990; Smith *et al.*, 1997). It also facilitates the arranging of interviews with key decision makers in the sample companies, and allows the researcher to feel more confident about identifying management issues that are of interest both to the academic and to the practitioner. The author in question had worked for more than four years in the wine and spirits industry as brand and sales manager in the three countries chosen for the study – the UK, Japan and Germany – and was able to use his contacts to obtain industry data as well as to arrange interviews with senior executives of the world's leading spirits companies.

The choice of the three national sample markets was influenced by relative market size,[1] the importance of the companies operating in these markets and the availability of industry data. The companies chosen for our three-country strategic group study were spirits companies with a sales volume of at least £100 million in 1995.[2] In addition, each of the intra-country groups of companies accounted for more than 70 per cent (volume and value) of their total national spirits markets, and in combination the companies held a 71.3 per cent share of the global market. Companies with sales of £100 million or more account for a significant proportion of the UK, US and German spirits industry and thus our sample provides a valid picture of the whole industry. The field research consisted of 47 semi-structured interviews with representatives of the sample companies and their trade organizations at both the corporate and the subsidiary level. The statistical research involved the build-up of a global database, and included information on the most relevant strategy and performance variables of the spirits industry and its industry players. The concentration ratio of the worldwide spirits market was used to classify the industry into global and pre-global time periods, and six strategy variables were used to conduct a hierarchical cluster analysis (at a 95 per cent confidence level) of the three national markets during the pre-global and global time periods.

EMPIRICAL FINDINGS

The SG concept was applied to domestic players in the UK, US and German spirits industries during the pre-global period 1982–86 (when according to the 'four phases' model the concentration level of the world's biggest four companies was below 40 per cent), and to players in the combined UK, US and German markets during the global period 1987–95 (when according to the 'four phases' model the concentration level of the world's biggest four companies was above 40 per cent). The cluster analysis of the sample companies identified five SGs in the UK, four in the US and two in Germany during the pre-global period, and three SGs in the global spirits market during the global period.

In the UK, there were 10 companies that fulfilled the criterion of at least £100 million in total sales. The ten companies were divided into five SGs with significant differences between them in terms of product breadth and international sales (Figure 17.1). Among the five SGs, three single-member groups (SG 3, SG 4 and SG 5) were closer to each other in terms of 'strategic space' (McGee and Segal-Horn, 1990) than the multimember groups. (SG 1 and SG 3). In the German spirits market nine companies fulfilled the sales criterion. These

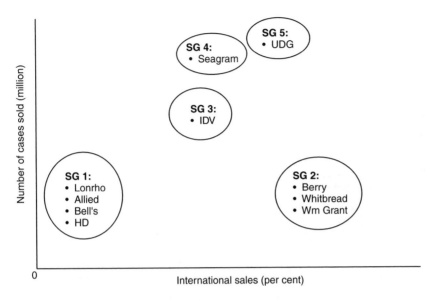

Figure 17.1   Hierarchical cluster analysis of the UK spirits market, 1982–86

were divided into just two SGs (Figure 17.2). Thus, with the exception of one single-member SG (SG 2), the companies were uniform in terms of product breadth and international sales. The strategic space between the multi-member group (SG1) and the single-member group (SG 2) was significant. In the US, 10 companies fulfilled the sales criterion. These were divided into four multi-member SGs with significant differences between them in terms of product breadth and international sales (Figure 17.3) but not in terms of strategic space. In the global spirits market 19 US, UK and German companies fulfilled the sales criterion. These were divided into three multi-member SGs, and again there were significant differences between then in respect of product breadth and international sales (Figure 17.4) but not in respect of strategic space.

This has three important implications. First, the cluster analysis confirmed the fundamental proposition that SGs do exist at the global level in the spirits industry – this was the first application and confirmation of its kind. Second, the total number of SGs and membership of SGs between the two time phases changed, probably reflecting the instability of SG membership during the globalization process. All but two SGs joined new SG constellations (that is, parted company with their previous SG co-members) during the transition from the preglobal to the global period. The membership pattern of SGs during the global period reveals a clear link between SG membership and country of origin, thus confirming proposition 2. Spirits companies chose their strategies (and thus their SGs) by joining or forming groups with competitors they had known for a considerable time, that is, competitor companies from their home markets.

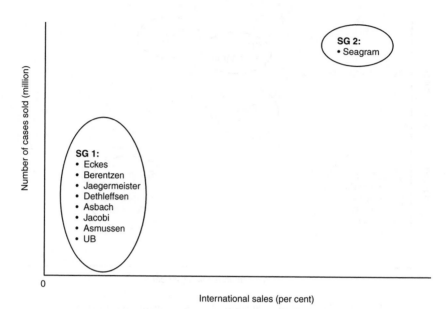

Figure 17.2   Hierarchical cluster analysis of the German spirits market, 1982–86

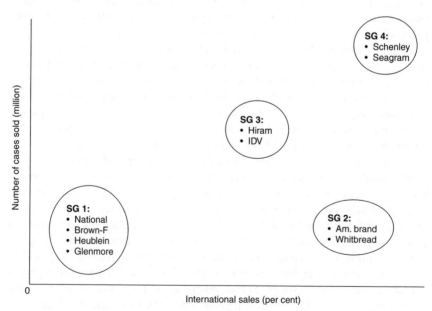

Figure 17.3   Hierarchical cluster analysis of the US spirits market, 1982–86

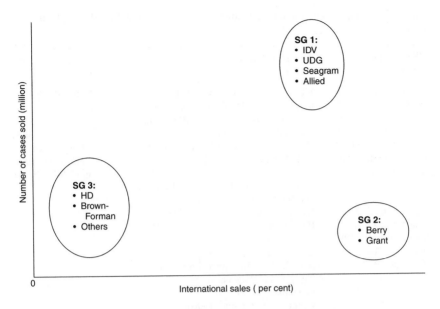

Figure 17.4 Hierarchical cluster analysis of the global spirits market, 1987–95

Consequently, in the global spirits market the co-members of an SG tended to have the same country of origin. Companies from one particular country of origin dominated two of the three SGs in the global market. Third, there was little change in terms of friendly or hostile relations between members of the same SG and members of different SGs Even though the majority of executives (76.7 per cent) described their relations with members of other SGs as somewhat friendlier, their relation with members of the same SG were predominantly seen as neutral (78.7 per cent). In contrast to this, 91.5 per cent of senior executives stated that strategy imitation had become commonplaces in the spirits industry. This confirms the proposition that strategy imitation plays a highly important role in strategic group interaction – until now this factor has been vastly underrated.

The globalization of the spirits industry was triggered by strategic moves and countermoves by United Distillers Guinness (UDG) and International Distillers and Vintners (IDV) as a result of declining profits and the launch of a global strategy by UDG's visionary chairman Ernest Saunders. IDV imitated UDG's strategy and both started to acquire their US distribution partners and other sizable foreign spirits companies in order to build up a global distribution network and a full product portfolio. The strategies moves and global strategies of UDG and IDV were soon taken up by the UK company Allied and the US–Canadian company Seagram. During the build-up of their global distribution networks and product portfolios between 1987 and the early 1990s the four companies followed each other from commitment to commitment to acquire

Table 17.2   Major international acquisitions/joint ventures by UDG, IDV and Allied, 1986–95

US/Canadian market	European/Far Eastern market	Latin American market
UDG Schenley (US 1986) IDV: Heublein (US, 1987), Almaden (US, 1987), La Salle (US, 1989) Allied: Hiram (US, 1987)	UDG alliance with LVMH (France 1986) and Caldbeck-Dodwell (Hong Kong, 1987), JVs with Jardines (Japan, 1987) and Inchcape (Hong Kong, 1987) IDV: Far East JV with Martell (1987) and JV with Cinzano (Italy, 1987)	UDG: Pampero (1991) IDV: JV in Colombia (1994) Allied: JV in Venezuela (1993) and Chile (1993)
UDG: Schenley (Canada, 1990), Glenmore (US, 1991) Allied: Corby (Canada, 1989)	Allied: JVs with IDV (Australia 1987) and Suntory (Japan, 1988) UDG: Asbach (Germany, 1991) IDV: Metaxa (Greece, 1989) AED (Spain, 1990) Emmet: (Ireland, 1991) Allied: JVs with Spirit (Italy, 1989), Costa Pina (Portugal, 1989), in Thailand (1990) and with Genka (Greece, 1990) IDV: Cinzano (Italy, 1992), JVs with Ekpac (Hong Kong, 1992), Young (Korea, 1992), Gonzalez (Spain, 1992), Buton (Italy, 1993) and Picon (France, 1995) Allied: JV in India (1993), with PJBG (France, 1993), R. Domecq (Spain, 1994) and Jacobi (Germany, 1994), JV in China (1995)	

Note: JV = joint venture.
Sources: Annual reports; *Finanical Times*; trade journals.

other companies or form joint-ventures with local spirits distribution companies (Table 17.2), again confirming the existence of a high degree of strategy imitation. Through their acquisitions the four companies built up a dominant position in the global spirits market, and by 1995 they owned more than half (52.3 per cent) of the world's million spirit brands.

Since its formation in 1987, the most globally orientated SG in our study had increased its world market share year by year. Because of the economies of scale and scope enabled by their full brand portfolios the SG members achieved major savings in production, distribution and marketing costs. Ownership of their distribution network made them independent of other distribution companies and gave them full control over the marketing of their own brands. In addition, because of their sheer size they were able to survive the global shakeout process. However, no statistically significant correlation could be found between strategic group membership and financial and market performance during the period

1987–95. This causes us to reject proposition 5 – that is, membership of one SG in the spirits industry does not lead to a significantly higher performance level than membership of another SG. Although the companies that pursued a global strategy belonged to the best performing SG in terms of return on sales and growth of market share, this was not at a statistically significant level – second-best-performing SG (companies pursuing an international strategy) came very close in both respects.

CONCLUSIONS

The general finding of our study is that in a dynamic, globalizing business environment the older more static, nationally orientated SG concept loses some of its power to predict the behaviour and performance of companies. In practice, most empirical studies have not incorporated international competitor moves. Globalization generally leads to major structural changes and greater diversity in strategic choices, and this demands a more flexible, internationally orientated SG concept that takes account of dynamic industry changes. We have demonstrated with our example of the spirits industry that SGs exist at the global level. Global concentration and consolidation has led to increased instability within the industry. A number of SGs broke up when the co-members started to pursue different strategies and consequently formed or joined new SGs.

Dramatic changes in the industry environment and the adoption of successful new strategies by innovative companies caused their fellow SG members to reconsider their own strategies and contemplate following their co-members' lead. Membership of SGs within a globalizing industry was found to be strongly influenced by the companies' country of origin. Country of origin effects lead to a wider range of strategies to choose from in order to become more competitive at the global level. Finally, no statistically significant relationship could be found between company performance and SG membership. This might be because the time period chosen for the study – 1982 to 1995 – coincided with the industry's globalization process. Once the latter is completed, SG membership and financial performance might prove to be statistically significant.

Notes

1. According to Euromonitor, in value terms the UK and Germany are by far the two largest European spirits markets, accounting for 52.8 per cent of the European total. The US is the biggest North and South American spirits market and equals 85 per cent of the total European spirits market.
2. A minimum sales volume of $100 million was chosen to limit the number of sample companies to a feasible number for the collection of quantitative collection and of qualitative data, and to ensure comparability and representativeness, both domestically and internationally.

18 Explaining Organizational Performance Through Psychic Distance

Jody Evans and Felix Mavondo

INTRODUCTION

In the substantial body of literature on firm internationalization the concept of psychic distance has been identified as a key factor in variations in expansion patterns and organizational performance (Johanson and Wiedersheim-Paul, 1975; Johanson and Vahlne, 1977; Vahlne and Wiedersheim-Paul, 1977; Nordstrom and Vahlne, 1994; Stottinger and Schlegelmilch, 1998). Psychic distance refers to the perceived degree of similarity or difference between the home market and a foreign market. The sequence of foreign expansion described in numerous models of internationalization implies that companies perform best in these foreign markets which are most similar to their domestic market (Bilkley and Tesar, 1977; Johanson and Vahlne, 1977; Cavusgil, 1980; Czinkota, 1982; Nordstrom and Vahlne, 1994). This negative relationship between psychic distance and organizational performance is attributed to the fact that psychically close countries are easier to learn about and understand (Nordstrom and Vahlne, 1994).

However, the existence of a negative relationship between psychic distance and organizational performance remains an assumption, as the direction of the relationship has yet to be empirically established. A number of recent studies have examined this relationship in a variety of contexts – including cross-border acquisitions (Morosini, 1994), international joint-ventures (Ali, 1995), export development (Stottinger and Schlegelmilch, 1998), exchanges between exporters and importers and foreign retail operations (O'Grady and Lane, 1996) – but they have failed conclusively to establish that the relationship is negative. On the other hand some evidence of a psychic distance paradox, where the perception of differences between the home and foreign markets actually enhances performance, has been found (O'Grady and Lane, 1996).

This chapter begins with a review of the current definitions of psychic distance and then goes on to examine the relationship between psychic distance and organizational performance. Details of the research methodology and empirical findings of our survey are presented, followed by a discussion of the results and implications.

PSYCHIC DISTANCE DEFINED

The definition of 'psychic distance' has changed substantially since it was first used in Beckerman's (1956) study of the distribution of international trade.

Vahlne and Wiedersheim-Paul (1973) defined psychic distance in terms of factors that prevent or disturb the flow of information between suppliers and customers. Nordstrom and Vahlne (1994: 42) subsequently redefined it as 'factors preventing or disturbing firm's learning about and understanding a foreign environment'. This refinement was justified on the basis that learning and understanding, rather than access to information, are essential to the development of appropriate operating strategies in foreign markets. In contrast, O'Grady and Lane (1996: 330) define psychic distance as 'a firm's degree of uncertainty about a foreign market resulting from cultural differences and other business difficulties that present barriers to learning about the market and operating there'.

While the continual redefinition of psychic distance has resulted in a deeper understanding of the concept the current definitions still fail to encapsulate the two elements: *psychic* and *distance*. 'Psychic' is derived from the word psyche, which refers to the mind or soul. According this definition it cannot be the simple presence of external environmental factors (as identified by Vahlne and Wiedersheim-Paul, 1973, Nordstrom and Vahlne, 1994, and O'Grady and Lane, 1996) that determines the degree of psychic distance, but rather the mind's processing, in terms of perception and understanding, of cultural and business differences.

O'Grady and Lane (1996) attempt to incorporate the 'distance' aspect into their conceptualization of psychic distance by referring to uncertainty. It is argued that uncertainty has been confused with distance. Distance relates to similarity or difference in terms of degree of separation between two points. In contrast uncertainty refers to a lack of sureness about something and ranges from a minor lack of certainty to a complete lack of knowledge. This focus on uncertainty is inconsistent with the way in which psychic distance is operationalized. Most research on psychic distance asks respondents to indicate the degree to which a foreign country is similar to or different from their home country in terms of certain environmental factors (Johanson and Wiedersheim-Paul, 1975; Johanson and Vahlne, 1977, 1990, 1992; Vahlne and Wiedersheim Paul, 1977; Nordstrom and Vahlne, 1994; Ali, 1995; O'Grady and Lane, 1996).

Research conducted by O'Grady and Lane (1996) highlights the need to specify the factors that combine to determine psychic distance. O'Grady and Lane (1996) argue that psychic distance should incorporate both cultural and business differences. Business differences include language, business practices, political and legal systems, education, economic development, marketing, infrastructure and industry structure (Vahlne and Wiedersheim-Paul, 1977; Nordstrom and Vahlne, 1994).

Hence, it is apparent that there is little consensus in the international business literature as to the precise definition and operationalization of psychic distance. On the basis of the above review of definitions it is proposed that psychic distance be defined as 'the distance between the home market and a foreign market, resulting from the perception of cultural and business differences'.

PSYCHIC DISTANCE AND ORGANIZATIONAL PERFORMANCE

The internationalization literature implies that businesses will achieve greater success in psychically similar markets, as similarities are easier to manage than differences (Vahlne and Wiedersheim-Paul, 1977; Nordstrom and Vahlne, 1994). It could also be argued, however, that the perception of cultural and business differences can enhance performance as firms will make a concerted effort to learn more about and fully understand the foreign market, which will ultimately improve strategic decision making. In contrast, assumed similarities between the home and the foreign market can lead to poor performance as subtle but important differences tend to be overlooked or underestimated (O'Grady and Lane, 1996).

The findings of research on the relationship between psychic distance and organizational performance have been contradictory. Most of the research efforts in this area have focused primarily on cultural distance. Franko (1971) and Li and Guisinger (1991) have studied the relationship between cultural distance and international joint-venture performance. Franko (1971) failed to find a significant relationship between cultural distance and the stability of US joint-ventures in foreign markets, although this could be attributed to the simplified and subjective measurement of cultural distance employed. In contrast, Li and Guisinger (1991) have found that the failure of US affiliates is significantly higher when the parent company is based in a culturally distant country in comparison with those where the parent company is in a culturally similar country.

In contrast to the previous studies, Ali (1995) has measured both cultural and business differences to test the relationship between psychic distance and international joint-venture performance in a developing country. Using measures of cultural distance, differences in business practices and communication, a composite index of psychic distance was computed. Ali found that a combined index of culture and business practices did not have a significant effect on either of the performance measures, that is, the stability of the joint-venture and satisfaction with the joint-venture. However, ease of communication was found to have a significant effect on international joint-venture stability. The psychic distance index was not found significantly to affect international joint-venture performance. Ali's study was limited, however, by a number of factors. One limitation was the small sample size – 59 international joint-ventures. Furthermore, the psychic distance construct was only measured using indices of cultural distance, business practices differences and communication differences. Factors such as the economic environment, legal and political environment and industry structure were not included, even though economic environmental differences, for instance, should have been an important consideration as the context of the study was a developing country.

O'Grady and Lane (1996) have also examined the relationship between cultural or psychic distance and organizational performance. They found that operating in a psychically close country does not necessarily lead to superior performance as the presumption of similarity prevents executives from noticing subtle but crucial differences in the foreign market. In fact, the presumption held by their sample of

Canadian retailers about the similarity between the US and Canadian markets was strongly associated with their poor performance in the US market. Thus, according to O'Grady and Lane a psychic distance paradox exists, where psychic closeness is negatively related to organizational performance. While these authors have contributed substantially to the psychic distance debate, application of their findings is limited by a number of factors. First, they examined two countries only. The problem with this is that cultural and psychic distance is often seen in relative terms. Canada and the US can be considered as more psychically similar than, say, Canada and Germany. In this context, any minor differences between Canada and the US will be magnified because of lack of comparison with other countries. Second, while O'Grady and Lane recognize that psychic distance is a superior concept to cultural distance in terms of its power to explain differences in organizational performance, the study only measures cultural differences. Thus, even though the authors recommend that psychic distance be measured by both cultural and business differences, their findings are limited by the fact that they have measured cultural distance only.

It is evident that empirical studies do not conclusively support either a positive or a negative relationship between psychic distance and organizational performance. Despite this, the intuitively appealing assumption that psychic distance is negatively related to organizational performance is often accepted without question. Stottinger and Schlegelmilch (1998) state that the results of their study challenge this assumption. They found that, in some cases, export sales to psychically distant countries are greater than to psychically close countries. As this finding does not support a negative relationship, the authors conclude that psychic distance has very limited explanatory power. Stottinger and Schlegelmilch are to be commended for their review of the theoretical and managerial relevance of psychic distance and for their attempt to test the concept empirically. Furthermore, they have made an important contribution to the internationalization literature with their attempt to operationalize psychic distance through the application of cognitive mapping and by conducting their study on a cross-national basis. However, an alternative interpretation of their findings is that psychic distance is still very relevant, but that the construct and its consequences need to be more accurately measured it significant relationships are to be identified.

It can be, therefore, argued that the *perception* of cultural and business differences may be positively related to organizational performance. The perception of differences between the home and foreign market can encourage expansion into distant markets because of the new opportunities they offer. Moreover, the perception of differences between the home and foreign markets can enhance performance as firms will make a concerted effort to learn more about these markets, which will improve their strategic decision making and ultimately their organizational performance. While this argument challenges the intuitively appealing presumptions of the internationalization models, it is justified by the fact that it incorporates both cultural and business differences. A careful and theoretically grounded conceptualization of psychic distance that includes cultural, legal and political, economic, retail structure, business practices and language differences enhances the explanatory power of the psychic distance construct. Thus:

- *Hypothesis 1:* psychic distance is significantly and positively related to organizational performance.

Knowledge of the perceived distance between the home market and a foreign market is of considerable value. However, if research in this area is to advance and to offer substantial managerial applications, the key factors that combine to create psychic distance and their effect on organizational performance must be examined individually.

In our study of international retailers the following differences will be examined: national culture, legal and political environment, economic environment, business practices, language and retail structure. These differences have been identified in the international retailing, international business and psychic distance literature as factors that have a considerable influence on the internationalization process and organizational performance (Vahlne and Wiedersheim-Paul, 1973, 1977; Johanson and Wiedersheim-Paul, 1975; Johanson and Vahlne, 1977, 1990, 1992; Cavusgil and Zou, 1994; Nordstrom and Vahlne, 1994; Dupuis and Prime, 1996; Alexander, 1997).

In terms of business differences, it is in factors such as enterprise density, market concentration, economic development and government regulations that the psychic distance paradox is evident. Differences do not necessarily lead to unfavourable results. Indeed, it can be argued that retailers whose home market is characterized by advanced economic development, a well-developed and concentrated retail structure and strict regulations will perform well, if not better, in a developing market because of the distinct opportunities that this market can offer. The perception of cultural, business-practice and language differences can also enhance performance, as firms operating in foreign markets will be more culturally sensitive and will strive to minimize misunderstandings. Thus:

- *Hypotheses 2–7:* perception of differences between the home and foreign market in respect of the following factors is significantly and positively related to organizational performance: national culture (hypothesis 2); legal and political environment (hypothesis 3); economic environment (hypothesis 4); retail structure (hypothesis 5); business practices (hypothesis 6); and language (hypothesis 7).

METHODOLOGY

Our sample consisted of randomly selected non-food retailers with shops in at least three foreign countries. The data was collected by means of a formally structured questionnaire mailed to senior executives based in the US, the UK, Europe and the Asia-Pacific region. A useable sample of 102 symmetrical responses was obtained (a 13 per cent response rate). This sample included 204 international retailing operations as the respondents were asked to answer all the questions twice, once for a retail operation in a psychically *close* market and once for a retail operation in a psychically *distant* market the respondents were provided with definitions of these concepts). These two nominated markets provided the basis for answers to the questions on psychic distance and organizational performance.

Psychic Distance

New measures were developed (based on a review of the international business and retailing literature) to capture perceived differences in the legal and political environment, economic environment, industry structure, business practices and language. The measures for cultural distance were based on Hofstede's (1991) dimensions of national culture. While the empirical validity of Hofstede's framework has been extensively critiqued in the cross-cultural literature, the model is generally accepted as the most comprehensive framework for national cultural values (Kogut and Singh, 1988; Sondergaard, 1994). The items for the five dimensions of national culture were based on Hofstede's (1991) descriptions of the dimensions rather than the actual measures, so that general aspects of national culture would be captured rather than work-related values. The respondents were asked to indicate the degree to which the foreign market was similar to or different from the home market on a seven-point Likert scale, ranging from 'totally the same' (1) to 'totally different' (7).

Indices for cultural distance and business distance were calculated and used as the basis for the psychic distance construct. These indices were based on Kogut and Singh's (1988) formula for cultural distance:

$$CD_j = \sum_{I=1}^{n} ([I_{ij} - 1]^2 / V_i) / n$$

where CD_j or BD_j is the cultural or business differences of the *j*th foreign market from the home market, I_{ij} is the index of the *i*th cultural or business dimension and the *j*th market, 1 is the home market and V_i is the variance of the index of the *i*th dimension. These two indices were then averaged to provide a composite index of psychic distance.

Organizational Performance

The measurement scales for organizational performance were based on existing measures (Cavusgil and Zou, 1994; Shoham, 1996) in terms of financial performance and strategic effectiveness. In the case of financial performance the respondents were asked to indicate the extent to which a number of financial indicators had changed in previous three years on a Likert scale ranging from 1 'decrease of more than 20 per cent' to 7 'increase of more than 20 per cent'. Likewise strategic effectiveness was measured using a Likert scale ranging from 1 'very unsuccessful' to 7 'very successful'.

The reliability of the scales satisfactorily met Nunally's (1978) recommendation as the Cronbach alphas exceeded 0.7 for all the constructs. Exploratory and confirmatory factor analyses were performed and all the items significantly loaded onto the hypothesized constructs.

RESULTS AND DISCUSSION

The composite index of psychic distance was subjected to a simple regression analysis to evaluate its predictive ability in respect of organizational performance (Table 18.1). For the close market, no significant relationship was found between psychic distance and financial performance. However, a significantly negative relationship was found between psychic distance and strategic effectiveness. Even for apparently close markets there was a great deal of variation in the perception of similarity and difference between the home and foreign markets. The implication here is that for close markets psychic distance explains a very small proportion of the variance in organizational performance.

However, hypothesis 1 was supported in the case of distant markets as there was evidence that psychic distance was significantly and positively related both to financial performance and to strategic effectiveness. Thus, the results lend support to the argument that differences do not necessarily lead to unfavourable results, rather the perception of cultural and business differences can in fact enhance organizational performance. This positive relationship can be attributed to the distinct opportunities presented by distant foreign markets, particularly in the case of our sample of retailers. The majority of the retailers surveyed were based in developed and highly concentrated retail markets. Sixty per cent of the respondents identified Asian countries and 28 per cent identified Eastern European countries as their most distant markets. These countries are usually characterized as less economically developed and as possessing less concentrated retail structures. The implications here are that foreign markets with very different cultural and business environments from those of the home market offer financial and strategic opportunities, and that recognition of the existence of psychic distance prompts retailers to take steps to

Table 18.1   Psychic distance and organizational performance

	Psychic distance (Beta t-values)	R^2	*Adj R^2*	*F-ratio*
Financial performance				
Close	0.073 (0.722)	0.005	−0.005	0.521
Distant	0.369*** (3.972)	0.136	0.128	15.776***
Strategic effectiveness				
Close	−0.213* (−2.165)	0.045	0.036	4.688*
Distant	0.485*** (5.547)	0.235	0.228	30.766***

Notes: * = $p < 0.05$; *** = $p < 0.001$.

ensure that they will succeed in despite these differences, or to take advantage of these differences as a source of differentiation.

The fact that our findings differ from those of previous studies is largely due to our operationalization of psychic distance. Our results challenge Stottinger and Schlegelmilch's (1998) argument that psychic distance as an explanatory construct is 'past its due-date' as the composite index of psychic distance explained approximately 14 per cent of financial performance and 24 per cent of strategic effectiveness in distant markets. These results can also explain the difference between the findings of this study and those of previous investigations of psychic distance and organizational performance. Franko (1971) did not find a significant relationship between cultural distance and organizational performance while Li and Guisinger (1991) found a negative relationship, and Ali (1995) did not find a significant relationship between psychic distance and joint-venture performance. None of these studies, however, measured both cultural and business differences. Thus it can be concluded that incorporating cultural and business differences enhances the explanatory power of psychic distance.

The individual dimensions of psychic distance were also subjected to a multiple regression analysis, the results of which are summarized in Table 18.2. These results provide support for hypotheses 2 and 7 in the case of close markets. While no significant relationships were found for strategic effectiveness, both cultural distance and language differences were found to be significantly and positively related to financial performance. Business-practice differences were also found to be significantly related to financial performance, however, the relationship was negative and therefore hypothesis 6 is rejected.

The findings indicate that cultural distance is the most important predictor of financial performance in close markets. It can be, therefore, argued, that cultural distance is advantageous for international retailers, as it provides a basis for differentiation. Retailers from other cultures can capitalize on their differences as the latter may insulate them from direct competition with local firms and possibly lead to improved performance. The findings also support O'Grady and Lane's (1996) assertion that the perception of cultural closeness is negatively related to organizational performance. The implication of this is that assumed cultural similarities between the home and foreign markets can lead to poor performance as subtle but important differences may be overlooked or underestimated. Another interpretation is that the perception of cultural difference improves performance because firms make a more concerted effort to understand the unique needs and tastes of the local market. This improves strategic decision making, which in turn enhances organizational performance.

Language differences were also found to be an important predictor of financial performance. Previous research has found that language differences often contribute to misunderstandings and diminish the effectiveness of communication (Vahlne and Wiedersheim-Paul, 1977; Ali, 1995). Consequently, it might be expected that language differences will have a negative effect on organizational performance. However, the findings of our study lend support to the

Table 18.2 Psychic distance dimensions and organizational performance

Psychic distance dimensions (Beta t-values)

CulDis	LegPol	RetStc	Eco	BusPrc	Lang	R^2	Adj R^2	F-ratio
Financial performance (close)								
0.437*	−0.207	0.102	0.012	−0.396*	0.286**	0.134	0.079	2.445*
(2.276)	(−1.606)	(0.926)	(0.086)	(−2.161)	(2.686)			
Financial performance (distant)								
0.215	−0.209	0.028	0.235	0.116	0.099	0.172	0.120	3.291*
(1.283)	(−1.242)	(0.226)	(1.407)	(0.788)	(0.951)			
Strategic effectiveness (close)								
−0.079	−0.086	0.061	0.071	−0.092	−0.131	0.061	0.002	1.035
(−0.395)	(−0.640)	(0.534)	(0.477)	(−0.484)	(−1.177)			
Strategic effectiveness (distant)								
0.105	−0.339*	−0.148	0.826***	0.108	0.015	0.443	0.407	12.330***
(0.742)	(−2.417)	(−1.423)	(5.619)	(0.867)	(0.173)			

Notes: * = $p < 0.05$; ** = $p < 0.01$; *** = $p < 0.001$.

view that when the languages of the home and foreign markets are perceived to be substantially different, firms will make a more determined effort to communicate effectively, and thereby minimize misunderstandings. This will improve both strategic decision making and day-to-day operations, resulting in superior organizational performance.

Interestingly, however, this argument is not supported in the case of business practices. Differences between business practices were found to have a significantly negative effect on financial performance in close markets. This can be attributed to the fact that business practices go to the very heart of a foreign retail operation. It is possible that the characteristics of our sample intensified the negative effect of business-practice differences on organizational performance. The majority (60 per cent) of the respondent firms had adopted entry strategies that involved a local firm; namely strategic alliances, joint-ventures and acquisitions. The dominance of these entry modes in the sample may highlight the importance of business-practice differences, as they play a more important role when separate businesses from different countries are combined.

With regard to distant markets, only hypothesis 4 was supported. Economic differences were found to be significantly and positively related to strategic effectiveness in distant markets. This is consistent with the finding of previous research that less developed markets with signs of economic growth offer substantial opportunities for international retailers (Myers and Alexander, 1996; Nagashima, 1999). The positive relationship between the perception of economic differences and organizational performance can be attributed to the benefits derived from being the first to establish a presence in a developing market.

While the combined group of cultural and business factors was found to explain a significant proportion of financial performance in distant markets, none of the separate factors proved to be an important predictor in its own. This highlights the importance of the composite index of psychic distance. Thus, it can be concluded that the combination of cultural and business differences has the most explanatory power in the case of financial performance.

CONCLUSIONS

This chapter has shown that it is necessary to investigate both close and distant markets as the results indicate substantial variation in the perception of differences between home and foreign markets, both within the close and distant markets and between the two markets. In terms of close markets, the results suggest that perception of distance has no significant effect on financial performance, but it does reduce the strategic effectiveness of the foreign operation. The relationship between psychic distance and organizational performance is much stronger in distant markets. Hence, it can be inferred that as the perception of distance between the home and the foreign market increases, the foreign retail operation will be more successful in terms of financial performance and strategic effectiveness.

Relationships between the disaggregated dimensions of psychic distance and organizational performance were also investigated. The results show that the dimensions differ in importance between close and distant markets. For close markets, cultural distance is the most important factor in organizational performance. Thus, it can be argued that retailers will perform better in close markets that are culturally distant from the home market. As the majority of retailers surveyed in our study are from highly developed and mature markets it can be expected that their closest markets will have similar characteristics. Consequently, the perception of legal and political, economic and retail structure differences will be less important and cultural distance will be more important. It is possible that the perception of cultural distance will provide retailers with a competitive advantage in close markets because it forms the basis for a differentiation strategy. For distant markets, the perception of economic differences is the most important predictor of organizational performance. Our findings suggest that retailers perform better in distant markets that are perceived to be economically different from the home market. This positive relationship can be attributed to the fact that economic differences represent substantial growth opportunities for retailers based in developed and mature markets. Retailers may expand into economically developing markets because competition is less intense and there are advantages to be had from being the first to establish a presence in the market.

Further research is required, however, into two aspects of our study. First, the perception of distance from apparently close markets warrants deeper investigation. It is evident that there is substantial variation in the perception of distance from close markets. Managers may identify a market as close, but when asked about specific environmental factors they point to significant differences between the home and the close market. It is recommended that further research be conducted on the perception of differences in respect of close markets and the effect of this on strategy formulation and performance. Second, while this study makes a substantial contribution to the existing literature by offering a more comprehensive operationalization of psychic distance, there is scope for further refinement. For instance, there is a need to explore whether language differences are an adequate indicator of communication differences. Finally, other dimensions of psychic distance could be included in the analysis, such as differences between educational standards and between more industry-specific factors.

Part Five

Internationalization of SMEs

19 Globalization and the Smaller Firm: Reconcilable Notions?

Maureen Berry, Pavlos Dimitratos and Michael McDermott

INTRODUCTION

> Globalisation in its economic aspect refers to the *increasing* integration of economies *around the world*, particularly through trade and financial flows. The term sometimes also refers to the movement of people (labour) and knowledge (technology) across international borders.
> (IMF, 2000: 36, emphasis added)

The term globalization is repeatedly encountered in the academic literature and business press nowadays. Although 'internationalization' and 'globalization' are frequently used interchangeably (Dicken, 1998), there is a degree of difference between them . The IMF definition printed above refers essentially to the macroeconomic level. At a microeconomic level one can argue that globalization is occurring when firms expand their international operations with firms and customers situated well beyond their own national borders. Internationalization can be viewed as a phenomenon of the 1950s, 1960s and much of the 1970s, while globalization a phenomenon of the 1980s and 1990s (OECD, 1999b).

It appears that when many authors refer to 'global' firms or 'global' strategies they are implying that the latter are better, more innovative or more successful than their international, exporting or domestic counterparts. In so doing they depict globalization as an end in itself, something that enterprises have to achieve if they wish to be truly successful. But ironically, this is a proposition for which there seems to be little empirical evidence, perhaps because there is no agreement on the constituents of globalization or the global firm.

Related to the statement that 'global is better' is the assertion by many researchers that possession of the label 'global' requires a large number of business assets and a substantial business presence. Hence, it is not surprising that globalization has customarily been associated with the international operations of large firms. It is a common belief that globalization needs a 'critical mass' in order to thrive, and that this is something larger firms can achieve more easily.

As will be shown, most authors use the terms global, transnational and multinational to refer explicitly or implicitly to the operations of large firms. However, an emerging trend in the literature is to label smaller firms with particular features as 'born globals' (Rennie, 1993; Knight and Cavusgil, 1996; Madsen and Servais, 1997), and occasionally the academic literature and the business press report instances of smaller firms seeking to 'go global' through exporting (for example Chittum, 1998). These examples imply that even smaller enterprises can be active participants in the globalization process, thus challenging the traditional 'large firm' view of globalization.

This begs the question of whether globalization and the smaller firm are compatible notions. In other words, what are the features of the smaller global firm, if any, and what are the practical implications of this? This topic merits attention, if only to clarify the tension that exists in the literature about the association between globalization and the business operations of the smaller firm. We argue that globalization and the smaller firm can be viewed as compatible and that international business researchers can work with the dimensions of the smaller global firm that this chapter will present.

In this chapter we define smaller firms as independently owned firms that do not have an influential market share in the industry in which they operate, although they may dominate a particular market segment or niche of that industry. For instance, a small plastics firm will capture only a minor share of the overall plastics market, but it may dominate the plastic hose segment or the flexible plastic hose niche. Smaller firms typically possess restricted amounts of human, financial, production and information resources, and concentrate on producing and marketing a limited number of product lines.

This chapter is organized as follows. The next section explores the representations in the literature of global strategies, the transfer of knowledge within the multinational enterprise and the 'born global' firm. In doing so it calls attention to the disagreement that exists in the literature with regard to the compatibility of globalization and the smaller firms. The third section examines the features of the smaller global firm and provides a theoretical framework that researchers may use to derive empirical taxonomies of such firms. Finally, the fourth section provides a synopsis and suggestions for future investigations.

MAIN ISSUES IN THE LITERATURE

The smaller firm faces difficulties with international growth in that it possesses limited resources (Yang *et al.*, 1992; Benito and Welch, 1994; Liesch and Knight, 1999). Incremental frameworks have often been used to explain the international development of the smaller firm (Johanson and Wiedersheim-Paul, 1975; Bilkey and Tesar, 1977; Johanson and Vahlne, 1977, 1990). The central notion is that a firm will proceed into the international market incrementally as experiential knowledge is acquired. Hence, the international development of small firms that are global from their inception is not explained by these frameworks (McDougall *et al.*, 1994).

In our examination of whether globalization and the smaller firm are compatible notions we shall consider well-known definitions in the literature of the terms global firm, transnational corporation and multinational enterprise (Table 19.1). As can be seen, there seems to be no agreement among authors about the meaning of these terms (cf. Ghoshal, 1987; Fleenor, 1993; Birkinshaw *et al.*, 1995; Harzing, 2000). Our purpose is to explore how this ambiguity has affected researchers' views on the globalization of smaller firms, starting with how the

Table 19.1 Key defining characteristics of global, transnational and multinational enterprises

	Source	*Characteristics*
Fully globalized small and medium-sized enterprise	OECD (1997)	Majority of inputs sourced across borders, large majority of outputs traded across borders; multiple establishments in all major international regions; markets in all major international regions
Global corporation	Bartlett and Ghoshal (1989)	Centralization of strategic planning and operations at headquarters' implementation of centralized strategy by subsidiaries abroad; development and maintenance of knowledge at headquarters
Global firm	Govindarajan and Gupta (2000)	Globalization of market presence, capital base, corporate mindset and supply chain
Born global firm	Knight and Cavusgil (1996), Rennie (1993)	Aims at markets worldwide from inception or soon after, often ignoring the home market
Born again global firm	Bell *et al.* (2000)	Well established in its home markets; with no apparent motivation suddenly embraces rapid internationalization
Transnational corporation	Bartlett and Ghoshal (1989)	Development of more independent subsidiaries to take advantage of distinctive local resources,mutual exchange of knowledge by subsidiaries and headquarters through a flexible organizational system
	UNCTAD World Investment Reports (e.g. 1999)	Incorporated or un-incorporated enterprise comprising parent enterprise and its foreign affiliates (subsidiary enterprises,associate enterprises and branches)
Multinational corporation	Hood and Young (1979)	Owns, controls and manages income-generating assets in more than one country
Multinational enterprise	Dunning (1991)	Orchestrates a set of geographically dispersed but independent assets
	Hout *et al.* (1982)	Has substantial operations and market interests abroad

global strategy issue has impinged on the association between globalization and the smaller firm.

Global Strategy

Yip (1989) provides one of the most comprehensive definitions of global strategy. He argues that such strategies have four constituents:

1. Competitive moves into the international market place materialize as part of a 'global competitive plan'.
2. Value-added activities such as marketing, sales, R & D and production are established in different places in order to maximize global efficiency.
3. Target countries are chosen on the basis of anticipated gains from a world-wide presence rather than single-country gains.
4. A standardized product and a homogeneous marketing mix are offered to all countries.

According to this definition, the main characteristic of a global strategy is the pursuit of economies of scale and scope worldwide. The former is achieved by establishing sales presence in major international markets, while the latter is achieved through the establishment of value-added activities worldwide, which also enables worldwide sourcing of essential inputs such as labour, management personnel, raw materials, accessories, capital and technological know-how (cf. the definitions by Govindarajan and Gupta, 2000, and OECD, 1997, in Table 19.1).

Many researchers consider that in order to be characterized a global firm, an enterprise must be implementing a global strategy. This is especially apparent in studies that deal with the operations of firms that have subsidiaries worldwide (Roth *et al.*, 1991; Sundaram and Black, 1992; Leong and Tan, 1993; Harzing, 2000). According to this perspective the global firm seeks to maximize its gains from economies of scale and scope worldwide, and configures its organizational structure (headquarters and subsidiaries) accordingly. The question of interest here is, if this proposition is accepted, can the smaller firm be characterized as a global one?

We argue that this is not often the case because smaller firms possess only limited resources. They might achieve a substantial market presence abroad, and hence significant economies of scale in the international market, particularly if they are strongly committed to their international operations. However, it is rather difficult for the smaller firm to spread its operations over sufficient countries to diversify its capital base fully, to source labour, management personnel and technological know-how to a significant degree, or to set up its value-added activities in a number of different countries (in line with constituent 2 of Yip's 1989 definition). Very few smaller firms have come close to implementing the comprehensive strategy, defined by Yip. In corroboration of this assertion, the OECD (1997) estimates that only 1 per cent of smaller firms, mainly operating in high-tech industries, can be characterized as fully globalized.

Transfer of Knowledge within the Multinational Enterprise

Global strategy has largely been associated with the operations of firms that have subsidiaries worldwide, that is, the multinationals. Therefore, another associated theme in the international business literature that is of relevance to our examination is the transfer of knowledge within the hierarchy of the firm across borders. Theoretical explanations in studies of large international firms are usually rooted in transaction cost frameworks, that is, the internalization approach and the eclectic paradigm. These frameworks view the international growth efforts of multinationals as an attempt to internalize markets for intermediate and tangible inputs (Hennart, 1991b; Dess *et al.*, 1995). The multinational is considered to possess rent-yielding, firm-specific advantages that can generate monopolistic power advantages, and it may choose to exploit these abroad by means of internalization through a subsidiary (Buckley and Casson, 1976; Teece, 1981a).

Implicit in this line of thought is the argument that a firm that does not internalize its international activities through subsidiaries (or quasi-internalize them through joint-ventures) cannot obtain proper information on or knowledge about foreign market conditions and idiosyncrasies. This could be the main reason why transaction cost theorists have paid no attention to exporting enterprises. It appears that multinational firms that pursue global strategies cannot be exporting enterprises since they do not obtain relevant knowledge about their international activities from their foreign distributors or partners. In light of this 'multinationality' aspect of global strategies (and firms), can smaller firms be characterized as global? The answer is that smaller enterprises only occasionally qualify as global firms because they do not usually proceed beyond the exporting stage. Only if they establish sales or production subsidiaries (or perhaps joint-ventures) to service foreign markets can they be characterized as global.

The 'Born Global' Firm

The intra-firm transfer of knowledge across borders is not without costs (Teece, 1981b; Gupta and Govindarajan, 2000). Furthermore, power struggles are a ubiquitous phenomenon in all organizations (Pfeffer, 1981). Hence, reliance on markets for knowledge about foreign market conditions is sometimes the only viable solution, something that can hold for the enterprises discussed in this section.

As stated previously, an increasingly discussed phenomena in the academic literature and business press are the 'born global' and 'global exporting' smaller firms. To a large extent these two enterprise categories often overlap, since 'born globals' often go international through exporting entry modes (Madsen and Servais, 1997). A characteristic of 'born globals' is that from their inception they seek to obtain substantial competitive advantages from their market presence in multiple countries (see the definition in Table 19.1). Their way of international expansion challenges the incrementalists' proposition that development initially takes place in the home country.

Found especially in high-tech industries,[1] small 'born globals', as well as exporting, may employ networks and strategic alliances as modes of foreign entry in order to overcome resource constraint barriers (Johnson, 1999). Because of standardization of demand and the high growth rate of the industries in which they operate, it is essential for small 'born globals' to establish a presence in the key foreign markets of their industries – mainly in the Triad region (Jolly *et al.*, 1992). We argue that these firms are likely to have been named global partly because this region is associated with the presence of the most demanding and sophisticated customers. This of course is related to the proposition discussed in the introductory section that if an enterprise can effectively vie in such a competitive context, it can be considered a successful, and therefore a global firm.

Hence, a feature of small 'born globals' is their presence in the key geographic markets of their industries and their consequent ability to achieve economies of scale. Because they mainly operate in environments in which the forces of global integration are relatively strong and local responsiveness is relatively weak, the industries in which they operate can also be described as global (cf. Ghoshal and Nohria, 1993).

Regardless of whether 'born globals' go international through exporting or other collaborative exercises, they rely heavily on specialized networks of firms that supplement their own competences (Jolly *et al.*, 1992). Because they often employ advanced information and technological systems to communicate with their foreign partners (Madsen and Servais, 1997), they can easily internationalize by internalizing *information* on external markets rather than actually internalizing these markets (Liesch and Knight, 1999). By doing so they are likely to achieve international outcomes similar to those of larger firms, such as a market presence in 'lead' markets.

The Internet has undoubtedly provided considerable opportunities for smaller firms to conduct transactions with partners and customers worldwide by significantly lowering the transaction costs involved (Etemad and Wright, 1999; Brock, 2000; Kleindl, 2000; Lituchy and Rail, 2000). Advanced information and technological communication systems can drastically diminish the advantages large multinationals have over small enterprises (Lituchy and Rail, 2000) as use of these systems can substantially lower the resource constraint barriers that smaller firms traditionally encounter.

Oviatt and McDougall (1994) argue that 'born global' firms may construct their value-added activities across the foreign countries in which they operate. This holds largely for the sales and marketing functions, especially in the case of global exporters. It appears that 'born global' firms may internationalize their value-added operations through networking activities in an attempt to attain economies of scope from these operations.

Closely related to 'born global' small firms are their 'born again global' counterparts (Bell *et al.*, 2000). Such firms are well established in their home markets but due to a 'critical incident' they show a sudden enthusiasm to internationalize. 'Critical incidents' include acquisition of the firm, change of ownership or following clients abroad. The existence of 'born again global' firms highlights the fact that internationalization is neither a linear nor a unidirectional process, but an irregular route that can be precipitated by specific episodes (Oesterle, 1997).

To sum up, born 'global small' firms are smaller enterprises that can be characterized as global because they cover key markets of the industry in which they operate by employing a large network of international partners and exploiting modern information and communication systems. The major characteristic of 'born global' smaller firms is that they seek a strong market presence or even dominance in the market segments or niches of the key foreign countries in which they operate. This market presence theme is fundamental to the discussion of the five features of the global smaller firm presented in the next section.

AN INTEGRATIVE FRAMEWORK: THE DIMENSIONS OF THE SMALLER GLOBAL FIRM

It is helpful to conceive the internationalization route of the smaller global firm as a temporal process (Figure 19.1). We argue that the main criterion for a smaller enterprise to be categorized as a global firm is that it has reached the 'end result' or *a posteriori* stage, that is, it has established a presence in the major foreign markets of the industry of which it is part. This is not to down play the importance of the earlier stages, but as discussed in the previous section a defining feature of small global firms is their presence in key industry markets. Since these firms are usually found in the high-tech sector, their presence in the lead markets of the Triad region can be vital, and they achieve economies of scale by expanding their operations worldwide.

It should be stressed that small firms' presence in these key markets by no means implies wide coverage of these markets. Instead they employ a 'deep niche' strategy, that is, they satisfy the needs of a well-defined and specific segment or niche of the foreign market (Simon, 1996). Hence, market presence is likely to be accompanied by pursuit of market dominance in particular segments or niches.

It has been argued that in order to achieve a worldwide market presence, small global firms have to position[2] their value-added activities in different countries, including their sales and marketing functions and, for some, stage their R & D and production facilities. This is mainly how they achieve economies of scope, and it is the first component of the process that global small firms go through to reach the *a posteriori* stage (Figure 19.1). The second component is the acquisition of foreign market knowledge, usually from networks of suppliers or partners as very few small firms have subsidiaries. The third and interrelated component is the sourcing of inputs worldwide to ensure global efficiency. We argue that this component is likely to be absent among small

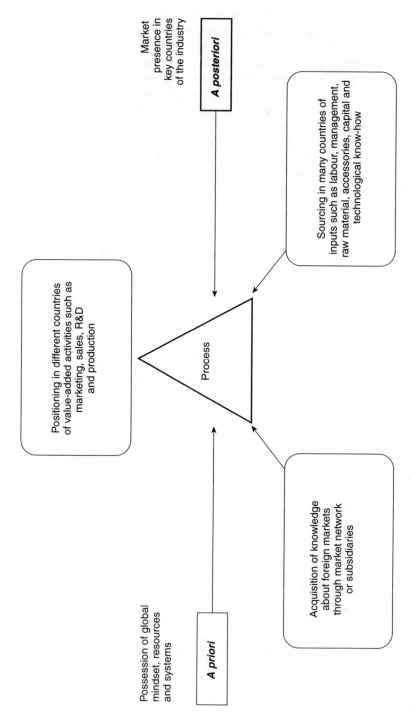

Figure 19.1   Dimensions of the smaller global firm

global firms, and there is little empirical evidence to the contrary. It should be stressed that here the sourcing of inputs should not be confused with the procurement of inputs through imports from countries abroad.

Many researchers insist that the major determinant of completion of the process stage and arrival at the *a posteriori* stage is possession of a 'global mindset' (for example Jolly *et al.*, 1992; Oviatt and McDougall, 1995; Madsen and Servais, 1997). This refers to the motivation of managers of smaller firms who would like their enterprises to secure a place in the international marketplace, that is, a market presence in the key countries of their industry, as we define it. Successful small global firms have leaders with an entrepreneurial vision who take a bold and proactive stance as far as international growth is concerned. It is posited that, for the process stage to take place and the *a posteriori* stage to be received, adequate human, financial, production and information resources (Yang *et al.*, 1992; Benito and Welch, 1994) and effective management systems for the planning and control of internationalization (Kirpalani and Macintosh, 1980; Burton and Schlegelmilch, 1987) must be accompanied by a global mindset. Hence, these factors constitute the *a priori* part of Figure 19.1.

We argue that small firms that, for any reason, do not have a market presence in the key countries of their industry are not global. For instance, if a small European software firm has achieved a market presence only in EU countries while the key markets of its industry are in the Triad countries, this firm is not a global but a 'regional' firm (cf. Baden-Fuller and Stopford, 1991; Morrison *et al.*, 1991; Roth, 1992). In similar vein, another small software firm that has achieved a market presence in several of the key countries of its industry but has not paid attention to the geography of this presence can better be called an 'internationalized' firm. Nonetheless, both firms can be classified as potential global firms if they satisfy the *a priori* criteria, that is if they have a global mindset and the resources and systems necessary for a market presence in the key countries of their industry.

CONCLUSIONS AND FUTURE RESEARCH

The question examined in this chapter was whether globalization and the smaller firm are compatible notions. We have shown that the two notions are reconcilable, we have described the dimensions of the smaller global firm, and we have stressed that presence in key markets all over the world is the main prerequisite for a firm to be characterized as global (Figure 19.1). Advances in information technology and other technological developments, plus an increasing trend towards collaborative arrangements, have made presence by small this more feasible than in the past. This market presence is likely to be accompanied by dominance of specific segments or niches of the key markets.

We have shown that the definitional differences in the literature are substantially due to the fact that authors tend to mix the *a posteriori* stage with the process and the *a priori* stages. Truly global small firms achieve a market (sales) presence in the key foreign markets of their respective industries (the *a posteriori* stage) by positioning their value-added activities in different countries, acquiring knowledge about these markets through networks of suppliers or partners, and sourcing inputs in many countries (the process). The forces behind the initiation of the process are possession of a global mindset and the resources and management systems needed for internationalization (the *a priori* stage). Elements of the 'global strategy', the 'multinational enterprise' and the 'born global firm' themes are included in these three stages.

The globalization model presented in Figure 19.1 shows a unidirectional process. One possibility that has not been investigated in the literature is that attainment of (the *a posteriori* stage by a) smaller firm might reinforce the *a priori* and process stages, thus, prompting a new round of international growth by that firm. Future studies could elaborate on this issue, as it is likely that the economies of scale generated from a worldwide market presence could also have a positive effect on a new round of internationalization.

Based on the dimensions shown in Figure 19.1, researchers could derive empirical taxonomies of global smaller firms. For instance firms that satisfy all five dimensions could be characterized as truly global firms, whereas if they only satisfy the *a priori* conditions they could be characterized as potential global firms. Intermediate stages of globalization could be also identified. The managerial and policy aspects of the connection between globalization and small firms could be strengthened through such empirical investigations and thereby acquire importance apart from its pure 'theoretical' association.

Future studies could also examine the association of the dimensions in Figure 19.1 with other firm- and environment-specific variables. The international operations of a smaller global firm are strongly affected by the parameters of the organization and of its foreign and domestic markets. For example, the global mindset of the firm depends significantly on the competences, knowledge and past experience of the management team (Madsen and Servais, 1997). Researchers could examine these issues thoroughly in order to acquire a comprehensive picture of the globalization of the smaller firm.

Finally, it would be interesting to investigate the degree to which the framework in Figure 19.1 depicts the full dimensions of global firms, irrespective of their size. As stated earlier, there is considerable disagreement in the literature about the defining characteristics of the global firm. With our framework we have gone beyond the simple view that a global firm is merely one that pursues a global strategy or acquires information through its subsidiaries in foreign countries. Future studies could apply this framework to the international operations of larger firms in order to investigate the extent of its overall validity and generalizability.

Notes

1. Born globals can also be found in low-tech industries, especially if they come from smaller countries where the domestic demand is small, such as Denmark (Knight *et*

al., 2000). However, Danish born global firms are not particularly global in orientation since they are mainly involved in exporting to the EU. Of course this raises a general definitional issue, to which we shall in the next section.

2. In the context of the smaller global firm we prefer the term 'positioning' rather than 'establishment' in the case of value-added activities because the latter term is likely to be associated with physical presence in the form of a joint venture or subsidiary abroad. Such a physical presence does not necessarily hold in the case of the smaller global firm.

20 Multiple Sales Channel Strategies in the Export Marketing of Small and Medium-sized Design Companies

Mika Gabrielsson and Zuhair Al-Obaidi

INTRODUCTION

A large contribution is made by small and medium-sized companies (SMEs) to national economies in the OECD countries in general and Finland in particular. In the OECD, SMEs represent 99.7 per cent of all companies (OECD, 1997). Finnish designer products are famous in many parts of the world, especially in the case of glassware and porcelain (Iittala, Arabia, Aalto), kitchenware (Hackman), furniture (Aalto), jewellery (Kalevala, Lapponia) and textiles and clothing (Marimekko). Finnish design companies benefit in many ways from their Scandinavian origin, but face a tremendous growth challenge due to their relatively small home market (a population of five million) and the difficulty of making individual designer products known internationally.

This leads us to the question to be addressed in this chapter: how can small and medium-sized Finnish design companies, with their limited resources and marketing skills, successfully export their products to foreign markets where customers are not familiar with Finnish design? In the following sections we shall describe the structure of alternative sales channels used by small and medium-sized design companies, examine the reasons for adopting the various alternatives, and analyze, in the light of empirical evidence, the propositions offered by current theories.

Earlier research on sales channels largely built on studies of the internationalization process (for example Luostarinen 1970, 1979; Johanson and Vahlne 1977; Leonidou *et al.*, 1996) and on the domestic-oriented marketing literature (for example Stern and Reve 1980). Within the latter stream, research has been based on various approaches, such as transaction cost analysis (Williamson 1975, 1985), product life cycles and long-term relations (Dwyer *et al.*, 1987).

Furthermore, earlier research examined channel choice mainly from a single channel approach (direct/indirect), so the use of multiple channels as means of international expansion tended to be neglected (Frazier 1990; Dutta *et al.*, 1995). Likewise there have been few empirical studies that take a longitudinal approach to channels in transition (Rangan *et al.*, 1993).

This prompts a number of interesting research questions. Do small and medium-sized design companies use different sales channel structures, and if so, why? What kinds of channel structure do small and medium-sized design companies use, and how have they developed over time? What are the motives for using these channels, and what factors have influenced their development? How have recent technological changes affected the sales channel strategies of small and medium-sized design companies? How adequate are current sales channel theories for predicting small and medium-sized companies' sales channel behaviour?

In this chapter, small companies are defined as those with fewer than 50 employees, and medium-sized firms as those with 50–250 employees.

MULTIPLE SALES CHANNEL STRATEGIES IN EXPORT MARKETING

The fields of international business and marketing have developed distinct definitions of sales channel structures, and this can easily give rise to confusion. Many of the factors underlying these definitions – such as the degree of directness of a channel, channel ownership, the variety and number of channels, and the degree of selectivity of a channel – are important in both research streams, but the international business literature views these factors from the internationalization perspective (Luostarinen, 1970, 1979) while the marketing literature views them from a domestic market or single market perspective (Mallen, 1977; Hardy *et al.*, 1988).

The internationalization literature identifies two main types of marketing operation, and these form the basis of channel strategies (Luostarinen 1979):

- Export operations, which utilize non-direct-investment marketing operation modes: indirect export mode, direct export mode and own export mode (Luostarinen, 1970, 1979).
- Sales and marketing subsidiary operations, which utilize direct-investment marketing operation modes (Luostarinen 1979; Luostarinen and Welch, 1990).

According to the marketing literature, 'Marketing channels can be viewed as sets of interdependent organisations involved in the process of making a product or service available for use or consumption. Not only do marketing channels satisfy demand . . ., but they also stimulate demand by the promotional activities by the units composing them' (Stern *et al.*, 1989: p. 57). Furthermore, sales channels can be indirect or direct (see for example Hardy *et al.*, 1988).

With the *indirect sales channel*, instead of goods going directly to the consumer they pass through the hands of an independent intermediary located in the target market. This type of channel can be one-tier or two-tier in structure. In the one-tier structure a reseller or retailer sells the goods to the consumer; and in the two-tier structure the goods go first to a distributor and then to the reseller or retailer. In a direct sales channel the producer sells directly to the consumer through its own sales force (Hardy *et al.*, 1988). The relationships between marketing modes and sales channel strategies are illustrated in Figure 20.1.

The usual internationalization path taken by companies located in small and open countries is first to internationalize their sales and marketing activities

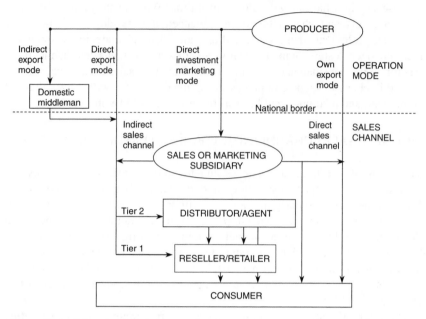

Figure 20.1   Sales channels for international expansion

Note: In tier 2 the agent either passes on the goods to the reseller/retailer or sells them directly to the consumer

Source: Adapted from Gabrielsson (1999: 23).

through a non-direct-investment marketing operation mode, and then to utilize a direct-investment marketing operation mode (Luostarinen, 1979). In the first stage the company can choose between three main alternatives: indirect exporting, direct exporting or own exporting. *Indirect exporting* involves another company located in the home market carrying out export activities on the producer's behalf. In *direct exporting* the producer takes care of its export activities with the help of an intermediary located in the target country. (Luostarinen and Welch, 1990). With the *own export* mode there is no domestic or foreign intermediary and the producer's own export marketing personnel sell to the customer. This naturally involves a lot of travelling (ibid.: 27).

As the operation expands and the company becomes more experienced in dealing with foreign markets, it may decide to establish a sales or marketing subsidiary. The sales subsidiary can be characterized as a middleman in the chain, and its activities can be compared to those of an importer or wholesaler (Hentola, 1994). A further possibility is for multiple sales channel strategies to be used simultaneously (Hardy *et al.*, 1988). This can take the form of either a dual sales channel or a hybrid sales channel. With the dual strategy a combination of direct and indirect strategies are used. In the hybrid strategy the sales and sales-promotion functions are shared between the producer and an intermediary. (Gabrielsson, 1999; see also Anderson *et al.*, 1997). The dual channel strategy can be characterized as adversarial, whereas the hybrid channel strategy is based more on cooperation and partnership (Figure 20.2).

In addition to choosing its sales channel strategy, the producer also has to consider a great variety of intermediaries for each channel. This can lead to a third type of multiple channel in which the goods reach the consumer via a number of intermediaries: distributors, agents, resellers and retailers. By definition distributors do not sell directly to the consumer, but utilize resellers or retailers as middlemen. Agents' sales contact can be either resellers/retailers or consumers. In the latter case they are called sales agents. Resellers sell to industrial customers whereas retailers sell to consumers through retail outlets. The titles given to intermediaries vary greatly from industry to industry and even from company to company, so it is more important for a producer to investigate the functions that particular intermediaries perform than to what they are called (Buckley *et al.*, 1994).

Having described the various sales channel strategies for international expansion, we turn now to the theoretical approaches to channel choice and development.

THEORETICAL APPROACHES

Four theoretical explanations of sales channel strategy choice and development are reviewed here: the internationalization process, sales channel economic structure (transaction cost analysis), long-term relations, and product life cycles.

The *internationalization process* literature focuses on the stages that companies go through as they gradually proceed towards more demanding products, operations and markets, both at the company level (Luostarinen 1979) and at the country level (Luostarinen, 1970; see also Johanson and Vahlne, 1977, and a review of other early models by Leonidou and Katsikeas, 1996). Each company has its own product–operation–market pattern and this affects its sales channel selection. The internationalization models are based on the behavioural theory of the firm (Cyert and March, 1963), growth of the firm (Penrose, 1959) and the concept of lateral rigidity (Vaivio, 1963). According to the latter, rigid lateral behaviour on the past of decision makers in firms can be overcome through the learning process (Luostarinen, 1979). This also applies to sales channel selection at the export or marketing-subsidiary level. In this model the producer is expected first to conduct its exporting activities through indirect sales channels, but as experience is gained a direct channel will be established. A positive experience of a particular channel strategy either in the home country or in foreign markets increases the probability that a similar strategy will be chosen for a new market entry.

The objective of the *sales channel economic structure* literature is to explain channel selection by considering cost and efficiency factors. One of the most

262

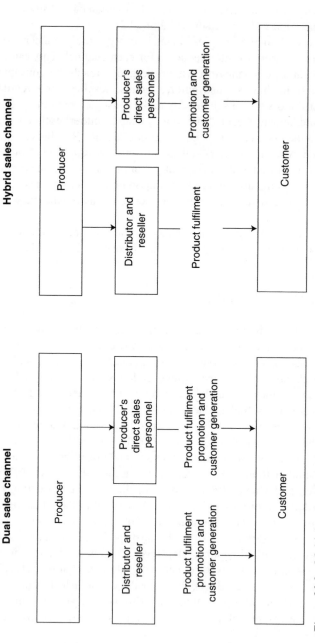

Figure 20.2   Multiple sales channels

Source: Adapted from Gabrielsson (1999: 28).

commonly used methods is the transaction cost approach, based on the early work of Coase (1937) and later Williamson (1975, 1985). The transaction cost approach suggests that the degree of vertical integration (market/hierarchical control) is based on the cost efficiency of transactions. Since it is difficult to measure such costs, the following proxies are utilized: asset specificity, external uncertainty, internal uncertainty and transaction volume (size multiplied by frequency) (Williamson, 1975, 1985). Transaction cost analysis also takes sociopolitical considerations into account. The approach's main suggestions are that direct sales channels make the most sense when the size of the transaction is large and asset specificity is high, and that multiple (dual or hybrid) sales channels are optimal for increasing sales volume in the case of highly diversified markets. The latter has to do with economies of scale and scope in handling a large number of transactions and with managing the external uncertainty caused by the diversity of these markets.

The *long-term channel relationship* literature's primary objective is to explain the development of this relationship over time (Dwyer *et al.*, 1987). It is argued that the channel relationship can lead either to partnership advantages (Sethuraman *et al.*, 1988) or to channel conflicts (Moriarty and Moran, 1990). This is moderated by several relationship variables, namely power (see Emerson 1962), trust and commitment (see Dwyer *et al.*, 1987). This study focuses on the influence that channel relationships have on channel selection (see also Thibaut and Kelley, 1959). It is argued that these are especially useful in explaining the choice of multiple channels (dual or hybrid). Hybrid channels will be chosen when trustworthy and committed partners are important, whereas a dual channel will be chosen when the relative power of the company is strong enough to overcome channel conflicts.

The objective of the *product life cycle* (PLC) model is to describe the stages through which a product passes. The theory of diffusion and innovation provides the rationale for the PLC model (Rogers, 1962). The question addressed is which channels are best for targeting customers at a particular PLC stage. According to this model, single (direct sales or indirect specialized sales) channels are used during the introductory stage, dual channels during the growth stage, multiple (dual or hybrid) channels during the the maturity stage dual channels and hybrid or direct (marketing) channels during the decline stage (see also Lele, 1986).

THE PRESENT STUDY

Framework and Methodology

The simple framework guiding our empirical study is based on the four theoretical approaches reviewed above. (Figure 20.3).

This study is based on four case studies, a methodology that allowed us to build our understanding inductively from data rather than deductively through

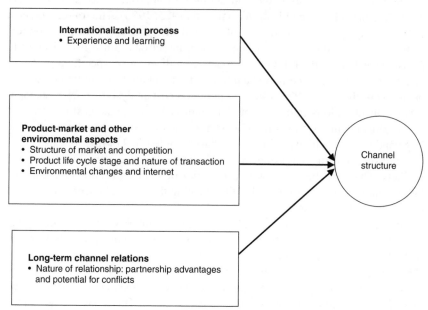

Figure 20.3   Dynamic framework for sales channel structure selection

Source: Adapted from Gabrielsson (1999: 112).

theory testing. The strengths of the case study method are the likelihood of it resulting in theory development (Eisenhardt, 1989) and its ability to answer 'how' and 'why' questions. Multiple case studies rather than a single one were used as this would allow better substantiation and replication of the evidence obtained (Yin, 1989). It would also offer a deeper understanding of the processes and outcomes than a single case (Miles and Huberman, 1994). The companies chosen for the study were Avarte, Designor, Kalevala Jewellery and Marimekko, all of which were leading design companies in Finland. They were selected from the 21 companies that participated in an exhibition called Design Forum Finland. The selection criteria were willingness to participate in the research project and a minimum of five years' export experience.

During the data gathering and analysis we borrowed many of the suggestions put forward by Eisenhardt (1989). In the initial phase, clearly expressed research questions were formulated. During the selection of companies to be studied we ensured that they exported designer products and were SMEs, therefore, following a 'theoretical sampling logic' (Yin, 1989). Multiple data collection methods were used to triangulate the findings (Miles and Huberman, 1994). The main instruments used for data collection were interviews and secondary sources – information published by the in question, companies statistical data and independent academic research, (for example, Eisenhardt, 1989; Yin, 1989). The interviews were conducted between autumn 2000 and spring 2001. The six inter-viewees were either the managing directors or the export managers/directors of the companies. The managing directors of Avarte and Kalevala Jewellery were interviewed by one interviewer, but the export managers of Designor and Marimekko were interviewed by two people to enhance the quality of the study.

The data was analyzed using techniques suggested by Yin (1989) and devel-oped by Miles and Huberman (1994) and Patton (1980), after which the evi-dence was tabulated for each construct and the search for evidence of the 'why' behind the relationships took place. The main analytical method was explanation building (Yin, 1989). The last two steps (as suggested by Eisenhardt, 1989, and Yin, 1989) were to compare our findings with those in the literature in terms of similar and conflicting findings, and to conduct a critical evaluation of the quality of the study. Validity was enhanced by having the interviewees review the draft case reports, by having more than one interviewer at some of the inter-views, and by properly analyzing the results. Reliability was enhanced by careful data collection and tape recording each interview.

SALES CHANNEL SELECTION BY THE CASE STUDY COMPANIES

This section examines the motives for and reasons why the sample companies used particular sales channels and the factors that influenced their development. The analysis follows the framework presented in Figure 20.3. Thus three ele-ments are reviewed: (1) the internationalization process, (2) product-market and other environmental aspects and (3) long-term channel relations.

The Internationalization Process

The degree of internationalization of the sample companies varied, although most were in the early stage of the process. We shall look at each four compa-nies in turn.

Kalevala Jewellery
This company was established in 1937 by a group of Finnish women for whom the manufacture of jewellery based on an ancient tradition and heritage was a way of honouring *Kalevala*, the Finnish national epic. The company specialized in the crafting of precious metals into jewellery resonant of the Viking era. There were four hundred or so items, including necklaces, brooches, earrings, rings, tiepins and cufflinks. All these items were sold under the brand name of Kalevala Jewellery. The owners of the company were motivated less by profit than by building up the company's reputation and giving customers the feeling that they were the supporting national culture. Kalevala's net sales grew steadily, rising from Fmk 13 million to Fmk 80 million between 1988 and 1996 and accounting for approximately 20 per cent of Finnish jewellery sales and about 20 per cent of the total jewellery exports. Kalevala's first export markets

were Sweden and Germany, and it later expanded its operations to include Norway, Denmark, Japan and the US. It followed the traditional internationalization process by first utilizing agents and later adopting more demanding modes, for instance it established its own sales subsidiaries in Sweden and Germany as well as utilizing independent retailers. Thus, its sales channel strategy was indirect in all target countries but Sweden and Germany, where a dual strategy was used.

Designer

In the early 1990s the Hackman group established an entity called Designor to market goods produced by itself (cutlery and cookware), Arabia (porcelain), Iittala (glassware) and Rörstrand (porcelain). The latter three brands, which had built up a strong position in their domestic markets, had been acquired earlier by the Hackman group.

Each brand range is produced in a separate factory and between them they employ about 1500 people. The brand managers of each entity are responsible for design and development; Designor is responsible for marketing and has become a world leader in Scandinavian designer tablewear and decorative household items. The operations are run from two central locations, one in Finland and the other in Sweden.

Hackman, the mother company, was established in 1790 as a trading house in Viborg. By the time of our study it had expanded its international operations to include manufacturing facilities in four countries and sales subsidiaries in seven countries: Sweden, Denmark, The Benelux countries, Estonia and the US. In these countries, where sales subsidiaries exist, independent retailers are used to sell the four brands and direct sales are made to large customers. In the US, in addition to the sales subsidiary sales agents are used to sell to retailers. In other countries where sales subsidiaries have not been established, either agents (Italy) or distributors (the UK, France and Japan) are used. Thus, Designor's sales channel strategy is dual where sales subsidiaries have been established and indirect where they have not.

Avarte

Founded in 1980 as a privately owned company, Avarte manufactures and markets designer furniture. Yrjö Kukkapuro has been the principal designer since the company's inception. Avarte makes original, aesthetic, ergonomically advanced furniture, primarily chairs. It specializes in furniture for offices and cultural and educational facilities. The quest of the designer is to find materials that are perfectly suited to the purpose and function of each item, and great emphasis is placed on carefully considered details that are in harmony with the overall appearance. This requires extensive cooperation with architects, who can bring strong influence to bear on prospective purchasers. The company exported its products right from the beginning, in line with its internationalization philosophy, and it seized opportunities wherever they existed. This has influenced its product design in that two additional factors have to be considered: national variations in requirements such as colour and size, and ease of packing and transport.

Exports have been boosted by the company's excellent reputation and the many international awards won by its principal designer, Yrjö Kukkapuro. The share of exports in total sales is 18 per cent. Sweden is the largest recipied, accounting for 29 per cent of export sales, followed by Germany (21 per cent), the US (20 per cent) and Japan (11 per cent). Avarte sailsits products via distributors in Japan and intermediary agents in Norway, the UK and Holland. The method of promoting the products among architects differs between countries. In Norway, the UK and Holland the company itself promotes the products, while in Japan this is the responsibility of the distributors. Thus Avarte's sales channels are hybrid in the former countries and indirect in Japan. The company has furthered its international involvement by forming a jointly owned sales subsidiary in Sweden, a fully owned one in Germany and a jointly owned production and marketing subsidiary in China. In these countries the products are promoted by architects. Resellers are used for product sales in Germany, but not in Sweden and China. Thus, the sales channels are direct in Sweden and China, and hybrid in Germany.

Marimekko

The Marimekko Corporation – a Finnish textiles and clothing company – was established in 1951. Its operations are based on the original Marimekko brand and the Marimekko concept, which reflects the company's lifestyle ethos. It has three product lines: clothing, interior decorations and accessories.

Between 1956 and 1968 the company experienced rapid growth and thereby achieved internationalization. Export sales began in 1956, when the first exhibition was arranged in Stockholm, followed by the opening of a Marimekko shop in Sweden in 1960 (Ainamo, 1996). In 1961, exhibitions were arranged in Boston, Paris and Stuttgart (ibid.; Kauranen and Kasanen, 1995). That year, Jacqueline Kennedy bought seven Marimekko dresses, an article about Marimekko appeared in *Vogue* and exports to the US began (Kauranen and Kasanen, 1995).

The internationalization process stepped up during the 1970s and 1980s. A licensing agreement was signed with the US company Fieldcrest for the manufacturing of textiles in 1972, and the next year licensing agreements were signed with Nishikawa Sangyo in Japan and Dan River in the US (Ainamo, 1996). Marimekko was listed on the Finnish Stock Exchange in 1974. In 1975, sales subsidiaries were founded in Germany and the US, followed by the opening of a design studio in the US in 1976 (these US operations are not active at the moment). In 1977, franchise stores were opened in Amsterdam (now suspended) and New York (Kauranen and Kasanen, 1995: 15). In addition, the company has 26 shops of its own, most of which are located in Finland. Domestic retailers number about 80 in all, foreign retailers around 700. Thus, the company's sales channels are indirect in all foreign countries but Sweden, where it is dual (although the volume of direct sales is limited).

The above discussion shows that the degree of internationalization of the four companies considerably varies. The least internationalized is Kalevala, followed by Avarte and then Marimekko. The most internationalized company is Designor. All four started their international activities by means of single, indirect channels. As they learned more about their markets they established sales/marketing subsidiaries and other operations, and sold their products either through retailers/resellers or directly through their own sales subsidiaries or retail outlets. Kalevala later established a dual sales channel arrangement for its most promising markets – Sweden and Germany – and Marimekko has a dual sales channel arrangement for Sweden. Avarte chose a hybrid sales channel arrangement for Germany, while designor has relied on dual sales channel arrangements for many of its main markets and a number of indirect sales channels for Japan. The latter accords with the assumptions drawn in the theoretical review of the internationalization process.

Product-Market and Other Environmental Aspects

Most of the sample companies began their export activities once the home market had been consolidated, and these activities were pursued aggressively. Their market offerings – designer products – have international appeal represent a unique life style. They reflect the Scandinavian ability to combine harmony with nature, simplicity and elegant craftsmanship, and they bear the hallmarks of Scandinavian design: timeless beauty combined with functionality. Since they are not mass-produced they also been the personal touch of the designers and craftsmen. They are made from high-quality (often natural) materials and are costly to produce.

During the early stages the products were safe from imitation, but once they became internationally known they became vulnerable to imitators using mass production methods and cheaper materials. Thus, the companies have worked hard to protect their brands and ensure brand loyalty, and they have continuously up-graded the design attributes of their brands. This has required careful selection of markets and sales channel arrangements. The enduring values inherent in designer products have to be strongly communicated to the interested consumer, not only by the firms but also by the members of their sales channels. Hence the latter have to be lovers of fine things. However, values, attitudes and life styles change, and dynamic forces in the market environment can produce many threats. The sample companies seem to be aware of these factors and their potential impact is watched carefully. The rest of this section addresses these aspects and their impact on sales channel arrangements.

The sample companies are in different phases of their product life cycles. Avarte's products are perhaps the most innovative, and it sometimes tailors them to specifications provided by architects. Therefore, it is necessary for its sales channels to be either direct (as in the case of Sweden) or hybrid (Norway and Germany) in order to ensure the success of its export marketing. Designor's products are also innovative, although they include more ordinary tableware products that appeal to a broader market segment and are sold through retailers. However, it also sell sits their products directly to large end-customers in some countries for reasons of scale and scope. The sales channels used by Marimekko – whose products are classic designs sold to a broader segment, and purchase requires the touch and feel consumer to be able to the goods – are of the dual type, consisting of independent retailers and company-owned retail outlets. Finally, Kalevala's Viking-inspired jewellery is purchased by a highly specialized market segment from specialist retailers in most of the company's export markets, but in Sweden and Germany it has its own outlets, and thus it employs a dual sales channel arrangement.

The markets these companies chose to enter clearly influenced their sales channel selection. Their home market characteristics and the potentially large export market led the companies to invest heavily in their channel arrangements, including the sales subsidiaries and/or own retail outlets mentioned above (Designor in the US, Marimekko, Avarte and Designor in Germany Kalevala, Marimekko and Designo in Sweden). The produce of some export markets forced the companies to alter their channel strategies to suit local conditions. In Japan, for instance, Designor and Marimekko use a number of indirect distributors rather than one. Avarte also uses an indirect distributor, thus deviating from its policy of direct control through hybrid sales channel arrangements.

Among the most interesting developments in the market environment is the rise of information technology in general and the Internet in particular. The sample companies view the Internet with mixed feelings, but most see it as a threat as it may allow cheap copies to compete, or enable channel members to manipulate prices. They all think that the nature of designer products is such that Internet users may not fully appreciate the unique features of the products they offer. Furthermore, they feel that conducting export sales through the Internet might endanger their relationship with their channel members. Therefore, only company and product information is provided on their Internet home pages, with consumer queries being passed on to the appropriate channel members in the case of Marimekko and Avarte. All this is in line with the research finding that although the Internet provides the potential for rapid entry into foreign markets, it can cause conflict when not well coordinated with channel members (Al-Obaidi *et al.*, 2000). Designor and Avarte leave it up to their channel members to decide whether to engage in Internet business, but Marimekko is discouraging this until to conduct the result have been carefully studied.

Long-term Channel Relations

Designer products, as explained above, are considered special and feature at the high end of the market. Therefore, channel arrangements exclude ordinary shops selling mass produced items. Rather the outlets chosen are more like studies and the products are artistically exhibited. Such outlets are often small and privately owned by entrepreneurs. (Department stores are difficult to enter and price negotiations are usually tough). These retailers or resellers are first approached and then supplied by importers, distributors or agents. Channel member relationships are usually characterized as sensitive and personal and long-term relationships are very important. When this relationship is developed by understanding each other's needs and offering trust and commitment, it can lead to partnership advantages. On the other hand, when there are conflicts of interest or changes in objectives, bargaining power may be brought to bear or channel structures may be changed to alleviate the conflict.

All our sample companies emphasize the importance of long-term relationships, and hence they do not directly compete with their channel members in any market (direct/indirect) channels. But Avarte's reliance on channel intermediaries for product placement and its strong dependence on sales promotion by architects means that it places great importance on its relationship with these actors. However, Designor's use of nunerous distributors in Japan offers the possibility of conflict. According to Designor this channel arrangement is necessary because in Japan different product lines are sold through different distributors. The second strand of Designor's dual sales channel strategy focuses on large accounts, which does not conflict with the interests of channel members who sell to smaller customers. While Kalevala and Marimekko's dual channel arrangements have a large conflict potential, the indirect retailers who sell the bulk of their exported products have not objected to the presence of the companies' own showrooms and shops, but rather appreciate the chance to familiarize themselves with the products offered there. This lack of conflict can be attributed to one of two reasons: the small volume of their direct sales, or their ability to wield power. In the case of both Kalevala and Marimekko the first explanation seems more logical as it is not likely that they will have a significant amount of power over their channel members.

SALES CHANNELS STRUCTURE

The sales channel structures of the sample companies are analyzed at the cross-case level, based on the data gathered from the companies. As discussed above, both single sales channels and multiple sales channel structures are utilized by the companies. These will be examined separately.

Single Sales Channels

Single sales channel strategies have been used by all the sample companies for at least some of their markets. These have taken three forms: (A1) exporting/indirect sales, (A2) direct investment/indirect sales and (A3) direct investment/direct sales (Figure 20.4).

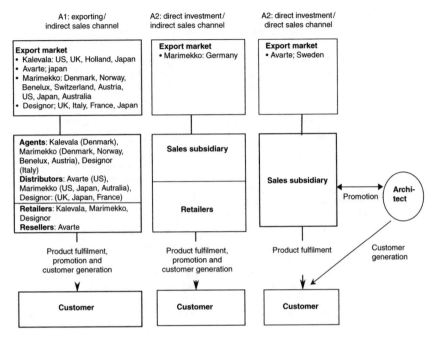

Figure 20.4   Single sales channel strategies

The most commonly used sales channel for all four companies is A1. The companies use either an agent or a distributor, depending on the foreign market entered, and then sell through retailers or resellers, depending on whether the customers are industrial buyers (Avarte) or consumers, thus utilizing an indirect sales channel. Two of the companies have either established a subsidiary for direct sales (A3, Avarte in Sweden) or sell indirectly (A2) through retailers (Marimekko in Germany).

Multiple Sales Channel Strategies

Multiple sales channel strategies have also been used by the sample companies, but only in certain markets. These channels consist of (B1) exporting/many indirect channels, (B2) exporting/hybrid sales channel, (B3) direct investment/dual sales channel and (B4) direct investment/hybrid sales channel (Figure 20.5).

The four companies seem to have taken individual approaches. Channel structure B1 was adopted by Designor and Marimekko when they entered the Japanese market due to the existing product-market structure. Structure B2 is used by Avarte in Norway, the UK and Holland, and B4 channel is used by Avarte in Germany.

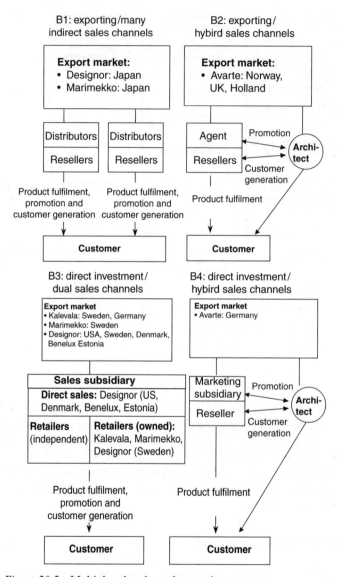

Figure 20.5   Multiple sales channel strategies

The hybrid sales channels thus involve either a local presence or no local presence. Direct investment is logical in large countries such as Germany, but it does not make sense in smaller countries such as Norway. Avarte intends to make greater use of the hybrid channel structure (B2) in the future, with Avarte's but will maintain its direct channel in Sweden. Both of these arrangements enable greater control. Avarte's direct contact with architects is also crucial. Finally, B3 is used by Kalevala and Marimekko. Designor too uses its own and independent retailers in Sweden, as well as providing catalogues and direct sales to large customer (US, Denmark, the Benelux countries and Estonia).

DISCUSSION

The above review of the sales channel structures used by the sample companies raises an interesting question: how well can the current sales channel theories predict small and medium-sized companies' sales channel behaviour?

The internationalization process literature focuses on the stages that companies go through as they proceed towards more suphisticated products, operations and markets (Luostarinen, 1970, 1979; see also Johansson and Vahlne, 1977). It was argued in the theoretical section above that exporters of designer products first export through indirect sales channels, but when experience is gained a direct channel is established. This study confirms this assertion as all the sample companies started their international operations by exporting through indirect sales channels. The expectation that greater internationalization will lead to the use of multiple channels is also confirmed. Furthermore, it was asserted in our review of the literature that a positive experience of a particular channel strategy, either in the home country or in foreign markets, increases the probability of a similar strategy being chosen for a new market entry. This too receives support from our study, for instance Marimekko and Kalevala use dual sales channel arrangements in their main export markets as well as in their home market.

The sales channel economic structure literature explains channel selection on the basis of the cost and efficiency considerations that lie at the heart of transaction cost analysis (Coase, 1937; Williamson, 1975, 1985). According to this theory, direct sales channels, especially when asset specificity is high, make the most sense when the transaction size is large. This accords with our findings, for instance Avarte has more direct sales channel arrangements (including hybrid) than the other companies, whose transactions are probably smaller in volume than Avarte's (due to the latter's focus on consumers) and have lower asset specificity (ordinary sales activities do not require the same expertise as Avarte's promotional activities with architects). Furthermore, the suggestion that multiple (dual or hybrid) sales channels are optimal for increasing sales volume in highly diversified markets receive, some support from our study. However, in the case of Avarte, hybrid channels are used in a very fragmented market (educational establishments and offices); and in the case of Designor, numerous distributors are used in Japan to reach different market segments.

The long-term channel relationship literature's focuses on the development of relationships over time (Dwyer *et al.*, 1987). It is argued that this is especially useful in explaining companies' choice of multiple channels (dual or hybrid). Hybrid channels will be selected when the partnership advantages that accrue from trustful and committed relationships are important, whereas a dual channel will be chosen when the relative power of the exporting company is strong enough to overcome channel conflicts. Our results support the former argument. The importance of good, long-term relations with architects and resellers led Avarte to opt for a hybrid sales channel arrangement. The importance of superior power in overcoming sales channel conflicts, especially in the case of dual sales channels, receives limited support, although in in our study the volume of direct sales may have been too small to spark conflicts.

The product life cycle model (Rogers, 1962) describes the stages through which a product passes. The assertion that different channels are used during different stages of the life cycle has proved somewhat difficult to examine as our sample companies are all innovative in nature. However, comparing them with each other seems to confirm the suggestion that the more innovative the product, the more that direct/hybrid channel arrangements will be utilized (Avarte). On the other hand, the broader the targeted market segment of our sample, the more they used either indirect sales channels (Designor and Marimekko) or dual sales channels (Designor, Marimekko and Kalevala). A novel finding was that hybrid sales channels were used in the early phases of the products' life cycles (cf. Gabrielsson, 1999: 97–99).

CONCLUSION

In this concluding section we shall evaluate the theoretical contribution and managerial implications of our study. The fact that the subject matter of our investigation is relatively under-researched means that it has been a fruitful area of study (see Dutta *et al.*, 1995; Frazier, 1990) and has produced some interesting results.

The use of multiple channels in the export activities of design companies has not previously been the object of explicit study. The conventional approach has been to consider sales channel decisions from a single channel viewpoint. Thus, our focus on multiple sales channel strategies and their development has helped to narrow this research gap (see also Gabrielsson, 1999). This study has applied and developed the existing theories, constructs and concepts to examine these channels. A variety of channel structures have been identified (Figures 20.4 and 20.5) and their selection has been explained.

Many of our research results may be applicable to other industries. Indeed, Turnbull and Ellwood (1986) have already found evidence of multiple sales channel arrangements among European information technology companies. Multiple sales channel arrangements have also been found in the personal computer industry (Gabrielsson, 1999), as well as in the hospital and health care equipment and air-conditioning equipment industries (see for example Corey *et al.*, 1989; Anderson *et al.*, 1997).

With regard to the managerial implications of our study, the increased use of e-commerce in sales channel strategies could lead to (1) increased use of hybrid sales channels due to the ease of communication between partners via the Internet, and (2) greater use of dual sales channels as producers will increasingly be able to dispense with channel intermediaries, thus drastically cutting costs. The possibility of the former happening receives more support than the latter in our study, or at least for the time being. In addition, we have increased the available knowledge on export channel strategies. This is important as inappropriate strategies are difficult to change and have a long-term impact on company performance.

References

Aaby, N. and Slater, S. F. (1989) 'Management influences on export performance: a review of the empirical literature 1978–1988', *International Marketing Review*, 6(4), pp. 7–23.

Aggarwal, R. (1999) 'Technology and Globalization as Mutual Reinforcers in Business: Reorienting Strategic Thinking for the Millennium', *Management International Review*, Special Issue 2/99, pp. 83–104.

Agarwal, S. and Ramaswami, S. N. (1992) 'Choice of foreign market entry mode: Impact of ownership, location and internalisation factors', *Journal of International Business Studies*, 23(1), pp. 1–28.

Ainamo, A. (1996) 'Industrial Design and Business Performance: A Case Study of Design Management in a Finnish Fashion Firm, doctored thesis: Helsinki School of Economics.

Akehurst, G. and Alexander, N. (1995) 'Developing a framework for the study of the internationalization of retailing', *Service Industries Journal*, 15(4), pp. 204–9.

Aldrich, H. and Zimmer, C. (1986) 'Entrepreneurship through Social Networks', in R. Smilor and D. Sexton (eds) *The Art and Science of Entrepreneurship* (New York: Ballinger).

Alexander, N. (1997) *International Retailing* (Oxford: Blackwell).

Ali, Y. (1995) 'Performance of International Joint Ventures (IJVs) in Developing Countries: A Study of IJVs in Bangladesh', unpublished doctoral dissertation (Wollongong, NSW: University of Wollongong).

Al-Obaidi, Z., Nahar, N. and Huda, N. (2000) 'A Framework for the Analysis of Barriers in IT-enabled Exporting of High-tech Firms', in R. Hackey (ed.), *Proceedings of the Business Information Technology Management: E-futures*, 10th Annual BIT Conference, (on CD-ROM), Manchester 1–2 November.

Alon, I. and McKee, D. L. (1999) 'The Internationalisation of professional business service franchises', *Journal of Consumer Marketing*, 16, pp. 74–85.

Alt, M. (1990) *Exploring Hyperspace: A Non-Mathematical Explanation of Multivariate Analysis* (Maidenhead: McGraw-Hill).

Amiti, M. (1998) 'New Trade Theories and Industrial Location in the EU: A Survey of the Evidence', *Oxford Review of Economic Policy*, 14(2), pp. 45–53.

Anderson, E. (1990) 'Two firms, one frontier: On assessing joint venture performance', *Sloan Management Review*, 19 (Winter), pp. 19–30.

Anderson, E. and Coughlan, A. T. (1994) 'International Market Entry and Expansion via Independent or Integrated Channels of Distribution', *International Market Entry and Expansion*, 51 (January), pp. 71–82.

Anderson, E., Day, G. S. and Rangan, V. K. (1997) 'Strategic Channel Design', *Sloan Management Review*, Summer, pp. 59–69.

Anderson, E. and Gatignon, H. (1986) 'Modes of foreign entry: A transaction cost analysis and propositions', *Journal of International Business Studies*, 17 (Fall), pp. 1–26.

Anderson, E. and Gatignon, H. (1988) 'Modes of foreign entry: a transaction cost analysis and propositions', *Journal of International Business Studies*, 17, pp 1–26.

Andersen, O. (1993) 'On the Internationalization Process of Firms: A Critical Analysis', *Journal of International Business Studies*, 24, pp. 209–32.

Andersson, U., Johanson, J. and Vahlne, J. (1997) 'Organic Acquisitions in the Internationization Process of the Business Firm', *Management International Review*, 37(2), pp. 67–84.

Axel, M. (1995) 'Toward an analysis of Japanese-style management: a psycho-cultural and socio-historical approach', *Management International Review*, 35(2), pp. 57–73

Aydalot, P. and Keeble, D. (eds) (1988) *High Technology Industry and Innovative Environments: The European Experience* (London: Routledge).

Baden-Fuller, C. and Stopford, J. (1991) 'Globalization frustrated: the case of white goods', *Strategic Management Journal*, 12, pp. 493–507.

Bagchi-Sen, S. and Kuechler, L. (2000) 'Strategic and functional orientation of small and medium sized enterprises in professional services: An analysis of public accountancy', *The Service Industries Journal*, 20, pp. 117–46.

Bailey, J. P. (1998) Intermediation and Electronic Markets: Aggregation and Pricing in Internet Commerce, PhD. thesis, Massachusatt, Institute of Technology.

Bailey, N. (1994) 'Towards a research agenda for public–private partnerships in the 1990s', *Local Economy*, 8(4), pp. 292–306.

Bain, J. (1956) *Barriers to New Competition* (Cambridge, Mass.: Harvard University Press).

Bakos, Y. and Brynjolfsson, E. (1999) 'Bundling information goods: pricing, profits and efficiency', *Management Science*, 45(12), pp. 1613–30.

Balabanis, G. I. (1998) 'Antecedents of co-operation, conflict and relationship longevity in an international trade intermediary supply chain', *Journal of Global Marketing*, 12(2), pp. 25–46.

Balabanis, G. I. (2000) 'Factors Affecting Export Intermediaries' Service Offerings: The British Example', *Journal of International Business Studies*, 31(1), pp. 83–99.

Barkema, H. G., Bell, J. and Pennings, J. M. (1996) 'Foreign Entry, Cultural Barriers, and Learning', *Strategic Management Journal*, 17, pp. 151–66.

Barney, J. B. (1991) 'Firm resources and sustained competitive advantage', *Journal of Management*, 17, pp. 99–120.

Barney, J. and Hoskisson, R. (1990) 'SGs: Untested Assertions and Research Proposals', *Managerial and Decision Economics*, 11, pp. 187–98.

Bartlett, C. (1981) 'Multinational structural change: evolution versus reorganization', in L. Otterbeck (ed.), *The Management of Headquarters–Subsidiary Relationships in Multinational Corporations* (Aldershot: Gower), pp. 121–45.

Bartlett, C. and Ghoshal, S. (1986) 'Tap your subsidiaries for global reach', *Harvard Business Review*, November/December, pp. 87–94.

Bartlett, C. G. and Ghoshal, S. (1987) 'Managing Across Borders: New Strategic Requirements', *Sloan Management*, 28, pp. 7–17.

Barlett, C. and Ghoshal, S. (1989/1994) *Managing Across National Borders: The Transnational Solution* (Cambridge, Mass.: Harvard Business School Press).

Barlett, C. and Goshal, S. (1991) 'Global Strategic management: impact on the new frontiers of strategy research', *Strategic Management Journal*, 12, pp. 5–16.

Baums, T. (1993) 'Takeovers versus institutions in corporate governance in Germany', in D. D. Prentice and P. R. J. Holland (eds), *Contemporary issues in corporate governance* (Oxford: Clarendon Press), pp. 151–83.

Beamish, P. W., Craig, R. and McLellan, K. (1993) 'The Performance Characteristics of Canadian versus U.K. Exporters in Small and Medium-sized Firms', *Management International Review*, 33, pp. 121–37.

Becattini, G. (1990) 'The Marshallian industrial district as a socio-economic notion', in F. Pyke, G. Becattini and W. Sengenberger (eds), *Industrial Districts and Inter-Firm Cooperation in Italy* (Geneva: International Institute for Labour Studies).

Beckerman, W. (1956) 'Distance and the Pattern of Intra-European Trade', *Review of Economics and Statistics*, 28, pp. 31–40.

Beechler, S. and Zhuang Y. J. (1994) 'Transfer of Japanese-style management to American subsidiaries: contingencies, constraints, and competencies', *Journal of International Business Studies*, 25(3), pp 467–93.

Bell, J. (1995) 'The Internationalisation of Small Computer Software Firms: A Further Challenge to Stage Theories', *European Journal of Marketing*, 29(8), pp. 60–75.

Bell, J., McNaughton, R. and Young, S. (2000) 'Born-again global firms: an extension to the "born global" phenomenon', Paper presented at the McGill Conference on International Entrepreneurship.

Bell, J. and Young, S. (1998) 'Towards an integrative framework of the internationalisation of the firm', in G. Hooley, R. Loveridge and D. Wilson (eds), *Internationalisation: Process, Context and Markets* (London: Macmillan).

Benito, G. R. G. (1997) 'Divestment of Foreign Production Operations', *Applied Economics*, 29, pp. 1365–77.

Benito, G. R. G. and Welch, L. S. (1994) 'Foreign market servicing: beyond choice of entry mode', *Journal of International Marketing*, 2(2), pp. 7–27.

Bennett, R. (1997) 'Export marketing and the Internet', *International Marketing Review*, 14(4), pp. 56–71.

Bennett, R. (1998) 'Using the WWW for International Marketing: Internet Use and perceptions of Export barriers among German and British Businesses', *Journal of Marketing Communications*, 4, pp. 27–43.

Bhat, S. S., Bonnici, J. L. and Caruana, A. R. (1993) 'Diversification strategies for the service sector', *Journal of Professional Services Marketing*, 9, pp. 59–70.

Bilkey, W. and Tesar, G. (1997) 'The Export Behaviour of Smaller-Sized Wisconsin Manufacturing Firms', *Journal of International Business Studies*, 8, pp. 93–8.

Birkinshaw, J. (1994) 'Approaching Heterarchy: A review of the literature on multinational strategy and structure', *Advances in Comparative Management*, 9, pp. 111–44.

Birkinshaw, J. (1996) 'How Multinational Subsidiary Mandates are Gained and Lost', *Journal of International Business Studies*, 27(3), pp. 467–95.

Birkinshaw, J. (2000) *Entrepreneurship in the Global Firm* (London: Sage).

Birkinshaw, J. and Hood, N. (1997) 'An empirical study of development processes in foreign-owned subsidiaries in Canada and Scotland', *Management International Review*, 37(4), pp. 339–64.

Birkinshaw, J. and Hood, N. (eds) (1998a) *Multinational Corporate Evolution and Subsidiary Development* (London: Macmillan).

Birkinshaw, J. and Hood, S. (1998b) 'Multinational Subsidiary Evolution: Capability and Charter Change in Foreign-Owned Subsidiary Companies', *Academy of Management Review*, 23, pp. 773–95.

Birkinshaw, J. M. and Morrison, A. J. (1995) 'Configurations of strategy and structure in subsidiaries of multinational corporations', *Journal of International Business Studies*, 26(4), pp. 729–54.

Birkinshaw, J., Morrison, A. and Hulland, J. (1995) 'Structural and competitive determinants of a global integration strategy', *Strategic Management Journal*, 16, pp. 637–55.

Black, B. S. (2000) 'The legal and institutional preconditions for strong stock markets', Stanford Law School Working Paper, no. 179, Stanford.

Blackwell, W. L. (1968) *The beginnings of Russian industrialization*, vol. 1. (Princeton, NJ: Princeton University Press).

Blackwell, W. L. (1970) *The industrialization of Russia: an historical perspective* (New York: Crowell).

Blasi, J. H., Kroumova, M. and Kruse, D. (1997) *Kremlin capitalism: privatizing the Russian economy* (Ithaca, NY: Cornell University Press).

Blomstrom M. and Kokko, A. (1998) 'Multinational Corporations and Spillovers', *Journal of Economic Surveys*, 2, pp. 247–8.

Boddewyn, J. (1979) 'Foreign Divestment: Magnitude and Factors', *Journal of International Business Studies*, 10, pp. 21–7.

Boddewyn, J. (1983) 'Foreign and Domestic Divestment and Investment decisions: Like or unlike?', *Journal of International Business Studies*, 14, pp. 23–35.

Bogner, W. (1991) 'Patterns of Intra-Industry Competition: A Dynamic Analysis of Theoretical Foundations of Strategic Groups', unpublished doctoral dissertation, University of Illinois.

Bogner, W., Thomas, H. and McGee, J. (1996) 'A Longitudinal Study of The Competitive Positions and Entry Paths of European Firms in the US Pharmaceutical Market', *Strategic Management Journal*, 17, pp. 85–107.

Bolton Committee (1971) 'Report of the Committee of Enquiry on Small Firms', Cmnd 4811 (London: HMSO).

Bolton, P. and Von Thadden, A. (1998) 'Blocks, liquidity and corporate control', *Journal of Finance*, 53, pp. 1–25.

Bonaccorsi, A. (1993) 'What do we know about Exporting by Small Italian Manufacturing Firms', *Journal of International Marketing*, 1, pp. 49–75.

Bowman, E. H. and Singh, H. (1993) 'Corporate Restructuring: Reconfiguring the Firm', *Strategic Management Journal*, 14, Special Issue, pp. 5–14.

Boyacigiller, N. (1990) 'The role of expatriates in the management of interdependence, complexity and risk in multinational corporations', *Journal of International Business Studies*, 21(3), pp. 357–81.

Brandt, W. K. and Hulbert, J. M. (1977) 'Headquarters guidance in marketing strategy in the multinational subsidiary', *Columbia Journal of World Business*, Winter, pp. 7–14.

Bresman, H., Birkinshaw, J. and Nobel, R. (1999) 'Knowledge transfer in international acquisitions', *Journal of International Business Studies*, 30(3), pp. 439–62.

Brock, J. K.-U. (2000) 'Information and communication technology in the small firm', in S. Carter and D. Jones-Evans (eds), *Enterprise and Small Business: Principles, Practice and Policy* (London: Prentice-Hall),

Brouthers, K. D. (1995) 'The Influence of International Risk on Entry Mode Selection in the Computer Software Industry', *Management International Review*, 35(1), pp. 7–28.

Brouthers, K. D. and Brouthers, L. E. (2000) 'Acquisition or greenfield start-up? Institutional, cultural and transaction cost influences', *Strategic Management Journal*, 21, pp. 89–97.

Brouthers, L. E., Brouthers, K. D. and Werner, S. (1999) 'Is Dunning's eclectic framework descriptive or normative?', *Journal of International Business Studies*, 30(4), pp. 831–44.

Brown, R. and Cook, D. (1990) 'Strategy and Performance in British Exporters', *The Quarterly Review of Marketing*, 15(3), pp. 1–6.

Brülhart, M. (1996a) 'Commerce et specialization geogaphique dans l'Union Europeenne', *Economie Internationale*, 65, pp. 169–202.

Brülhart, M. (1996b) 'Economic Geography, Industry Location and Trade: The Evidence', *World Economy*, 21, pp. 775–801.

Brush, T. H. and Artz, K. W. (1999) 'Toward a Contingent Resource-Based Theory: The impact of information asymmetry on the value of capabilities in veterinary medicine', *Strategic Management Journal*, 20, pp. 223–50.

Brynjolfsson, E. and Smith, M. (2000) 'Frictionless commerce? A comparison of internet and conventional retailers', *Management Science*, 46(4), pp. 563–85.

Buck, T. and Cole, J. (1987) *Modern Soviet economic performance* (Oxford: Blackwell).

Buck, T., Filatotchev, I., Wright, M. and Zhukov, V. (1999) 'Corporate governance and employee ownership in an economic crisis: enterprise strategies in the former Soviet Union', *Journal of Comparative Economics*, 27, pp. 459–74.

Buck, T. and Tull, M. (2000) 'Anglo-American contributions to German and Japanese corporate governance after WW2', *Business History*, 42(2), pp. 119–40.

Buckley, P. J. (1989) 'Foreign Direct Investments by Small- and Medium-Sized Enterprises: The Theoretical Background', *Small Business Economics*, 1, pp. 89–100.

Buckley, P. J. (1995) *Foreign Direct Investment and Multinational Enterprises* (Basingstoke: Macmillan).

Buckley, P. J. and Casson, M. (1976) *The Future of Multinational Enterprises* (London: Holmes and Meier).

Buckley, P. J. and Casson, M. (1988) 'A Theory of Co-operation in International Business', in F. J. Contractor and P. Lorange (eds), *Co-operative Strategies in International Business* (Lexington, Mass.: Lexington).

Buckley, P. J. and Mucchielli, J. L. (eds) (1997) *Multinational Firms and International Relocation* (Cheltenham: Edward Elgar).

Buckley, P. J., Pass, C. L. and Prescott, K. (1990) 'Measures of International Competitiveness: Empirical Findings from British Manufacturing Companies', *Journal of Marketing Management*, 6(1), pp. 1–13.

Buckley, P. J., Pass, C. L. and Prescott, K. (1994) 'Foreign Market Servicing by Multinationals: an Integrated Treatment', in P. J. Buckley, and P. Ghauri (eds) *The Internationalisation of the Firm: A Reader* (London: Dryden), pp. 273–88.

Burgel, O. and Murray, G. C. (2000) 'The International Market Entry Choices of Start-Up Companies in High-Technology Industries', *Journal of International Marketing*, 8(2), pp. 33–62.

Burton, F. N. and Schlegelmilch, B. B. (1987) 'Profile analyses of non-exporters versus Exporters grouped by export involvement', *Management International Review*, 27(1), pp. 38–49.

Byrne, B. M. (1994) *Structural Equation Modeling with EQS and EQS/Windows* (Thousand Oaks, CA: Sage).

Cannon, T. and Willis, M. (1981) 'The Smaller Firm in Overseas Trade', *European Small Business Journal*, 1(3), pp. 45–55.

Cantwell, J. A. and Mudambi, R. (2000) 'MNC competence-creating subsidiary mandates: an empirical investigation', paper presented at the 29th Annual Conference of the European International Business Academy, Maastricht.

Casson, M. (1986) *International Divestment and Restructuring Decisions (with special reference to the motor industry)*, Multinational Enterprises Programme Working Paper no. 40 (Geneva: International Labour Office).

Casson, M. (1992) 'Internalisation Theory and beyond', in P. J. Buckley (ed.), *New Directions in International Business: Research Priorities for the 1990s* (Aldershot: Edward Elgar), pp. 4–27.

Casson, M. (1993) 'Cultural determinants of economic performance', *Journal of Comparative Economics*, 17, pp. 418–42.

Caves, R. E. (1974) 'Causes of direct investment: foreign firms shares and Canadian and United Kingdom manufacturing industries', *Review of Economic and Statistics*, 56, pp. 272–93.

Caves, R. E. (1996) *Multinational Enterprise and Economic Analysis*, 2nd edn (New York: Cambridge University Press).

Caves, R. and Porter, M. (1997) 'From Entry Barriers to Mobility Barriers – Conjectural Decisions and Contrived Deterrence to New Competition', *Quarterly Journal of Economics*, 91, pp. 241–62.

Cavusgil, S. T. (1980) 'On the Internationalisation Process of the Firm', *European Research*, 8(6), pp. 273–81.

Cavusgil. S. T. (1984) 'Differences in Exporting Firms Based on Their Degree of Internationalisation', *Journal of Business Research*, 12, pp. 195–208.

Cavusgil, S. T. and Zou, S. (1994) 'Marketing Strategy–Performance Relationship: An Investigation of the Empirical Link in Export Market Ventures', *Journal of Marketing*, 58 (January), pp. 1–21.

Chapters Online (2000) Annual Report (www.chapters.ca/ir).

Chaudhry, S. and Crick, D. (1998) 'Export information providers: are they meeting the needs of SMEs?', *Marketing Intelligence and Planning*, 16(3), pp. 141–9.

Cheng, J. L. C. and Bolon, D. S. (1993) 'The management of multinational R&D: a neglected topic in international business research', *Journal of International Business Studies*, 24(1), pp. 1–18.

Chesnais, F., Ietto-Gilles, G. and Simonette, R. (eds) (2000) *European Integration and Global Corporate Strategies* (London: Routledge).

Chesnais, F. and Soilleau, A. (2000) 'FDI and European Trade', in F. Chesnais, G. Ietto-Gilles and R. Simonette (eds), *European Integration and Global Corporate Strategies* (London: Routledge).

Chetty, S. K. and Hamilton, R. T. (1993) 'Firm-level Determinants of Export Performance: A Meta-analysis', *International Marketing Review*, 10, pp. 26–34.

Chittum, J. M. (1998) 'How do I go global?', *Business America*, 119(4), pp. 17–18.

Christensen, P. R. and Lindmark, I. (1993) 'Location and Internationalisation of Small Firms', in L. Lundqvist and L.-O. Persson (eds), *Visions and Strategies in European Integration* (Berlin: Springer-Verlag).

Chu, W. and Anderson, E. M. (1992) 'Capturing ordinal properties of categorical dependent variables: A review with application in modes of foreign entry', *International Journal of Research in Marketing*, 9(2), pp. 149–60.

Clark, T. and Mallory, G. (1997) 'The Impact of Strategic Choice on the Internationalisation of the Firm', in G. Chryssochoidis, C. Millar and J. Clegg (eds), *Internationalisation Strategies* (London: Macmillan), pp. 193–206.

Coase, R. H. (1937) 'The Nature of the Firm', *Economica*, 4, pp. 386–405.

Cohen, W. M. and Levinthal, D. (1990) 'Absorptive capacity: A new perspective on learning and innovation', *Administrative Science Quarterly*, 35(1), pp. 128–52.

Cooke, P. and Morgan, K. (1994) 'The Regional Innovation System in Baden-Wurttemberg', *International Journal of Technology Management*, 9(3), pp. 394–429.

Cool, K. and Dierickx, I. (1993) 'Rivalry, Strategic Groups and Profitability', *Strategic Management Journal*, 14, pp. 47–59.

Cool, K. and Schendel, D. (1987) 'Strategic Group Formation and Performance: US Pharmaceutical Industry (1963–1982)', *Management Science*, 33, pp. 1102–24.

Cooper, A. (1994) 'Having ideas will travel', *Adweek*, 35, pp. 28–35.

Coppel, J. (2000) 'E-Commerce: impacts and policy challenges', OECD Economics Department Working Paper, ECO/WKP (Paris: OECD).

Corey, R. E., Cespedes, F. V. and Rangan, K. V. (1989) *Going to Market: Distribution Systems for Industrial Product* (Boston, Mass.: Harvard Business School).

Coviello, N. and Martin, K. A.-M. (1999) 'Internationalisation of Service SMEs: An Integrated Perspective from the Engineering Consulting Sector', *Journal of International Marketing*, 7(4), pp. 42–66.

Coviello, N. E. and McAuley, A. (1999) 'Internationalisation and the Smaller Firm: A Review of Contemporary Research, *Management International Review*, 39(3), pp. 223–56.

Coviello, N. and Munro, H. (1995) 'Growing the entrepreneurial Firm: Networking for International Market Development', *European Journal of Marketing*, 29(7), pp. 49–62.

Cray, D. (1984) 'Control and coordination in multinational corporations', *Journal of International Business Studies*, 15(2), pp. 85–98.

Crick, D. (1992) 'UK Export Assistance: are we supporting the best programmes', *Journal of Marketing Management*, 8, pp. 81–92.

Crick, D. (1995) 'An investigation into the targeting of UK export assistance', *European Journal of Marketing*, 29(8), pp. 76–94.

Crick, D. (1999) 'An investigation into SMEs' Use of Languages in Their Export Operations', *International Journal of Entrepreneurial Behaviour and Research*, 59(1), pp. 19–31.

Crick, D. and Bradshaw, R. (1999) 'The Standardisation Versus Adaptation Decision of "Successful" SMEs: Findings from a Survey of Winners of the Queen's Award for Export', *Journal of Small Business and Enterprise Development*, 6(2), pp. 191–9.

Crick, D. and Chaudhry, S. (1995) 'Export Practices of Asian SMEs: some preliminary findings', *Marketing Intelligence and Planning*, 13(11), pp. 13–21.

Crick, D. and Chaudhry, S. (1996) 'Export Behaviour of Asian and indigenous-owned SMEs in the UK clothing industry: a research note', *International Journal of Entrepreneurial Behaviour and Research*, 2(1), pp. 77–84.

Crick, D. and Chaudhry, S. (1997a) 'Small businesses' motives for exporting: the effect of internationalisation', *Journal of Marketing Practice: Applied Marketing Science*, 3(3), pp. 156–70.

Crick, D. and Chaudhry, S. (1997b) 'Export problems and government assistance required by UK exporters: an investigation into the effect of ethnicity', *International Journal of Entrepreneurial Behaviour and Research*, 3(1), pp. 3–18.

Crick, D. and Chaudhry, S. (1999) 'Cultural Diversity and Export Growth in the UK: Comparative Evidence of Asian and Indigenous-Owned Firms' Motives for Exporting', *Journal of Transnational Management Development*, 4(2), pp. 49–64.

Crick, D. and Chaudhry, S. (2000a) 'UK SMEs' awareness, use and perceptions of selected government export assistance: an investigation into the effect of ethnicity', *International Journal of Entrepreneurial Behaviour and Research*, 6(2), pp. 72–89.

Crick, D. and Chaudhry, S. (2000b) 'UK agricultural exporters' perceived barriers and government assistance requirements', *Marketing Intelligence and Planning*, 18(1), pp. 30–8.

Crick, D., Chaudhry, S. and Batstone, S. (2000) 'Revisiting the concentration versus spreading debate as a successful export growth strategy: the case of UK SMEs exporting agricultural-related products', *Entrepreneurship and Regional Development*, 12(2), pp. 49–67.

Crick, D. and Czinkota, M. R. (1995) 'Export Assistance: Another look at whether we are supporting the best programmes', *International Marketing Review*, 12(3), pp. 61–72.

Crick, D. and Jones, M. V. (1999) 'Design and Innovation Strategies within Successful High-Tech Firms', *Marketing Intelligence and Planning*, 17(3), pp. 161–8.

Crick, D. and Jones, M. V. (2000) 'Small High-Technology Firms and International High-Technology Markets', *Journal of International Marketing*, 8(2), pp. 63–85.

Crick, D., Jones, M. V. and Hart, S. (1994) 'International Marketing Research Activities of UK Exporters: An Exploratory Study', *Journal of Euromarketing*, 3(2), pp. 7–26.

Crick, D. and Katsikeas, C. S. (1995) 'Export Practices of UK Clothing and Knitwear industry', *Marketing Intelligence and Planning*, 13(7), pp. 13–22.

Crisp, O. (1976) *Studies in the Russian economy before 1914* (London: Macmillan).

Cromie, C., Clarke, B. and Cromie, S. (1997) 'The Use of Foreign Languages by Irish Exporters', *Irish Business and Administrative Research*, 18, pp. 16–33.

Cyert, R. M. and March, J. G. (1963) *A Behavioral theory of the Firm* (New York: Blackwell).

Czinkota, M. (1982) *Export Development Strategies: US Promotion Policy* (New York: Praeger).

Danson, M. and Whittam, G. (1998) 'Networks, innovation and industrial districts: the case of Scotland', in M. Steiner (ed.), *Clusters and Regional Specialisation* (London: Pion).

da Rocha, A., Christensen, C. H. and da Cunha, C. E. (1990) 'Aggressive and Passive Exporters: A Study in the Brazilian Furniture Industry', *International Marketing Review*, 7(5), pp. 6–15.

Das, M. (1994) 'Successful and Unsuccessful Exporters from Developing Countries: Some Preliminary Findings', *European Journal of Marketing*, 28(12), pp. 19–33.

D'Cruz, J. (1986) 'Strategic Management of Subsidiaries', in H. Etemad and L. S. Dulude (eds), *Managing The Multinational Subsidiary: Response to Environmental Changes and to Host Nation R&D Policies* (London: Croom Helm).

Delios, A. and Beamish, P. W. (1999) 'Ownership strategy of Japanese firms: Transactional, institutional, and experience influences', *Strategic Management Journal*, 20, pp. 915–33.

De Meyer, A. (1993) 'Management of an international network of industrial R&D laboratories', *R&D Management*, 23(2), pp. 109–20.

De Meyer, A. (1995) 'Tech talk', in J. Drew (ed.), *Readings in International Enterprise* (London: Routledge).

Department of Trade and Industry (DTI) (1997) *Export Winners: How the Best Companies are Winning in World Markets* (London: DTI).

Dess, G. and Davis, P. (1984) 'Porter's (1980) generic strategies as determinants of strategic group membership and organizational performance', *Academy of Management Journal*, 27, pp. 467–88.

Dess, G. G., Gupta, A., Hennart, J. F. and Hill, W. L. (1995) 'Conducting and integrating strategy research at the international corporate and business levels: issues and directions', *Journal of Management*, 21, pp. 357–93.

Dess, G. G. and Robinson, R. B. (1984) 'Measuring organisational performance in the absence of objective measures: The case of the privately held firm and conglomerate business unit', *Strategic Management Journal*, 5, pp. 265–73.

Devlin (2000) *Webpsych for Websites*, Devlin Applied Design, www.devlin.ca.

Diamantopoulos, A. (1998) Editorial, *Journal of International Marketing*, 6(3), pp. 1–9.

Diamantopoulos, A. and Schlegelmilch, B. B. (1994) 'Linking Export Manpower to Export Performance: A Canonical Regression Analysis of European and US Data', in S. T. Cavusgil and C. Axinn (eds), *Advances in International Marketing*, vol. 6 (Greenwich, CT: JAI Press), pp. 161–181.

Diamantopoulos, A. and Souchon, A. L. (1996) 'Instrumental, Conceptual and Symbolic Use of Export Information: an exploratory study of UK firms', *Advances in International Marketing*, 8, pp. 147–63.

Dichtl, E. (1990) 'International Orientation as a Pre-Condition for Export Success', *Journal of International Business Studies*, 21(1), pp. 23–40.

Dicken, P. (1998) *Global Shift: Transforming the World Economy* (London: Paul Chapman).

Dickerson, A. P., Gibson, H. D. and Tsiakalotos, E. (1995) 'Short-termism and under-investment: the influence of financial system', *Manchester School*, 63, pp. 1–22.

DiMaggio, P. J. and Powell, W. W. (1983) 'The iron cage revisited: institutional isomorphism and collective rationality in organizational fields', *American Sociological Review*, 48, pp. 147–60.

Doz, Y. L. (1980) 'Strategic Management in Multinational companies', *Sloan Management Review*, 21, pp. 27–46.

Doz, Y. L. and Prahalad, C. K. (1991) 'Managing DMNCs: a search for a new paradigm', *Strategic Management Journal*, 12, pp. 145–64.

Driffield, N. (1999) 'Regional and Industry Level Spillovers from FDI', paper presented at the NIESR Conference on Inward Investment, Technological Change and Growth, London.

Dunn, G., Everitt, B. and Pickles, A. (1993) *Modelling Covariances and Latent Variables Using EQS* (London: Chapman & Hall).

Dunning, J. H. (1977) 'Trade, location of economic activity and the multinational enterprise: a search for an eclectic approach', in B. Ohlin, P. O. Hesselborn and P. M. Wijkman (eds), *The International Allocation of Economic Activity* (London: Macmillan).

Dunning, J. H. (1991) 'Governments–markets–firms: towards a new balance?', *The CTC Reporter*, 31 (Spring), pp. 2–7.

Dunning, J. (1992) 'The Competitive Advantages of Nations and the Activities of Transnational Corporations', *Transnational Corporations*, 1, pp. 135–68.

Dunning, J. (1997) 'The European Internal Market Programme and Inbound Foreign Direct Investment – Parts I and II', *Journal of Common Market Studies*, 35(1), pp. 1–30, 35(2), pp. 189–223.

Dunning, J. H. (1998) *American Investment in British Industry*, 2nd edn (London: Routledge).

Dupuis, M. and Prime, N. (1996) 'Business Distance and Global Retailing: A Model of Analysis of Key Success/Failure Factors', *International Journal of Retail and Distribution Management*, 24(1), pp. 30–8.

Dutta, Shantanu, Bergen, Mark, Heide, Jan B. and John, George (1995) 'Understanding Dual Distribution: The Case of Reps and House Accounts', *The Journal of Law, Economics and Organisation*, 11(1), pp. 189–204.

Duysters, G. and Hagedorn, J. (1995) 'Strategic Groups and Inter-Firm Networks in International High-Tech Industries', *Journal of Management Studies*, 32, pp. 359–81.

Dwyer, R. F., Schurr, P. H. and Oh, S. (1987) 'Developing Buyer–Seller Relationships', *Journal of Marketing*, 51 (April), pp. 11–27.

Dyer, J. H. and Nobeoka, K. (2000) 'Creating and managing a high-performance knowledge-sharing network: The Toyota case', *Strategic Management Journal*, 21, pp. 345–67.

Earle, J. S. and Estrin, S. (1996) 'Employee ownership in transition', in R. Frydman, C. W. Gray and A. Rapaczynski (eds), *Corporate governance in Russia: Vol. 2, Insiders and the State* (London: World Bank/CEU Press).

The Economist (1997), 21 June.

Egelhoff, W., Gorman, L. and McCormick, S. (2000) 'How FDI Characteristics Influence Subsidiary Trade Patterns: The Case of Ireland', *Management International Review*, 40(3), pp. 203–30.

Eisenhardt, K. M. (1989) 'Building Theories from Case Study Research', *Academy of Management Review*, 14(4), pp. 532–50.

Emerson, R. M. (1962) 'Power-Dependence Relations', *American Sociological Review*, 27 (February), pp. 31–41.

Engel, C. and Rogers, J. (1996) 'How wide is the border', *American Economic Review*, 86(5), pp. 1112–25.

Engelbrecht, H. (1997) 'International R&D Spillovers, Human Capital and Productivity in OECD Economies', *European Economic Review*, 41, pp. 1479–88.

Enright, M. (2000) 'Globalization of competition and the localization of competitive advantage: Policies towards regional clustering', in N. Hood and S. Young (eds), *Globalization of Multinational Enterprise Activity and Economic Development* (London: Palgrave).

Erickson, T. J. (1990) 'Worldwide R & D management: concepts and applications', *Columbia Journal of World Business*, Winter, pp. 8–13.

Erramilli, M. K. and Rao, C. P. (1990) 'Choices of Foreign Market Entry Modes by Service Firms: The Role of Marketing Knowledge', *Management International Review*, 30(2), pp. 135–50.

Erramilli, M. K. and Rao, C. P. (1993) 'Service firms' international entry-mode choice: A modified transaction-cost analysis approach', *Journal of Marketing*, 57 (July), pp. 19–38.

Etemad, H. and Wright R. W. (1999) 'Internationalization of SMEs: management responses to a changing environment', *Journal of International Marketing*, 7(4), pp. 4–10.

Euromonitor (1997) *Impact International Drinks Bulletin* (London: Euromonitor Publications).

European Commission (1996) 'Economic Evaluation of the Internal Market', *European Economy*, no. 4, (Luxembourg: Office for the Official Publications of the EC).

Eyre, P. and Smallman, C. (1998) 'Euromanagement competencies in small and medium-sized enterprises: a development path for the new millennium?', *Management Decision*, 36(1), pp. 34–42.

Falkus, M. E. (1972) *The industrialisation of Russia, 1700–1914* (London: Macmillan).

Farnham, D. and Horton, S. (1996) *Managing the New Public Services*, 2nd edn (London: Macmillan).

Ferdows, K. (1997) 'Making the Most of Foreign Factories', *Harvard Business Review*, 75(2), pp. 73–88.

Feser, E. (1998) 'Old and new theories of industry clusters', in M. Steiner (ed.), *Clusters and Regional Specialisation* (London: Pion).

Fiegenbaum, A., Sudharshan, D. and Thomas, H. (1987) 'The Concept of Strategic Time Periods in Strategic Group Research', *Managerial and Decision Economics*, 8, pp. 139–48.

Fiegenbaum, A. and Thomas, H. (1993a) 'Strategic Groups and Performance: The US Insurance Industry, 1970–1984', *Strategic Management Journal*, 11, pp. 197–215.

Fiegenbaum, A. and Thomas, H. (1993b) 'Industry and Strategic Group Dynamics: Competitive Strategy in the Insurance Industry, 1970–1984', *Journal of Management Studies*, 30, pp. 69–105.

Filatotchev, I., Dyomina, N., Wright, M. and Buck, T. (2000) 'Export Orientation in the Former Soviet Union: Strategies after Privatization', CREEM Discussion Paper, University of Nottingham.

Filatotchev, I., Wright, M., Buck, T. and Zhukov, V. (1999) 'Corporate Entrepreneurs and Privatised Firms in Russia, Ukraine, Belarus', *Journal of Business Venturing*, 14, pp. 475–92.

Fleenor, D. (1993) 'The coming and going of the global corporation', *Columbia Journal of World Business*, 28(4), pp. 6–16.

Ford, D. (1989) 'One More Time, What Buyer–Seller Relationships are all about', 5th IMP Conference Proceedings, Pennsylvania State University, Ohio, 7 September.

Ford, D. and Leonidou, L. (1991) 'Research Developments in International Marketing', in S. J. Paliwoda (ed.), *New Perspectives on International Marketing* (London: Routledge).

Forsgren, M., Holm, U. and Johanson, J. (1992) 'Internationalisation of the second degree: the emergence of European-based centres in Swedish firms', in S. Young and J. Hamill (eds), *Europe and the Multinationals* (Aldershot: Edward Elgar), pp. 241–65.

Foss, N. and Pedersen, T. (2000) 'Transferring Knowledge in MNCs: The Role of Sources of Subsidiary Knowledge in Organizational Context', paper presented at the 29th Annual Conference of the European International Business Academy, Maastricht.

Franko, L. (1971) *Joint Venture Survival in Multinational Corporations* (New York: Praeger).

Franks, J. and Mayer, C. (1997) 'Corporate ownership and control in the UK, Germany and France', *Journal of Applied Corporate Finance*, 9, pp. 30–45.

Frazier, Gary, L. (1990) 'The Design and Management of Channels of Distribution', in G. Day, B. Weitz and R. Wensley (eds), *The Interface of Marketing and Strategy, Strategic Management Policy and Planning: A Multivolume Treatise*, vol. 4 (London: JAI Press).

Freeman, C. and Soete, L. (1997) *The Economics of Industrial Innovation* (London: Pinter).

Gabrielsson, M. (1999) 'Sales Channel Strategies for International Expansion: The Case of Large Companies in the European PC Industry', doctoral thesis, Helsinki School of Economics.

Garnier, G. H. (1982) 'Context and decision making autonomy in the foreign affiliates of U.S. multinational corporations', *Academy of Management Journal*, 25(4), pp. 893–908.

Gates, S. R. and Egelhoff, W. G. (1986) 'Centralization in headquarters–subsidiary relationships', *Journal of International Business Studies*, 17(2), pp. 71–92.

Gatignon, H. and Anderson, E. (1988) 'The multinational corporation's degree of control over foreign subsidiaries: An empirical test of a transaction cost explanation', *Journal of Law, Economics, and Organisation*, 4(2), pp. 305–36.

Gatrell, P. (1986) *The Tsarist economy 1850–1917* (London: Batsford).

Gemunden, H. G. (1991) 'Success Factors of Export Marketing: A Meta-Analytic Critique of the Empirical Studies', in S. J. Paliwoda (ed.), *New Perspectives on International Marketing* (London: Routledge).

General Agreement on Trade in Services (GATS) (2000) *International trade and statistics 2000*, www.WTO.org/services/resources.

Geringer, M. J. and Hebert, L. (1991) 'Measuring performance of international joint ventures', *Journal of International Business Studies*, 22(2), pp. 249–63.

Ghose, S. (1994) 'Hierarchical and overlapping structure, representations of perceptions of professional service providers', *Journal of Professional Services Marketing*, 10, pp. 55–74.

Ghoshal, S. (1987) 'Global strategy: an organizing framework', *Strategic Management Journal*, 8, pp. 425–40.

Ghoshal, S. and Bartlett, C. A. (1988) 'Creation, adoption and diffusion of innovations by subsidiaries of multinational corporations', *Journal of International Business Studies*, 19(3), pp. 365–88.

Ghoshal, S. and Moran, P. (1996) 'Bad for practice: A critique of the transaction cost theory', *Academy of Management Review*, 21, pp. 13–47.

Ghoshal, S. and Nohria, N. (1993) 'Horses for courses: organizational forms for multinational corporations', *Sloan Management Review*, 34(2), pp. 23–35.

Gnan, L. and Songini, L. (1995) 'Management styles of a sample of Japanese manufacturing companies in Italy', *Management International Review*, 35(2), pp. 9–26.

Goodman, L. W. (1987) *Small Nations, Giant Firms* (New York: Holmes and Meier).

Govindarajan, V. and Gupta, A. (2000) 'Analysis of the emerging global arena', *European Management Journal*, 18(3), pp. 274–84.

Grabher, G. (1993) 'The weakness of strong ties: the lock-in of regional development in the Ruhr area', in G. Grabher (ed.), *The Embedded Firm: On the Socioeconomics of Industrial Networks* (London: Routledge).

Grant, R. (1999) 'The Resource-Based Theory of Competitive Advantage: implications for strategy formulation', in S. Segal-Horn (ed.), *The Strategy Reader* (Milton Keynes: Blackwell).

Gray, H. P. (1998) 'Globalization and the Relocation of S-Good Activities', Working Paper no. 98.010, The Rutgers Center for International Business Education and Research (Newark, NJ: Rutgers).

Green, H. (1999) 'Twas the season for e-splurging', *Business Week*, 18 January 1999, p. 40.

Grein, A. and Ducoffe, R. (1998) 'Strategic responses to market globalisation among advertising agencies', *International Journal of Advertising*, 17, pp. 301–19.

Gupta, A. K. and Govindarajan, V. (2000) 'Knowledge flows within multinational corporations', *Strategic Management Journal*, 21, pp. 473–96.

Hair, J. F., Anderson, R. E., Tatham, R. L. and Black, W. C. (1998) *Multivariate Data Analysis* (Englewood Cliffs, NJ: Prentice-Hall).

Halkier, H. and Danson, M. (1997) 'Regional development agencies in Western Europe: a survey of key characteristics and trends', *European Urban and Regional Studies*, 4(3), pp. 243–56.

Hamel, G. and Prahalad, C. K. (1993) 'Strategy as Stretch and Leverage', *Harvard Business Review*, 71, pp. 75–84.

Hamill, J. (1997) 'The internet and international marketing', *International Marketing Review*, 14(5), pp. 300–23.

Hamill, J. and Gregory, K. (1997) 'Internet Marketing in the Internationalisation of UK SMEs', *Journal of Marketing Management*, 13, pp. 9–28.

Hansen, M. T., Nohria, N. and Tierney, T. (1999) 'What's your strategy for managing knowledge?', *Harvard Business Review*, March–April, pp. 106–16.

Hardy, Kenneth, Magrath G. and Allan, J. (1988) *Marketing Channel Management; Strategic Planning and Tactics* (USA: Scott, Foresman and Company).

Hart, S. and Tzokas, N. (1999) 'The impact of marketing research activity on SME export performance: Evidence form the UK', *Journal of Small Business Management*, 37(2), pp. 63–76.

Hart, S., Webb, J. R. and Jones, M. (1994) 'Export Marketing Research and the Effect of Export Experience in Industrial SMEs', *International Marketing Review*, 11(6), pp. 4–22.

Harzing, A.-W. (2000) 'An empirical analysis and extension of the Bartlett and Ghoshal typology of multinational companies', *Journal of International Business Studies*, 31, pp. 101–20.

Hatten, K. and Hatten, M. (1987) 'Strategic Groups, Asymmetrical Mobility Barriers and Contestability', *Strategic Management Journal*, 8, pp. 329–42.

Hatten, K., Schendel, D. and Cooper, A. (1977) 'Heterogeneity Within an Industry: Firm Conduct in the US Brewing Industry', *Journal of Industrial Economics*, 26, pp. 97–113.

Hedlund, G. (1981) 'Autonomy of subsidiaries and formalization of headquarters–subsidiary relationships in Swedish MNCs', In Lars Otterbeck (ed.), *The Management of Headquarters–Subsidiary Relationships in Multinational Corporations* (Aldershot: Gower), pp. 25–78.

Hedlund, G. (1986) 'The hypermodern MNC: a heterarchy?', *Human Resource Management*, 25, pp. 9–36.

Hedlund, G. (1994) 'A model of knowledge management and the N-form corporation', *Strategic Management Journal*, 15, Summer Special issue, pp. 73–90.

Hedlund, G. and Rolander, D. (1990) 'Actions in heterarchies: new approaches to managing the MNE', in C. A. Bartlett, Y. L. Doz and G. Hedlund (eds), *Managing the Global Firm* (London: Routledge), pp. 195–214.

Heischmidt, K. A. and Hekmat, F. (1991) 'Professional Services: Application of the Service-Market-Cost model of Strategy Development', *Journal of Professional Services Marketing*, 8, pp. 67–83.

Helliwell, J. F. (1998) *How Much Do National Borders Matter?* (Washington, DC: Brookings Institution).

Hellström, T., Kemlin, P. and Malmquist, U. (2000) 'Knowledge and competence management at Ericsson', *Journal of Knowledge Management*, 4(2), pp. 99–110.

Helpman, E. and Krugman, P. (1985) *Market Structure and Foreign Trade* (Cambridge, Mass.: MIT Press).

Hennart, J. F. (1991a) 'The transaction costs theory of joint ventures: An empirical study of Japanese subsidiaries in the United States', *Management Science*, 37(4), pp. 483–97.

Hennart, J. F. (1991b). 'The transaction cost theory of the multinational enterprise', in C. Pitelis and R. Sudgen (eds), *The Nature of the Transnational Firm* (London: Routledge).

Hennart, J. F. and Park, Y. R. (1994) 'Location, governance, and strategic determinants of Japanese manufacturing investment in the United States', *Strategic Management Journal*, 15, pp. 419–36.

Hentola, H. (1994) *Foreign Sales Subsidiaries and Their Role within the Internationalisation Process of a Company: A Study of the Finnish Manufacturing Firms*, CIBR research reports, series X–2 (Helsinki: Helsinki School of Economics and Business Administration).

Hof, R. (1998) 'Amazon.com: the wild world of e-commerce', *Business Week*, 14 December, p. 37.

Hofstede, G. (1980a) *Culture's consequences: international differences in work-related values* (Beverly Hills, CA: Sage).

Hofstede, G. (1980b) 'Motivation, leadership and organization: do American theories apply abroad?', *Organizational Dynamics*, Summer, pp. 42–63.

Hofstede, G. (1991) *Cultures and Organizations: Software of the Mind* (Berkshire: McGraw-Hill).

Hofstede, G. and Bond, M. H. (1988) 'The Confucian connection: from cultural roots to economic growth', *Organizational Dynamics*, 16, pp. 4–21.

Hogarth, R. and Hillel, E. (1992) 'Order effects in belief updating: the belief adjustment model', *Cognitive Psychology*, 24(1), pp. 1–55.

Holmlund, M. and Kock, S. (1998) 'Relationships and the Internationalisation of Finnish Small and Medium-Sized Companies', *International Small Business Journal*, 16(4), pp. 46–63.

Hood, N. and Taggart, J. H. (1997) 'German Direct Investment in the UK and Ireland: Survey Evidence', *Regional Studies*, 31(2), pp. 139–150.

Hood, N., Taggart, J. H. and Young, S. (1999) 'German manufacturing investment in the UK: survey results and economic impact', in R. Barrell and N. Pain (eds), *Innovation, Investment and the Diffusion of Technology in Europe: German Direct Investment and Economic Growth in Postwar Europe* (Cambridge: Cambridge University Press).

Hood, N. and Young, S. (1979) *The Economics of Multinational Enterprise* (London: Longman).

Hood, N. and Young, S. (1988) 'Inward investment and the EC: UK evidence on corporate integration strategies', in J. H. Dunning and P. Robson (eds), *Multinationals and the European Community* (Oxford: Basil Blackwell).

Hood, N. and Young, S. (1997) 'The United Kingdom', in J. H. Dunning (ed.), *Governments, Globalization, and International Business* (Oxford: Oxford University Press).

Hood, N. and Young, S. (1998) 'Multinational subsidiary development in an integrated Europe', in P. J. Buckley, F. Burton and H. Mirza (eds), *The Strategy and Organisation of International Business* (Basingstoke: Macmillan).

Hood, N., Young, S. and Lal, D. (1994) 'Strategic evolution within Japanese manufacturing plants in Europe: UK evidence', *International Business Review*, 3(2), pp. 97–122.

Hout, T., Porter, M. E. and Rudden, E. (1982) 'How global companies win out', *Harvard Business Review*, 60(5), pp. 98–108.

Hubert, F. and Pain, N. (1999) 'Inward Investment and Technical Progress in the UK', paper presented at the NIESR Conference on Inward Investment, Technological Change and Grow (London).

Hundley, G. and Jacobson, C. K. (1998) 'The effects of the Keiretsu on the export performance of Japanese companies: help or hindrance?', *Strategic Management Journal*, 19, pp. 927–37.

Hunt, M. (1972) 'Competition in the Major Home Appliance Industry 1960–1970', unpublished doctoral dissertation (Harvard University).

Ibeh, K. I. N. (2001) 'On the resource-based, integrative view of small firm internationalization: an exploratory study of Nigerian firms', in M. Berry, M. McDermott and J. Taggart (eds), *The Multinational in the New Era* (London: Macmillan).

IMF (2000) *Annual Report – Making the Global Economy Work for All* (Washington, DC: IMF).

International Labour Office (ILO) (1981a) *Employment Effects of Multinational Enterprises in Developing Countries* (Geneva: International Labour Organisation).

International Labour Office (ILO) (1981b) *Employment Effects of Multinational Enterprises in Industrialised Countries* (Geneva: International Labour Organisation).

Isard, P. (1977) 'How far can we push the law of one price?', *American Economic Review*, 67(5), pp. 942–8.

Jaeger, A. M. (1983) 'The transfer of organizational culture overseas: an approach to control in the multinational corporation', *Journal of International Business Studies*, 14(2), pp. 91–114.

James, E. (2000) 'Services: US Firms are Leaders in the Global Economy', *Business America*, http:////www.stat-usa.gov.

Jarillo, J. C. and Martínez, J. I. (1990) 'Different roles for subsidiaries: the case of multinational corporations in Spain', *Strategic Management Journal*, 11, pp. 501–12.

Johanson, J. and Mattsson, L.-G. (1988) 'Internationalization in industrial systems – a network approach', in N. Hood and J.-E. Vahlne (eds), *Strategies in Global Competition* (New York: Croom Helm).

Johanson, J. and Vahlne J. (1977) 'The internationalisation process of the firm: a model of knowledge development on increasing foreign commitments', *Journal of International Business Studies*, Spring–Summer, pp. 23–32.

Johanson, J. and Vahlne, J. (1990) 'The Mechanism of Internationalisation: The Internationalisation of Business: Theory and Evidence', *International Marketing Review*, 7(4), pp. 11–24.

Johanson, J. and Vahlne, J. E (1992) 'Management of Foreign Market Entry', *Scandinavian International Business Review*, 1(3), pp. 9–27.

Johanson, J. and Wiedersheim-Paul, F. (1975) 'The Internationalisation of the Firm – Four Swedish Cases', *The Journal of Management Studies*, 12, pp. 305–22.

Johnson, J. E. (1999) 'Towards a success factor framework for global start-ups', *Global Focus*, 11(3), pp. 73–84.

Johnson, J. H. (1995). 'An empirical analysis of the integration-responsiveness framework: US construction equipment industry firms in global competition', *Journal of International Business Studies*, 26(3), pp. 621–35.

Jolly, V. K., Alahuhta, M. and Jeannet, J. P. (1992) 'Challenging the incumbents: how technology start-ups compete globally', *Journal of Strategic Change*, 1, pp. 71–82.

Jones, M. V. (1990) 'Market Orientation: An Empirical Analysis of Market Intelligence Generation by British Industrial Exporters', MSc dissertation, University of Strathclyde.

Jones, M. V. (1999) 'The Internationalisation of Small UK High Technology Firms', *Journal of International Marketing*, 7(4), pp. 15–41.

Jones, M. V. (2000) 'First Steps: An Examination of the First Cross-Border Business Activities of a Sample of Small, UK, High Technology Firms', paper presented at The Third McGill Conference on Globalization and Emerging Businesses. McGill University, Canada.

Jones, M. V. and Tagg, Stephen K. (2000) 'The Internationalisation of Small UK High Technology Based Firms: A Value Chain Analysis', paper presented at The Academy of International Business Annual UK Conference, University of Strathclyde.

Kagono, T. (1981) 'Structural design of headquarters–division relationships and economic performance: an analysis of Japanese firms', in Lars Otterbeck (ed.), *The Management of Headquarters–Subsidiary Relationships in Multinational Corporations* (Aldershot: Gower), pp 147–85.

Kamath, S., Rosson, P. J., Patton, D. and Brooks, M. (1987) 'Research on Success in Exporting: Past, Present and Future', in P. J. Rosson and S. D. Reid (eds), *Managing Export Entry and Expansion* (New York: Praeger), pp. 398–421.

Katsikeas, C. S., Al-Khalifa, A. and Crick, D. (1997) 'Manufacturers' Understanding of their Overseas Distributors: the relevance of export involvement', *International Business Review*, 6(2), pp. 147–63.

Katsikeas, C. S., Piercy, N. F. and Kaleka, A. (1998) 'Sources of competitive advantage in high performing export companies', *Journal of World Business*, 3(4), pp. 378–93.

Kauranen, I. and Kasanen, E. (1986) 'Marimekko – The post-turn-around direction' (Helsinki: Helsinki School of Economics).

Kawai, K. (1960) *Japan's American interlude* (Chicago, Ill: University of Chicago Press).

Kilburn, D. (1999) 'Growing pains', *Marketing Week*, 22, pp. 45–47.

Kim, W. C. and Hwang, P. (1992) 'Global strategy and multinationals' entry mode choice', *Journal of International Business Studies*, 23(1), pp. 29–54.

Kim, W. C. and Mauborgne, R. A. (1991) 'Implementing global strategies: the role of procedural justice', *Strategic Management Journal*, 12, pp. 125–43.

Kim, W. C. and Mauborgne, R. A. (1993a) 'Procedural justice, attitudes and subsidiary top management compliance with multinationals' corporate strategic decisions', *Academy of Management Journal*, 36(3), pp. 502–26.

Kirpalani, V. H. and Macintosh, N. B. (1980) 'Internal marketing effectiveness of technology-oriented small firms', *Journal of International Business Studies*, 11(3), pp. 81–90.

Kleindl, B. (2000) 'Competitive dynamics and new business models for SMEs in the virtual marketplace', *Journal of Developmental Entrepreneurship*, 5(1) pp. 73–85.

Knight, G. A. and Cavusgil, S. T. (1996) 'The born global firm: a challenge to traditional internationalization theory', *Advances in International Marketing*, 8 (Greenwich, CT: JAI Press).

Knight, G., Madsen T. K., Servais, P. and Rasmussen, E. (2000) 'The born global firm: description and empirical investigation in Europe and the United States', paper presented at the American Marketing Association Conference, New York.

Ko, K. K. (1995) 'Spreading the net: The consolidation process of large transnational advertising agencies in the 1980s and early 1990s', *International Journal of Advertising*, 14, pp. 195–218.

Kobrin, S. J. (1991) 'An empirical analysis of the determinants of global integration', *Strategic Management Journal*, 12, pp. 17–31.

Kobrin, S. J. (1994) 'Is there a relationship between a geocentric mind-set and multinational strategy?', *Journal of International Business Studies*, 25(3), pp. 493–511.

Kogut, B. and Singh, H. (1988) 'The Effect of National Culture on the Choice of Entry Mode', *Journal of International Business Studies*, 19(3), pp. 411–32.

Kogut, B. and Zander, U. (1992) 'Knowledge of the firm, combinative capabilities, and the replication of technology', *Organization Science*, 3(3), pp. 383–97.

Kogut, B. and Zander, U. (1993) 'Knowledge of the Firm and the Evolutionary Theory of the Multinational Corporation', *Journal of International Business Studies*, 24(4), pp. 625–41.

Kotha, A. (1998) 'Competing on the internet: how amazon.com is rewriting the rules of competition', *Advances in Strategic Management*, 15, pp. 239–65.

Kotha, S. and Rindova, V. (1999) *Building Reputation on the Internet: Lessons From Amazon.Com and Its Competitors* (University of Washington Business School).

Krugman, P. (1991) 'Increasing Returns and Economic Geography', *Journal of Political Economy*, 99, pp. 484–99.

Krugman, P. and Venables, A. (1990) 'Integration and the Competitiveness of Peripheral Industry', in C. Bliss and J. Braga de Macedo (eds), *Unity with Diversity in the European Community* (Cambridge: Cambridge University Press).

Lagendijk, A. (1999) *Good Practice in Cluster Development Initiatives: Summary of an ADAPT Funded Analysis of Cluster Initiatives* (Newcastle: Centre for Urban and Regional Development Studies).

Lane, C. (1989) *Management and Labour in Europe* (Cheltenham: Edward Elgar).

La Porta, R., Lopez-De-Silanes, F., Shleifer, A. and Vishny, R. W. (1997) 'Legal determinants of external finance', *Journal of Finance*, 52, pp. 1131–50.

Lele, Miland (1986) 'Matching Your Channels to Your Product's Lifecycle', *Business Marketing*, 71(12), pp. 61–9.

Leonard-Barton, D. (1995) *Wellsprings of Knowledge* (Boston, Mass.: Harvard Business School Press).

Leong, S. M. and Tan, C. T. (1993) 'Managing across borders: an empirical test of the Bartlett and Ghoshal organizational typology', *Journal of International Business Studies*, 24, pp. 449–64.

Leonidou, L. S. and Adams-Florou, A. S. (1998) 'Types and Sources of Export Information: Insights from Small Business', *International Small Business Journal*, 17(3), pp. 30–48.

Leonidou, Leonidas C. and Katsikeas, Constantine S. (1996) 'The export development process: an integrative review on empirical models', *Journal of International Business Studies*, 27(3), pp. 517–49.

Lewis, P. and Thomas, H. (1990) 'The Linkage Between Strategy, Strategic Groups and Performance in the UK Retail Grocery Industry', *Strategic Management Journal*, 11, pp. 384–99.

Li, J. and Guisinger, S. (1991) 'Comparative Business Failures of Foreign-Controlled Firms in the United States', *Journal of International Business Studies*, 22(2), pp. 209–24.

Liesch, P. W. and Knight, G. A. (1999) 'Information internalization and hurdle rates in small and medium sized enterprise internationalization', *Journal of International Business Studies*, 30, pp. 383–94.

Liouville, J. and Nanopoulos, C. (1996) 'Performance factors of subsidiaries abroad: lessons in an analysis of German subsidiaries in France', *Management International Review*, 36, pp. 101–21.

Lippman, S. and Rumelt, R. (1982) 'Uncertain imitability: An analysis of interfirm differences in efficiencies under competition', *Bell Journal of Economics*, 13, pp. 418–38.

Lituchy, T. R. and Rail, A. (2000) 'Bed and breakfasts, small inns, and the Internet: the impact of technology on the globalization of small businesses', *Journal of International Marketing*, 8(2), pp. 86–97.

Lovelock, C. S. and Yip, G. S. (1996) 'Developing Global Strategies for Service Businesses, *California Management Review*, 38, pp. 64–86.

Lovering, J. (1999) 'Theory led by policy: the inadequacies of the "new regionalism" (illustrated from the case of Wales)', *International Journal of Urban and Regional Research*, 23(2), pp. 379–95.

Lowe, R. and Doole, I. (1997) 'The characteristics and development of exporting firms at different stages of internationalisation', in I. Doole and R. Lowe, *International Marketing Strategy: Contemporary Readings* (London: Thomson Business Press), pp. 163–79.

Lowendhal, B. R. (1997) *Strategic Management of Professional Service Firms* (Copenhagen: Copenhagen Business School Press).

Luostarinen, R. (1970) 'Foreign Operations of the Firm', liceneiate thesis, Helsinki School of Economics.

Luostarinen, R. (1979) 'Internationalisation of the firm: An empirical study of the internationalisation of firms with small and open domestic markets with special emphasis on lateral rigidity as a behavioral characteristic in strategic decision-making', doctoral thesis, Helsinki School of Economics.

Luostarinen, R. and Marschan-Piekkari, R. (2001) 'Strategic evolution of foreign-owned subsidiaries in a host country: a conceptual framework', in M. McDermott, and J. H. Taggart (eds), *Multinationals in the Millennium: Changes and Choices* (Basingstoke: Palgrave).

Luostarinen, R. and Welch, Lawrence (1990) *International Business Operations* (Helsinki: Kyriiri).

Lyles, M. A. and Salk, J. E. (2000) 'Knowledge acquisition from foreign parents in international joint ventures: An empirical examination in the Hungarian context', *Journal of International Business Studies*, Special Issue, pp. 877–903.

Lynch, J. G. and Ariely, D. (2000) 'Wine-online: search costs and competition on price, quality and distribution', 19(1), *Journal of International Marketing* pp. 83–103.

Maddy, C. G. and Ickes, B. (1998) 'Russia's virtual economy', *Foreign Affairs*, 77, pp. 53–68.

Madhok, A. (1997) 'Cost, value and foreign market entry mode: The transaction and the firm', *Strategic Management Journal*, 18, pp. 39–61.

Madsen, T. K. (1987) 'Empirical Export Performance of Studies: A Review of Conceptualisations and Findings', in S. T. Cavusgil (ed.), *Advances in International Marketing*, vol. 2 (Greenwich, CT: JAI Press).

Madsen, T. K. and Servais, P. (1997) 'The internationalization of born globals: an evolutionary process?', *International Business Review*, 6, pp. 561–583.

Majkgard, A. and Sharma, D. D. (1998) 'Client-Following and Market-Seeking Strategies in the Internationalisation of Service Firms', *Journal of Business-to-Business Marketing*, 4, pp. 1–41.

Mallen, B. (1977) *Principles of Marketing Channel Management, Interorganisational Distribution Design and Relations* (Toronto: Lexington Books, D. C. Heath).

Markusen, A. (1996) 'Sticky Places in a Slippery Place: A Typology of Industrial Districts', *Economic Geography*, 72, pp. 293–313.

Martin, X. and Salomon, R. (1999) 'Knowledge transfer capacity: implications for the theory of the multinational corporation', paper presented at the Annual Academy of Management Conference, Chicago.

Martinez, J. I. and Jarillo, J. C. (1989) 'The Evolution of Research on Coordination Mechanisms in Multinational Corporations', *Journal of International Business Studies*, 20(3), pp. 489–514.

Martínez, J. I. and Jarillo, J. C. (1991) 'Coordination demands of international strategies', *Journal of International Business Studies*, 22(3), pp. 429–44.

Mascarenhas, B. (1986) 'International strategies of non-dominant firms', *Journal of International Business Studies*, 17(1), pp. 1–25.

Mascarenhas, B. and Aaker, D. (1989) 'Mobility Barriers and Strategic Groups', *Strategic Management Journal*, 10, pp. 475–85.

Mattson, L. (1998) 'Dynamic of Overlapping Networks and Strategic Actions by International Firms', in A. Chandler, P. Hagstrom and O. Sölvell, *The Dynamic Firm: The Role of Technology, Strategy, Organisation and Regions* (Oxford: Oxford University Press).

Mazzarol, T. (1998) 'Critical Success Factors for international education marketing', *International Journal of Educational Management*, 12(4), pp. 163–75.

McAuley, A. (1993) 'The Perceived Usefulness of Export Information Sources', *European Journal of Marketing*, 27(1), pp. 52–64.

McAuley, A. (1999) 'Entrepreneurial Instant Exporters in the Scottish Arts and Craft Sector', *Journal of International Marketing*, 7(4), pp. 67–82.

McCallum, C. (1999) 'Globalisation, Developments and Trends in the Changing New International Division of Labour', *Research Papers in International Business*, 19–99, Centre for International Business Studies (London: South Bank University).

McCallum, J. (1995) 'National borders matter: Canada–US regional trade patterns', *American Economic Review*, 85(3), pp. 615–23.

McDonald F., Heise, A. and Tüselmann H. J. (2000) 'Does Foreign Investment Improve Employment in Host Regions?', paper presented at the 29th Annual Conference of the European International Business Academy, Maastricht.

McDougall, P. P., Shane S. and Oviatt, B. M. (1994) 'Explaining the formation of international new ventures', *Journal of Business Venturing*, 9, pp. 469–87.

McGee, J. and Segal-Horn, S. (1990) 'Strategic Space and Industry Dynamics: The Implications for International Marketing', *Journal of Marketing Management*, 6(4), pp. 175–93.

McGee, J. and Thomas, H. (1986) 'Strategic Groups: Theory, Research and Taxonomy', *Strategic Management Journal*, 3, pp. 77–98.

McGuinness, N., Campbell, N. and Leontiades, J. (1991) 'Selling Machinery to China: Chinese Perceptions of Strategies and Relationships', *Journal of International Business Studies*, Second Quarter, pp. 171–207.

Mediametrix (2000) Media Metrix Canada press releases, www.mediametrix.ca.

Meschi, P. X. (1997) 'Longevity and cultural differences of international joint ventures: Toward time-based cultural management', *Human Relations*, 50(2), pp. 211–27.

Meyer, J. W. and Rowan, B. (1977) 'Institutional organizations: formal structure as myth and ceremony', *American Journal of Sociology*, 83, pp. 340–63.

Michailova, S. and Anisimova, A. (1999) 'Russian voices from a Danish company', *Business Strategy Review*, 10(4), pp. 65–78.

Miesenbock, K. J. (1988) 'Small Business and Exporting: A Literature Review', *International Small Business Journal*, 6(2), pp. 42–61.

Miles, M. M. and Huberman, A. M. (1994) *Qualitative Data Analysis: An expanded source book*, 2nd edn (New York: Sage).

Monks, R. A. G. and Minow, N. (1995) *Corporate governance* (Oxford: Blackwell).

Moon, W. C. (1994) 'A revised framework of global strategy: extending the coordination–configuration framework', *International Executive*, 36(5), pp. 557–74.

Moore, R. A. (1990) 'The Conflict Gap in International Channel Relationships', *Journal of Marketing Management*, 6(3), pp. 225–37.

Moore, R. A. (1991) 'Relationship States in an International Marketing Channel', *European Journal of Marketing*, 25(5), pp. 47–59.

Moore, R. A. (1992) 'A Profile of UK Manufacturers and West German Agents and Distributors', *European Journal of Marketing*, 26(1), pp. 41–51.

Morgan, R. E. and Katsikeas, C. S. (1997a) 'Export Stimuli: Export Intention Compared with Export Activity', *International Business Review*, 6(5), pp. 477–99.

Morgan, R. E. and Katsikeas, C. S. (1997b) 'Obstacles to Export Initiation and Expansion', *Omega*, 25(6), pp. 677–90.

Morgan, R. E. and Katsikeas, C. S. (1998) 'Exporting Problems of Industrial Manufacturers', Industrial Marketing Management, 27, pp. 161–76.

Moriarty, Rowland T. and Moran, Ursula (1990) 'Managing Hybrid Marketing Systems', *Harvard Business Review*, Nov.–Dec., pp. 146–155.

Morosini, P. (1994) 'Effects of National Culture Differences on Post-Cross-Border Acquisition Performance in Italy', unpublished doctoral thesis, University of Pennsylvania.

Morrison, A. J., Ricks, D. A. and Roth, K. (1991) 'Globalization versus Regionalization: Which way for the multinational?', *Organizational Dynamics*, 19(3), pp. 17–29.

Morwitz, V. G., Greenleaf, E. A. and Johnson, E. J. (1998) 'Divide and prosper: consumers' reactions to partitioned prices', *Journal of Marketing Research*, 35(4), pp. 453–63.

Myers, H. and Alexander, N. (1996) 'European Food Retailers' Evaluation of Global Markets', *International Journal of Retail & Distribution Management*, 24(6), pp. 34–43.

Nachum, L. (1996) *Firm Specific and Home Country Determinants of Ownership Advantages of Multinational Professional Service firms: A Case Study of the Advertising Industry*, Samfunslitteratur Ph.D. Series 12.96 (Copenhagen: Copenhagen Business School, Institute of Organisation and Industrial Sociology).

Nachum, L. (1998) 'Danish Professional Service Firms: Why Are They Not Competitive Internationally? A Comparative Analysis between Danish and UK Management Consultancy Firms', *Scandinavian Journal of Management*, 14, pp. 37–51.

Nachum, L. (2000) 'Economic Geography and the Location of TNCs: Financial and Professional Service FDI to the USA', *Journal of International Business Studies*, 31(3), pp. 367–85.

Nagashima, S. (1999) *The Advance of European and American Foods/General Merchandise Retailers into Asia* (Tokyo: The Distribution Economics Institute of Japan).

Narula, R. (1996) *Multinational Investment and Economic Structure; Globalisation and Competitiveness* (London: Routledge).

Naumov, A. I. (1996) 'Hofstede's measures in Russia: the influence of national culture on business management', *Menedzhment*, 3, pp. 70–103.

Neale, C. W. and Schmidt, R. A. (1991) 'Exporters' Credit Policy: an Anglo-West German Comparative Policy', *European Journal of Marketing*, 25(5), pp. 7–19.

Nelson, R. and Winter, S. (1982) *An Evolutionary Theory of Economic Change* (Cambridge, Mass.: Harvard University Press).

Nitsch, D., Beamish, P. W. and Makino, S. (1996) 'Entry mode and performance of Japanese FDI in Western Europe', *Management International Review*, 36(1), pp. 27–43.

Nonaka, I. (1994) 'A dynamic theory of organizational knowledge creation', *Organization Science*, 5, pp. 15–37.

Nonaka, I. and Takeuchi, H. (1995) *The Knowledge-Creating Company: How Japanese Companies Create the Dynamics of Innovation* (New York: Oxford University Press).

Nordstrom, K. (1990) *The Internationalisation Process of the Firm – Searching for New Patterns and Explanations* (Stockholm: Stockholm School of Economics).

Nordstrom, K. A. and Vahlne, J. E. (1994) 'Is the Globe Shrinking? Psychic Distance and the Establishment of Swedish Sales Subsidiaries During the Last 100 Years', in M. Landeck, (ed.), *International Trade: Regional and Global Issues* (New York: St Martin's Press).

North, D. C. (1990) *Institutions, Institutional Change and Economic Performance*. (Cambridge: Cambridge University Press).

Noteboom, B. (1999) 'Voice- and exit-based forms of corporate control: Anglo-American, European and Japanese', *Journal of Economic Issues*, 33, pp. 845–60.

Nunally, J. C. (1978) *Psychometric Theory*, 2nd edn, (New York: McGraw-Hill).

Oakley, P. (1996) 'High-tech NPD success through faster overseas launch', *European Journal of Marketing*, 30(8), pp. 75–91.

Obstfeld, M. and Rogoff, K. (1999) *The Six Major Puzzles in International Macroeconomics: Is There a Common Cause?* (Cambridge, Mass.: National Bureau of Economic Research).

O'Donnell, S. (2000) 'Managing foreign subsidiaries', *Strategic Management Journal*, 21, pp. 525–48.

OECD (1997) *Globalisation and Small and Medium Enterprises (SMEs), Volume 1: Synthesis Report, Volume 2: Country Studies* (Paris: OECD).

OECD (1998) 'Public Management Reform and Economic and Social Development', OECD Working Papers, VI.22, (Paris: OECD).

OECD (1999a) *Boosting Innovation: The Cluster Approach*, (Paris: OECD)

OECD (1999b) *Session on Globalisation – Manual on Globalisation Indicator*, (Paris: OECD).

OECD (1999c) 'Corporate Governance in Russia', Conference Synthesis Note, Moscow (Paris: OECD).

OECD (2000) *The OECD Guidelines for Multinational Enterprises*, (Paris: OECD) (www.oecd.org/daf/investment/guidelines/mntext.htm).

Oesterle, M. J. (1997) 'Time span until internationalisation: foreign market entry as a built-in mechanism of innovation', *Management International Review*, 37(2), pp. 125–49.

O'Farrell, P. N. (1995) 'Manufacturing Demand for Business Services', *Cambridge Journal of Economics*, 19, pp. 523–43.

O'Farrell, P. N., Wood, P. and Zheng, J. (1996) 'Internationalisation of Business Services: an Inter-regional analysis', *Regional Studies*, 30(2), pp. 101–18.

O'Farrell, P. N., Wood, P. and Zheng, J. (1998a) 'Internationalisation by business SMEs: An inter-industry analysis', *International Small Business Journal*, 16, pp. 13–33.

O'Farrell, P. N., Wood, P. and Zheng, J. (1998b) 'Regional Influences on Foreign Market Development by Business Service Companies: Elements of a Strategic Context Explanation', Regional Studies, 32(1), pp. 31–48.

O'Grady, S. and Lane, H. (1996) 'The Psychic Distance Paradox', *Journal of International Business Studies*, 27(2), pp. 309–33.

Ohmae, K. (1985) *Triad Power: The Coming Shape of Global Competition* (New York: Free Press).

ONS (Office of National Statistics) (2000) *Sector Review of Service Trade* (London: HMSO).

Osborne, D. and Gaebler, T. (1992) *Reinventing Government: How the Entrepreneurial Spirit is Transforming the Public Sector* (New York: Addison-Wesley).

Ostgaard, T. A. and Birley, S. (1996) 'New Venture Growth and Personal Networks', *Journal of Business Research*, 36(1), pp. 37–50.

Ottavianno, G. and Puga, D. (1998) 'Agglomeration in the Global Economy: A Survey of the New Economic Geography', *World Economy*, 21, pp. 707–31.

Ouchi, W. C. (1978) 'The transmission of control through organizational hierarchy', *Academy of Management Journal*, 21(2), pp. 173–92.

Oviatt, B. M. and McDougall P. P. (1994) 'Toward a theory of international new ventures', *Journal of International Business Studies*, 25, pp. 45–64.

Oviatt, B. M. and McDougall P. P. (1995) 'Global start-ups: entrepreneurs on a world-wide stage', *Academy of Management Executive*, 9, pp. 30–43.

Oviatt, B. M. and McDougall, P. P. (1997) 'Challenges for Internationalisation Process Theory: The Case of New Ventures', *Management International Review*, Special Issue 2, pp. 85–99.

Padmanabhan, P. (1993) 'The Impact of European Divestment Announcements on Shareholder Wealth: Evidence from the UK', *Journal of Multinational Financial Management*, 2, pp. 185–208.

Pan, Y., Li, S. and Tse, D. K. (1999) 'The Impact of Order and Mode of Market Entry on Profitability and Market Share', *Journal of International Business Studies*, 30(1), pp. 81–103.

Panitz, E. (1995) 'Strategic types and growth strategies used by public accounting firms', *Journal of Professional Services Marketing*, 13, pp. 135–40.

Papanastassiou, M. and Pearce, R. (1999) *Multinationals, Technology, and National Competitiveness* (Cheltenham: Edward Elgar).

Patton, Michael Quin (1980) *Qualitative Evaluation and Research Methods* (New York: Sage).

Pearce, R. (1992) 'World Product Mandates and MNE Specialization', *Scandinavian International Business Review*, 1(2), pp. 38–57.

Pearce, R. D. (1999a) 'The evolution of technology in multinational enterprises: the role of creative subsidiaries', *International Business Review*, 8, pp. 125–48.

Pearce, R. D. (1999b) 'Decentralised R & D and strategic competitiveness: globalised approaches to generation and use of technology in multinational enterprises', *Research Policy*, 28, pp. 157–78.

Pearce, R. D. (2001) 'Multinationals and industrialisation: the bases of "inward investment" policy', *International Journal of the Economics of Business*, 8(1), pp. 51–73.

Pearce, R. D. and Papanastassiou, M. (1997) 'European markets and the strategic roles of multinational enterprise subsidiaries in the UK', *Journal of Common Market Studies*, 35(2), pp. 241–66.

Pearce, R. D. and Tavares, A. T. (1998) 'Strategies of multinational subsidiaries in a context of regional trading blocs', University of Reading Discussion Papers in International Investment and Management, XI, Series B, no. 257.

Peng, M. (2000) *Business strategies in transition economies* (London: Sage).

Penrose, E. (1959) *The Theory of the Growth of the Firm* (Oxford: Basil Blackwell).

Peoples, J. and Sugden, R. (2000) 'Divide and Rule by Transnational Corporations', in C. N. Pitelis, and R. Sugden (eds), *The Nature of the Transnational Firm* (London and New York: Routledge).

Peteraf, M. (1992) 'The Cornerstones of Competitive Advantage: A Resource-Based View', *Strategic Management Journal*, 14, pp. 179–91.

Peteraf, M. (1993) 'Intra-Industry Structure and the Response Toward Rivals', *Managerial and Decision Economics*, 14, pp. 519–28.

Peteraf, M. and Shanley, M. (1997) 'Getting to Know You: A Theory of Strategic Group Identity', *Strategic Management Journal*, 18 (Summer special issue), pp. 165–86.

Peters, E. and Hood, N. (2000) 'Implementing The Cluster Approach. Some Lessons from the Scottish Experience', *International Studies of Management and Organization*, 30(2), pp. 68–92.

Pfeffer, J. (1981) *Power in Organizations* (Marshfield, Mass.: Pitman).

Pfeiffer, R., Burgemeister, H., Hibbert, E. and Spence, M. (1998) 'A Comparative Survey of Trade Fairs in the UK and Germany in three Industry Sectors', *Journal of European Business Education*, 7(2), pp. 52–69.

Picard, J. (1997) 'Factors of variance in multinational marketing control', in L. Mattson and F. Weidsheim-Paul (eds), *Recent Research on the Internationalization of Business*, (Uppsala: Almqvist and Wiksel).

Piercy, N. F., Kaleka, A. and Katsikeas, C. S. (1998) 'Sources of Competitive advantage in high performing exporting companies', *Journal of World Business*, 33(4), pp. 53–67.

Pipes, R. (1995) *Russia under the old regime* (Harmondsworth: Penguin).

Polanyi, M. (1962) *Personal Knowledge: Towards a Post-Critical Philosophy* (New York: Harper Torchbooks).

Pollara (2000) Pollara Internet Survey, *Canadian Internet Holiday Spending Exceeds Expectations* (www.pollara.ca).

Porter, M. (1980) *Competitive Strategy* (New York: Free Press).

Porter, M. E. (1985) *Competitive Advantage: Creating and Sustaining Superior Performance* (New York: Free Press).

Porter, M. E. (1986a) 'Competition in global industries: a conceptual framework', in: M. E. Porter (ed.), *Competition in Global Industries* (New York: Free Press).

Porter, M. E. (1986b) 'Changing patterns of international competition', *California Management Review*, 28, pp. 9–40.

Porter, M. E. (1990a) *Competitive Strategy* (New York: Free Press).

Porter, M. E. (1990b) *The Competitive Advantage of Nations* (New York: Free Press).

Porter, M. E. (1997) 'The Structure Within Industries and Companies Performance', *Review of Economics and Statistics*, 61, pp. 214–27.

Porter, M. E. (1998) 'Clusters and the new economics of competition', *Harvard Business Review*, November/December, pp. 77–90.

Porter, M. and Sölvell, O. (1998) 'The Role of Geography in the Process of Innovation and the Sustainable Competitive Advantage of Firms', in A. Chandler, P. Hagstrom and O. Solvell (eds), *The Dynamic Firm: The Role of Technology, Strategy, and Regions* (Oxford: Oxford University Press).

Prahalad, C. K. and Doz, Y. (1987) *The Multinational Mission: Balancing Local Demands and Global Vision* (New York: Free Press).

Quelch, J. A. and Hoff, E. J. (1986) 'Customizing global marketing', *Harvard Business Review*, 64(3), pp. 59–68.

Quelch, J. and Klein, L. (1996) 'The internet and international marketing', *Sloan Management Review*, 37(3), pp. 60–75.

Raines, P. (2000) 'Developing Cluster Policies in Seven European Regions', Regional and Industrial Research Paper, 42 (Glasgow: European Policies Research Centre, University of Strathclyde).

Rangan, K. V., Corey, R. E. and Cespedes, F. (1993) 'Transaction Cost Theory: Inferences from Clinical Field Research on Downstream Vertical Integration', *Organisation Science*, 4(3), pp. 454–77.

Reed, R. and DeFillippi, R. J. (1990) 'Causal ambiguity, barriers to imitation and sustainable competitive advantage', *Academy of Management Review*, 15, pp. 88–102.

Reger, G. (1997) 'Internationalisation and coordination of R & D of western European and Japanese multinational corporations', in K. Macharzina, M.-J. Oesterle and J. Wolf (eds), *Global Business in the Information Age*, pp. 573–604.

Reid, S. (1981) 'The Decision-maker and Export Entry and Expansion', *Journal of International Business Studies*, 12(2), pp. 101–12.

Reid, S. (1983) 'Firm Internationalisation Transaction Costs and Strategic Choice', *International Marketing Review*, 1, pp. 45–55.

Rennie, M. W. (1993) 'Born Global', *McKinsey Quarterly*, 4, pp. 45–52.

Reuber, A. R. and Fischer, E. (1999) 'Understanding the Consequences of Founders' Experience', *Journal of Small Business Management*, 25 (1) pp. 30–45.

Ricci, L. (1999) 'Economic Geography and Comparative Advantage: Agglomeration versus Specialisation', *European Economic Review*, 43, pp. 357–77.

Roe, M. J. (1993) 'Some differences in corporate governance in Germany, Japan and the United States', *Yale Law Journal*, 102, pp. 1927–2003.

Rogers, E. M. (1962) *Diffusion of Innovations* (New York: Free Press).

Rogoff, K. (1996) 'The purchasing power parity puzzle', *Journal of Economic Literature*, 34(2), pp. 647–68.

Rosenau, P. (1999) 'Introduction: the strengths and weaknesses of public–private policy partnerships', *American Behavioral Scientist*, 43(1), pp. 10–34.

Rosenbloom, B. (1995) *Marketing Channels: A Management view* (London: Dryden Press).

Roth, K. (1992) 'International configuration and coordination archetypes for medium-sized firms in global industries', *Journal of International Business Studies*, 23, pp. 533–49.

Roth, K. and Morrison, A. J. (1990) 'An empirical analysis of the integration–responsiveness framework in global industries', *Journal of International Business Studies*, 21(4), pp 541–64.

Roth, K. and Morrison, A. J. (1992) 'Implementing Global Strategy: Characteristics of global subsidiary mandates', *Journal of International Business Studies*, 23(4), pp. 715–36.

Roth, K., Schweiger D. M. and Morrison, A. J. (1991) 'Global strategy implementation at the business unit level: operational capabilities and administrative mechanisms', *Journal of International Business Studies*, 20, pp. 369–402.

Rothwell, R. (1991) 'External Networking and Innovation in Small and Medium-Sized Manufacturing Firms in Europe', *Technovation*, 11(2), pp. 93–112.

Rugman, A. M. and Bennett, J. (1982) 'Technology transfer and world product mandating in Canada', *Columbia Journal of World Business*, 17(4), pp. 58–62.

Rugman, A. M. and D'Cruz, J. R. (1997) 'The Theory of the Flagship Firm', paper presented at the 5th International Conference on Competitive Strategy, Oxford.

Rugman, A. R. (2000) *The End of Globalization* (London: Random House).

Ruigrok, W., Pettigrew, A., Peck, S. and Whittington, R. (1999) 'Corporate Restructuring and New Forms of Organizing: Evidence from Europe', *Management International Review*, Special Issue 2/99, pp. 41–64.

Sachs, J. D. and Warner, A. (1995) 'Economic reform and the process of global integration', Brookings Papers on Economic Activity, 2 (Washington, DC: Brookings Institution), pp. 1–118.

Salmon, W. J. and Tordjman, A. (1989) 'The internationalization of retailing', *International Journal of Retailing*, 4(2), pp. 3–16.

Schlegelmilch, B., Diamatopoulos, A. and MacDonald, T. (1991) '1992 and the Scottish Whisky Industry: A Survey of Company Expectations and Planned Responses', *Journal of Euromarketing*, 1(1–2), pp. 59–83.

Schmid, S. (1999) 'Foreign Subsidiaries as Centres of Competence – Empirical Evidence from Japanese MNCs', paper presented at the 5th Workshop on International Business, Vaasa.

Schwittay, B., Davies, G. and Carr, C. (1999) 'Applying Strategic Groups in the Static and Dynamic Analysis of Market Behaviour', paper presented at Monchester, the British Academy of Management Annual Conference: Managing Diversity.

Scottish Enterprise (2000) *Inward Investment Benefits for the Scottish Economy* (Glasgow).

SEC filings (10-K) (various years) www.edgar-online.com.

Sethuraman, R., Anderson, J. C. and Narus, J. A. (1988) 'Partnership Advantage and its Determinants in Distributor and Manufacturer Working Relationships', *Journal of Business Research*, 17, pp. 327–47.

Sharma, S. (1996) *Applied Multivariate Analysis* (New York: Wiley).

Shaw, H. (2000) 'Curbing costs key to Chapters Online', *National Post*, 8 September, www.nationalpost.com.

Sheenan, P. and Grewal, B. (2001) 'Growth Strategy in a Diverging World', in A. R. Rugman and T. L. Brewer (eds), *Oxford Handbook of International Business* (Oxford: Oxford University Press).

Shleifer, A. and Vishny, R. W. (1997) 'A survey of corporate governance', *Journal of Finance*, 52, pp. 737–83.

Shoham, A. (1996) 'Marketing-Mix Standardisation: Determinants of Export Performance', *Journal of Global Marketing*, 10(2), pp. 53–73.

Simmonds, P. G. (1998) 'The Combined diversification breadth and mode dimensions and the performance of large diversified firms', *Strategic Management Journal*, 11 pp. 399–410.

Simon, H. (1996) *Hidden Champions: Lessons from 500 of the World's Best Unknown Companies* (Boston, Mass.: Harvard Business School Press).

Simonin, B. L. (1999) 'Transfer of marketing know-how in international strategic alliances: An empirical investigation of the role and antecedents of knowledge ambiguity', *Journal of International Business Studies*, 30(3), pp. 463–90.

Simpson, E. M. and Thorpe, D. I. (1995) 'A conceptual model of strategic considerations for international retail expansion', *Service Industries Journal*, 15(4), pp. 16–24.

Smith, A. W. (2000) 'Making globalisation work', *Consulting to Management*, 11, pp. 18–20.

Smith, K., Grimm, C. and Wally, S. (1997) 'Strategic Groups and Rivalrous Firm Behaviour: Towards a Reconciliation', *Strategic Management Journal*, 18, pp. 149–57.

Sondergaard, M. (1994) 'Hofstede's Consequences: A Study of Reviews, Citations and Replications', *Organization Studies*, 15(3), pp. 447–56.

Souchon, A. L. and Diamantopoulos, A. (1997) 'Use and Non-use of Export Information: Some Preliminary Insights into the Antecedents and Impact on Export Performance', *Journal of Marketing Management*, 13, pp. 135–51.

Spender, J. (1998) 'The Geographies of Strategic Competence: Borrowing from Social and Educational Psychology to Sketch an Activity and Knowledge-Based theory of the Firm', in A. Chandler, P. Hagstrom and O. Solvell (eds), *The Dynamic Firm: The Role of Technology, Strategy, and Regions* (Oxford: Oxford University Press).

SPSS. (1998) *SPSS Base 8.0 Syntax Reference Guide* (Chicago, Ill.: SPSS).

Steiner, M. (1998) *Clusters and Regional Specialisation* (London: Pion).

Stern, L. W., El-Ansary, A. I. and Brown, J. R. (1989) *Management in Marketing Channels* (Englewood Cliffs, NJ: Prentice-Hall).

Stern, L. W. and Reve, T. (1980) 'Distribution Channels as Political Economies: A Framework for Comparative Analysis', *Journal of Marketing*, 44, (Summer), pp. 52–64.

Stewart, D. B. and McAuley, A. (1999) 'The Effects of Export Stimulation: Implications for Export Performance', *Journal of Marketing Management*, 15, pp. 505–18.

Stiglitz, J. and Wallsten, S. (1999) 'Introduction: the strengths and weaknesses of public–private policy partnerships', *American Behavioral Scientist*, 43(1), pp. 52–73.

Storper, M. (1995) 'The Resurgence of Regional Economies, Ten Years Later: The Region as a Nexus of Untraded Interdependencies', *European Urban and Regional Studies*, 2(3), pp. 191–221.

Storper, M. (1997) *The Regional World* (London: Guilford Press).

Stottinger, B. and Schlegelmilch, B. (1998) 'Explaining Export Development Through Psychic Distance: Enlightening or Elusive?', *International Marketing Review*, 15(5), pp. 357–72.

Styles, C. (1998) 'Export Performance Measures in Australia and the UK', *International Marketing Review*, 6 (3), pp. 12–36.

Styles, C. and Ambler, T. (1994) 'Successful Export Practice: The U.K. Experience', *International Marketing Review*, 11(6), pp. 68–79.

Styles, C. and Ambler, C. (2000) 'The Impact of Relational Variables on Export Performance: An empirical investigation in Australia and the UK', *Australian Journal of Management*, 25(3), pp. 515–28.

Sullivan, D. and Bauerschmidt, A. (1989) 'Common Factors Underlying Barriers to Export: A Comparative Study in the European and US Paper Industry', *Management International Review*, 29(2), pp. 17–32.

Sundaram, A. K. and Black, J. S. (1992) 'The environment and internal organization of multinational enterprises', *Academy of Management Review*, 17(4), pp. 729–57.

Surlemont, B. (1996) 'Types of centers within multinational corporations: an empirical investigation'. *Proceedings of the European International Business Academy* (Stockholm): pp. 745–66.

Szulanski, G. (1996) 'Exploring internal stickiness: impediments to the transfer of best practice within the firm', *Strategic Management Journal*, 17 (Winter Special Issue), pp. 27–43.

Taggart, J. H. (1996a) 'Multinational manufacturing subsidiaries in Scotland: strategic role and economic impact', *International Business Review*, 5, pp. 447–68.

Taggart, J. H. (1996b) 'Evolution of multinational strategy: evidence from Scottish manufacturing subsidiaries', *Journal of Marketing Management*, 12, pp. 535–49.

Taggart, J. H. (1996c) 'Autonomy and Procedural Justice: A Framework for Evaluating Subsidiary Strategy', *Journal of International Business Studies*, 28(1), pp. 51–76.

Taggart, J. H. (1997a) 'US MNC affiliates in the UK: a special relationship', in P. J. Buckley, M. Chapman, L. J. Clegg, and A. Cross (eds) *The Organisation of International Business*

Taggart, J. H. (1997b) 'Mapping stability and evolution of subsidiary strategy on the integration–responsiveness framework', in P. J. Buckley. Buckley, P. and Mucchielli, J. W. (ed) *Multinational Firms and International Relocation* (Cheltenham: Edward Elgar).

Taggart, J. H. (1997c) 'An evaluation of the integration-responsiveness framework: MNC manufacturing subsidiaries in the UK', *Management International Review*, 37(4), pp. 295–318.

Taggart, J. H. (1997d) 'R & D complexity in UK subsidiaries of manufacturing multinational corporations', *Technovation*, 17(2), pp. 73–82.

Taggart, J. H. (1997e) 'Autonomy and procedural justice: a framework for evaluating subsidiary strategy', *Journal of International Business Studies*, 28(1), pp. 51–76.

Taggart, J. H. (1997f) 'Identification and development of strategy at subsidiary level', in J. Birkinshaw, and N. Hood (eds), *Multinational Corporate Evolution and Subsidiary Development*, (London: Macmillan), pp 33–52.

Taggart, J. H. (1998) 'Strategy shifts in MNEs' subsidiaries', *Strategic Management Journal*, 19, pp. 663–81.

Taggart, J. H. (ed.) (1999) 'Special Issue, Subsidiary Strategy', *International Business Review*, 8(2), pp. 77–85.

Taggart, J. H. and Berry, M. M. J. (1997) 'Second Stage Internationalisation: evidence from MNC manufacturing subsidiaries in the UK', *Journal of Marketing Management*, 13(1), pp. 179–94.

Taggart, J. M. and Taggart, J. H. (1997a). *International Competitiveness of Exporters: A Comparison of UK and Irish Firms (Glasgow:* Business Unit, Strathclyde University).

Taggart, J. and Taggart, J. (1997b) 'Subsidiary Strategy from the Periphery', in B. Fines and S. Ennis, *Competing from the Periphery: Core Issues in International Business* (Dublin: Oak Tree Press).

Takeuchi, H. and Porter, M. E. (1986) 'Three roles of marketing in global strategy', in Michael E. Porter (ed.), *Competition in Global Industries* (Boston, Mass.: Harvard Business School Press), pp 111–47.

Tan, J. J. and Litschert, R. J. (1994) 'Environment-strategy relationship and its performance implications: an empirical study of the Chinese electronics industry', *Strategic Management Journal*, 15, pp. 1–20.

Tang, M. J. and Thomas, H. (1992) 'The Concept of Strategic Groups: Theoretical Construct or Analytical Convenience', *Managerial & Decision Economics*, 13, pp. 323–29.

Tavares, A. T. (2001) 'Multinational enterprises in Ireland: the dynamics of subsidiary strategy', in M. McDermott and J. H. Taggart (eds), *Multinationals in the Millennium: Changes and Choices* (Basingstoke: Palgrave).

Tavares, A. T. and Pearce, R. D. (1999) 'The industrial policy implications of the heterogeneity of subsidiaries' roles in a multinational network', Industrial Development Policy Discussion Paper no. 5 (Ferrara and Birmingham: Institute for Industrial Development Policy).

Tavares, A. T. and Pearce, R. D. (2001) 'European integration and structural change in the multinational: evidence from foreign subsidiaries operating in Portugal', in M.

Hughes and J. H. Taggart (eds), *International Business: European Dimensions* (Basingstoke: Palgrave).

Taylor, S. and Raines, P. (2001) *Learning to Let Go: The Role of the Public Sector in Cluster Building in the Basque Country and Scotland*, Paper presented at the Regional Studies Association Gdansk.

Taylor, C. R., Zou, S. and Osland, G. E. (1998) 'A transaction cost perspective on foreign market entry strategies of US and Japanese firms', *International Business Review*, 40(4), pp. 389–412.

Teece, D. J. (1977) 'Technology transfer by multinational firms: The resource costs of transferring technological know-how', *Economic Journal*, 87, pp. 242–61.

Teece, D. J. (1981a) 'The multinational enterprise: market failure and market power considerations', *Sloan Management Review*, 22(3), pp. 3–17.

Teece, D. J., (1981b) 'The market for know-how and the efficient international transfer of technology', *Annals of the AAPSS*, 45, pp. 81–96.

Thibaut, John W. and Kelley, Harold H. (1959) The *Social Psychology of Groups* (New York: John Wiley and Sons).

Thill, G., Leonard-Barton, D. (1993) *Hewlett-Packard: Singapore*, Case 694-037 (Boston, JH: Harvard Business School).

Thomas, H. and Venkatraman, N. (1988) 'Research on Strategic Groups: Process and Prognosis', *Journal of Management Studies*, 25(6), pp. 537–55.

Tookey, D. A. (1964) 'Factors Associated with Success in Exporting', *The Journal of Management Studies*, 1(1), pp. 48–66.

Tricker, R. (1994) *International Corporate Governance: Text, Readings and Cases* (London: Blackwell).

Tse, D. K., Pan, Y. and Au, K. Y. (1997) 'How MNCs choose entry modes and form alliances: The China experience', *Journal of International Business Studies*, 28(4), pp. 779–805.

Tuncalp, S. (1990) 'Export Marketing Strategy to Saudi Arabia: The Case of British Exporters', *Quarterly Review of Marketing*, 15(2), pp. 65–78.

Turnbull, P. W. and Doherty-Wilson, L. (1990) 'The Internationalisation of the Advertising Industry', *European Journal of Marketing*, 24, pp. 7–16.

Turnbull, P. W. and Ellwood, S. (1986) 'Internationalisation in the Information Technology Industry', in Peter W. Turnbull and Stanley J. Paliwoda (eds), *Research in International Marketing* (Australia: Croom Helm).

Tversky, A. and Daniel K. (1974) 'Judgement under uncertainty: heuristics and biases', *Science*, 18(5), pp. 1124–31.

Tzokas, N., Hart, S., Argouslidis, P. and Saren, M. (2000a) 'Strategic Pricing in Export Markets: empirical evidence from the UK', *International Business Review*, 9, pp. 95–117.

Tzokas, N., Hart, S., Argouslidis, P. and Saren, M. (2000b) 'Exporting Practices of UK Industrial Manufacturers', *Industrial Marketing Management*, 9, pp. 95–117.

UNCTAD (1989) *The Role of Foreign Direct Investment on Trade*, E88.II.A.7 (New York: United Nations).

UNCTAD (1999) *World Investment Report – Foreign Direct Investment and the Challenge of Development* (New York and Geneva: UNCTAD).

US Department of Commerce, Bureau of Economic Analysis (1998) *International Accounts Data*, http:////www.bea.doc.gov/bea/di1.htm, and USDOC, BEA, *Survey of Current Business*, July.

US Internet Council (2000) *State of the Internet 2000*, www.usic.org.

Vahlne, J. E. and Wiedersheim-Paul, F. (1973) 'Economic distance: model and empirical investigation, in E. Hornell, J. E. Vahlne, and F. Wiedersheim-Paul (eds), *Export and foreign establishments* (Uppsala: University of Uppsala), pp 81–159.

Vahlne, J. E. and Wiedersheim-Paul, F. (1977) *Psychic distance – An Inhibiting Factor in International Trade*, (Uppsala: University of Uppsala).

Vaivio, F. (1963) 'Sivusuuntainen jäykkyys yrityksen käyttäytymispiirteenä' (Rigid Adherence to Plans as an Element of Business Behaviour), *The Finnish Journal of Business Economics*, 3, pp. 17–31.

Valos, M. and Baker, M. (1996) 'Developing an Australian model of export marketing performance determinants', *Marketing Intelligence and Planning*, 14(3), pp. 11–20.

Valtonen, M. (1999) 'The role of the regional centres of expertise in business networks', in G. Schienstock and O. Kuusi (eds), *Transformation Towards a Learning Economy: The Challenge of the Finnish Innovation System* (Helsinki: Finnish National Fund for Research and Development).

Van den Bulcke, D., Boddewyn, J. J., Martens, B. and Klemmer, P. (1979) *Investment and Divestment Policies of Multinational Corporations in Europe* (Farnborough: Saxon House).

Venkatraman, N. and Prescott, J. -E. (1990) 'Environment–strategy coalignment: an empirical test of its performance implications', *Strategic Management Journal*, 11, pp. 1–23.

Vernon, R. (1966) 'International Investment and International Trade in the Product Cycle', *Quarterly Journal of Economics*, 80, pp. 255–67.

Von Hippel, E. (1994) ' "Sticky in formation" and the locus of problem solving; Implications for innovation', *Management Science*, 40(4), pp. 429–39.

Wakelin, K. (1998) 'Innovation and export behaviour at the firm level', *Research Policy*, 26, pp. 829–41.

Weintraub, J. (1997) 'The theory and politics of the public/private distinction' in J. Weintraub and K. Kumar (eds), *Public and Private in Thought and Practice: Perspectives on a Grand Dichotomy* (Chicago, JH.: University of Chicago Press).

Welch, L. (1992) 'The Use of Alliances by Small Firms in Achieving Internationalisation', *Scandinavian International Business Review*, 1(2), pp. 21–37.

Welch, L. S. and Luostarinen, R. (1988) 'Internationalisation: Evolution of a Concept', *Journal of General Management*, 14, pp. 34–55.

Welch, L. S. and Welch, D. E. (1996) 'The Internationalisation Process and Networks: A Strategic Management Perspective', *Journal of International Marketing*, 4, pp. 11–28.

Wernerfelt, B. (1984) 'A resource-based view of the firm', *Strategic Management Journal*, 5, pp. 171–80.

Westhead, P. (1995) 'Exporting and non-exporting small firms in Great Britain', *International Journal of Entrepreneurial Behaviour and Research*, 1(2), pp. 6–36.

Westhead, P., Wright, M. and Ucbasaran, D. (2001) 'The Internationalization of New and Small Firms: A Resource-Based View', *Journal of Business Venturing*, 16, pp, 333–358.

White, R. E. and Poynter, T. A. (1984) 'Strategies for Foreign-owned Subsidiaries in Canada', *Business Quarterly*, Summer, pp. 59–69.

Whitley, R. (1992) 'Societies, firms and markets: the social structuring of business systems', in R. Whitley (ed.), *European Business Systems* (London: Sage), pp. 5–45.

Whitelock, J. and Jobber, D. (1999) 'An Exploratory Investigation into the Impact of Competitor Environment and the Role of Information on the Decision to Enter a New, Non-Domestic Market', *Journal of Global Marketing*, 13(2), pp. 67–83.

Wiedersheim-Paul, F., Olson, H. C. and Welch, L. S. (1976) 'Pre-Export Activity: The First Steps in Internationalisation', *Journal of International Business Studies*, 9(1), pp. 47–58.

Wild, John J., Wild, Kenneth L. and Han, Jerry C. (2001) *International Business: An Integrated Approach, E-Business Updated Edition* (Englewood Cliffs, NJ: Prentice-Hall).

Williams, D. E. (1992) 'Retailer internationalization: an empirical inquiry', *European Journal of Marketing*, 26(8), pp. 8–24.

Williams, D. (1999) 'Foreign Manufacturing Firms in the UK: Effects on Employment, Output and Supplier Linkages', *European Business Review*, 99(3) pp. 393–8.

Williamson, O. (1975) *Markets and Hierarchies: Analysis and Antitrust Implications* (New York: Free Press).

Williamson, O. (1985) *The Economic Institutions of Capitalism* (New York: Free Press).

References

Williamson, P. (1991) 'Successful Strategies for Export', *Long Range Planning*, 24(1), pp. 57–63.

Wilson, B. D. (1980) *Disinvestment of Foreign Subsidiaries*, Research for Business Decisions no. 25 (Ann Arbor, Mich.: UMI Research Press).

Winch, G. and Schneider, E. (1993) 'Managing the knowledge-based organisation: The case of architectural practices', *Journal of Management Studies*, 30, pp. 923–37.

Winklhofer, H. and Diamantopoulos, A. (1996) 'First insights into sales forecasting practice: a qualitative study', *International Marketing Review*, 13(4), pp. 55–68.

Withey, J. J. (1980) 'Differences between Exporters and Non-exporters: Some Hypotheses Concerning Small Manufacturing Business', *American Journal of Small Business*, 4(3), pp. 29–37.

Woodcock, C. P., Beamish, P. W. and Makino, S. (1994) 'Ownership-based entry mode strategies and international performance', *Journal of International Business Studies*, 25(2), pp. 253–73.

World Trade Organization (2000) www.wto.org/wto/ecom/ecom.htm.

Wright, M., Hoskisson, R., Filatotchev, I. and Buck, T. (1998) 'Revitalizing privatized Russian enterprises', *Academy of Management Executive*, 12, pp. 74–85.

Voudouris, I., Lioukas S., Makridakis S. and Spanos Y. (2000) 'Greek hidden champions: lessons from small, little-known firms in Greece', *European Management Journal*, 18(6), pp. 663–74.

Yang, Y. S., Leone R. P. and Alden D. L. (1992) 'A market expansion ability approach to identify potential exporters', *Journal of Marketing*, 56(1), pp. 84–96.

Yeoh, P. L. (2000) 'Information Acquisition Activities: A Study of Global Start-Up Exporting Companies', *Journal of International Marketing*, 8(3), pp. 36–60.

Yin, Robert K. (1989) *Case Study Research: Design and Methods* (Newbury Park, CA: Sage).

Yip, G. S. (1989) 'Global strategy in a world of nations', *Sloan Management Review*, 31(1), pp. 29–41.

Yip, G. S. (1992) *Total Global Strategy: Managing for Worldwide Competitive Advantage* (Englewood Cliffs, NJ: Prentice-Hall).

Young, S. (1987) 'Business Strategy and the Internationalization Business: Recent Approaches', *Managerial and Decision Economics*, 8, pp. 31–40.

Young, S. (1995) 'Export Marketing: Conceptual and Empirical Developments', *European Journal of Marketing*, 29(8), pp. 7–16.

Young, S. (2000) 'The Multinational Corporation: The Managerial Challenge of Globalization and localization', in J. Legewie and H. Meyer-Ohle (eds), *Corporate Strategies for South-east Asia after the Crisis* (London: Macmillan).

Young, S., Hood, N., and Dunlop, S. (1989) 'Global strategies, multinational subsidiary roles and economic impact in Scotland', *Regional Studies*, 22(6), pp. 487–97.

Young, S., Hood. N. and Hamill, J. (1985) *Decision-making in Foreign-owned Multinational Subsidiaries in the United Kingdom*, Multinational Enterprises Programme Working Paper no. 35 (Geneva: International Labour Office).

Young, S., Hood, N. and Peters, E. (1994) 'Multinational Enterprises and Regional Economic Development', *Regional Studies*, 28(7), pp. 65–71.

Zou, S. and Stan, S. (1998) 'The determinants of export performance: a review of the empirical literature between 1987 and 1997', *International Marketing Review*, 15(5), pp. 333–56.

Zou, S., Taylor, C. R. and Osland, G. E. (1998) 'The EXPERF Scale: A Cross-National Generalized Export Performance Measure', *Journal of International Marketing*, 6(3), pp. 37–58.

Name Index

Subject Index